The Rise and Fall
of the American Left

Other Books by John Patrick Diggins

Mussolini and Fascism: The View from America

The American Left in the Twentieth Century

Up from Communism: Conservative Odysseys in
American Intellectual History

The Bard of Savagery: Thorstein Veblen and
Modern Social Theory

The Problem of Authority in America (coeditor)

The Lost Soul of American Politics: Virtue,
Self-Interest, and the Foundations of Liberalism

The Proud Decades: America in War and in Peace,
1941–1960

THE RISE
AND FALL
OF THE
AMERICAN
LEFT

John Patrick Diggins

W. W. NORTON & COMPANY
NEW YORK LONDON

First published as a Norton paperback 1992

The text of this book is composed in 11/13 Walbaum Regular with the
display set in Serifa. Manufacturing by the Haddon Craftsmen, Inc.
Book design by Charlotte Staub.

Library of Congress Cataloging-in-Publication Data
Diggins, John P.
    The rise and fall of the American left / John Patrick Diggins.
        p.   cm.
    Expanded version of: The American left in the twentieth century.
    Includes bibliographical references and index.
    1. Radicalism—United States—History. 2. Socialism—United
States—History. 3. New Left—United States—History. I. Diggins,
John P. American left in the twentieth century. II. Title.
    HN90.R3D556   1992
    303.48″4—dc20   91-22508

ISBN 0-393-30917-7

W. W. Norton & Company, Inc., 500 Fifth Avenue, New York, N.Y. 10110
W. W. Norton & Company Ltd, 10 Coptic Street, London WC1A 1PU

    4 5 6 7 8 9 0

To the Memory of
Max Eastman and
Sidney Hook

They made themselves a fearful monument!
The wreck of old opinions—things which grew,
Breathed from the birth of time: the veil they rent,
And what behind it lay all earth shall view.
But good with ill they also overthrew,
Leaving but ruins, wherewith to rebuild
Upon the same foundation, and renew
Dungeons and thrones, which the same hour refilled,
As heretofore, because ambition was self-willed.

But this will not endure, nor be endured!
Mankind have felt their strength, and made it felt.
They might have used it better, but, allured
By their new vigor, sternly have they dealt
On one another; pity ceased to melt
With her once natural charities. But they,
Who in oppression's darkness caved had dwelt,
They were not eagles, nourished with the day;
What marvel then, at times, if they mistook their prey?

Lord Byron, *Childe Harold*

Contents

Acknowledgments

Among the other things historians do, or try to do, is to bring back the ideas of dead men and women and describe the events that have shaped their lives. Any success in this dialogue with the dead depends upon clarity of language, and when one deals with those still living, accuracy of interpretation remains important no matter how that goal has been derided in contemporary literary criticism. In my efforts to deal with the past I have benefited from the astute editorial work of Jeanette Hopkins, the comprehensive reading and stylistic suggestions of Christina von Koehler, the helpful criticisms of Paul Berman, and the research assistance of Melissa Nickle.

The book is dedicated to the memory of Max Eastman and Sidney Hook, two thinkers who gave the American Left philosophical respectability, integrity, witty polemics, and the joy of ideas.

Preface

"A Fearful Monument"

This work, a substantially expanded version of a book published in 1973, *The American Left in the Twentieth Century*, offers the opportunity to delve more thoroughly into historical episodes and theoretical issues only touched upon in the slender, original volume. Sections on new topics have been added, and the interim period between the death of one Left and the birth of another has been discussed to highlight generational tensions. The story has now been brought up to 1990, a curious time when the Left in the United States has no political significance but considerable educational influence, no power to affect immediate events but considerable authority to shape the minds of the young. Having lost the class war in the factories and the fields, the American Left continues the battle for cultural hegemony in the classroom.

Much of the Left today, derived from the sixties generation, remains an anomaly living on college campuses on memory. Whereas previous radical movements experienced a sense of being ascendant because of hopes of reaching the working class, the contemporary Left must be described as being in a state of decline and fall. However prolific in publications, the Left's ranks have been dwindling and it has no basis in the working class and seemingly little sympathy for the "bourgeois" middle class. More seriously, it has become excessively intellectual and academic and hooked on European "postmodern" theories that have more to do with domination than with liberation. Earlier in the century the Left fought power with ideas provided by knowledge; today knowledge is suspect in its claims to efficacy and objectivity, and ideas are simply "discourses" about this and that. A Left without power is familiar and perhaps a defining characteristic of its historical predicament; a Left without knowledge loses its excuse for being.

When the term "Left" is mentioned, many Americans think of the sixties, some with a smile of affection, the great majority with a shudder of disdain. For those who have no personal identity with it, the decade offers a convenient explanation of all that has come to bedevil America: abortion, pornography, gay rights; the deterioration of educational standards and the "closing" of the American mind; the promises of "pot" and hence the beginning of the drug problem; the breakup of family and community; the decline of America as a world power; moral relativism and the loss of respect for authority and the work ethic; and, in the universities, the bashing of Western civilization, with alternative education by feminists and third world activists on the grounds that nothing is universal, eternal, or neutral and everything is contingent, contextual, and political.

Those who do focus on such acrimonious issues scarcely consider what America would have been like had not the sixties generation opposed the Vietnam War and awakened the country's conscience to poverty, racism, and the ecological fragility of the environment. Nor can one assume that America's political leaders would have faced such problems if young Americans had not compelled them to do so. In recent years the youth of Eastern Europe and China took to the streets and braved bullets and tanks in their demonstrations for freedom, while America's political leaders worried about stability, the China "market," public opinion, and reelection. Contemporary neoconservatives complain that the sixties generation has "corrupted" higher education by, among other treacheries, denying the possibility of teaching truth. The great American historian Henry Adams, who called himself a "Conservative, Christian, Anarchist," concluded that truth could not thrive in American politics, where corruption was a sign of good manners. If academics cannot seem to find truth in the pursuit of knowledge, politicians cannot seem to remember it in the pursuit of power. But the burden today's academic radical faces is greater since the Left has historically looked to knowledge as emancipatory. How can one deny the possibility of knowing truth and at the same time deal with the deceptions of power?

The American Left was born in the United States. Contrary to popular belief, it was not the product of foreign powers and alien ideologies. Although each Left generation would have its rendezvous with European Marxism, Marxist ideas were usually embraced to support a radical movement that had already come into being. Most Left intellectuals and activists in America read Thomas Jefferson and Walt Whitman before they read Karl Marx or, later, Mao Zedong, and many caught the flame of William Jennings Bryan or John Fitzgerald Kennedy before they felt the fascination of V. I. Lenin or Fidel Castro. Sprouting from native soil, the Left often erupted in a fury of radical innocence and wounded idealism so peculiar to American intellectual history. We need only listen to the opening dialogue in the first major confrontation of the New Left. At the height of the Berkeley free-speech movement in 1964, the student leader Mario Savio denounced the university "system" as a technological grotesquerie: "It becomes odious so we must put our bodies against the gears, against the wheels and machines, and make the machine stop until we're free." The image of man throwing his body against the mechanistic institution has always touched a rebellious impulse deeply rooted in the American mind and character. In the nineteenth century Ralph Waldo Emerson cursed the "corpse-cold" nature of institutions and protested a society in which "man is thus metamorphosed into a thing"; Whitman called upon young Americans to "sing" of themselves and to "resist much, obey little"; and Henry David Thoreau formulated his classic doctrine of civil disobedience in the metaphors of human resurrection and mechanistic doom: "Let your life be a counter friction to stop the machine." Marx told us a great deal about the nature of society against which man rebels; Emerson's "The American Scholar" may tell us even more about the emotional and intellectual sources of alienation and idealism that have characterized the American Left.

Yet having been born on native ground, the Left wanted to see itself as Byron's "fearful monument" that would make the ruling classes tremble. The three Lefts, of the twentieth century especially, looked abroad for revolutionary models of monumental dimensions. For the radicals of the First World War years, the fearful symbol would be Lenin, the Bolshevik leader whose dramatic moves created "the ten days that shook the world," the theorist of power who synthesized thought and action, the supreme monument of the revolutionary dynamism latent in the body of Marxist doctrine. For many intellectuals of the thirties, that image would be assumed by Leon Trotsky. Hero of the Red Army, brilliant historian and polemicist, Trotsky became an anti-Stalinist outcast who, even as the "unarmed prophet," could make regimes fearful of the "Mephistophelian character" who traveled throughout the world preaching permanent revolutionary struggle. For the student New Left of the sixties, the monumental symbol became Castro, the Cuban revolutionary who seized power with both hands, defied yanqui imperialism, and seemingly dramatized the insurrectionary potential in what would come to be called "the third world."

The American Left has generally been approached as a footnote to the history of the American labor movement, or as an aspect of the socialist and communist experiences in the United States, or as an episode in the rich chronicle of American literary radicalism. To integrate these several dimensions into an interpretive synthesis, I have drawn especially upon the excellent studies of Daniel Bell, Theodore Draper, and Daniel Aaron. My own focus is primarily on intellectual history as expressed through generational experience. By intellectual history I mean not the disembodied "history of ideas" but rather the mind and moral temper of a generation as it arose from the crucible of concrete historical experience.

In recent years New Left scholars like Todd Gitlin, Maurice Isserman, Russell Jacoby, and James Miller have written excellent studies of the sixties and their historical background. They, too, want to make sense of their radical past, to know what went wrong and why. I have benefited from their works, some of which call to mind Emerson's dictum that there is no history, only biography.

Years ago I showed up at a conference of radical historians. "What are you doing here?" asked an eminent scholar, half in jest. "You are a troublemaker!" The nuns used to say the same thing. I do confess to the sin of poaching. For my position is to the right of the Left and to the left of the Right. Essentially a Niebuhrian position, it is critical of the anticapitalist Left for seeing in the abolition of property an end to oppression and the birth of freedom, and critical of the antigovernment Right for seeing in the elimination of political authority the end of tyranny and the restoration of liberty. If indeed *les extrêmes se touchent*, one might say with Byron that both Left and Right "mistook their prey."

The book has three aims: to describe the sensibilities and styles of thought that a radical intellectual movement assumes as a means of mobilizing its emotional energies; to explain the philosophical posture that movement adopts as a means of negating prevailing sentiments that sustain the existing order; and to analyze the historical developments that account for the "deradicalization" of the Left as a generation phenomenon. The main focus, therefore, will be not on the Left in general but on three different American Lefts and a fourth Left that represents a curious after-life of the third.

These are the Lyrical Left of the First World War era, the Old Left of the thirties, the New Left of the sixties, and the Academic Left of our times. The Lyrical Left had its emotional and intellec-tual roots in the joyous, rhapsodic milieu of New York's Green-wich Village. The Old Left's desperate hopes and anxieties derived from the Depression and the rise of a malevolent Euro-pean totalitarianism. The New Left's impulse arose out of a deep sense of personal alienation in an affluent society as well as politi-cal frustration produced by a cold war abroad, with the unpopular Vietnam conflict, and a racial crisis at home. The Academic Left is actually a continuation of the New Left by other means—the college classroom and scholarly journal instead of the campus confrontation and street demonstration. The first three Lefts had unlike social origins and evolved from different historical con-texts; and each projected its own self-images, political objectives, ideologies, and life-styles. Lacking historical continuity, each is best approached generationally, for each tended to deny paternity to its predecessor and enduring legacy to its successor. Revolutions may devour their children; in the rites of political passage that characterize generational rebellions, it is the children who slay their fathers. Only in the case of the fourth Left, the Academic, can it be said that a generational revolt succeeded in perpetuating itself for life, or at least for the duration of tenure.

Although generational hostility characterizes the American Left, one figure remained a towering presence to all—the philoso-pher John Dewey. In the First World War era Randolph Bourne expounded Dewey's educational ideas, and Max Eastman saw in Lenin a scientific embodiment of revolution as an empirical "ex-periment." In the thirties Sidney Hook tried to convert Dewey to Marxism as a "critique" instead of a "system." Dewey remained unconvinced, but he valiantly defended Trotsky during the Mos-cow trials and then engaged him in a brilliant debate on the theme "Means and Ends." C. Wright Mills, a hero of the sixties generation, wrote his doctoral dissertation on pragmatism and demonstrated its relevance to social thought, and Tom Hayden drew on Dewey's ideas of community and participatory democracy when drafting the SDS's Port Huron statement. Today some members of the Academic Left are turning to Dewey again in order to find a way out of the epistemological crisis brought on by poststructuralism and deconstruction. Whether one can resolve in practice what cannot be explained in theory is an issue addressed in the final chapter.

The American Left resists precise definition, but there are ways of approaching a historical understanding of its role in past and present society.[1] Part 1, "Theory," devoted mainly to historical background and theoretical and problematical issues, attempts to explain why simple definitions sacrifice nuance for neatness, why the Left may be interpreted as an intellectual and generational phenomenon, and why the American Left found itself without a real revolutionary "proletariat." Part 2, "History," deals specifically with the three American Lefts of the twentieth century. Part 3, "Anomaly," involves the Academic Left that survives in America in defiance of Darwin's law of evolutionary adaptation.

Webster's defines "anomaly" as "a departure from the regular arrangement," a definition that could apply to the Left in general as a phenomenon of protest, resistance, and rebellion. But the Academic Left is anomalous in deviating from previous Lefts in several ways. It is the first Left with no social constituency beyond the college campus, no sustained hope in the Enlightenment and the promises of reason and science, and seemingly no faith in the spirit of freedom but instead a gloomy preoccupation with the structures of domination in a universe of power and oppression, a murky universe of causeless events in which the oppressor is not necessarily identified.

The Academic Left can be ambiguous as well as anomalous. Radical scholars under the spell of poststructuralism portray the contemporary world not as the story of class struggle or moral progress but as the systematic victimization of people as "objects" to whom things happen. When writing about the distant past, however, radical historians frequently depict people as subjects whose actions defy structural determinism. Some historians even go so far as to portray people of the past as freer, more consciously involved and more disposed to virtue and community, than present Americans supposedly numbed into passivity by corporate capitalism, telecommunications, and the culture of mindless consumption. In both poststructuralism and radical historiography the idea of progress is often questioned and the values of the Enlightenment exposed as Eurocentric, the foundation not of human rights but of racist and sexist assumptions embedded in linguistic conventions. Where it was once assumed that people grasped Enlightenment ideas to overcome their misery, it is now argued that such progressive ideas offered a snare and a delusion and that the masses could rely upon their own collective identity in an attempt to sustain a "premodern" moral sensibility. Such a retrogressive interpretation of history would have perplexed both Marx and Dewey, who saw in the Enlightenment the emergence of such emancipatory developments as reason, science, and technology. In writing about workers and peasants resisting the forces of domination, the contemporary radical scholar often sees technology as threatening and reason as part of a rationalizing, integrating process culminating in social control. Thus the anomalous Academic Left departs from the legacies of Marxism and pragmatism: looking forward in fear, it looks backward to hope.

Whatever their differences, all the Lefts have one thing in common; their respective histories hardly represent a success story. Yet in America, where "the bitch-goddess of success," in William James's words, has its price, one can perhaps learn from failure. Even while the Marxist Left drew its "poetry" from the perfect future, we must not ignore the imperfect past. Marx stated the lesson well in the preface to *Das Kapital*: "We suffer not only from the living but from the dead. *Le mort saisit le vif!*"

Why study the American Left if it is little more than a record of foibles and frustration? In part because the Left has always identified itself in opposition to the actual state of things and thus affirmed the possibility of hope. True, the Left often betrayed its ideals or abandoned them. But the Left's saving remnant is the tension between its promises and its failures. It may be that the failures are inherent in its promises, particularly if one sees the goals of the Left as impossible to realize. At this point the temptation arises to taunt the Left with the label "utopian," pinned on those who are supposedly out of touch with reality. Yet striving after another world in defiance of reality is the Left's categorical imperative. One might say of members of the Left what Reinhold Niebuhr said of the fate of moral man and woman in immoral society: they must seek after an "impossible victory" and adjust themselves to an "inevitable defeat." No matter how often defeated, the American Left was born to seek and to struggle.

John Patrick Diggins
New York City, 1990

One

THEORY

The Left as a Theoretical Problem

> He belonged to the left, which, as they say in Spain, is the side of the heart, as the right is that of the liver.
> George Santayana, 1920

> The true Left is that which continues faithfully to invoke, not liberty or equality, but fraternity—in other words, love.
> Raymond Aron, 1957

The Problem of Definition

The first obstacle in a study of the American Left in the twentieth century is the difficulty of discovering precisely what the American Left is. One of the most elusive of all political categories, the Left does not lend itself to tidy, fixed definitions. The following discussion attempts to illustrate some of the fallacies and limitations contained in common notions about the Left.

ADVOCACY OF CHANGE   In the simplest terms "the Left" has generally designated those who wish to change an existing order and "the Right" those who wish to preserve it. This formu-

The Oneida leader John Humphrey Noyes had women forsake traditional dresses for skirts and pantaloons as one way to overcome gender differences. (Oneida Community Mansion House)

lation does not tell us very much. For what is at issue is not the demand for change but the motive for change. Indeed, when viewed in historical perspective, the Left may be seen less as an agent of change than as a response to it. More often than not the social and political changes demanded by the Left were primarily reactions to vast, disruptive economic and technological changes wrought by the Right. Capitalists on the Right may not have created their own "gravediggers" when they produced an industrial working class, as Marx prophesied, but in drastically transforming the character of modern society, capitalists did more than anyone else to give birth to the Left. Nineteenth-century industrialization, in particular, brought not only soot and squalor but human atomization, depersonalization, and exploitation, reducing society to what Emile Durkheim called "a dust of individuals." In the United States in the late nineteenth century it was the men and women of the Left, the utopian and Christian socialists, who protested the rapid economic changes that were destroying the intimate bonds of human community. Significantly, one finds in the twentieth-century American Left a curious ambiguity on the question of change; one is never sure whether it desires to transform society in order to realize new values or to restore lost ideals. By midcentury this ambivalence seemed to have been resolved in favor of the values of the past. At times the New Left of the 1960s, with its pastoral idyll of small, self-sufficient communities pursuing simple crafts, appeared to have turned its back on change and modernity.

In the decades following the sixties, many veterans of that generation found themselves in the academic world, and the task now seemed to be not primarily to advocate political change but to rediscover what had been lost to the forces of historical change. As historians and political theorists, New Left academics would write about the American past with a romantic determination to find there what they could never find in the American present outside their own enclaves: moral community, feminine consciousness, and a radical working class. History would now be studied "from the bottom up," and truth and virtue would be found among racial minorities, ethnic groups, and others previously excluded from the mainstream of American life. Whatever the future may hold, the past could be seen to belong to those ignored and "marginalized" by history itself.

In respect to social theory this reorientation is novel in the history of the Left. Marxists and pragmatists alike believe that the past is the past and that not much can be done about it. Yet while New Left academics, too, might advise students and teachers to understand the past only to the extent that such historical knowledge will help bring about change in the present and future, they sought also to change the past itself by "redescribing" new, radical ways of looking at it, that is, devising a vocabulary to change our view of reality. Thus change would signify not so much realization as conceptualization. Marx once complained that philosophers were content to interpret the world, whereas the whole

Scene in a West Coast commune of the 1970s. (Dennis Stock/Magnum)

point of knowledge is to change it. Much of the later New Left, influenced by French poststructuralist thought, reinterpreted the past and the present world to show how hidden conditions of power and domination defeat any possibility of genuine change.

POLITICAL IDEALS   Since a political phenomenon may be defined in light of its ideals, it may be useful to consider whether the American Left possessed an exclusive and coherent set of political ideals. The political principles generally associated with the historical European Left are: liberty, justice, equality, and democracy. Liberty, as one of the great ideals of the French Revolution, developed in response to the classic antagonism between the aristocracy and the bourgeoisie, a postfeudal stage of historical conflict that was not part of colonial America's political experience. Americans were "born free," as Tocqueville observed, and did not have to struggle for the political liberties Europeans achieved only after years of revolutionary turmoil. Moreover, the Anglo-Saxon idea of liberty was essentially "negative liberty"—

constitutional freedoms designed not to enable humankind to realize its "higher nature" or "true self," but to protect it *against*
encroachments by the state.[1] The Left sometimes resorts to constitutional rights like free speech, as did the Lyrical Left when it was
harassed by the government during the First World War, or it
may repudiate these "bourgeois" liberties as a form of "repressive
tolerance," as did some elements of the New Left.[2] Love of liberty
has been an occasional affair of the Left, not a marriage.

It is also difficult to establish justice and equality as ideals
peculiar to the Left. For when we try to define these concepts, we
find that they are as elusive to the Left as they have always been
to the political philosopher. If justice is understood as a legal
principle, as fair and equitable treatment, conservative lawyers
and jurists may have as much claim to it as the Left. If justice is
understood as a social ideal, as sympathy for the poor and oppressed, the Left can hardly deny that many twentieth-century
liberal reformers and humanitarians have had a commitment to
social justice—and one that appeared more capable of enduring
setbacks and defeats. Equality is also a perplexing issue. It was
Thomas Jefferson, not Karl Marx, who announced that "all men
are created equal," and the meaning of that ringing statement has
troubled intellectual historians ever since. When equality is cast
as an economic proposition—as equality of opportunity—it suggests an ethos of competition, achievement, and merit that the
twentieth-century Left rejected when it turned its back on liberal
capitalism. On the other hand, equality invoked as a moral injunc-
tion, according to which it becomes a "duty" to treat one's fellows
as equal while raising them from an unequal station, was taken by
some sensitive radical intellectuals to be patronizing.

Duty, like sacrifice and service, always implies a personal relation
of individuals. You are always doing your duty to somebody or
something. Always the taint of inequality comes in. You are morally superior to the person who has duty done to him. If that duty is
not filled with good-will and desire, it is morally hateful, or at very
best, a necessary evil,—one of those compromises with the world

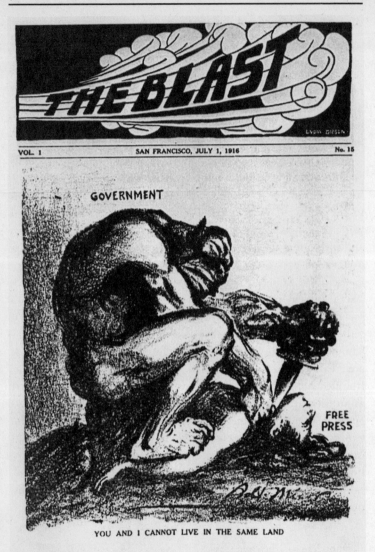

YOU AND I CANNOT LIVE IN THE SAME LAND

The Left defends the liberal cause of a free press during the repressions of the First World War.

which must be made in order to get through it all. But duty without good-will is a compromise with our present state of inequality, and to raise duty to the level of a virtue is to consecrate that state of inequality forevermore.[3]

Democracy, another ideal of the historical European Left, is even more difficult to use in reference to the twentieth-century American Left. In nineteenth-century Europe the Left fought alongside the working class to gain the ballot and win political power from the bourgeoisie. These goals had largely been realized in America long before the appearance of the first modern Left. Moreover, the peculiar sequence of American political and economic history has worked to frustrate the American Left. In many parts of continental Europe, where democracy lagged behind industrialization, or where, as in southern and eastern Europe, it failed to penetrate conditions of economic backwardness, workers became class conscious before they became politically conscious. In America, however, mass democracy developed at the same time as bourgeois capitalism. The "specter" of a democratic class war against capitalism and property that haunted European conservatives turned out to be more shadow than substance in America.

Early in the nineteenth century the conservative Federalist and Whig parties did fear unlimited suffrage as a threat to property rights. Then, in the tumultuous "cider campaign" of 1840, the Whigs, finally realizing there were no class-conscious "mobs" in America, nominated the popular military hero General William Henry Harrison for president. Stooping to conquer, wealthy New England Whigs sent Harrison around the country in a large wagon with a log cabin on top and a barrel of hard cider on tap for the crowds of workmen. The Whigs won the popular vote from the Jacksonians, and democracy was safely domesticated. Thus, in contrast to Europe, where the struggle for democracy often accompanied the struggle for socialism, democracy in America never posed a direct threat to capitalism, since many Americans owned some property, and even those who did not could dream of doing so. The one exception to this is to be found in the South, where demands for the ballot by disenfranchised blacks represent a struggle to alter both class and political structures. But this exception also illustrates the dilemma of using democracy as a defining goal of the Left. In the late nineteenth century American radicals could look upon the struggles of the working class as a genuine democratic expression because workers appeared to constitute a growing majority of the population. The New Left, however, became involved with the civil rights and social goals of powerless minorities. If the historical European Left, as David Caute has argued is to be defined as the attempt to realize "popular sovereignty," the New Left in America may have to be defined as the attempt to realize the sovereignty of the unpopular.[4]

ADVOCACY OF ECONOMIC DEMOCRACY Although nineteenth-century American history deprived the twentieth-century American Left of political democracy as a goal, the ideal of economic democracy was still far from realization. Liberalism may have succeeded in democratizing political institutions and expanding suffrage, but the Left recognized that the masses would remain without effective power as long as work, wages, and welfare were controlled by those who owned the means of production. To extend democracy from the political to the economic sphere became, therefore, the characteristic goal of the Left. Whether economic democracy is automatically realized when private enterprise is socialized remains a speculative proposition. Nevertheless, in the past, the American Left assumed that true freedom begins only when capitalism ends. Hence the Left was nothing if not anticapitalist. All the Lefts of the twentieth century were influenced by socialism; all advocated various programs calling for public ownership of the means of production and democratic control of economic activity. However the new social order was envisioned, competitive individualism would be replaced by some version of the cooperative ideal in which human beings, freed from the economic necessity of engaging in coerced labor, would realize their full nature in creative work. Using anticapitalism as an exclusive categorical definition of the Left, however, creates some difficulties. In America liberal reformers also have advocated public control of private enterprise, and, indeed, some of the sharpest critics of capitalism have been of the Right. The attacks on the inhumanity of the "free" economy by slavery apologists like John C. Calhoun and George Fitzhugh, the penetrating critiques of industrial capitalism by conservative writers like Allen Tate and Irving Babbitt, and the diatribes against Wall Street by protofascists like Ezra Pound and Lawrence Dennis are as caustic as any editorial in *Pravda* or the *Daily Worker.* Anticapitalism has more than one meaning; it is not necessarily synonymous with the Left.

TRADITION OF DISSENT   The American Left may lay claim to a long and rich tradition of radical dissent.[5] The challenge of individual conscience against authority and majority rule began in this country with the Puritan antinomians of the seventeenth century; it was carried forward by the abolitionists of the nineteenth century; and it found its most recent expression in the activities of civil rights workers and draft resisters of the 1960s. Yet dissent itself cannot serve to define the Left in any meaningful sense. Dissent is not a social philosophy but a tactic, a method of protesting and communicating to the public in order to bring law more into congruence with some ideal or higher law. Nor is dissent compatible with democracy, for dissent involves conflict between autonomous individual morality and political allegiance. Like liberty, dissent is basically negative, an assertion of the integrity of the individual's private conscience against both the coercion of the state and the "tyranny of the majority." Moreover, the dissent tradition is highly individualistic, occasionally anarchistic, and at times even spiritual and mystical, whereas the Left comes alive in collective action and seeks material solutions to social problems. The Left may hail Thoreau as the most noble dissenter of all, the heroic "majority of one," who went to jail rather than support a war and who dropped out of society rather than conform to it, but the philosopher-poet of Walden Pond deliberately refused to offer any radical program for transforming society other

Henry David Thoreau, nineteenth-century dissenter whose ideas could never be assimilated by the Marxist Left. (Library of Congress)

than advising men of "quiet desperation" to "simplify" their needs.[6] The twentieth-century American Left could find moral inspiration in the dissent tradition; it had to look elsewhere for political direction.

RATIONALISM AND IDEOLOGY Is it possible to define the Left by its belief systems and mental habits? Does the Left

Tom Paine, Revolutionary War patriot and theoretician who believed in human liberation through the exercise of reason and common sense. This eighteenth-century champion of bourgeois radicalism has become a hero of contemporary neoconservatives. (Library of Congress)

possess a common worldview and a common theory of knowledge? Is there, in short, a systematic "mind" of the Left? It is a widespread notion that the Left stands for rationality and intelligence and has an optimistic belief in the essential goodness of human nature. On the other side, the Right is said to assume the primacy of emotion over reason, elemental sinfulness inherent in conduct, and hence the imperfections of the "human condition." This dichotomy may have some validity for the Revolutionary era, when men of the Enlightenment like Tom Paine proclaimed the infinite capacities of human intelligence, and conservatives like John Adams tried to demonstrate the infinite illusions of reason. But in the nineteenth century radical reform movements were often inspired by religious "awakenings," philosophical idealism, or the romantic cult of moral intuition; and the first Left in the twentieth century stressed the passions of poetry and "feeling" as much as the power of reason. Not until the full impact of Marxism in the 1930s was there a marked return to the worship of reason, science, and technological progress. It was this philosophical legacy of the Old Left, however, that the New Left repudiated, and in doing so the young radicals of the 1960s displayed a deep uncertainty about rationalism, even while invoking the political ideals that had been born in the eighteenth-century Age of Reason. The antagonist remained bourgeois society, which had disfigured original human nature by its demands for social conformity, economic competition, and sexual repression. Yet, the New Left had few illusions about the liberating power of the Enlightenment. At the turn of the century American socialists read Julius Weyland's *Appeal to Reason;* in the 1960s "reason" was the enemy and the vibrations of "soul" the real test of truth.

If rationalism does not define the mentality of the Left, neither does ideology. In the United States "ideology" is a bad word. Supposedly it is a European habit alien to the "pragmatic" wisdom of the American character. This understanding of the term is curious, for it was Marx who first analyzed ideology as a deception and an "illusion." From the Marxist viewpoint, ideology is a rationalization, a verbal "cloak" of ideas behind which true "reality" lies. The American Left, insofar as it has sought to "unmask" ideas like the "laws of the market place" and to lay bare the harsh social realities hidden therein, can rightly be described as antiideological. But there is another meaning to "ideology," one that emerged in the late 1930s when jaded radicals, having lost faith in the "apocalyptic" prophecies of Marx, dismissed Marxism itself as an ideology. "Ideology" now took on an invidious connotation and came to mean a set of fixed ideas derived from unworkable philosophical systems and unproved scientific laws. Henceforth, to be labeled "ideological" meant that one was hooked on "blueprints," on abstract principles and theoretical doctrines that had nothing to do with reality. In this respect the announcement of the "end of ideology" by veterans of the Old Left after the Second World War was a way of confessing that they themselves had been out of touch with reality.[7] Yet if the description "ideological" may be applied to the Old Left because of its rigid commitment to Marxist doctrines, this description cannot be applied to the American Left in general. The Lyrical Left of 1913 rose up in revolt against abstract doctrine, embraced a pragmatic socialism that was as open-ended as free verse, and proudly heralded itself as conqueror without a creed. Similarly the New Left originally saw itself as the first generation of existential radicals who could live without doctrinal illusions. Ideology was the "brain disease" of the Old Left, taunted some young radicals of the 1960s, and Marxism was its "head trip." With the Academic Left that emerged in the late seventies, Marxism again asserted itself as an all-embracing theory, and terms like "hegemony" were used to explain why oppression persisted even if the oppressor could not be identified. "Ideology" now meant the sowing of suspicion.

Historical Roles

The characteristics most often used to define the Left—the demand for change; political ideals like justice, equality, and democracy; anticapitalism and the tactic of dissent; the mentalities of rationalism and ideology—are either so broad as to include many other political elements or so narrow as to apply to one American Left and not to others. Nevertheless, there are some ways of thinking about the Left that may enable us to approach a historical understanding of its function and role in twentieth-century America.

THE LEFT AS OPPOSITION   Without a Right and a Center there most likely would be no Left. For the Left is born and takes its shape as an opposition. Since it defines itself by what it rejects as well as by what it affirms, the Left is better understood when seen against the background of other political philosophies. In America the two philosophies against the Left have been conservatism and liberalism. The conservative Right has generally stood for the primacy of family, religion, authority, and property. The radical Left, in contrast, has called for the liberation of the young, the demystification of religious beliefs, the destruction of traditional authority, and the abolition of private property. The liberal Center—the Left's chief antagonist—has generally been committed to a pluralistic balance of power, an equilibrium of class interests, an ethic of opportunity and achievement, and a realistic vision of human limitations. The Left, in contrast, has demanded the liquidation of institutionalized power and interest politics, the elimination of social classes, the replacement of competitive life with one of fraternal participation and cooperative fulfillment, and unlimited visions of human possibility. Even as a political opposition, however, the Left cannot be understood in terms of traditional American politics. The American Left has never, on the national level, been a political party or an effectively organized political movement. Nor has it ever enjoyed political power. Rather, it has been something of a spontaneous moral impulse, mercurial and sporadic, suspicious of power and distrustful of politics.

THE LEFT AS NEGATION   Just as the political position of the Left may be identified by its role in opposition, so its philosophical temperament may also be characterized by a sense of negation. The Left has opposed its enemies by refusing to engage in their practice of politics as the "art of the possible," and it has tried to negate their philosophical foundations by affirming its own vision of an "impossible ideal" as a truth about to be realized.

What do we mean by the concept of negation? In simplest terms, to negate is to deny that the prevailing understanding of reality is valid.[8] Whereas some conservatives or some liberals may regard war, poverty, or alienation as permanent features of historical reality, the Left regards such phenomena as transitory features of the stages of history—real aspects of immediate historical experience, but not ultimate reality itself. Thus, rather than defending existing conditions, as do conservatives, or reforming them, as do liberals, the Left has sought to transform present society in the hope of realizing "unborn ideals" that transcend historical experience. Unceasing and uncompromising in its attack on present reality, the Left has a mentality fraught with tension. The left-wing intellectual is acutely sensitive to the gap between the real and the ideal, between what *is* and what *ought* to be. The perpetual dilemma of the Left is that it has had to treat the impossible as if it were possible, to accept the huge gap between the real and the ideal and yet struggle to realize the ideal. The philosophical burden the Left has historically assumed would be appreciated by William James as well as by Marx, for the Left recognizes that ideals presently unattainable will never be realized unless they are first articulated as an act of belief.

In attempting to articulate their visionary ideals, and thereby negate the accepted view of reality, different American Lefts have displayed different intellectual resources and temperaments. The Lyrical Left tended at first to rely more upon the regenerating force of culture and the imaginative power of poetry as a means of manifesting "premature truths"; the Old Left saw in the "science" of Marxism a method of historical understanding that would enable man to triumph over the "contradictions" of capitalism; the New Left at first embraced an existential ethic of moral choice and human commitment as a way of overcoming the paradoxes of alienation; and the Academic Left sought to expose the structures of power and domination.

THE LEFT AS A GENERATIONAL EXPERIENCE   The concept of negation is also useful in understanding the Left as a generational experience. There is little historical continuity and even less political sympathy among different generations of the American Left. The ex-radicals of the 1930s and the young radicals of the 1960s often spoke past one another whenever they did not shout one another down. The hostility that separated these two Lefts was due not only to different values and attitudes but also to profoundly different perceptions of reality and history. When the Old Left emerged from the 1930s and underwent the experience of deradicalization, it gradually came to terms with the imperfections of American society, reembraced American institutions and values, and politically (though not culturally) reconciled itself to existing reality. Certainly not all veterans of the Old Left engaged in what C. Wright Mills called the "great American celebration." Still, we must ask why the New Left saw so clearly the injustices that many members of the Old Left tended to ignore. How did it happen that human minds concerned with the same environment perceived that environment so differently?

It is not enough to say that people of different age groups will see some things differently. How one interprets existing conditions is largely determined by whether one believes they can be fundamentally changed. When the Old Left lost its belief that existing historical reality could be radically transformed, it lost its capacity for negation. To call this behavior of the Old Left a "cop-out" is as uncharitable and misleading as to describe the activities of the New Left as a "nihilistic ego trip"—epithets often hurled across the generational barricades. From the perspective of intellectual history, what divided these two radical generations was an implicit debate involving two ponderous questions: What is real? What is possible? When the Old Left intellectuals abandoned all hope of radical transformation, they tended to accept what existed as the true reality to which all human ideals must conform if they are to be realized. The New Left, innocent of the burden of historical experience, rejected this definition of reality and defiantly invoked a new sense of the possible. Thus the institutions that ex-radicals embraced as real represented to younger radicals the very system that was rejected as unreal because of its alleged irrationality and immorality. Moreover, in denying that war, poverty, racism, and alienation were inherent in the structure of historical reality or in the nature of human existence, the New Left also challenged the concept of reality and human nature that had morally numbed America during the time of the "silent generation" of the 1950s. In so doing, the New Left had done for its generation what the Old Left and Lyrical Left had once done for theirs: it articulated a new historical vision, a new sense of reality and possibility that transcended the given state of things, a new consciousness of the negating ideal—that which *ought* to exist, but does not.

A generation is not simply a people coexisting in the same time

Scene at the Homestead strike, an early instance of Left-supported working-class assertion. (Library of Congress)

period. What identifies a group as belonging to a particular generation is both a shared perspective on common historical problems and a similar strategy of action taken as a result of that perspective. For the Left, in particular, cultural forces and historical crises operate as a "formative experience" upon the mind of a new generation, which in turn shapes its impressions of the world, crystallizes its awakening convictions, and brings into focus its distinct self-consciousness as participating in a common destiny. A radical nucleus of a generation is formed when some young intellectuals or students, as a result of common "destablizing" experiences, begin to feel, articulate, and defend the identity of certain values and ideals in a society that is indifferent or hostile.[9] Thus the Lyrical Left rebelled against the philistinism of nineteenth-century Victorian culture and the tawdry machine politics of the two-party system; the Old Left, against the political defeatism and cultural despair of the "lost generation" of writers of the 1920s and the "normalcy" politics of the Coolidge era; the New Left, against the alienating mass culture of corporate life and the apathetic "consensus" politics of the 1950s. Similarly the common historical ordeals faced by each Left served to unify radical perspectives and create a generational identity. For the Lyrical Left those ordeals were the labor struggle, the First World War, the Bolshevik Revolution, the Red Scare, and the socialist-communist split; for the Old Left they were the Depression, the threat of fascism, the Spanish civil war, Stalinism and the Moscow trials, the Russo-German nonaggression pact; for the New Left they were the domestic racial crisis, the wars in Southeast Asia, Cuba, and China, and the politics of confrontation with the resultant fear of repression. These ordeals left deep and lasting impressions on each generation of the twentieth-century American Left. And the very uniqueness of these experiences explains in part why radicals of different generations see themselves as dissimilar, why they often refuse to listen to one another, why they will not deign to learn from one another.

Ally of the Working Class?

When we speak of the Left, two different social strata come to mind: the intellectuals and the workers. Historically the Left in the United States as well as in Europe has attempted to synthesize a single political force out of these two, forging something of an intellectual-worker alliance that would fuse culture and life, thought and action, truth and power. Indeed, one of the most persistent characteristics of the American Left in the twentieth century is this effort of young intellectuals and students to sink their idealistic roots into the material struggles of the working class and to find common cause with the oppressed and exploited. Thus at first glance it might seem as though the Left could be defined by identifying those social groups it supports and those it opposes. Using this mode of analysis, the sociologist and political scientist Robert MacIver located the Left as follows:

> The right is always the party sector associated with the interests of the upper or dominant classes, the left with the sector expressive of lower economic or social classes, and the center that of the middle classes. Historically this criterion seems acceptable. The conservative right has defended entrenched prerogatives, privileges and powers; the left has attacked them. The right has been more favorable to the aristocratic position, to the hierarchy of birth and wealth; the left has fought for the equalization of advantage or of opportunity, for the claims of the less advantaged. Defense and attack have met, under democratic conditions, not in the name of class but in the name of principle; but the opposing principles have broadly corresponded to the interests of different classes.[10]

There are some difficulties with this class-representation analysis of the Left. Most left-wing intellectuals do not come from the working class, and it is questionable whether their ideals "always" correspond to those of the "lower economic or social classes." On occasion radical writers may have struck a sympathetic response when they addressed themselves to the economic concerns of industrial workers. But on such issues as racism, nationalism, culture, religion, and sex they often found themselves in another world. Even the immediate economic interests of the working class can be contrary to the ideals of the Left. At the turn of the century, Left intellectuals failed to instill a spirit of class consciousness in the working class, while labor leaders successfully propounded more conservative principles of opportunity and upward social mobility. Since its cultural ideals are scarcely a replica of the class interests of labor, the Left cannot simply be defined by asserting that it will always be in support of working-class demands.

Why, then, did radical intellectuals in America seek the comradeship of the lower class? One interpretation has been offered by the historian Christopher Lasch. According to Lasch, "the rise of the new radicalism coincides with the emergence of the intellectual as a distinctive social type." Focusing on the changing nature of the social order at the turn of the century, Lasch attempts to show that the "intellectual class . . . is a distinctly modern phenomenon, the product of cultural fragmentation that seems to characterize industrial and post-industrial societies." This cultural disintegration resulted from the decline of tradition, community, and, above all, parental authority, which explains why "the revolt of the intellectuals so often took the form of a rebellion against the conventional family." And this "estrangement" of the intellectuals from the "middle class" and from the "dominant values of American culture" also explains why the intellectual "identified himself with other outcasts and tried to look at the world from their point of view" and to "see society from the bottom up."[11]

Lasch's sociological explanation is richly suggestive but historically limited. The rise of the radical intellectual did not necessarily coincide with the emergence of the "cultural fragmentation" that characterized the social structure of "industrial or post-industrial societies." Well before the full impact of industrialism, the transcendentalists and utopian reformers of the 1830s and 1840s felt themselves at odds with the prevalent values of American society, and several Brook Farm utopians tried to identify with the plight of the lower class. Moreover, some of the leading intellectuals of the Lyrical Left neither broke with their parents nor rebelled against their familial heritage. Floyd Dell, Max Eastman, and John Reed had the fondest memories of their parents and family upbringing. "When I was sixteen," Reed recalled,

> I went East to a New Jersey boarding school, and then to Harvard College, and afterward to Europe for a year's travel; and my brother followed me through college. We never knew until later how much our mother and father denied themselves that we might go, and how he poured out his life that we might live like rich men's sons. He and mother always gave us more than we asked, in freedom and understanding as well as material things.[12]

Eastman described his father as "kind, reasonable, patient, courageous, sweet-tempered, generous, truthful, just, tempered," and his beloved mother as "heroic" and "saintly."[13] As for the Old Left intellectuals of the Depression, they scarcely questioned the family as a repressive social institution. Indeed, it is not easy to find a direct causal relationship between social origin and political position. Many middle- and upper-class American intellectuals of the First World War generation experienced social estrangement in one form or another, but not all estranged intellectuals became radicals of the Left. One of the most estranged writers of the era, the social philosopher Thorstein Veblen, remained aloof from politics, while another, the poet Ezra Pound, denounced America as a "botched civilization" and went off to Europe to become the rhapsodist of Italian fascism. Until we understand the mysteries of character and personality, we probably will not know why some alienated intellectuals became Left radicals and others did not. Meanwhile, rather than explain the Left intellectual as a social type, perhaps it is best to try to see the Left as it saw itself—as a new intellectual class with a profoundly radical view of the nature of history and reality.

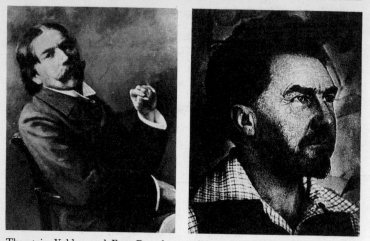

Thorstein Veblen and Ezra Pound, two alienated intellectuals whose radical critiques of society did not lead to the radical politics of the Left. (*Left*, Culver Pictures; *right*, Library of Congress)

2

The New Intellectuals

How awful for the world . . . that there are 40,000
revolutionary students in Russia, without a proletariat
or even a revolutionary peasantry behind them and
with no career before them except the dilemma:
Siberia or abroad—to western Europe. If there is
anything which might ruin the western European
movement, then it would have been this import of
40,000 more or less educated, ambitious, hungry
Russian nihilists; all of them officer candidates without
an army.   Engels to Marx, 1870

Marxism and the Intellectuals

To see the Left as an intellectual class is to accept the Left on its
own terms, for it was with this self-image that several young
radical writers and college graduates first attempted to ally themselves with the socialist movement in the United States. The appearance of the first Left of the twentieth century as an intellectual class raises three important questions: What exactly was
meant by "intellectual"? Why did many socialists at first resist the
efforts of intellectuals to enter their ranks? Who were these radical, upper-class intellectuals who were finally hailed as a van-

guard and recognized as the first genuine American Left of the twentieth century?

The term "intellectual" first came to be used to describe a group at the time of the Dreyfus affair (1898–1906), when the radical French intellectual community rose to defend the Republic against the reactionary anti-Dreyfusards. From the beginning, the term conveyed clear political implications: ethically it implied that men of ideas should serve as the authentic conscience of society; socially it described a class of writers, artists, journalists, and professors who felt themselves separated from society; ideologically it suggested that those who choose intellectual life as a vocation should repudiate the interests of their bourgeois class and remain forever independent of the corrupting power of institutions. William James, the first American known to use the term, touched upon some of these implications when he wrote in response to the Dreyfus affair: "We 'intellectuals' in America must all work to keep our precious birthright of individualism and freedom from these institutions [church, army, aristocracy, royalty]. *Every* great institution is perforce a means of corruption—whatever good it may do. Only in the free personal relations is full ideality to be found."[1]

Several radical intellectuals who graduated from college between the turn of the century and the First World War tried to find their full ideality in the American socialist movement. They were young writers whose first commitment was to culture, to those elevating pursuits that deepen the mind and heighten the imagination. This commitment created a *mesalliance*, for the Marxist socialists who came to dominate American radicalism after the turn of the century possessed no theory of a cultural class. Indeed, the idea that a revolutionary movement needed an intellectual class appeared almost alien to Marxist theory—or at least to the American version of Marxism that prevailed in the years preceding the First World War. American Marxism was characterized by an optimistic faith in natural science and historical progress. Since history was unfolding rationally according to predetermined "laws," society could be studied through the same empirical methods used in natural science. This deterministic view of history presented an awkward problem for the cultural intellectuals who wanted to become socialists and yet remain exponents of ideas. If socialism would develop automatically from the natural laws of history, what role could the radical intellectual perform? If history is determined by economic changes, what role could ideas play in the transformation of society? In the struggle to liberate the working class, Marx saw no crucial function for the moral idealism and cultural criticism of the intellectual class. It is one of the curious ironies of history that Marx, the greatest radical thinker of the nineteenth century, developed a theory of history that offered no decisive or central role for the radical mind of the intellectual.[2]

In the 1920s this problem would be addressed by the Italian Marxist Antonio Gramsci. The discovery of his prison notebooks, which Gramsci's wife smuggled out of a fascist cell after his death in 1937, lifted the spirits of Marxist intellectuals everywhere in the Western world after the Second World War. Yet even had Gramsci's writings been known in America, it is difficult to see how relevant they would be since he exhorted Marxist intellectuals to do what would surely have sounded strange to American rebels—repudiate their aloof cosmopolitanism, return to the roots from which they sprang, and merge their identity with the local masses. Would John Reed have been able to become what Gramsci called an "organic intellectual"? When the czar fell from power, Reed wanted to rush to St. Petersburg, not return to Portland, Oregon, his hometown. The Jewish radical intellectual in America would also have found strange Gramsci's description of cosmopolitanism as the curse of modernism. So too some black intellectuals and feminists who wanted to escape racism, provincialism, nativism, chauvinism, and other "organic" ties. The question of the usefulness of Gramsci's ideas will be discussed with respect to different generations of the American Left.

The problem of the role of the intellectual occupied socialist theorists from the turn of the century to the outbreak of the First World War. In 1900 the *International Socialist Review,* a scholarly

Daniel DeLeon, leading American Marxist theoretician, critic, and opponent of emerging middle-class Left intellectuals. (Library of Congress)

journal edited in Chicago by the historian A. M. Simons, published an essay entitled "Socialism and the Intellectuals," by the French writer Paul Lafargue, son-in-law of Karl Marx. Simons and Lafargue warned against the "bourgeois intellectual" who would enter the workers' movement not as a combatant in the class struggle but as a *déclassé* "aristocrat" and "mandarin," a "brain worker" who wanted to open the movement to "all amiable exploiters." The volatile Daniel DeLeon, the most militant of

American Marxists, took up the attack against the intelligentsia. Stressing the need for working-class unity, DeLeon lashed out at the "pernicious influence" of the intellectual who "is incapable of learning; of seeing that he joins the Movement, not for the Movement's sake, but for his own." At every critical moment, complained DeLeon, the intellectual betrays the movement, sacrificing its "interests to his own crossed malevolence." This curious attack on intellectuals by intellectuals did not go unanswered. John Spargo, one of the first Americans to write a book on Marx, described the leaders of the anti-intellectual campaign as "unsuccessful 'intellectuals'—lawyers without clients, authors without publishers, professors without chairs, ministers without pulpits." But intellectuals continued to be attacked from both sides of the Left, the radical wing depicting them as dispossessed professionals seeking soft positions in the labor movement, the conservative wing as dangerous adventurers and extremists who joined the movement to overcome the boredom of bourgeois existence. And perhaps both sides could agree with a coal miner who charged that the "radical bourgeois" was more concerned with such goals as free love than with the "stomach ideals" of the workers. Even more disturbing, intellectuals potentially had feet of clay: "They can steal over into the capitalist camp at any time—we can't. They can retire from the firing line—we can't."[3]

"Hail to the New Intellectuals!"

Above the crossfire of polemics hovered a deeper philosophical debate—that between materialism and idealism. Many party socialists unsympathetic to intellectuals were steeped in a crude concept of economic determinism and mechanical materialism, a scientific philosophy of history that precluded subjective ideas and creative imagination. The independent radical intellectuals, on the other hand, insisted that their function was to infuse the movement with idealism and theoretical vision, thereby making the implicit claim that they possessed a consciousness that transcended the working class. The intellectuals' case gained a better hearing shortly before the First World War. With the rising prestige of French socialism, which stressed Jean Jaurès's ethical idealism and a radical version of Henri Bergson's *"élan vital,"* the role of moral will and intuition found a place in radical theory. The intellectual could now be regarded as an active and creative force. And if ethical consciousness was a determining influence, perhaps revolutions could originate within the mind, even the mind of the avant-garde intellectual.[4]

Yet by no means had the issue been resolved in 1914 when Robert Rives LaMonte published his provocative essay called "The New Intellectuals" in the *New Review,* a theoretical journal of American Marxism. The essay celebrated the appearance of a new radical intelligentsia that emerged just before the war. These young rebels differed from two distinct previous radical types: the eager provincial who, LaMonte said, failed to build a socialist movement because, "sneering" at the doctrine of "scientific socialism," he "contemptuously" dismissed Marxism; and the enthusiastic immigrant student from New York's East Side, a "one-book man" who failed because "his intensity of concentration upon Marx deprived him of that broad general culture without which it is impossible to use the Marxian viewpoint and method fruitfully." But the younger radicals, the author pointed out, were free of textual dogmatism, eager to absorb Nietzsche along with Marx and thus become "steeped in the culture of the day and generation." Still, it was doubtful that the young radicals had successfully resolved the issue of determinism versus freedom and materialism versus idealism. They advocated a "pragmatic" socialism that was "anthropocentric," that placed the "conscious, willing individual" at the center of history. Quoting from a book by one of the young intellectuals, LaMonte noted that what they meant by socialism was not the economic system but "the will, the will to beauty, order, neighbourliness, not infrequently a will to health." Nevertheless, what impressed LaMonte was the free-spirited pragmatism of their "winsome open-mindedness," their "breadth of vision," and their "intellectual and moral receptivity." He thus welcomed the new liberators of the mind: "Hail to the New Intel-

Walter Lippmann, prominent among the New Intellectuals. (Culver Pictures)

Max Eastman, eloquent feminist and socialist. (Library of Congress)

lectuals! May they increase and flourish!"⁵ And flourish they did.

LaMonte had singled out William English Walling, Walter Lippmann, and Max Eastman. These "New Intellectuals" represented a new breed of radical: intellectuals of upper-class sensibilities and lower-class sympathies, original thinkers capable of turning easy answers into harder questions and stimulating new trains of thought, advocates of action as well as ideas. Walling, a founder of the National Association for the Advancement of Colored People, was one of the few American socialist intellectuals willing to face squarely the theoretical difficulties of socialism. Lippmann, a brilliant young Harvard graduate who had run as a socialist mayoralty candidate in upstate New York, wrote his first book on political philosophy in 1913, at the remarkable age of twenty-three. Eastman, a handsome, flamboyant poet, a Columbia University philosophy teacher, and an organizer of the early feminist and pacifist movements, was one of the dominant figures in American cultural life between 1913 and 1922. These three intel-

The philosopher William James, whose pragmatic vision of an "unfinished reality" was particularly congenial to the intellectuals of the Lyrical Left who believed that life had no limits. (Library of Congress)

lectuals represented a nucleus of important writers who had joined with other young radicals to publish the *New Review* and the *Masses*, the organs of the first American Left of the twentieth century. Around 1913 many of these writers flocked to New York's Greenwich Village and formed a colony of infidels and iconoclasts who spoke of the coming American "renaissance" and celebrated everything and anything that was new. Here, for a brief moment in American history, cultural rebellion and social revolution seemed to have come together in a thrilling synthesis of art and activism. The radiant illusion was short-lived, but while it lasted it gave the first Left its distinct bohemian flavor.

The Historical Consciousness of the Left

This Lyrical Left is discussed in a subsequent chapter. At this point it is necessary to say something about the historical consciousness that characterized the Left and distinguished it from other expressions of political and cultural radicalism.

Eastman, Lippmann, and Walling had been influenced by various doctrines of European socialism. Their commitment to socialism, however, was conditioned by a deeper commitment to a pragmatic and existential conception of the nature of reality and history. From Dewey, they had learned that knowledge was essentially experimental and that truth was to be realized in practice. As a technique of inquiry, Dewey's philosophy of "instrumentalism" liberated American thought from abstraction and contemplation, making the intellect not a talent to be admired but a tool to be applied to social problems. Yet Dewey's faith in scientific intelligence and empirical methodology seemed to drain human thought of its emotional currents. Far more congenial to the poetically minded Left intellectuals was the thought of James, a pragmatic philosopher with an existential temperament, a "mystic in love with life," as George Santayana remarked, and one who knew the meaning of "alienation" long before the term became a boring cliché.

No one agonized more over the problem of knowledge and reality than did the young William James. In his early years he was struck by a "fear of [his] own existence" that felt like "a horrible dread at the pit of [his] stomach." A psychologist interested in the soul and spirit, James later overcame his morbid depression by turning to the mysterious powers of belief. He also brought all abstract philosophical issues together under the immediate phenomenon of "experience": the world may be without ultimate metaphysical meaning, and man may be a creature without ultimate essence; yet in experiencing the world, in the process

Karl Marx, the German philosopher who inspired various generations of the American Left with his brilliant writings. (Library of Congress)

of expanding his consciousness, man can impose meaning upon it and thereby create his own essence. What counted was will, purpose, and effort. Thus James made the emotions a source of energy that could influence objective reality. He advised a group of Harvard students, "Believe that life *is* worth living, and your belief will help create the fact." James's philosophy enabled the alienated intellectual to overcome scientific skepticism and moral paralysis, for life could now be conceived as an "adventure" that involved "passional decisions" and even a "leap" to faith. After James's classic essay "The Will to Believe" (1896), it was no longer necessary to struggle over hairsplitting metaphysical squabbles like determinism, for reality was essentially "unfinished" and man was as free as he chose and "willed" to be. Although James was far from a politically minded philosopher, the implications of his thought were profoundly radical: believe that the world can be changed, and your belief will help change it.[6]

For the upper-class intelligentsia Dewey and James played an important role in making intellectual radicalism possible. Their worldview eliminated a closed, rational order, a harmonious system in which humans must find their proper place in the structure of reality as ordained by God or nature. Nor was history, as the determinists argued, a mere succession of events that proceeded along the plane of natural causation, independent of human desires and will. On the contrary, reality was dynamic and unfolding, and humanity active and creative. It is this conception of historical reality and human nature that Walling conveyed in *The Larger Aspects of Socialism* (1913), where James's idea of poetic imagination and Dewey's idea of social experimentation are combined to present Marxism as a creative adventure as well as a pragmatic science. Lippmann and Eastman shared this view. Lippmann, a former student of James, who admired Marx as a demanding thinker who "set the intellectual standards of socialism on the most rigorous intellectual basis he could find," defended Walling when he was criticized by LaMonte for his pragmatic interpretation of Marxism. Lippmann was too skeptical a thinker to accept either pragmatism or Marxism as a flawless intellectual proposition. But his brief commitment to socialism was characterized by the Jamesian imperative that one must believe in the historically impossible to overcome the corrosive effects of critical doubt. To those who drew upon history to show that socialism would only replace bourgeois exploitation by proletarian domination, Lippmann replied, "That may be true, but it is no reason for being bullied by it into a tame admission that what has always been must always be. I see no reason for exalting the unconscious failure of other revolutions into deliberate models for the next one."[7]

One of the chief characteristics of the historical consciousness of the first Left was its willingness to believe that what "has always been" can be negated, that reality can be acted upon and transformed through conscious human effort. What tended to set left-wing thinkers apart from radical literary innovators like the poet Ezra Pound, or radical disturbers of convention like the journalist H. L. Mencken, was the conviction that the world could be remade by carrying theoretical and moral thought over into the field of practical action. Along with older cultural pessimists like Henry Adams and Mark Twain, the "New Intellectuals" of 1913 also felt estranged from the prevalent values of American society; but whereas the morose historian and the brooding novelist tried to find solace in a lost, mythical past, the younger radicals believed their thoughts could be made useful in contemporary society. Similarly the Left felt itself linked with the literary bohemians by a common hatred of bourgeois hypocrisy; but whereas the artists tended to limit themselves to contemplating and expressing aesthetic ideas, the Left insisted upon the political actualization of ideas. Finally, the Left shared with the socialists a revulsion against capitalism; but whereas the "scientific socialists" awaited the unfolding of the objective "laws" of economics, the young rebels were convinced that truth was not so much found or discovered as created and made actual.

All these tendencies came to fruition in the brilliant mind of Max Eastman, the poet-philosopher of the Lyrical Left. Significantly, liberals and reformers were Eastman's favorite targets. Liberals were "soft-headed idealists" who believed in the virtue of nationalism and the efficacy of class cooperation. Accepting pragmatism but rejecting Marxism, liberals used their "minds to mitigate the subjective impact of unpleasant facts instead of defining the facts with a view to drastic action." Specifically, liberals ruled out the "drastic" weapon of working-class struggle:

Between revolutionist and reformer there is . . . a flat contradiction of wish, belief, and action. The reformer wishes to procure for the workers their share of the blessings of civilization; he believes in himself and his altruistic oratory; he tries to multiply his kind. The revolutionist wishes the workers to take their blessings of civilization; he believes in them and their organized power; he tries to increase in them the knowledge of their situation and the spirit of class conscious aggression.[8]

Eastman criticized liberals for trying to "mitigate" and "blur" the existence of class conflict, for idealizing the real instead of realizing the ideal, for interpreting existing conditions instead of drastically changing those conditions through the will to believe and the will to act. Putting Marx's notion of "praxis" into verse, Eastman expressed eloquently the idea of negation:

> Mind's task is not to blur the real
> With mimic tints from an ideal
> But to change one into another by an act.[9]

Arising as an opposition to liberalism and conservatism, possessing the will to negate reality, perceiving itself as a new generation with a new historical consciousness of freedom and possibility, the first Left of the twentieth century set out to conquer the world armed not with a systematic ideology but with a vague strategy of class conflict and working-class struggle. This strategy confronted the Lyrical Left with a problem that would continue to confound every American Left in the twentieth century—the problem of the proletariat.

3

Strangers in the Land: The Proletariat and Marxism

> Morally and spiritually I was sickened. I remembered
> my intellectuals and idealists, my unfrocked preachers,
> broken professors, and clean-minded class-conscious
> workingmen, . . . a spiritual paradise of unselfish and
> ethical romance. And I saw before me, ever blazing
> and burning the Holy Grail. So I went back to the
> working class.   Jack London, 1907

Farmers and Industrial Workers

Whatever its social or psychological origins, the modern intellectual's fascination with the working class derives in large part from
the doctrines and ideas of Karl Marx. Marx saw the laboring
masses as the vehicle of social transformation because they possessed the sheer weight of numbers, felt the economic crises more
acutely than other classes, and were strategically located in the
industrial system. Moreover, it was not the intellectuals but the
proletariat that was destined to liberate mankind: philosophers
only interpret the world; the proletariat can change it. In Marx's
theory of knowledge, to think is to act, and to work and produce is

Senator William Jennings Bryan, a great orator who aroused young radicals with his attacks on the corruptions of wealth. (Library of Congress)

to know the world by laboring upon it and transforming it. Glorifying work as an activity higher than thought itself, Marx came close to believing that the proletariat would be able to grasp "the self-awareness adumbrated in the speculations of the philosophers."[1] As the agency of historical consciousness, the proletariat would fulfill its predetermined mission by struggling to emanci-

63

pate human society from capitalist domination, peacefully if possible, violently if necessary.

This chapter is concerned with two questions: Why did the first American Left of the twentieth century fail to find a true revolutionary proletariat in the organized farmer and labor movements? Why did that Left reject the nineteenth-century tradition of American radicalism and turn to Marxism as the true revolutionary ideology?

In the opening years of the twentieth century the United States was still primarily an agricultural country. Neither backward nor underdeveloped, rural America did not have the volatile peasantry and agrarian anarchism that characterized many countries with revolutionary traditions or tendencies. Yet, toward the end of the nineteenth century, the most exciting and powerful expression of radical protest in America came from the farmers' populist movement. Populism had its origins in the sporadic discontent of western and southern growers who began to see themselves as victims of landlords and of exploitation by wealthy interests. Caught between the familiar squeeze of declining commodity prices and rising farm costs, gouged by inequitable rail rates, and harassed by eastern creditors and bankers, the growers struck back by organizing one of the most aggressive political movements of the late nineteenth century. In the early nineties the populist People's party could control or influence a dozen state legislatures and claim four senators and over fifty congressmen. The programs it advocated made it appear a radical force of the Left. Populists demanded government ownership or regulation of railroads and telegraph systems, lower tariffs, a graduated income tax, control of monopolies, direct election of senators, and low-interest government loans to farmers. Radical proposals of this sort shook the conservative classes everywhere. When the eloquent William Jennings Bryan won the Democratic presidential nomination in 1896 and adopted parts of the populist platform, the urban press headlined prophecies of doom.

Since populism antagonized the industrialists, it aroused the imagination of many young radicals. Several prominent Ameri-

Labor leader Samuel Gompers, antagonist of the socialists and defender of workers' demands for the comforts of capitalist consumption as well as the fruits of their labor. (Library of Congress)

can socialists passed through a populist phase on their way to Marxism; the title of the autobiography of the communist William Z. Foster—*From Bryan to Stalin*—reflects this. Yet serious ideological differences existed between populism and socialism. Populists rightly stressed the dangers of concentrated industrial power, but Marxists regarded the farmers' single-minded attacks upon the trusts as a misreading of history. Most Marxists accepted industrial centralization as inevitable and progressive, since business growth and consolidation would produce more industrial workers and tend to drive out the petit entrepreneur, thereby swelling the ranks of the proletariat and setting the stage for revolution. Social and ethnic issues also separated radical intellectuals from populists. Left intellectuals were at home in the cosmopolitan life of the city; southern and western farmers feared the city as alien, parasitical, and subversive to the traditional institutions of family and religion. Although populist leaders cooperated with labor in a few states, and even won the support of the "Colored Alliance," an organization of black field workers in the South, they displayed little understanding of the needs of urban workers and the aspirations of immigrants. Populist monetary policy also alienated the radical Left. Convinced that money was power, populists advocated easy credit and the free coinage of silver in order to alleviate the burden of debts and to challenge the gold standard of eastern bankers. To the socialist Left such programs merely confused the symptom and the cause by equating the "curse of gold" with the crime of capitalism.

The limitations of agrarian radicalism as a potential component of the Left can better be seen in the "contradictions" of populism. Populist leaders desired to destroy the national banking system but to preserve local state banks; they attacked industrial property but not private property; they demanded government control of railroads and monopolies but stopped far short of calling for the nationalization of the means of production, which would include the sacrosanct farm itself. Populists and socialists did tend to have a common vocabulary and common targets. Populists matched the Marxist theory of "surplus value" with their own notion of the "labor-cost theory of wealth," thereby juxtaposing the real "producing classes" against the corporate "interests." Yet the populist appeal to the dignity and justice of human toil scarcely echoed Marx's hope of doing away with the "alienated labor" that he saw as a product of capitalism, although one historian has maintained that it did.[2] Actually, populist values sprang from a traditional Protestant ethic that made hard, honest work the expression of high moral character. Indeed, the influence of that conservative ethic could be seen in the fact that farmers frequently attacked socialism as well as industrial capitalism. Socialism threatened "the love of title deeds to home [which] is inbred among the people," stated one midwesterner. Hence socialism "inevitably destroys all independence of individual action and love of country." Committed to individualism and patriotism, many populists shared the fundamental premises of American capitalism: the "sacredness" of property, the value of opportunity, and the virtue of work. "Socialism would only replace one master by another, the monopolist by the community," declared a journal of the western populists. "All the systems of anarchy and socialism are based upon a supposed quality innate in man which history from the earliest moment of his existence has disproved." Moving from the lessons of history to the principles of psychology, the journal raised the most troubling question of all: "Without individual competition and rivalry what is there to emulate? The answer must inevitably be nothing."[3]

Young radicals who had read Veblen's sociology of rural life knew what the populists wanted to "emulate." For populism ultimately betrayed a love-hate relationship with capitalism wherein the "interests" of Wall Street were opposed in order that the "higher interests" of Main Street might prevail. The acid test was Marxism, and the "inflexible reluctance" of the Midwest to tolerate "Marxian ideas," stated the Lyrical literary intellectual Randolph Bourne, revealed "its robust resistance to . . . self knowledge."[4] Steeped in Jeffersonian individualism and Protestant morality, populism could attack capitalism politically but never transcend it intellectually. Since its leitmotif was restoration rather than revolution, populism waxed and waned with the rise and decline of economic grievances.

The Lyrical Left never placed much hope in the farmers, but the failure of industrial workers to produce a radical proletariat raises a question that has troubled radicals and scholars since the turn of the century: Why is the American working class so conservative? If this question could be answered we might better understand why socialism failed in the United States and why the life of each Left has been so feeble and short.

Several answers have been suggested: the existence of the American frontier, which, while it may not have offered a safety valve to the propertyless workers in eastern cities, did keep the labor supply limited (and unemployment low) by slowing the growth of urban populations; America's advanced economic development and national income, which, while grossly maldistributed, enabled Americans to enjoy relative prosperity long before most Europeans; the American labor force, which, while perhaps materially no better off than German workers before the First World War, was characterized by the ethnic heterogeneity of immigrant groups, a factor that hindered development of class identity and promoted the desire of their descendants to exceed the status of their parents and prove themselves "respectable" Americans; and, finally, the fluid nature of the U.S. social structure, which, while not offering a universal "rags to riches" ladder to success, may have offered meaningful low-level mobility. The factor of upward social mobility is crucial, and although the paucity of historical data makes it hazardous to generalize about working-class attitudes, curiosity impels us to speculate. If American workers believed in the capitalist ideology of opportunity and mobility, did those who failed to rise see the cause of their failure as personal inadequacy rather than social inequity and thereby suffer guilt and self-deprecation? On the other hand, if workers remained skeptical of the ideology, why did they fail to develop a radical class consciousness as a means of penetrating the deception? Or were economic opportunity and occupational mobility not myth, but in some measure plausible reality? However these questions will be answered by further research, one fact seems incontestable: the American working class was far from experiencing what Marx called the "increasing misery" of the proletariat—and no one was more aware of this fact than Samuel Gompers.[5]

As president of the American Federation of Labor, Gompers was the bane of the Left. Earlier in the nineteenth century the American labor movement had seemed to offer a radical alternative to the status quo. The militant Knights of Labor, an idealistic

Victor Berger, leader of the right wing of the Socialist party in the controversy over how to establish socialism in America. (Library of Congress)

fraternity of toilers organized after the Civil War, attempted to forge the unity of all who labored—black and white, women and children, the skilled and unskilled. This experiment in working-class solidarity soon petered out, and by the end of the century the AFL dominated the labor movement in the United States. Under Gompers's powerful leadership, the AFL concentrated on organizing skilled workers, and its membership grew increasingly elitist and exclusive. In contrast to the Knights' comprehensive reform unionism, the AFL's "pure and simple" trade unionism aimed not so much to liberate by humanizing the work process as to secure greater economic gains from management. To machinists, shoe-makers, typesetters, and hardworking craftsmen living on the edge of survival, a wage increase was a godsend. But to the left-wing intellectuals, the AFL offered no ideological challenge to capitalism other than demanding more of its profits so that work-ers could purchase more of its products. Gomperism, as George Bernard Shaw said of trade unionism, was the capitalism of the proletariat.

American socialists attempted to challenge Gompers's leader-ship. But a key to the weakness of that challenge may be seen in the famous debate in 1914 between Gompers and Morris Hillquit. A Latvian immigrant, Hillquit became one of the chief spokes-men for the philosophy of socialism in America. A leading popula-rizer of Marxism, he effectively answered the attacks by critics who feared collective ownership as a threat to individual liberty. Yet, in his debate with Gompers, he was reluctant to define an "end" or "ultimate goal" of socialism other than to say that social-ists' demands went "further" and "higher" than those of the AFL. The basic difference between socialism and trade unionism was, Hillquit admitted, "a quantitative one—that the Socialist Party wants more than the American Federation of Labor."[6] Such a formulation had serious limitations. Without an enduring ideal toward which labor must struggle, without a theoretical vision that would guide everyday decisions, it was difficult for socialists to check practice against theory and even more difficult for work-ers to know how to distinguish the "quantitative" promises of socialism from those of capitalism.

Hillquit aside, other socialist intellectuals did hold out for invi-olable ideals regardless of the possibility of their realization. In this respect, Gompers may have possessed a better "materialist" grasp of historical forces than even sophisticated Marxists like Daniel DeLeon. Shunning all vague ideals, Gompers believed that "only the concrete and the immediate were material"— higher wages, shorter hours, better working conditions. As Draper has shrewdly observed, "Whatever success Gompers had, and the Socialists did not have, was scarcely a repudiation of the Marxist

emphasis on material interests. It might have indicated the need
for American Marxists to take their materialism a little more
materialistically."[7] There lay one predicament confronting intellectual radicals: to meet the immediate, material needs of the
American working class they ran the risk of settling for less than
socialism, which is not so much a demand for "more" as a demand
for the humanization of life. Yet the obverse is also true: as long as
the socialist-labor dialogue confined itself to material matters,
capitalist values would prevail. For a subtle change would take
place in America that the Left had not fully anticipated: as Veblen
perceived at the time, the United States would pass from a society
of producers to a society of buyers and spenders in which the
impulse toward "conspicuous consumption" could possibly influence even the working class. Unable to find satisfaction in routine
production, American workers could very well assume that they
would find it in burgeoning consumption. Veblen's *The Theory of
the Leisure Class* (1899) presented Marxism with a paradox: the
United States was a society with a class structure but without any
decisive conflict over the very materialistic values that kept the
structure intact. For the pervasive "pecuniary canons of taste"
would beguile the working class into believing that one finds
fullest happiness not in productive effort but in grasping for the
material symbols of status and achievement, for articles like clean
and expensive clothing, which show that the wearer does not
engage in manual labor. (The fashionable corset, Veblen observed, rendered women physically unfit for work.) As capitalism
held out the promise of more and more material goods, American
workers could mistake the abolition of scarcity for the abolition of
capitalism. Since the boosters of capitalism could claim to have
brought about the miracles of abundance, there was danger that
America's "proletariat" would accept the ruling class's power and
values.

One problem facing the American Left, then, was the problem
of consciousness. The fact that a broad class consciousness would
emerge in the working class was an article of faith to most Marxist socialists. Gompers had an answer to this eternal dream of the

Left. "I told [the socialists] that the *Klassen Bewusstsein* [class consciousness] of which they made so much was not either a fundamental or inherent element, for class consciousness was a mental process shared by all who had imagination." The real sense of workers' solidarity, argued Gompers, was "that primitive force that had its origins in experience only," the gut emotion of "class feeling" that developed among organized workers who had a common stake in their craft and position. By a strange coincidence Gompers arrived at somewhat the same conclusion Lenin had been propounding in his struggle with his Russian opponents. Lenin, too, maintained that no inherent quality of "socialist consciousness," no revolutionary vision of "what must be done," resided in the workers. Like Gompers, Lenin believed that class consciousness could be appreciated and nurtured only by those capable of understanding "philosophical, historical, and economic theories." But where Gompers obviously accepted the "primitive force" of "class feeling," Lenin believed socialist theorists must wage a strenuous *"struggle with elementalness"* and combat the workers' tendency toward either acquiescence or blind, rebellious "spontaneity" that would not lead to coherent revolutionary action. Since workers on their own would develop only a "trade union consciousness," the task of instilling true class consciousness was the unique function of the intellectuals.[8]

The Utopian Tradition

Lenin was not the first to demonstrate the role of the intellectual in the reformation of society. Indeed, in the midnineteenth century Friedrich Engels, colleague of Marx, thought he had discovered "the existing practice of communism" in various American communities like the "one at Brook Farm, Massachusetts, where fifty members and thirty pupils live on about 200 acres, and have founded a distinguished school under the leadership of a Unitarian preacher, G. Ripley."[9]

In the 1830s and 1840s America spawned a number of small socialist communes—early experiments in what a later generation would call "countercultures." The utopian colonies were headed by an odd mixture of spiritualists and sensualists: Christian communists like the Shaker Mother Ann, who called upon her followers to withdraw from the polluted world of the flesh and practice celibacy in order to prepare for the Day of Judgment; secular communists like John Humphrey Noyes, who advocated the "complex marriage" system of free love in accordance with the laws of physical and spiritual nature. Many intellectuals and utopians believed, with the French socialist Charles Fourier, that modern society had distorted original human nature. Emerson, an admirer of Fourier, best described the fragmentation of the self: "The state of society is one in which the members have suffered amputation from the trunk, and strut about as so many walking monsters,—a good finger, a neck, a stomach, an elbow, but never a man." Fourier's solution was to liberate the "passions" in order to allow the natural force of "attraction" to govern human behavior. Thus, since man is as attracted to different objects of desire as to different objects of labor, he should be tied down to neither the delight of a single woman nor the drudgery of a single job. Although Fourier's American followers (the Associationists) shied away from his pansexualism, utopians like George Ripley believed that the release of passion "will call forth, as from a well-tuned instrument, all those exquisite modulations of feeling and intellect, which were aptly termed by Plato, the 'music of his being.' "[10]

Pre–Civil War utopian socialism elicited the enthusiastic response of many intellectuals, and it influenced a wide variety of campaigns for educational reform, women's rights, pacifism, and the abolition of slavery. Significantly, the romantic utopians were the first generation of American intellectuals to try to integrate socialism with culture, to unify the life of work with the life of mind, and, in Ripley's words, "insure a more natural union between intellectual and manual labor than now exists; to combine the thinker and the worker, as far as possible, in the same individual." Utopians as well as transcendentalists believed that only when this fusion of culture and social regeneration took place could man become truly conscious of his essence and realize what Emerson called "a perfect unfolding of individual nature." The first issue of Brook Farm's *Harbinger* passionately stated this theme. After discussing literature, painting, music, sculpture, architecture, drama, "and all arts which seek the Good, by way of the Beautiful," the editorial concluded:

> We shall suffer no attachment to literature, no taste for abstract discussion, no love of purely intellectual theories, to seduce us from our devotion to the cause of the oppressed, the down-trodden, the insulted and injured masses of our fellow men. Every pulsation of our being vibrates in sympathy with the wrongs of the toiling millions, and every wise effort for their speedy enfranchisement will find in us resolute and indomitable advocates. If any imagine from the literary tone of the preceding remarks, that we are indifferent to the radical movement for the benefit of the masses, which is the crowning glory of the nineteenth century, they will soon discover their egregious mistake. To that movement, consecrated by religious principle, sustained by an awful sense of justice, and cheered by the brightest hopes of future good, all our powers, talents, and attainments are devoted. We look for an audience among the refined and educated circles, to which the character of our paper will win its way; but we shall also be read by the swart and sweaty artisan; the laborer will find in us another champion; and many hearts, struggling with the secret hope which no weight or care and toil can entirely suppress, will pour on us their benedictions as we labor for the equal rights of All.[11]

The utopian impulse also infused the writings of late-nineteenth-century thinkers. In Henry George's *Progress and Poverty*, Edward Bellamy's *Looking Backward*, and William Dean Howells's *A Traveler from Altruria*, Americans could find schemes for redistributing nonproductive wealth (unearned income) and visions of a future world of social felicity. Together with muckraking journalists and progressive scholars, utopian novelists subjected America to a ferment of social criticism that effectively exposed the injustices of capitalism and the power of the business class. Moreover, going beyond the populists and trade unionists, the utopians consciously sought to alter the conditions of work and the quality of life. Nevertheless, despite its humane impulses and enormous popularity, the whole tradition of utopian socialism seemed inadequate to most radicals of the twentieth century.

As models of social conscience, the pre—Civil War utopian communes offered a mirror of self-criticism and a mechanism of escape. But as movements for social change, they produced little of enduring value. Looking back, later generations of radicals would claim that the romantic communitarians failed because they lacked an understanding of economics and a commitment to politics. Setting up fragile enclaves in a brave but innocent attempt to escape the grasping paws of society, utopians assumed they could insulate their communities from the ubiquitous pressures of capitalism. Shunning institutions such as political parties, labor organizations, the law, the church, and the professions, they disengaged themselves from political life. Hopelessly naive about the nature of power ("power ceases in the instant of repose"—Emerson), the transcendentalists in particular appeared to be formulating useless aesthetic solutions to pressing social problems.

Late-nineteenth-century utopians also seemed to have no grasp of economic realities. Approaching socialism as an ethical force, the inevitable result of moral progress, many utopians believed they could elicit from men of power the funds with which to build pastures of cooperation within a jungle of competition. Moreover, the utopians had no direct ties to the unorganized and unskilled workers. Though deeply moved by the plight of industrial workers, novelists like Bellamy and Howells were more concerned with the devastating impact of competitive capitalism upon traditional values. Both writers wanted to replace rampant individualism with some version of the cooperative community, and also to keep the virtues of the country safe from corruption by a "foreign" socialism that, in Bellamy's telling words, "smells to the average American of petroleum, suggests the red flag, and all manner of sexual novelties, and an abusive tone about God and religion, which in this country we at least treat with decent respect." This concern for the moral health of the traditional American character linked the two (pre- and post-Civil War) generations of uto-pian socialists. Defending Fourierism, the journalist Horace Greeley spoke of the need for "education and training," which will lead men to the habits of "Industry, Virtue, Self-Respect, instead of those which naturally lead to Idleness, Dissipation, Vice and Debasement." The politics of middle-class self-preservation, uto-pian socialism was an attempt to reform the circumstances of economic life in order better to affirm the principles of moral life. Humane, civilized, sincere, genteel, proper, and upright, reform socialism appeared to younger radicals to be the false conscious-ness of the "starched collar" class.[12]

Few members of the Left could find an inspiring political vi-sion in traditional nineteenth-century liberalism and radicalism. Organized farmers and industrial workers never constituted a rev-olutionary proletariat; utopians never questioned the sanctity of private property; liberals never took up the strategy of class strug-gle; and humanitarian reformers could never transcend a genteel legacy of polite idealism. Yet there remained one doctrine that supposedly would fill all these needs—Marxism.

The Marxist Background

The doctrines of Marx were first brought to America by immi-grants who fled Germany after the ill-fated uprisings of 1848. Steeped in the problems of class consciousness, German-American Marxists like Joseph Weydemeyer and Friedrich Sorge opposed utopianism as an idle dream completely out of touch with immi-grant and proletarian life. The German leaders also organized American branches of the International Workingmen's Associa-tion, the First International, established in London with the sup-port of Marx. A second generation of German immigrants brought with them the ideas of the founder of German social democracy, Ferdinand Lassalle. Later in the century, as successive waves of Italian, Jewish, and east European immigrants arrived, and the labor struggle in the United States grew more intense, American socialism took on a variety of expressions, including anarchism and syndicalism. These groups divided not over the goal of socialism but over how to achieve it.

Drastically reduced, the arguments revolved around three issues. The first was the argument over politics versus economics. Although positions were never clear and consistent, in general the Lassalleans believed workers and intellectuals must win over the state through political activity. The Marxists, in contrast, maintained that economic struggle through union organization took precedence over electoral politics.

The second issue, involving the pace and nature of historical change, divided the gradualists from the extremists. The right-wing socialists believed the goals of Marx could be realized step-by-step through piecemeal changes, while the left wing held out for an almost apocalyptic leap to socialism. Hence the left wing castigated the palliative reforms sponsored by progressives, claiming that socialism could not be legislated into existence until capitalism was abolished. Similarly, on the issue of trade unionism, the left wing advocated setting up organizations to rival established unions, even though the tactic of "dual unionism" jeopardized efforts at unifying the labor movement, and the right wing advocated entering established unions and "boring from within" in order to educate the workers to socialism. The chief theoretical spokesman for the left wing was DeLeon, dubbed an *impossibiliste* by his opponents because of his scorn for immediate programs. The chief practical spokesman for the right wing was Victor Berger, the first American socialist elected to Congress. Their disagreements represented something of a pale repetition of the intense dialogue over "orthodoxy" versus "revisionism" that had occupied the international socialist movement in Europe. DeLeon adhered to the traditional version of class struggle and the triumph of the proletariat, while Berger tried to adapt Marxist principles to American conditions. One saw the birth of socialism in the revolutionary power of the workers, the other in the evolutionary reforms of the government. Moderates accused DeLeon of indulging in revolutionary fantasy, while militants accused Berger of subscribing to an evolutionary fallacy.

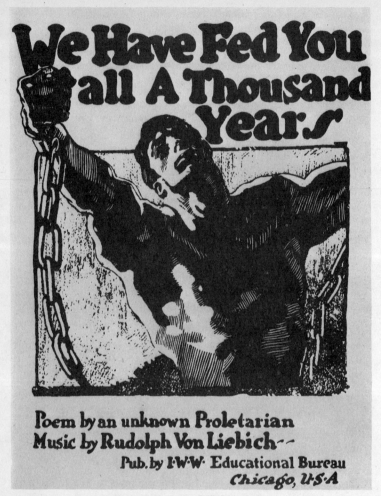

Cover of sheet music distributed by the IWW in 1918.

The third dispute among socialists arose over the use of violence. Contrary to the myth of peaceful and orderly progress, the United States had been the scene of one of the most ravaging social struggles in the Western world. Between 1881 and 1906 some 30,000 strikes and lockouts occurred, affecting almost

200,000 businesses and over 9.5 million workers. From the coal mines of Pennsylvania, where Irish Molly Maguires would methodically murder the management's police spies, to the mine fields of Colorado, where management hired state authorities to terrorize and lynch migrant coal workers, class warfare became a daily reality. After Chicago's famous Haymarket Riot of 1886 socialists disagreed sharply over the tactic of violence. Violence was associated with the idea of anarchism, a simple and yet complex doctrine opposed to all forms of authority and coercion, what Max Nomad has called an elusive "political daydream" of total statelessness and classlessness. Psychologically as well as politically, anarchist terrorism reflected the utter hopelessness and desperation of the disinherited. By the time of the First World War six chiefs of state had been assassinated in the name of anarchism, including, in the United States, President William McKinley.

There were thousands of anarchists among the Italian-American followers of Enrico Malatesta and the German-American disciples of Johann Most. What troubled the American labor movement, however, was not the sporadic deeds of violence by isolated foreign terrorists, but the sustained doctrine of class warfare of the Industrial Workers of the World. The IWW sprouted in the western states mainly among unorganized, seminomadic lumbermen and miners. The Wobblies, as they were called, were tough, boisterous, and defiant. Appropriately, their songs have become part of the idiom of radical folk music, their courageous exploits legendary in the annals of the American Left. A grand brotherhood of drifting hoboes and daring heroes, the Wobblies had more than their share of political martyrs: Wesley Everst, a northwestern lumberman riddled with bullets by the American Legion after one true patriot castrated him; Carlo Tresca, a colorful agitator gunned down by an unknown political assassin; Joe Hill, a Utah construction worker arrested on a spurious murder charge, who exclaimed while facing a firing squad, "Don't mourn for me. Organize!" Occasionally the IWW organized as many as 30,000 workers; and, in 1912, during the height of its fame, it won a dramatic, long-fought textile strike in Lawrence, Massachusetts.

Krylenko

Carlo Tresca, an anarchist folk-hero of the Left who antagonized fascists and communists until he was assassinated in New York City in 1943. (Courtesy Yvette Eastman)

The Wobblies believed in syndicalism, originally a French doctrine that held that completely autonomous workers' unions (or syndicates) could lead the masses to socialism. Because of their great faith in the spontaneous, creative character of the proletariat, syndicalists were often at odds with Marxists, who had less

Big Bill Haywood, *right*, leader of the anarcho-syndicalist Wobblies, in Moscow with Max Eastman, *left*, and James D. Cannon, founder of the Socialist Workers party, an American Trotskyite faction. (Courtesy Yvette Eastman)

faith in the untutored political consciousness of the workers.

What disturbed American socialists was not so much the European issue of "spontaneity" versus "consciousness" as the tactics employed by the IWW. The tactics were a variation on the anarcho-syndicalist theme of "propaganda by the deed": "direct action," "sabotage," and the magic of the "general strike," which supposedly would bring down all authority in a single blow. Yet the Wobblies' use of violence has been greatly exaggerated. Wobblies were convinced that power comes from the barrel of a gun, but they also knew that the ruling class possessed more guns. Although they occasionally resorted to Winchester rifles or dynamite sticks to defend themselves or to retaliate, seldom did Wobblies as an organization use violence as a strategic weapon, and rarely did their leaders really believe—despite the rhetorical bombast of their declarations—that violence alone could lead to power. "I, for one," the Wobbly leader Bill Haywood remarked during the Lawrence strike, "have turned my back on violence. It

Troops hold workers in check at a demonstration during the crucial textile strike in Lawrence, Massachusetts. (Library of Congress)

wins nothing. When we strike now, we strike with our hands in our pockets. . . . Pure strength lies in the overwhelming power of numbers."[13] Nevertheless, the issue was fiercely debated at various socialist conferences; and in 1912 the rising tension between the socialists and the syndicalists came to a head when the Socialist party amended its constitution to prohibit the use of "sabotage." The repudiation of violence made socialism more respectable, but the expulsion of the IWW from the SP made Wobblyism more attractive to the Left in its fight against respectability.

Despite the factionalism, socialism grew rapidly after the turn of the century. In 1901 the newly formed Socialist party broadened the base of the movement under the inspiring leadership of Eugene Debs. Between 1902 and 1912 the SP's membership grew from 10,000 to 118,000, and its electoral power from 95,000 to the nearly 900,000 votes that Debs gathered as presidential candidate in 1912. During this period it could claim one congressman, 56

Eugene V. Debs, who during his 1920 campaign (conducted from a jail cell) won almost a million votes. (Library of Congress)

A Greenwich Village (New York City) gathering place of the early 1920s. The inscription reflects the sense of the "Village" as a center of artistic and political ferment of the time. Jessie Tarbox Beals, "Polly's Restaurant." (Courtesy Museum of the City of New York)

mayors, 160 councilmen, and 145 aldermen. The socialist press in America circulated 5 English and 8 foreign-language dailies, 262 English and 36 foreign-language weeklies, and 10 English and 2 foreign-language monthlies. Several developments account for the dramatic rise of American socialism during its "golden years" (roughly 1902–12): the absorption of populist elements, particularly after 1910 when the SP reversed its 1908 resolution calling for nationalization of farm land; the influx of immigrants and the SP's policy of ethnic pluralism, which allowed Italians, Jews, Germans, Poles, Hungarians, Slavs, Slovaks, and Finns to establish autonomous branches; and the increasing prestige of European socialist parties, some of which appeared to be on the verge of securing an absolute parliamentary majority before the First World War.

Historians differ over when the SP began its decline. According to James Weinstein, the expulsion of the syndicalist Left in 1912 did not impair the growth of socialism, which continued to win the political vote of urban ethnic groups, radical intellectuals, and some middle-class elements discontented with the Democratic and Republican parties. As the research of John Laslett shows, however, the SP lost the support of many important trade unionists like the brewery, shoe, garment, machinist, and mine workers, who began to align with the Democratic party in support of the social and labor reforms of the Wilson administration.[14] Whatever the reasons for the rise and decline of American socialism, its history included some of the most towering figures in twentieth-century American radicalism. Three deserve special mention.

Three Leaders in American Socialism

DEBS   Most magnetic was Eugene Debs. Straight from the Indiana heartland of America, lanky and bald, his forehead weighted with worry and cheeks crinkled with laughter, Debs was the symbol of integrity. His life history reads almost like a socialist morality tale. At work on the railroads at the age of fifteen, he

Big Bill Haywood, leader of the Wobblies, (second from left) marching with fellow comrades in opposition to the war in 1918. (Wayne State University, Archives of Labor and Urban Affairs)

later gave up stoking locomotives to organize the American Railway Union. In 1893 his union won a crucial strike against James J. Hill's powerful Great Northern Railroad; but instead of following in Gompers's footsteps Debs then used his organizing talents to "eliminate the aristocracy of labor," to try to open up the union movement to all workers. In his early years he had been deeply stirred by the writings of Bellamy and George and later by the speeches of Bryan. He also read Marx while serving a prison term

85

for his activities in the bloody Pullman strike of 1894. Debs often recalled the government's intervention in that strike as his conversion experience: "At this juncture there were delivered, from wholly unexpected quarters, a quick succession of blows that blinded me for an instant and then my eyes opened—and in the gleam of every bayonet and the flash of every rifle *the class struggle revealed itself.*" Actually Debs's conversion to socialism was much less melodramatic, for despite the Pullman experience he kept faith in democratic reformism until the populist debacle of 1896. Thereafter he entered the SP and emerged as its titular head for almost twenty years. As late as 1920, once again in jail, this time for alleged antiwar propaganda, he drew nearly one million votes as the SP's presidential candidate. Debs had the martyr's charisma, but he also possessed tremendous oratorical power, a "sort of gusty rhetoric," wrote Dos Passos, that made workers "want the world he wanted, a world brothers might own where everybody would split even. . . ." "His tongue," recalled Eastman, "would dwell upon a *the* or an *and* with a kind of earnest affection for the humble that threw the whole rhythm of his sentence out of conventional mold, and made each one seem a special creation of the moment." Although Debs tried to remain above ideological battles, occasionally he criticized the SP's two extreme wings. Chiding "the spirit of bourgeois reform" on the Right, he insisted that "voting for socialism is not socialism any more than a menu is a meal"; opposing the saboteur rhetoric of the syndicalist Left, he maintained that "American workers are law-abiding and no amount of sneering or derision will alter the fact." Debs had his party enemies, but to the Left in general he was a "poet," a "saint," the "sweetest strongman," and a "lover of mankind."[15]

DELEON   Debs became the missionary of American socialism; Daniel DeLeon, its metaphysician. DeLeon was an impressive figure. His massive head, with its piercing black eyes and carefully trimmed white beard, seemed precariously balanced on his short neck and narrow shoulders. An educated scholar and masterful theoretician, he seemed to carry the whole blueprint for revolution in his brain. After the Bolshevik uprising in 1917, the Lyrical radical John Reed, back from Russia, reportedly told his American comrades that Lenin was a "great admirer of Daniel DeLeon" and regarded him as "the only one who had added anything to socialist thought since Marx."[16] Although the story may be apocryphal,[17] Lenin and DeLeon did have much in common. Studying the same developments after the turn of the century, they wrestled with similar problems: the strategy of party organization and control of its press, the "bourgeoisification" of the workers, and the effect of imperialism on the coming revolution. Like Lenin, DeLeon faced the crucial problem of the road to power. Should socialists overthrow the existing order through the efficacy of the ballot (Lassalleans), through the leadership of a mass party (Marxists), or through the economic struggle of radical industrial unions (syndicalists)?

In theory DeLeon attempted a formulation that would reconcile all sides: the SP would be voted peacefully into power but, once established, would liquidate itself and turn over the administration of the state to the workers themselves—a foreshadowing of Lenin's *State and Revolution.* In practice DeLeon was far to the left of the Debsian socialists and the reformists. Nothing was more repugnant to DeLeon than the revisionist argument that "the movement is everything, the goal nothing." A movement without a clearly defined goal could secure only piecemeal reforms that would leave the structure of capitalist power intact. DeLeon could tolerate economic reforms only if they were accompanied by sustained revolutionary consciousness. What he feared most was Gompersism—the corruption of the working class by bourgeois values and comforts. Ultimately he placed his faith in revolutionary industrial unions that would educate workers and cultivate their class consciousness. Organized like syndicates, the unions would be led by a dedicated cadre.

In all revolutionary movements, as in the storming of fortresses, the thing depends on the head of the column—upon that minority

that is so intense in its convictions, so soundly based in its principles, so determined in its actions, that it carries the masses with it,
storms the breastworks and captures the fort.[18]

HAYWOOD   DeLeon's finely spun theories made socialism appear as the perfection of an idea. The socialism of Big Bill Haywood, in contrast, symbolized the beauty of deed and the power of
action. Haywood captured the Lyrical Left's imagination, for he
came as close as any radical to embodying the proletarian-intellec-
tual, a workingman whose mind and conscience transcends his
condition and thereby makes him an articulate spokesman for
those who labor with their hands. Haywood was born in a board-
inghouse in Salt Lake City in 1869. As a youth he worked as a
bellhop, a messenger boy, and an usher; by age fifteen he was
hefting a pick and shovel as a hard-rock miner in Nevada, outfit-
ted with "overalls, a jumper, a blue shirt, mining boots, two pairs
of blankets, a set of chessmen, boxing gloves and a big lunch of
plum pudding his mother fixed for him," wrote Dos Passos. Restless and footloose, he wandered from town to town, working the
mines by day and sampling the saloons and brothels by night. He
came to know the West not as a land of opportunity but as a brutal
terrain for class warfare in which the conflict between labor and
capital was irrepressible. In the late nineties he joined the Western Federation of Miners and rose rapidly as an effective union
organizer and strike tactician. Shortly afterwards he joined the
IWW, and in 1905, during a protracted industrial war in the
Colorado coalfields, Haywood and two other union men were kidnapped by Pinkerton agents and brought to Boise to be tried for
complicity in the murder of Governor Frank Steunenberg of
Idaho. The entire labor movement came to their defense, and
after the great criminal lawyer Clarence Darrow won their acquit-
tal, Haywood became a national figure and a confirmed revolutionary. "Those of us who are in jail," Haywood later wrote to
fellow socialists, "those of us who have been in jail—all of us who
are willing to go to jail. . . . We are the Revolution!"[19]

A broad-shouldered man, over six feet tall, with a dark mat of hair and a black patch over a maimed right eye, Haywood seemed the élan vital of the wretched of the earth. The British socialist J. Ramsay MacDonald perceived in him the embodiment of Georges Sorel's revolutionary will, "a bundle of primitive instincts, a master of direct statement. . . . I saw him addressing a crowd in England, and there his crude appeals moved his listeners to wild applause. He made them see things, and their hearts bounded to be up and doing."[20] Haywood could move the intellectual Left in much the same way, and when the SP adopted its antisabotage resolution in 1912 and expelled Haywood the following year, several radical intellectuals sided with "Comrade Haywood." By that time Haywood himself had repudiated violence, but the actions of the socialists indicated no understanding of the needs of helpless miners and lumbermen who moved too often to become registered voters. Haywood, the "Polyphemus from the raw mining camps of the West [who] dedicated himself to the organization of the unskilled, the poverty stricken and forgotten workers," symbolized the real poverty and suffering that the intellectuals had never known. He also appealed to the intelligentsia because he seemed to be a poet of the proletariat, the harbinger of a new socialist culture. In Max Eastman's novel *Venture*, Haywood addresses a salon of America's literati. After explaining why there can be no art for the Pittsburgh steelworker, he expounds the nature of a true working-class culture:

"Not only is art impossible to such a man," he said, "but life is impossible. He does not live. He just works. He does the work that enables you to live. He does the work that enables you to enjoy art, and to make it, and to have a nice meeting like this and talk it over."

Bill used "nice" without irony: he meant it.

"The only problem, then, about proletarian art," he continued, "is how to make it possible, how to make life possible to the proletariat. In solving that problem we should be glad of your understanding, but we don't ask your help. We are going to solve it at your expense. Since you have got life, and we have got nothing but work, we are going to take our share of life away from you, and put you to work."

"... When we stop fighting each other—for wages of existence on one side, and for unnecessary luxury on the other—then perhaps we shall all become human beings and surprise ourselves with the beautiful things we do and make on the earth. Then perhaps there will be civilization and a civilized art. But there is no use putting up pretenses now. The important thing ... is that our side, the workers, should fight without mercy and win. There is no home for humanity anywhere else."[21]

By and large, American socialism was a movement not of but on behalf of the working class. Although it presumed to speak for the workers and to articulate their needs, the doctrines and tactics had been developed by intellectuals and party leaders. The Wobblies, the embodiment of a working class that spoke for itself and struggled for its own class interests, gave the Left its opportunity to reconcile the aristocracy of intelligence with the nobility of labor. Whereas the earlier Brook Farm utopians hoped that the "swart and sweaty" laborers would rise to culture, the New Intellectuals of 1913 were willing to sit at the feet of Haywood, the authentic voice of a genuine American proletariat, while he expounded the creation of a new and superior culture by the working class. Eastman's image of the Wobbly leader may have been more romantic than real, and likewise the Left's need to believe in a revolutionary proletariat may have been nurtured more by faith than by fact. The idea of the proletariat, as the agency of historical transformation, as the ascending class that enables the radical intellectual to maintain a dynamic contact with the masses, lives and dies in the mind of the Left.

Two

HISTORY

4

The Lyrical Left

When I was up at Columbia University, one of the
most unforgettable and most glamorous experiences I
recall in my student life was the first lecture I heard by
Max Eastman before the Socialist Study Club. He came
before us then as the fair-haired apostle of the new
poetry, the knight errant of a new and rebellious
generation, the man who was making his dreams come
true—as poet, as thinker, as editor, as teacher, as
psychologist, as philosopher, as a yea-sayer of the joy
and adventure of living in the fullest and richest sense
of the word. Even then Max was already a glamorous,
exciting figure in the world of letters and in the world
of adventure. Life was bursting in all its radiance all
around him. For him existence was a fight, a song, a
revolution, a poem, an affirmation.

> Lincoln Schuster to Victor Gollancz, 1936

The fiddles are tuning as it were all over America.

> John Butler Yeats, 1912

The Greenwich Village Rebellion

Unlike other American Lefts, the first Left of the twentieth century was born in a mood of unparalleled optimism. "One's first
strong impression," recalled Malcolm Cowley, "is one of the bus-
tle and hopefulness that filled the early years from 1911–1916.
. . . Everywhere new institutions were being founded—magazines, clubs, little theatres, art or free-love or single-tax colonies,
experimental schools, picture galleries. Everywhere was a sense of
comradeship and immense potentialities for change." The new
intellectuals' open-air habitat was Manhattan's Greenwich Village, which Floyd Dell, the chronicler of Village life, called "a

moral health resort"; their spiritual home was Twenty-three Fifth Avenue, Mabel Dodge's notorious apartment, where anyone and everyone who had a plan to remake the world was welcomed: "Socialists, Trade-Unionists, Anarchists, Suffragists, Poets, Relations, Lawyers, Murderers, 'Old Friends,' Psychoanalysts, I.W.W.'s, Single Taxers, Birth-Controlists, Newspapermen, Artists, Modern-Artists, Clubwomen, Women's-Place-is-in-the-Home Women, Clergymen, and just plain men all met there" to experience "freedom" and exchange "opinions."[1]

Dell caught the atmosphere of 1912 when, responding to the poet Edna St. Vincent Millay, he labeled it the "Lyric Year." The period seemed an intellectual saturnalia in which everything was possible and nothing prohibited, a joyous springtime in which, Mabel Dodge recalled, "barriers went down and people reached each other who had never been in touch before." The mood of America's "New Renaissance" was supremely lyrical, an outpouring of emotions and creative energy that had long been repressed. Responding to the thrilling labor strikes that spread from Lawrence, Massachusetts, to Ludlow, Colorado, the literary Left saw itself as the "music-makers" and "movers and shakers" of a revolutionary culture that aimed to break down the dualism between contemplative life and active life. This poetic passion for releasing the emotions and at the same time unifying thought, feeling, and action gave the first Left its distinctive lyrical style and tone. "Our eyes trained for every seeing," wrote Eastman in 1913, "our ears catching the first murmur of a new experience, we ran after the world in our eagerness, not to learn about it, but to taste the flavor of its being." No wonder Eastman could define himself as "the American lyrical Socialist—a child of Walt Whitman reared by Karl Marx."[2]

The Lyrical radicals went further than any previous generation in attempting to fuse politics and art. Whereas Emerson and Thoreau had looked upon collective action with disdain, the young intellectuals embraced it with delight. Whereas the transcendentalists had believed politics the realm of opinion and poetry the realm of truth, the new cultural rebellion denied all dichotomies.

Mabel Dodge, whose home in Greenwich Village became a kind of salon for radical thinkers in the arts and politics. (Bettmann Archive)

The Lyrical Left rejected Yeats's contention that poetry and politics, imagination and truth, private vision and public life must inevitably be in eternal opposition. Rather, the appeal of the prewar Left was its all-encompassing "integration of conflicting values . . . : politics, poetry, and science; justice, beauty, and knowledge."[3] The lyrical impulse to synthesize influenced even the sober-minded Walter Lippmann; in *A Preface to Politics* (1913), he sought to humanize government, to elevate it from "routine" procedures and stale formulas so that "the ideals of human feel-

Isadora Duncan, one of the many stars of the cultural and intellectual world seen by the Left as a symbol of sensual and artistic liberation. (Library of Congress)

ings" would "place politics among the genuine, creative activities of men." Making man the measure of politics, Lippmann realized, "amounts to saying that the goal of action is in its final analysis aesthetic and not moral—a quality of feeling instead of a conformity to rule."[4]

The young intellectuals cheerfully presided over the death of the "genteel tradition" as they attacked its Victorian standards, its polite manners and haut-bourgeois tastes, its Puritan heritage and decorous Brahmin literature, and, above all, its condescending certainty that it had found ultimate truth and absolute value. Forsaking the traditional quest for permanent truth and value, the young intellectuals embarked upon a life that embraced change and flux, a new life that had to be experienced before it could be analyzed. Their odyssey often brought them to Bergson, James, Nietzsche, Freud, and D. H. Lawrence, heralds of the antirationalist power of intuition, desire, will, dream, and instinct. Proclaiming a new ethic of gaiety and sensuality, the Lyrical rebels proudly declared themselves to be reckless and irresponsible. "A feeling of power that translates itself into duty is no fun," advised Mabel Dodge, who believed that "consciousness is more important than heroism or than any given ethical or political point of view, and I believe it more desirable to be ignoble and know it than to be noble and not know it." The "superb modern healthiness" of Dostoevsky, announced Randolph Bourne, is his ability to draw no "dividing line between the normal and the abnormal, or even between the sane and insane." Despite the cult of irresponsibility, many intellectuals who had been brought up in a religious environment carried with them the heritage against which they rebelled. Their passion for social justice, their quest for love and friendship, and their thirst for aesthetic experience reflected the internalized values of their Protestant backgrounds. If they rejected the capitalist ethos of striving to make good, many retained the religious ethic of striving to *be* good. In essence, theirs was a Christian culture without Christianity. Even so pagan a libertine as Mabel Dodge could, between taking John Reed as a lover and peyote as an offering, admit in a moment of doubt, "Finally I believed the lack to be in myself when I found myself perpetually unassuaged—and, I thought, only religion will fill me, someday I will find God." But God was dead, and no one knew this better than the generation of 1913.[5]

Although a certain sense of orthodox values and a vague spiritual hunger lingered on, with the collapse of religious beliefs the young intellectuals tried to find meaning and fulfillment in culture, sex, or politics—in many cases all three. Some turned to radical politics for a surrogate religion. For Max Eastman, Marxism would put an end to spiritual anguish: "I need no longer extinguish my dream with my knowledge. I need never again cry out: 'I wish I believed in the Son of God and his second coming.' "[6] Until 1917, when the Bolshevik Revolution challenged evolutionary democratic socialism, the Lyrical Left's radicalism drew on British Fabian and Guild socialism as well as on Marxism. The Left's socialism was also an outgrowth of a self-conscious youth culture that, at Harvard and Columbia especially, gave the blasé high school graduate the option of radical activism or *Kulturpessimismus*. Students debated socialism in classrooms, fraternities, and at the meetings of the Intercollegiate Socialist Society, where wealthy young scions from the Ivy League listened to Jack London, the golden-boy dropout who was becoming America's first millionaire novelist, lecture on the beauties of the social revolution.

Socialism appealed to intellectuals for diverse reasons. Eastman saw socialism both as a science and as an aesthetic liberation that would bring forth a life of creative leisure. The whimsical playboy John Reed hoped that struggling for socialism would overcome the *mauvaise foi* that plagued him and other middle-class intellectuals: "My happiness is built on the misery of others . . . that fact poisons me, disturbs my serenity, and makes me write propaganda when I would rather play."[7] Lippmann, precocious social philosopher and leading figure in the Harvard Socialist Club, considered socialism the only alternative to the corruption of Tammany Hall and the power of big business. Yet it is significant that Lippmann, one of the first American intellectuals to see the relevance to politics of the new irrationalist psychology, was also one of the first of the Lyrical Left to have reservations about socialism. Convinced that any political movement must be built upon a realistic theory of human nature, Lippmann found socialism wanting in two respects: its idolization of the masses ignored the widespread visceral need for heroic leaders, and its faith in the inevitable polarization of classes scarcely took into account the complexity of America's multiclass structure. At the same time, Lippmann rejected the argument of Walling's *Progressivism and After,* that the transition to socialism would be gradual, proceeding from the state capitalism of the industrialists to the progressive reforms of the middle class. Dismissing Walling's reasoning as an expression of the "American Dream," Lippmann believed that socialism could be achieved, if at all, only by organized pressure from the lower classes. That conviction attracted him to the IWW. Although the Wobblies scorned political activity, ignored the probability that the state would not disappear after capitalism, and seemed not to realize that workers' syndicates could exploit consumers as much as industrialists could, Lippmann still believed the IWW possessed tremendous potential because, unlike all other radical movements, "it has practiced actual solidarity." Lippmann refrained from glorifying the IWW, which he regarded as capable of only "insurrection," but he could agree with Eastman that it was "the only genuinely *proletarian* or revolutionary organization that ever existed in America."[8]

The first twentieth-century American Left advertised itself in two different publications, the *New Review* and the *Masses.* The former reflected its sober mind and the latter its soaring spirit. In the *New Review* the Left debated the basic issues facing socialism, carried symposia on the feminist movement, and explored the relatively new field of Negro history. But this sophisticated theoretical journal was overshadowed by the *Masses,* perhaps the heartiest journal in the history of American radicalism. Free of doctrinal strain, the *Masses* gave radicalism a well-needed lift of laughter. Satirical but not cynical, audacious but not self-righteous, it was animated by eight passions: "fun, truth, beauty, realism, freedom, peace, feminism, revolution."[9] Its masthead promised the *Masses* would please no one and delight everyone:

A REVOLUTIONARY AND NOT A REFORM MAGAZINE: A MAGAZINE WITH A SENSE OF HUMOR AND NO RESPECT FOR THE RESPECTABLE: FRANK, ARROGANT, IMPERTINENT, SEARCHING FOR THE TRUE CAUSES: A MAGAZINE DIRECTED AGAINST RIGIDITY AND DOGMA WHEREVER IT IS FOUND: PRINTING WHAT IS TOO NAKED OR TRUE FOR A MONEY-MAKING PRESS: A MAGAZINE WHOSE FINAL POLICY IS TO DO AS IT PLEASES AND CONCILIATE NOBODY, NOT EVEN ITS READERS.

Edited by Eastman with the help of Dell and Reed, the *Masses* featured young poets and novelists, reputable journalists, and talented artists and cartoonists who depicted the foibles of the rich and the frustrations of the poor. The breezy combination of bohemianism and radicalism was too much for the stolid labor Left and the old-time socialists like W. J. Ghent, who complained of the *Masses*, "It is peculiarly the product of the restless metropolitan coteries who devote themselves to the cult of Something Else; who are ever seeking the bubble Novelty even at the door of Bedlam."[10] One wit wondered how the *Masses* ever expected to reach the masses:

> They draw nude women for the *Masses*
> Thick, fat, ungainly lasses—
> How does that help the working classes?[11]

Socialist attacks failed to dampen the confident bravado of the Lyrical Left, which did its best to help the lower classes by raising funds for striking coal and textile workers, by publicizing the plight of immigrants and blacks, and by speaking truth to power. What would undermine its optimism was the subsequent challenge of historic events.

War and the State

The first challenge to the ideals of the Left came with the outbreak of the First World War in August 1914. From the establishment of the First International in 1864 to Trotsky's attempt to
start a Fourth International in 1939, the ideal of an international
working-class community loomed as the great hope of the Left. In
the years before the war, when the ideal seemed close to realization, American radicals assumed that European workers had
achieved the political strength and maturity to oppose war and
declare their solidarity with the Second International. When war
came, however, most socialist parliamentarians approved military
budgets in their respective governments, while workers responded
to the call of nationalism. Radicals had earlier been able to mount
antiwar demonstrations, but once war was declared there were no
mass protests, no general strikes, no worldwide labor boycotts.
The proletariat marched off to battle with the rest of the human
race.

In December 1914 the American SP issued a manifesto condemning the war, announcing its neutrality, and declaring it the
"supreme duty" of socialists to rededicate themselves to the "im-
perishable principles of international socialism." The manifesto
created bitter inner-party debate. To moderates like Hillquit and
Spargo the crisis of European socialism made it clear that workers
ultimately placed their country before their class and that, thus,
the concept of proletarian internationalism was a "frail wand."
The more militant Marxists, like Louis Fraina and Louis Boudin,
however, now began to trace the origins of the war to imperialism, an exercise that enabled them to sustain some faith in the
misguided masses and to suggest that a new International, purged
of all prowar elements, could be organized. The majority of socialist intellectuals and labor leaders changed their positions for various reasons. Some shifted to intervention because of a simple
concern for national security; others feared that a Prussianized,
imperialistic Germany presented a threat to democracy and the

till others believed that the war might hasten the coming of
sm as the government nationalized industry. For three
years the Left continued to debate the nature and consequences of
the war. By April 1917, when President Wilson went before Congress to ask for a declaration of war, most leading socialist writers
had already advocated U.S. intervention. Despite the defection of
intellectual luminaries like Walling, London, Simons, and Upton
Sinclair, the SP convention issued another antiwar resolution the
day after Wilson's address to Congress. The resolution, approved
by three-fourths of the delegates, had the support of political
leaders like Debs, Hillquit, and Berger. The SP's courageous action proved to be a short-run triumph and a long-run disaster.
Shortly afterwards the SP increased its membership by more than
12,000, and in various municipal elections in June socialist candidates gained new support from antiwar voters. But ultimately the
SP suffered a psychic wound as members began to accuse one
another of class betrayal or national treason. The prowar socialist
Charles E. Russell thought his former comrades "should be driven
out of the country," and the millionaire socialist J. G. Phelps
Stokes suggested they be "shot at once without an hour's delay."[12]

Though the government did not go that far, it went far enough.
In June 1917 Congress passed the Espionage Act (supplemented in
1918 by the Sedition Act), which forbade all obstruction of the
war effort. Immediately the U.S. Post Office denied mailing privi-
leges to socialist publications, and while editors tried vainly to
fight their case in court, the government moved against the SP
itself. Before the war was over, almost every major SP official had
been indicted for antiwar activity. Enraged mobs had also cracked
down on radical dissent everywhere. Throughout the country
IWW headquarters were raided. In Oklahoma, Wobblies were
rounded up and tarred and feathered; in Arizona they were
packed into cattle cars and abandoned in the desert; and in Mon-
tana, Frank Little, a crippled IWW leader, was kidnapped and
hanged from a railway trestle. The repression bore down heavily
on antiwar liberals as well. At Columbia University three profes-

sors were fired for having criticized U.S. intervention, whereupon the eminent historian Charles Beard resigned in protest. Watching this affair, the Columbia graduate Randolph Bourne visited one of the dismissed professors, his friend Harold C. Dana.

> "And now that you have been expelled, Harry, will you make the scandal?"
>
> "Certainly not," Dr. Dana said. "I've given my word as a gentleman."
>
> "That's the trouble," Bourne replied with a wide grin. "You look upon all this as a gentlemen's quarrel. You lack Homeric anger."[13]

Gentlemen scholars were not the only ones who disappointed the Lyrical Left. Everywhere the intellectual community seemed to be capitulating. Isadora Duncan, who once symbolized the liberating joys of the body, was now performing patriotic dances in the Metropolitan Opera House. Former *Masses* contributors had gone to work for the Committee on Public Information, Wilson's official propaganda agency; honored intellectuals like Veblen, Dewey, and the former socialist Lippmann had also come out strongly in support of America's entry into the war.

The *Masses* staff continued to oppose the war while the government prosecuted its editors for sedition and conspiracy to obstruct enlistment. During the trial in fall 1917, Eastman spoke eloquently about socialism, civil liberties, and the errors of U.S. foreign policy as another indicted staff member, the artist Art Young, impressed the jury by dozing off at the defendants' table. When his counsel awakened him, he opened his eyes, yawned, reached for his pad, and sketched a cartoon of himself napping, which he entitled "Art Young on Trial for His Life."

Eastman drew on the pulpit-oratory talents he had learned from his minister parents. In his summing up, an extemporaneous three-hour speech later distributed as a pamphlet, he told the jury, "I was brought up with the utmost love for the character and the beauty of the teachings of Jesus of Nazareth, and I count Him much nearer in His faith and His influence to the message of the Socialists than to the message of any other political body of men." Socialists are also good citizens, he said, and by no means unpatriotic; indeed, they believe in "liberty and democracy exactly in the same way" as Jefferson and the "rest of the true revolutionary fathers." Although his thoughts were on events in revolutionary Russia, Eastman knew socialism had no chance in America unless it could be rendered compatible with some cherished native conceits. His speech made a memorable impression on younger radicals in the courtroom and perhaps on a few solid citizens in the jury box. The jury could reach no verdict and the government dropped the case now that the *Masses* had ceased circulating.[14]

The Lyrical Left, always an uneasy alliance of disparate radicals with different causes, was now hopelessly divided by the war. Randolph Bourne leveled the most devastating attack on the prowar intellectuals. Bourne, who had once studied under Dewey, could not accept his argument that the conscientious objector

From left: Crystal Eastman, Art Young, Max Eastman, Morris Hillquit, Merrill Rogers, Jr., and Floyd Dell outside courthouse at the time of the first sedition trial in 1917 for opposing America's entry into the war. (National Archives)

should "attach his conscience and intelligence to forces moving in another direction" in order to assure that the war be elevated toward democratic ends. "War," Bourne pointed out, "determines its own end—victory, and government crushes out automatically all forces that deflect, or threaten to deflect, energy from the path of organization to that end." Similarly Eastman could not accept Walling's argument that intellectuals must "adjust themselves to events." A war based upon "blind tribal instincts," Eastman said, rendered events beyond rational control. Like Bourne, Eastman saw "no connection with its causes or the conscious purposes of those who fight. . . . It is a war of national invasion and defense— nationalism, the most banal of stupid idol-worships." John Reed also warned of the "judicial tyranny, bureaucratic suppression, and industrial barbarism, which followed inevitably the first care- less rapture of militarism." What remained of the Lyrical Left, then, rejected both the assumption, held by some socialists, that a war economy offered the possibility of industrial collectivism and the hope, held by many liberals, that the war could bring about worldwide democracy. "For once the babes and sucklings seem to have been wiser than the children of light," observed Bourne.[15]

The behavior of prowar writers like Walling and Lippmann also revived the Marxist distrust of a young "intellectual proletar- iat." The New Intellectuals who had earlier been hailed as a potential revolutionary vanguard now appeared to be "a corrupt and corrupting influence [whose] petty bourgeois souls scent the flesh pots of Imperialism. . . . In every imperialistic country it is precisely these 'workers of the brain' who manufacture and carry into the ranks of the workers the ideology and the enthusiasm of Imperialism."[16] Although the Lyrical Left's idealism was severely damaged by the defection of the intellectuals, the real deathblow came from the response of the masses to the war. The popular upsurge of nationalism was a source of repression that the Left had not fully anticipated. Eastman and Bourne pondered the so- cial and psychological meaning of war and nationalism in two significant essays: "The Religion of Patriotism," which Eastman wrote in 1916, and "The State," which Bourne started in 1917 but did not finish before his untimely death the following year. Both Eastman and Bourne believed that the war had laid bare the "gregarious instinct" and "herd impulse" of the human animal and, by transforming man's aggressive drives into illusions of power and idealism, had brought about a nationalistic solidarity that strangled critical intelligence. "There is nothing more copiously able to bind into its bosom the multiple threads of human impulse, and establish that fixed and absolute glorious tyranny among our purposes, than military patriotism," wrote Eastman. "The nation in war-time," observed Bourne, "attains a uniformity of feeling, a hierarchy of values culminating at the undisputed apex of the State ideal. . . . The individual as a social being in war seems to have achieved almost his apotheosis." More than culture or class conflict, war was the real catalyst that moved the masses to idealistic acts of self-sacrifice and delusions of "organic" wholeness. In despair, Bourne penned an epigram for a whole generation when he shrewdly commented, "War is the health of the State."[17]

The Bolshevik Revolution

Four thousand miles away an obscure Russian exile, Vladimir Ilich Lenin, reached the opposite conclusion. In his anarcho-syndicalist *State and Revolution* (1917) Lenin seemed to show that war was the sickness of the state and the health of revolution. In the eyes of the American Left, Lenin would soon emerge as the prophet who proved his theory of power.

In February 1917 the Russian czarist government collapsed with the dull thud of a historical anachronism; in October the Bolsheviks swept into power. The American Left reacted enthusiastically to the first event and ecstatically to the second. Although the triumph of Lenin defied the "laws" of Marxism, it answered the needs of American radicals. The last place a proletarian revolution was expected to occur was Russia, a backward country that lacked the industrial base to make the transition to socialism. Moreover, the revolution appeared to have been "made" by the

In its art as in its poetry, the Lyrical Left was moved to rapture by the example of Lenin's achievement.

determined imagination and will of a small minority of twelve thousand party leaders and intellectuals. It seemed that in Russia the radical intelligentsia had found at last a way to socialism that bypassed the long, arduous route of reform. If Russian intellectuals could create a revolution in an agricultural country, what could stop American intellectuals from doing the same in an industrialized society? To America's Left, dejected and rendered powerless by the war, Lenin's stunning achievement was Marx's second coming.

Not surprisingly, the American Left interpreted the revolution in its own disparate ideological images and every faction identified with the Bolsheviks. Eastman believed that even the February Revolution created in one blow a "Syndicalist-Socialist Russia." When the Bolsheviks triumphed over the Provisional Government, the DeLeonists claimed that the wisdom of revolutionary industrial unionism had been proven. Reed's eyewitness account, *Ten Days That Shook the World,* was later smuggled to the Wobbly prisoners in Leavenworth penitentiary, and the old Wobbly official Harold Varney announced that "Bolshevism was but the Russian name for I.W.W." Even reformist socialists who had denounced the doctrine of violence came to the defense of the violent Bolsheviks. James Oneal ridiculed those who protested that "there has been violence in Russia. Some violence in a revolution! Just imagine! Do they think a revolution is a pink tea party?" Moderate leaders like Hillquit defended the "dictatorship of the proletariat" as democratic; and Debs, the most gentle radical of all, proclaimed, "From the crown of my head to the soles of my feet I am Bolshevik, and proud of it." Emma Goldman and Alexander Berkman immediately sailed off to Russia to witness what they assumed would be the glorious birth of anarchism, and Lincoln Steffens returned from Russia to tell Americans, "I have been over into the future, and it works."[18]

What gave bolshevism its cataclysmic image was its brilliant leader Lenin. Nowhere is Byron's metaphor of "a fearful monument" better seen than in the portraits of Lenin drawn by Reed and Eastman. Reed depicted Lenin, with his solid muscular body, high forehead, and steely eyes, entering the cheering Duma as a moral force, the bringer of light who would shake the world with the truths that reside in power. "A strange popular leader," Reed mused, thinking, no doubt, of his shabby clothes and stubbled chin. "Unimpressive, to be the idol of a mob, loved and revered as perhaps few leaders in history have been. . . . A leader purely by virtue of intellect; colourless, humourless, uncompromising and detached, without picturesque idiosyncrasies—but with the power of explaining profound ideas in simple terms, of analysing a concrete situation. And combined with shrewdness, the greatest intellectual audacity." Eastman saw in Lenin the undoctrinaire engineer of the revolution, the one leader who had the nerve to defy Marxism by imposing his will on history. In 1918, when the Bolshevik leader lay stricken by an assassin's bullet, Eastman published a poem in praise of Lenin's steadiness of will and fluidity of mind:

> Men that have stood like mountains in the flood
> Of change that runs like ruin through the earth,
> When murder takes the sanctity of birth,
> When food is fire and harvest-treasure blood,
> Men that like fixed eternal stars have stood,
> Their faith clear-shining sadly, and their mind
> Unmaddened by the madness of their kind—
> They were the godlike, they the great and good.
> With light, and mountain steadiness, and power,
> And faith like theirs in this all-fluid hour,
> You to the dreadful depth of change descend,
> And with its motions moving it, you blend
> Your conquering purpose as blue rivers roll
> Through all the ocean's waters toward the pole.[19]

One cannot overemphasize the utopian, democratic image that surrounded bolshevism in its first months in power. The image of a "people's democracy" and a "commune state" enraptured the entire spectrum of the American Left: anarchists, syndicalists, revolutionary socialists, democratic socialists, and even a number of pacifists, social reformers, and liberal intellectuals. One by one most of these elements grew disenchanted with bolshevism, and within a few years its remaining American admirers dwindled to a small circle of comrades whose infatuation with Soviet power bore little resemblance to the original ideals of the American Left. Two developments account for the change of attitudes toward Russia: the centralization of the American communist parties, and the Stalinization of international communism.

When the Bolsheviks seized power, American radicals wanted to prove that they, too, were revolutionaries and not timid "mensheviks" or discredited reformers. This impulse led native radicals to look to the Russian-language Federation in the SP as the organic tie to bolshevism. The Russian Federation was composed of recent Slavic immigrants who knew almost nothing about bolshevism, but the Russian-Americans encouraged the illusion that only they could speak for Lenin and Trotsky. The left wing began to champion the Russian Federation, which, together with the Polish, Hungarian, Ukrainian, Lithuanian, Lettish, and Dutch federations, made up a majority in the SP. The spokesman for the left wing was Louis Fraina. A brilliant young Marxist and one of the founding fathers of American communism, Fraina had developed a new theory of "mass action" in *Revolutionary Socialism* (1918). In February 1919, militants issued Fraina's "Left-Wing Manifesto," which condemned the right wing for its tepid "sausage socialism" and, in the spirit of Russian bolshevism, called upon Americans to organize workers' councils as a means of taking power and establishing a proletarian dictatorship in the United States. The following month the Third International was born in Moscow. In order to disassociate themselves from the social democrats, the Bolsheviks revived Marx's use of the term "communism." The new Communist International (soon condensed to "Comintern") ordered every socialist party in the world to split from its right-wing factions. A fierce struggle now ensued for control of American socialism. A national referendum indicated that the majority of socialists desired to join the Third International, and another referendum for the election of a new national executive committee gave a decisive majority to the left wing. But the right wing simply dismissed the vote and began to suspend the seven left-wing, foreign-language federations. Within six months the SP lost two-thirds of its membership, declining from 109,589 to 39,750. Disgusted, left-wing leaders bolted and formed a separate communist organization, which immediately broke into two factions, the Communist party and the Communist Labor party. The larger CP was made up of the foreign-language federations and headed by Fraina and Charles Ruthenberg; the smaller CLP of native American radicals was led by

Reed and Benjamin Gitlow. Although the CP and CLP fought incessantly over organizational questions and over the "correct" interpretation of Marxist-Leninism, both groups espoused the revolutionary imperative of "mass action."[20]

In the year 1919, which Dos Passos likened to "the springtime of revolution," things did seem ripe for a radical solution. Labor unrest had gripped the country as longshoremen, printers, switchmen, tailors, garment workers, telephone personnel, streetcar conductors, and garbage collectors walked off their jobs. Outside the numerous plants of United States Steel some 367,000 workers took turns on the picket line for a period of four months; in Seattle a citywide strike was called; and in Boston policemen did not report for work, whereupon scores of college students, answering Governor Coolidge's call to God and country, helped maintain law and order. Yet while one of the greatest strike waves in U.S. history was taking place, communists remained on the sidelines, scorning the reforms demanded by workers and condemning trade unionism. The Bolshevik Revolution taught American communists to hold out for nothing less than revolution. But as they awaited the "inevitable" revolution, the predictable reaction set in. Wartime espionage and sedition laws were now used against communists and anarchists as Attorney General A. Mitchell Palmer directed unannounced raids against their homes and headquarters. During the Red Scare of 1919 and the early 1920s the membership of both communist parties declined from over 60,000 to under 10,-000. The remaining dedicated communists decided to go underground. Life in secret cell meetings increased their revolutionary fervor. Now American communists could regard themselves as real Bolsheviks, hounded by the police just as Lenin and Trotsky had been hounded by the Czar's Ochrana. Repression in America, as in czarist Russia, was merely further proof that revolution was just around the corner.

By the time the Red Scare had passed and the communists surfaced in late 1921, the international situation had begun to change. Even though American communists could not give up their revolutionary illusions, Lenin was shrewd enough to realize that while it still might be inevitable, revolution was no longer imminent. In *"Left-Wing" Communism: An Infantile Disorder* (1920), Lenin lashed out at the revolutionary impatience of the ultra-Left communists in the West. The two American parties, the CP and the CLP, had already been ordered by the Comintern to bury their differences and unite into one organization. American communists willingly accepted this directive from Moscow. But Lenin's tactical shift to the right came as a shock to many members. For communists were now told to establish a legitimate party, engage in electoral activity, and later to form "united fronts" with other progressive groups. Even more stunning, they were ordered to work within rather than against unions, not to destroy the AFL but to infiltrate it. This was the most painful irony of all. Lenin, the uncompromising revolutionary, was now ordering American radicals to practice what they had denounced the SP for engaging in since the turn of the century—political activity and trade unionism. These decisions bewildered left-wing leaders like Haywood and Fraina, who were to become increasingly disenchanted with the Moscow-dominated CP. But others stayed in the CP and subordinated themselves to the Comintern.

The remaining history of the CP during the twenties is a grotesque story of inner-party struggle, ego rivalry, and character assassination. The *Communist, Workers Monthly,* and *Revolutionary Age* occasionally featured high-level theoretical discussions. The controversy over "American exceptionalism"—can America's historical and economic development be understood solely in Marxist terms; and, if not, must America find its own way to the goals of Marx?—laid the groundwork for a half century of subsequent debate among American radical intellectuals. Yet what is significant about the factional debates of the 1920s is the manner in which they were resolved. In almost every instance the disputes were settled, despite the majority will of the American CP, either by a cablegram from the Comintern or by a trip to Moscow. This deference made the American CP an instrument that Joseph Stalin, the new dictator of the Soviet Union, gladly exploited to further Russia's interests. "Can anyone in his right mind," the

Trotskyist Max Shachtman would later lament, "imagine leaders of socialism like Lenin, Trotsky, Plekhanov, . . . Debs, DeLeon, Haywood . . . racing back and forth between their countries and the seat of the Second International, appealing to its Executive to make the decision on what policy their parties should be commanded to adopt?"[21] The generation of 1913 could not have imagined such a spectacle. The Stalinization of the American Left was the end of radical innocence.

During the 1920s communism had few admirers among those who had been the prewar intellectual rebels. Lenin's *State and Revolution* was compatible with the anarcho-syndicalist visions of the *Masses* circle; but his *"Left-Wing" Communism* could hardly inspire those who had once believed that "infantile disorder" was part of revolutionary adventure. Older socialists like Hillquit and liberals like Steffens continued to defend the Soviet Union against its conservative critics in the United States. But those closer to the spirit of the prewar rebellion found nothing to defend. Emma Goldman, the anarchist heroine of the Lyrical Left, watched in horror as Lenin crushed the Russian anarchists in the Kronstadt uprising in 1921, and embattled Wobblies soon gave up hope that Russian workers would have their own independent unions under bolshevism or that U.S. workers would have their own voice in the CP. Ultimately communism became a repudiation of two basic ideals that had inspired the Lyrical Left: the autonomy of the intellectual and the self-liberation of the working class. Under Stalin political "truth" became the test of culture and the intellectual was forced to defend, not the unorganized U.S. workers, but the tightly organized Communist party.

The Odysseys of Reed and Eastman

Typical of the disillusionment of what remained of the Lyrical Left were the reactions of John Reed and Max Eastman.

John Silas Reed's transformation from a lonely, insecure, wealthy student to a dedicated revolutionary who died in Russia of malnutrition and typhus is an experience in some ways unique, in some typical of the Left intellectual of the period. A robust, pleasure-loving rebel who would become an acquaintance of Lenin and Trotsky, an important American figure in the early Comintern, a patron saint of the American Communist party, and a hero buried near the Kremlin wall along with the fallen heroes of 1917, Reed seemed in his early years the epitome of genteel conformity.

Unlike most early American communists, Reed was neither an immigrant, a city-bred easterner, a self-educated worker-intellectual, nor a stern Marxist ideologue. Born and raised in an elegant mansion in Portland, Oregon, Reed attended prep school and then Harvard, where his greatest thrill was becoming the star cheerleader and enjoying "the blissful sensation of swaying two thousand voices in great crashing choruses during the football games." He was indifferent to politics and regarded his courses as insipid exercises one had to endure while gaining a place in the prestigious social clubs. When Lincoln Steffens came to interview him about a position in journalism, Reed told his idol of his ambitions: "To make a million dollars . . . to get married . . . to write my name in letters of fire against the sky." Reed's ambition for fame and fortune sprang from a deeper romantic desire, a restless, Byronic temperament that enabled him to become, without much ideological reflection, the poet-playboy of the Lyrical Left. Reed inherited his father's sympathy for the underdog, and his passionate commitment to verse suggests that his radicalism also grew out of an aesthetic temperament, a Faustian hunger for the fullness of life. He was easily moved by the drama of history and the majesty of great men and great deeds. "History was my passion, kings strutting about and armored ranks of men," he recalled. Later, in Venice with Mabel Dodge, he repeated to her the beauties of history. "The things *men* have done! But I wish that *I* could have been there at the *doing* of it, or that they were doing it now."[22]

When Reed moved to Greenwich Village, he instantly fell in love with the bohemian culture, New York's "wild ungovernable youth" whose "monuments uncouth" produced in him "a fierce

John Reed, poet-journalist and revolutionary, the romantic hero of the Lyrical Left whose possible second thoughts about bolshevism remain a matter of controversy. (Library of Congress)

joy of creation." Here he also fell in love with Mabel Dodge. "His olive green eyes glowed softly," sighed Dodge, "his high forehead was like a baby's with light brown curls rolling away from it and two spots of shining light on his temples, making him lovable. His chin was the best . . . the real poet's jawbone . . . eyebrows always lifted . . . generally breathless!"[23] During the joyous years before the war Reed wrote winsome verse, participated in the Paterson, New Jersey, garment workers' strike (during which he was jailed and organized the subsequently famous Paterson strike pageant), tried peyote ("these nauseatingly bitter buttons"), lived with various Village girls, and, on a trip to Paris, showed Mabel Dodge "what a honeymoon should be." But he soon became absorbed by the course of world events and in 1913 abandoned "man-eating Mabel" to see and write about war and revolution. His career from this point on reads like a Hemingway postscript to *Huckleberry Finn*. With an army of *companeros* he rode through Mexico to write about the exploits of the Robin Hood revolutionary Pancho Villa; a year later, when war broke out in Europe, he was off to France and then to the dreary eastern front; and after returning to the United States in 1917, he again rushed off to Russia as soon as he heard that the Romanov dynasty had crumbled.[24]

Reed arrived in Russia two months before the Bolsheviks came to power. Immediately he visited the liberal democrats' Duma, made his way into the Bolshevik headquarters and interviewed its leaders, then addressed bewildered Russian workers in English, sped around Petrograd in a truck passing out Russian-language leaflets he could not read, and participated in the storming of the Winter Palace, smuggling out a jewel-handled sword for a souvenir. Reed's sympathy for the downtrodden and his attraction to bold, dynamic leaders moved him to side with the Bolsheviks. As he watched them seizing power, he collected every item he could find—leaflets, newspapers, reports, resolutions, interviews, press clippings, peeled-off posters—to use in writing his vivid account of the greatest social cataclysm in modern history, *Ten Days That Shook the World*. Reed came back to the United States a confirmed Bolshevik, but just how long he remained so is a matter of controversy. In 1919 he returned to Russia to seek a solution to the factionalism that had split the two American communist parties. He arrived suffering from scurvy and malnutrition after two months of hunger and filth in a Finnish jail. Already distraught because of his illness, he became demoralized when he saw the suffering of the Russian people. The final blow was his treatment by Zinoviev and Radek, the Comintern's two leading officials. Reed had been at odds with the Comintern since it had announced its new trade-union line. To Reed the Bolshevik Revolution had been like the fulfillment of a Wobbly dream, an egalitarian uprising that put an end to all authority. Now new authorities were ordering American radicals to forsake the IWW and join the AFL. When officials tried to prevent Reed from presenting his case before the Second Congress of the Comintern, he resigned in disgust from its executive committee. No doubt he was appalled by the high-handed methods of the Comintern, but whether he had made a complete break with communism before his death is another question.

In an authoritative analysis, "The Mystery of John Reed," Theodore Draper concluded that there was no evidence of a "final accounting" and "definitive break" with communism. "But if disillusionment is understood intellectually and emotionally, Reed was probably as disillusioned as it was possible to be and still remain in the movement. His disillusionment was cumulative, and it was heading toward a break on both sides if he had persisted on his course." Had Reed lived, he would most likely have resigned from the CP, if the CP would not have expelled him first. Yet it is doubtful that Reed would have become a renegade from radicalism, as did much of the Old Left of the 1930s. As Draper put it, "Disillusionment there was, deeply implanted, but . . . John Reed had probably paid for his faith too dearly to give it up without another struggle."[25] This struggle might have brought him to side with Trotsky (a hero of *Ten Days That Shook the World*), the course taken by the other remaining spirit of the Lyrical Left, Max Eastman.

Like Reed, Eastman came from a Protestant, upper-middle-class background, and he too experienced all the tensions that parental dependency, sexual awareness, and religious doubt could produce in a sensitive adolescent. Unlike Reed, with his youthful romantic egotism, Eastman expressed a combination of paganism and piety. His "heroic" mother and "sainted" father were both Congregational ministers, and their "Christian ideal," he later recalled, "demands that life itself, as we live it, be transcended and superseded and changed. It is a utopian ideal, and ethically, at least, revolutionary."[26] This evangelical environment was the source of Eastman's social radicalism and of his moral conservatism, which made him uncomfortable with the flaunting libertinism of some of his comrades. Eastman was also more learned than the younger Reed and the other *Masses* writers. Something of a Renaissance radical, he would write over twenty books dealing with art, science, poetry, philosophy, humor, journalism, aesthetics, anthropology, religion, Marxism, German politics, and Freudian psychology, as well as five volumes of verse, a novel, two volumes of brilliant biographical portraits, and a study of the young Trotsky. After mastering Russian in a little more than a year, he translated the works of Pushkin and Trotsky, edited Marx's momentous *Das Kapital*, and clipped together a film documentary on the Russian revolution.

Tall, lean, tanned, and strikingly handsome with his blond wavy hair and deep, pensive eyes, Eastman was the best-known literary radical of his generation. "He looked Beauty and spoke Justice," exclaimed a close friend.[27] Eastman's life before the war was one continual round of cultural and political activities. He brought the Wobblies' struggle to public attention, championed the radical feminists, and, together with his sister, Crystal, organized the American Union against Militarism. Before the Bolsheviks came to power, none of the *Masses* group had heard of Lenin, and even afterwards so little was known of him in the United States that his name was frequently misspelled. But Eastman immediately sensed the man's greatness. To Eastman, Lenin was a philosopher-king and a social engineer whose language "was that of astute, flexible, undoctrinaire, unbigoted, supremely purposive, and, I judged, experimental intelligence." Eastman came to believe that Marxism's "dialectical reason" implied a practical mode of thought unencumbered by the constricting demands of abstract theory, and he would later quote Lenin as saying, "Flexibility of conception, flexibility to the point of the identity of opposite—that is the essence of the dialectic." All this was seductive. No doubt Lenin was a practical genius who acted pragmatically and realistically, but Eastman assumed that Marxism itself represented an open-ended, pragmatic philosophy. "To me the procedure was experimental, and the ideas were subject to correction." At bottom, Marxism appealed to Eastman's two contradictory impulses—his idealism and his realism, his yearning for the imaginative world of the possible beyond the actual, and his dispassionate scientific respect for the actual world of facts and experience. "It was this clash of impetuosities, the thirst of extreme ideals and the argumentative clinging to facts, which led me to seize so joyfully upon Marx's idea of progress through class struggle." As a philosophical proposition, Marxism seemed the resolution of the eternal dualism of facts and values, science and aesthetics, reality and desire. Marxism also appeared to have resolved one of the greatest problems in social theory: how to attain a perfect society with imperfect human beings. Eastman recalled Mark Twain's answer when the novelist was asked what he thought about socialism: "I can't even hope for it. I know too much about human nature." Marxism offered a solution to Twain's and Eastman's dilemma. While acknowledging the limitations of historical man, it enabled contemporary man "to line up fiercely with the ideal against the real." As a dialectical philosophy that negated all dualisms, Marxism resolved all contradictions.

This man Marx seemed to offer a scheme for attaining the ideal based on the very facts which make it otherwise unattainable. Instead of trying to change human nature, I said to myself, he takes human nature as it is, and with that as a driving force tries to change the conditions that make it work badly. Far from glorying in a new "conversion," I was loath even to call my new-found equilibrium socialism. I called it "hard-headed idealism."[28]

Yet even during the early Greenwich Village years Eastman had grown impatient with Marxism. In its orthodox formulation, Marxism meant waiting for history to develop its predetermined stages and reveal the inevitable. The socialist leaders of the Second International reassured themselves that the logical contradictions in capitalist development would lead to heightening crises and then to revolution itself. The Second International's version of socialism based itself on the canons of historical materialism, which left everything to the movement of objective forces and almost nothing to the power of subjective factors of consciousness, will, purpose, and effort. To Eastman a true scientific imagination required intervention and eschewed resignation. The scientist's experimentation introduces change into the world and brings about calculated results. Lenin appealed to Eastman more as scientist than as Marxist. In his *Liberator* (1918–24), the successor to the *Masses*, which had been suppressed by the government, Eastman portrayed Lenin as a daring innovator who defied Marxism by imposing his own will on historical events. Eastman's portrait would influence Gramsci, the young leader of the Italian Communist party, whose officials avidly read and relied upon the *Liberator*, the only journal smuggled passed fascist censorship to report on the Bolshevik Revolution.[29]

The precise meaning of Leninism, as a modification of orthodox Marxism, became a subject of debate within the European Left in the early twenties. Gramsci saw Lenin as the philosopher-prince of praxis, who realized that truth cannot be known in thought but only embodied in practice. To the Hungarian philosopher Georg Lukács the Bolshevik party, as the subject of history, and the masses, as its object, found a synthesis in Lenin. Marx never expected workers in a backward country to be sufficiently conscious to lead a revolution, and Lenin chose to instill revolutionary consciousness from above rather than await its spontaneous emergence from below. In the philosophical writings of

Gramsci and Lukács, Bolshevik claims of a party-led proletarian revolution took on universal significance.

Eastman himself never made such philosophical claims for the proletariat. He focused on Lenin's "colossal" brain, as though it represented the triumph of mind over matter. Eastman's hero-worship of the single leader contrasts strikingly with John Reed's view that the revolution dramatized the collective will of the masses of workers, peasants, and soldiers. In the first years of the revolution Reed saw no widening gulf between the party and the masses, and in *Ten Days That Shook the World* he wrote of Lenin without sensing any contradiction between genius and democracy. If Eastman attributed Bolshevik successes to leadership experimentation, Reed attributed them to mass mobilization. Eastman valued science and Reed solidarity.

How scientific was Marxism-Leninism? This question occupied Eastman later in the twenties when he reexamined his own views, and again in the thirties when he contested Sidney Hook's "Americanization of Marxism." But meanwhile he enthusiastically supported the left-wing socialists who wanted to break with the SP, and his new paper, the *Liberator,* endorsed the Comintern. Like Reed's, Eastman's ardor began to cool when he visited Russia in 1922—"to find out whether what I have been saying is true." At first he was impressed by the Red Army and by the energy and health of the Russian people. Bolshevik leaders gratefully received him as a trusted ally, and Trotsky befriended him as an intellectual comrade. While he toured the countryside and studied Russian in the Marx-Engels Institute Library, Stalin began to launch his campaign against Trotsky. Eastman attended the 1923 Party Congress, but he was "unaware of the beastlike struggle for power that was in progress behind the scenes of this high-minded discussion." With Lenin's death in January 1924, party hacks or "apparatchiks" began their move against the anti-Stalin opposition. Trotsky advised Eastman to leave the country with documents that would expose Russia's internal struggle for power; those documents included a section of Lenin's last "Testament," in which the premier, dictating from his deathbed, called for

Stalin's removal from the post of general secretary. Eastman published these documents in 1925, in *Since Lenin Died*, and defended Trotsky as a "genius" whose "superior moral and intellectual revolutionary greatness" made him Lenin's logical successor. Trotsky's subsequent failure to act upon those revelations and the defeat of the opposition in Russia made the Stalinization of American communism a certainty.[30]

Unlike Reed, Eastman had been untroubled by Lenin's shift to the right on the trade union issue, which could be regarded as evidence of Lenin's ideological flexibility. Actually it was Trotsky, Eastman's hero, who turned out to be the hesitating Hamlet, the "unarmed prophet" who failed to act pragmatically and decisively. The defeat of the anti-Stalinist opposition was not the only cause of Eastman's disillusionment. He had always been uneasy because Russian Bolsheviks relied upon Marxism as a body of "sacred scripture" instead of a "working hypothesis." He now began to explore the philosophical foundations of Marxism by studying its most esoteric premise: "dialectical materialism." In *Marx and Lenin: The Science of Revolution* (1927), and in several other essays, running debates, and books, he posed two simple but embarrassing epistemological questions: How did Marx come to know what he knew? How do we know that it is true?

Marx, said Eastman, did not arrive at his understanding of the meaning and direction of history from an objective, scientific study of present and past societies. He saw Marx's conviction that society moves, through determined stages, toward an inevitable goal as derived from Hegel. The dialectical philosophy of Hegel postulated an "inner logic" in history, a universal law of motion that revolved around the principle of contradiction and reconciliation. Marx transferred this principle of change through conflict and resolution from the realm of abstract ideas to the world of concrete social reality. Thus he assumed that capitalism harbored the "seeds of its own destruction," that it produced its own "contradiction" when it created an industrial proletariat, which in turn would revolt against capitalism and usher in the final resolution, the "end of pre-history"—socialism. To Eastman such historical reasoning seemed like "animistic thinking." Just as primitive man attributed human values and ideals to trees and other natural objects, so Marx attributed to the natural processes of history the unfolding of human ideals. Marx accepted Hegel, Eastman argued, much as nonscientific man accepts "religion"—as a means of reconciling himself to a universe in which he feels alienated. Marx believed in the coming of revolution because his belief enabled him to foresee a solution to estrangement from a world without justice, meaning, or value. Thus he read into history his own purposes and desires, telling it not like it was but as he wished it to be. He identified the desirable with the inevitable—an identification Eastman rejected as a Freudian expression of the "rationalization of wish." The crux of Eastman's critique of dialectical materialism was that belief in the inevitability of communism was a dubious scientific proposition. That capitalism morally "ought" to collapse was no basis for predicting that it would.[31]

Neither John Reed nor Max Eastman, the original spirits of the first Left of the twentieth century, provided an inspiring legacy to future generations of the American Left. In the thirties Reed, the "lost revolutionary," would be rediscovered by a younger generation as a symbol of bohemian radicalism while communists manipulated his legend to suit the party line. Eastman, now a pariah to the communists, would gain the respect of a few anti-Stalinist Left intellectuals of the late thirties for his support of Trotsky and his critiques of dialectical philosophy[32]—yet, in the early phase of the New Left, the Berkeley activist Mario Savio could say, "A lot of Hegel got mixed in with Marx's notion of history. Max Eastman pointed this out. The dialectic was a way in which Marx made the course of history coincide with his own unconscious desires."[33] But by and large, like the Old Left of the 1930s, the New Left of the 1960s knew little or nothing of the experiences of the founding generation of the American Left. Much of the Old Left would willingly accept the Comintern domination Reed so vigorously resisted, and the New Left would later, with the help of Herbert Marcuse, celebrate the very Hegelianism in Marx that Eastman so deftly exposed. Perhaps each generation must reenact the ceremony of innocence; each must repudiate the past even while repeating it.

Feminists and Black Intellectuals

Two aspects of the Lyrical Left did, however, represent an abiding legacy in America's political culture. One was feminism, which thrived in the teens and would, even though suffering a premature death in the twenties, remain a proud heritage to which subsequent generations of women returned for inspiration. The other was black intellectual life, which flirted with radicalism in the Greenwich Village era and flowered in the postwar Harlem Renaissance.

The various expressions of radicalism that animated the Left—socialism, anarchism, pacifism—were all influenced by women's perspectives. But since the years of the Second International the relationship of women to radicalism created problems and tensions in America as well as in Europe. The socialist leader Morris Hillquit complained that the woman question was unduly troublesome and distracting. Yet the editors of the *Masses* championed all women's causes, whether the fight against child labor, prostitution, or sexual discrimination or the fight for equal pay for women teachers, birth control, or free love.[34] Nonetheless, some women activists who did accept Engels's thesis, spelled out in *The Origins of the Family, Private Property, and the State,* that division of labor explained the subordinate status of women and children within the household and within society, could not accept the Marxist proposal to abolish the monogamous family. Also, many of the women who were struggling for temperance and child labor reforms were nativist moral crusaders who sought to purge society of its evils more in order to purify its character than in order to transform its conditions. And while radical feminists, especially those of immigrant background, saw the relevance of socialism to the emancipation of women, together with men, as victims of capitalist exploitation, some activists, like Kate Richards O'Hare, doubted whether women's liberation required women to take their place alongside of men in public industry instead of remaining within the family as wives and mothers.

Women radicals had been active in the protest movements of the late nineteenth century. The populist Mary E. Lease, who sought to receive equal pay for equal work, called upon farmer-husbands to raise less corn and more hell. The Christian socialists Mary Livermore and Frances Willard crusaded against booze and Mammon in the name of the Gospel. In *Women and Economics* (1898), Charlotte Perkins Gilman predicted an end of the male-dominated, androcentric culture and the entry of women into the productive life of the work force. Driven almost to madness by the mindless duties of domesticity, Gilman well understood the seriousness of Thorstein Veblen's sardonic *The Theory of the Leisure Class* (1899). Both authors believed that the modern culture of capitalism had turned middle-class women into idle consumers,

The birth control advocate Margaret Sanger, leaving a Brooklyn courthouse in 1917. (Library of Congress)

when their deepest need was to be doers and makers in the service of society. But Gilman wrote within the polite context of reform and uplift in which women would continue to serve as custodians of morality.[35]

Far bolder in action was Emma Goldman, the fiery anarchist who advised young women to keep their minds open and their wombs closed. Born in Russia in 1869, daughter of a violent, despotic father, Goldman had fled to the United States as a teenager; she worked in a coat factory for $2.50 a week, had a brief, disillusioning marriage, and determined to become a revolutionary as an organizer and agitator. An electrifying speaker, she lectured on the virtues of atheism and free love and the vices of property and marriage to an audience that regarded the latter as sacred and the former as scandalous. Goldman was forever being bailed out of jail by Reed and Eastman, after arrest for advocating birth control or opposing the war. Long before the Lyrical Left, Goldman anticipated the dictatorial direction the Bolsheviks would take, her anarchist distrust of all forms of centralized power leading her to declare in 1919, "The triumph of the state meant the defeat of the Revolution."[36]

Goldman's fear of the political state partly accounted for her skepticism about the suffragist movement. Like the German socialist August Bebel, she denied that the vote would transform the institution of marriage, abolish the economic dependency of women, or rid society of prostitution and venereal disease.

> The right to vote, or equal civil rights, may be good demands, but true emancipation begins neither at the polls nor in courts. It begins in woman's soul. History tells us that every oppressed class gained true liberation from its masters through its own efforts. It is necessary that women learn that lesson, that she realize that her freedom will reach as far as her power to achieve her freedom reaches. It is, therefore, far more important for her to begin with her inner regeneration, to cut loose from the weight of prejudices, traditions, and customs. The demand for equal rights in every vocation of life is just and fair; but, after all, the most vital right is the right to love and be loved. Indeed if partial emancipation is to

Emma Goldman, the fiery anarchist and feminist, one of the first to admire and one of the first to be disillusioned by the Soviet Union. (Library of Congress)

become a complete and true emancipation of woman, it will have
to do away with the ridiculous notion that to be loved, to be sweet-
heart and mother, is synonymous with being a slave or subordinate. It will have to do away with the absurd notion of the dualism
of the sexes, or that a man and woman represent two antagonist
worlds.[37]

To Max Eastman the women's movement for gaining recognition and influence in the public sphere was a family affair. His
mother, Annis Ford Eastman, had been the first female Congrega-
tionalist minister in New York State. It was she, his "first great
companion," who taught him "the essential secret of the joyous
life . . . to be ever in a state of growth." His sister, Crystal, organized the Feminist Alliance and drafted legislation for the New
York State Labor Committee. His first wife, Ida Rauh, worked
with the Labor Defense Council and the National Birth Control
League. Eastman himself founded the Men's League for
Women's Suffrage.[38]

The term "feminism" first emerged in America around 1910.
Although feminists were suffragists, not all suffragists were feminists; many who demanded political rights continued to uphold
orthodox values and considered feminists too risqué and "new
women" more interested in opportunities than in duties. Conflict
also arose between suffragists and socialists, as Gilman observed in
a witty poem:

> Said the Socialist to the Suffragist:
>   "My cause is greater than yours!
>   You only work for a special class,
>   We for the gain of the General Mass,
> Which every good ensures!"
>
> Said the Suffragist to the Socialist:
>   "You underrate my Cause!
>   While women remain a Subject Class,
>   You never can move the General Mass,
> With your Economic Laws!"
>
> Said the Socialist to the Suffragist:
>   "You misinterpret facts!

There is no room for doubt or schism
In Economic Determinism—
It governs all our acts!"[39]

Some of those who called themselves "feminists" were a part of Greenwich Village's rebellion against everything proper and respectable in favor of a life of disreputable adventure. All women activists, whether socialists or suffragists, claimed, as Goldman put it, "a right to love and be loved." However love might be defined, it remained one of the unfulfilled dreams of the Left. To Bertrand Russell, the principal aspiration behind the female emancipation movement was women's determination to be just as immoral as men were. Yet if some women sought fulfillment not in the duties of marriage and motherhood but in the delights of romance and even illicit raptures, women in general could not overcome the constraints of conscience. Some might speak of free love but condemn their husbands' extramarital affairs and cling to the nineteenth-century norm of female chastity. Some feminists struggled between their need for independence and a career and their need for nurturing and motherhood. Crystal Eastman, trying to overcome her maternal impulses, recognized what was at stake: "Women, more than men, succumb to marriage. They sink so easily into that fatal habit of depending on one person to rescue them from themselves. And this is the death of love."[40]

Marriage the graveyard of love! That sinking thought could not be denied by those who lived for experience. Crystal Eastman sought to keep the love of her marriage alive by living apart from her husband. Mabel Dodge, having failed in love, marriage, and the quest for happiness, went to Arizona in search of God. The feminist Agnes Smedley, who would court the Chinese communist leader Mao Zedong in the thirties, wondered whether a man with whom she enjoyed love and companionship was capable of responding to a free, independent woman. Mary Heaton Vorse, after being widowed for a second time, fell in love with the *Masses* illustrator Robert Minor. Minor showed up at the hospital, where she was recuperating after she miscarried their baby, to tell her he was involved with a younger woman. Mary Vorse took to morphine. Edna St. Vincent Millay often eased her romantic pain with a round of martinis and sublimated her frustration in lyrical deftness:

> I would indeed that love were longer-lived,
> And oaths were not so brittle as they are,
> But so it is, and nature has contrived
> To struggle on without a break thus far,—
> Whether or not we find what we are seeking
> Is idle, biologically speaking.[41]

Male feminists had their own troubles with the "new women" of Greenwich Village. John Reed, Max Eastman, Floyd Dell, and the journalist Hutchins Hapgood all engaged in self-scrutiny and psychoanalysis, and succumbed to possessiveness and bouts of anxiety in their inability to rise above their ego and merge their identity with that of the opposite sex. Hapgood feared strong women, whereas Dell feared that women claimed freedom but really wanted security. Eastman's first marriage, to the feminist Ida Rauh, ended in divorce; his second, to the actress Florence Deshon, ended in a separation, followed by her suicide. Eugene O'Neill had an affair with Reed's wife, Louise Bryant; he later used marriage and family as the subject of his tragedies. Some Leftists concluded that autonomy was more important than intimacy; others settled for a return to a Victorian marriage of monogamy and fidelity and dependence. By the end of the twenties three who had been Village authors—Dell, Walter Lippmann, and Joseph Wood Krutch—subjected the whole concept of romantic love to a devastating critique, depicting it as little more than an emotion extinguished at the moment of consummation. Adultery came to be seen less as an erotic adventure than as a debilitating neurosis. Eastman had once declared, "Lust is divine!" Krutch now called sexual ecstasy "an obscene joke."[42]

For men and women alike the cult of passionate love that had animated young Greenwich Village radicals ended in desultory middle age. The myth of romance could no more be sustained than could the myth of revolution. Once dependent upon both myths, the Lyrical Left lost the will to believe in either.

Together with feminism another abiding legacy of the Left to America's political culture was the contributions of black poets, writers, actors, and musicians. The black historian James Weldon Johnson observed in the twenties that the Provincetown Playhouse, started in that Cape Cod resort town in the prewar years, opened the way for blacks to enter the American theater. Eugene O'Neill made use of the materials of black experience in his drama at the time the "Negro Renascence" was beginning to emerge. Both black and white writers sought to challenge the "Sambo" and "Uncle Tom" images that had lingered since the time of slavery and been reinforced in the popular film *Birth of a Nation.* Certain Greenwich Village figures, including Eastman, O'Neill, Van Wyck Brooks, and Carl Van Vechten, championed the cause of both high black culture and folk, spiritual, and jazz music. Even the conservative, iconoclastic H. L. Mencken supported young black writers. A hero to some Village rebels, Mencken had disdain for Marxist socialism but shared the Lyrical Left's delight in the Nietzschean critique of sweet sentiment and facile formulas. His advice to black writers was to see themselves as the creators of culture, not as victims of history.

When Crystal Eastman died in 1928, at forty-six, among the many friends who mourned the passing of so noble a spirit was the black writer Claude McKay. When McKay first read the news, he took from his wallet a note from Crystal he had been carrying for years and cried for this "great-hearted woman."[43]

McKay, "the enfant terrible of the Harlem Renaissance," who was born in Jamaica, had attended Booker T. Washington's Tuskegee Institute briefly before arriving in Greenwich Village during the years of the First World War. Novelist, poet, and essayist, he was one of the first intellectuals to write about the culture of the black masses and to explore the idea of negritude as the recognition of self-identity in a white world. He was attracted to the Lyrical Left, which had been fighting racism while some socialist labor organizations defended segregation in public facilities and excluded black workers from trade unions. He befriended Max Eastman, wrote for the *Liberator,* and attended the Fourth Congress of the International in Moscow in 1922. Yet his restless, anarchic temperament was ill suited to communist discipline, although he scorned the gradualist reformist objectives of America's black leadership. He was, above all, a sensitive lyric poet. His antiwar protest "If We Must Die" brought him fame in intellectual circles.[44]

Jean Toomer, another black writer associated with the Left, in the twenties opted for art over politics. Deeply conscious of the "frigidization of the self," sensing the cold loss of what the intellect was helpless to find, he eventually chose mysticism over Marxism and religion over race. For Countee Cullen, a Harvard-educated poet who studied at the Sorbonne on a Guggenheim Fellowship, the romantic John Keats was the ideal and the cult of beauty the consummate experience, "a joy forever." He eschewed politics for art until the Depression led him to join the poet Langston Hughes in endorsing the Communist party candidacy of William Z. Foster and James W. Ford (the first black American to run for the vice-presidency of the United States). Cullen shared the Lyrical Left's conviction that the poet can awaken the world with surprising thoughts:

> Yet do I marvel at this curious thing:
> To make a poet black and bid him sing.[45]

Poetry as imaginative realization affirmed what political radicalism condemned. Like white writers of the "lost generation," black writers of the Harlem Renaissance, in the postwar years, felt themselves alienated from an American society at once prejudiced and philistine. All looked to art as salvation, some experimenting with new forms of modernist writing. Each noted the tension between cosmopolitanism and nativism, between a longing to reach out to the avant-garde culture of Paris as defiant exiles and a longing to return to their own roots as native sons.

Concern about one's central identity troubled radical intellectuals, black and white. In the twenties the imprisoned Italian Marxist Gramsci was formulating a new role for the intellectual. Convinced that the ruling class had prevailed in Italy not because of power but because of its cultural authority, Gramsci argued that intellectuals must overcome "hegemonic" domination by winning over the hearts and minds of the masses. Such an essentially educational role could be fulfilled only to the extent that writers renounced any aspirations toward "cosmopolitanism" and became "organic intellectuals" identifying with native traditions and articulating the needs and hopes of their own people. But Gramsci's message, a beacon of wisdom in the post–Second World War years, could have made little sense to white American radical intellectuals, to whom everything organic and native was reactionary. Even black writers, like W. E. B. DuBois, whose search for native roots carried them to all corners of the earth, would have found a rejection of cosmopolitanism uncongenial.[46]

Raised in New England, DuBois was educated at Harvard; he became a pioneer in the study of black history, organizer of numerous international conferences, and author of nineteen books, several of them translated into many languages. He was the living embodiment of the cosmopolitan spirit. A student of philosophy under William James, he retained from pragmatism the expectation that science would prevail over prejudice and superstition, and a similar Jamesian sense of the self as buffeted by contrary forces. "One even feels his two-ness," observed DuBois of the black scholar. "An American, a Negro; two souls, two thoughts, two unreconciled strivings, two warring ideals in one dark body, whose dogged strength alone keeps it from being torn assunder."[47]

After making his reputation as a writer with the publication of *The Souls of Black Folks* (1903), DuBois soon worked with the National association for the Advancement of Colored People (NAACP), editing its journal, the *Crisis*. He supported the suffrage movement. Although his later seminal work *Black Reconstruction* (1935) offered the first major interpretation of American race relations from a Marxist perspective, his commitment to Marxism had always been qualified by his recognition that the American working class had failed to move toward the universal class consciousness prophesied by Marx and Engels. In the 1930s he warned American blacks to stay clear of the Communist party, lest they be used as "shock troops" and find themselves in jail as martyrs for the Soviet Union. By time of the cold war, DuBois, disgusted with the Red Scare and racial discrimination, fled America. He was welcomed and lionized in communist Eastern-bloc countries. But even there the insults of white supremacy drove him to search for familial roots, an odyssey that took him first to Haiti and ultimately to Ghana; he died there on August 27, 1963, the day before the momentous civil rights march on Washington.

Throughout his career DuBois, America's greatest black radical scholar, could find no clear role for himself in the ranks of the Left. An elitist who believed in the leadership of "the talented tenth," a skeptic who saw little hope in organized labor, a separatist who broke with the NAACP and advocated self-segregation and all-colored schools, and yet a universalist who aspired to the ideals of pan-Africanism and world socialism, DuBois frustrated many potential allies with his complex positions, which had little relevance to the day-to-day struggles of America's black masses. DuBois's intellectual odyssey took him farther away from America and finally to his ancestral continent, there to die with his dreams.

The career of Paul Robeson, another black of towering talent and power, also offers an intriguing chapter in the annals of the black Left. The story of a man who did so much to break down the barriers of a racist society with his contributions to culture, only to be brought down in the end by the controversies sparked by his own radical politics, is at once an American triumph and an American tragedy.

Paul Leroy Robeson, born in Princeton, New Jersey, in 1898, was the youngest son in a family of five children. His father, an escaped slave, had earned a bachelor's degree in theology at Philadelphia's all-black Lincoln University and become the esteemed pastor of the Witherspoon Presbyterian Church in Princeton. His mother was a schoolteacher, who traced her regal family roots to the African Bantu people; she died after a stove-fire accident when Paul was six. He was raised thereafter by his loving but exacting father. Although he excelled in school and was respected by white classmates as a student and athlete, he experienced enough racial rebuffs to conclude that winning applause was not the same as gaining acceptance. On a scholarship to Rutgers University, he earned varsity letters in four sports and became the school's first all-American football player. He also dominated the debating and glee clubs and earned the post of valedictorian. The graduating-class "prophecy" of 1919 proclaimed that by 1940 Robeson would be governor of New Jersey and "the leader of the colored race of America."

At Columbia University Law School, Robeson worked as a football coach and played professionally, but his real passion was culture. His marriage to Eslanda Goode, a remarkable woman who had been educated in science and in medicine, fueled his ambitions to be an actor and singer. He gained some theatrical experience in London and then was approached by the Provincetown Players to act in Eugene O'Neill's *All God's Chillun Got Wings*. Rumors of a black's playing the leading role opposite a white actress sparked fears of riots on opening night, and to deflect trouble the Players decided to put on instead O'Neill's *The Emperor Jones*, for which Robeson received sterling reviews from prominent drama critics. By the late twenties Robeson's fame extended from the clubs of the Harlem Renaissance to the citadels of European culture; he became known not only as a powerful actor but also as a sonorous, soul-touching singer of Negro spirituals and other songs. His opening in *Show Boat* in Paris brought out the literati to hear him sing the mournfully vibrant "Ol' Man River." In London he made theater history in his performance as Othello. In Russia he became a close friend of Sergei Eisenstein and planned to collaborate with him on a film, never made, about Toussaint L'Ouverture, the nineteenth-century liberator of Haiti.

Robeson's growing interest in the Soviet Union and in communism seemed at first more anthropological than ideological, a desire more to discover old lost cultures than to impose new political systems. He convinced himself that American blacks as descendants of slaves had a common culture with Russian workers as descendants of serfs. Engrossed in "the minority question" in the Soviet Union, he became fluent in Russian. He saw Afro-American spirituals as congenial to Russian folk traditions. After a trip to Moscow in 1934, the first of several in which he and his wife were feted, Robeson concluded that the country was wholly free of racial prejudice. "Here, for the first time in my life," he said of his stay in Russia, "I walk in full human dignity."

Robeson's support of the Soviet Union, his fear of the spread of fascism, and his disgust with Western democracies for refusing to support Loyalist Spain were positions typical of many Western

Paul Robeson, the talented actor and singer who became controversial for his pro-communist views and defense of the Soviet Union. (Culver Pictures)

intellectuals of the thirties, a number of whom, however, became disillusioned by events. Robeson's position only hardened; he defended the purges, the nonaggression pact between Stalin and Hitler, Russia's war against Finland, America's nonintervention in 1940 and its intervention in June 1941 (after Hitler attacked Russia), and even the postwar Soviet occupation of Eastern Europe. Campaigning for the Progressive party in 1948, Robeson reiterated his conviction that England and other Western democracies were imperialist powers determined to bring back fascism. In 1949 he upset NAACP leaders when he urged black youths to refuse to fight in any further American wars. In Peekskill, in upstate New York, a riot broke out during his appearance at a concert. Several years later, in the McCarthy era, the State Department denied him a passport and the FBI kept close surveillance on his movements and activities. With his right to travel restored in the late fifties, Robeson returned to Europe, welcomed as a hero by communists and anti–cold war activists. In the Lenin Sports Stadium in Moscow, he sang in Russian a patriotic paean with this refrain: "I know no other land where people breathe so free." Robeson, aware that many Jews were among the millions who either disappeared or perished in Stalin's Russia, tried to investigate the fate of Jews in the Soviet Union but concluded, as he told reporters on his return to America, that the Soviet Union "had done everything" for its ethnic minorities.

Robeson knew well the meaning of racial oppression in America. Even as a talented celebrity he had had to control his rage when forced to use freight elevators and denied entrance to hotels and restaurants. Like Max Eastman, Robeson cut a dashingly handsome figure and beautiful women found the "ebony Apollo" irresistible, but when he crossed the color line he risked insulting stares and jeers; once his white woman companion was spat upon. No doubt memories of such slurs and his fury at the plight of other blacks in America influenced his desperate optimism about the Soviet Union.

Like a character out of a tragic novel, Robeson repressed his thoughts and emotions publicly, but privately, in unguarded expressions and comments, he had painful second thoughts about the Soviet Union. Plagued by a variety of physical and mental ailments as he grew older, he suffered from what a physician described as "endogenous depression in a manic depressive personality." On two occasions he attempted suicide. He died in New York City in 1976, the loss of his faculties perhaps easing the loss of his illusions.[48]

Intermezzo: The Lost Generation

In the 1920s the dreams of the Lyrical Left lost their bravado but not necessarily their breadth. Historians have generally interpreted the post–First World War years as a period of political reaction and ideological apathy. While an apt description at the national level of politics during the Republican administrations of Warren Harding, Calvin Coolidge, and Herbert Hoover, it is far from the whole truth. In some respects the mood of the lost generation of writers of the 1920s maintained the spirit of the earlier Greenwich Village rebellion. If all hope of revolutionary change had expired, cultural criticism and social alienation remained as alive as ever. Intellectuals had yet to make their peace with America.

Ironically, writers on the Left remained less radically alienated from America than did conservatives like the philosopher George Santayana and the poet Ezra Pound, who left their native country to settle in Italy. The few remaining Left radicals could take some satisfaction in an America that had committed itself to science and technology. Not only did the advance of industrialism promise to extirpate capitalism, but a scientific reading of the modern world seemed to reinforce Marxism as an empirical proposition. In the early twenties Eastman sparred with the literary critic Van Wyck Brooks in the *Liberator* on the status of science, insisting that poets and artists would soon be supplanted by engineers and scientists, the only thinkers capable of changing the conditions of life by experimenting upon them. To Brooks the radical celebration of science merely betrayed a naive bourgeois faith in material progress shared by American capitalists.

In the twenties intellectuals continued to provide a critique based upon the four villains of the Lyrical Left: Puritanism, capitalism, nationalism, and the frontier. Puritanism continued to be cited as the primary force that had made the American character repressed, guilt ridden, and censorious. With capitalism stronger than ever in the "New Era" of triumphant business leadership, most intellectuals saw prosperity as real and permanent, yet they lamented the pursuit of wealth as crass and meretricious. They regarded nationalism and devotion to nativist institutions and values as a source of pseudo-patriotic hysteria from the days of the Red Scare. Finally, the frontier, the fourth villain in the view of Brooks and other Village writers, was no longer a historical reality but still a psychological legacy nurturing a bias against high culture and the life of the mind. In *The Ordeal of Mark Twain* (1920), Brooks argued that this potential genius turned out to be a failure, his imagination stunted by the anti-intellectual mentality of the western frontier. The pioneer, the patriot, the profiteer, and the Puritan combined to produce the "philistine," the nemesis of the Left in its struggle to awaken consciousness.[49]

Ironically, all four villains have been cited by scholars as the historical forces that made possible the American Revolution and Jacksonian democracy. Even sophisticated Marxists see capitalism's role in overcoming mercantilism and feudalism as progressive. But writers of the lost generation felt too alienated from American history and society to see that change could arise from native grounds. Those intellectuals still interested in politics remained haunted by the ghost of the prophetic Randolph Bourne.

Bourne, who died in 1918, had been a hero to the Lyrical Left for his keen refutations of John Dewey's defense of America's entry into the war, but even more enduringly for his critique of nativism and nationalism in the name of universal values founded in what he termed "trans-nationalism." In the *Dial, Seven Arts,* and *Atlantic Monthly,* Bourne proposed that American writers adopt the "cosmopolitan spirit" as a means of escaping everything provincial and puritanical. An "organic intellectual" would return to America's constricting roots instead of fleeing them. Other writers could hail the "melting pot"; he urged immigrants to retain their ethnic identity and, in so doing, raise America's consciousness beyond its "repressions" and "old inbred morbid problems." Only such a differentiated cosmopolitanism could provide "liberation from the stale and familiar." As a radical thinker he was challenging a long-established liberal dualistic conceit—that Europe was old, tired, and decadent and America new, fresh, open, and tolerant. Bourne reversed the imagery of the Old World and the New, in effect telling intellectuals what Marx had told workers: that they have no native country.[50]

Many American writers and artists felt homeless in the twenties. "Where are our intellectuals?" asked Harold Stearns, editor of the anthology *Civilization in the United States* (1922). Here several authors explained why American intellectuals must flee their country: because of its emotional sterility, its commercial hegemony, its puritanical morality—all death to the creative artist and the life of the mind. Many did indeed abandon the United States and adopt France as their new home. To Montparnasse and to the Left Bank, American expatriates imported the Greenwich Village rebellion with its passionate commitment to novelty and innovation. "Make it new!" declared the poet Ezra Pound, who moved first to London and then to Paris, before settling in northern Italy. Mabel Dodge continued "to try things out," both in a new habitat and with a new lover. In *Exile's Return* (1934), Malcolm Cowley, chronicler of the lost generation, itemized its eight-point code of liberation: salvation by the energies of youth; self-expression; paganism and the body as temple; living for the moment; liberty as freedom from all restraint; female equality; psychological readjustment by resort to Freud; changing place and country and living as free-floating exiles. While the Marxist Gramsci dreamed of an "organic intellectual" and the Comintern of leadership of all intellectuals everywhere, American writers and artists looked to Paris as the new International of culture.[51]

In culture the spirit of criticism and rebellion remained; in politics, however, the lost generation had forsaken many of the Lyrical Left's ideals despite the participation of its followers in the same movements. One such abandoned ideal was democracy. In the twenties Lippmann concluded that democracy was as unrealizable as it was undesirable—especially the will of a majority that could prohibit access to the temptations of liquor and that had sought to stem the influx of immigrants and to make the teachings of Darwinism a crime. The sardonic Mencken ridiculed democratic man as the "booboisie" of the Bible Belt. T. S. Eliot cautiously explored royalism and Catholicism as alternatives to modern democracy; Pound embraced Mussolini and fascism. *New Republic* liberals like Herbert Croly and Charles Beard found promise in Il Duce's blackshirt Italy. Whatever else it wanted, the jazz age felt no obligation to make the world "safe for democracy."[52]

The ideal of socialism was another casualty. The journalist Lincoln Steffens, who in the Progressive Era had inveighed against the abuses of big business, now hailed capitalism as more efficient and productive than socialism, as an unplanned economic system that would bring forth abundance and thereby abolish poverty and social injustice. Thorstein Veblen promised Greenwich Village rebels that the enlightened engineer would supplant the irrational price system. An engineer, Herbert Hoover, was elected to the presidency, offering the same hope for technological expertise.

So too, the philosophy of pragmatism, the great earlier theory of the Lyrical Left, came under criticism in the twenties. Lewis Mumford and Joseph Wood Krutch spoke of pragmatism as an anemic expression of Protestantism and of capitalism. Had not William James referred to the "cash nexus" of philosophy and Oliver Wendell Holmes, Jr., to the competition of "the market place of ideas"? Ironically, while the Italian Gramsci offered the Marxist principle of "praxis," such cultural critics in America preached that a pragmatic approach to life exalted the practical at the expense of the moral. William Y. Elliott's *The Pragmatic*

Revolt in Politics (1928) and Julian Benda's *The Betrayal of the Intellectuals* (1927) maintained that pragmatism's worship of power and the cult of success could lead only to fascism.[53]

The final casualty of the twenties ideals was feminism. Scholars today still debate why the feminist movement ebbed after women gained the right to vote with the passage of Nineteenth Amendment. Did the vote make a difference? The election of the conservatives Harding, Coolidge, and Hoover indicated that formal political equality would not, as some Greenwich Village rebels had hoped, result in the radicalization of America. It now seemed that the anarchists and Marxists were right to insist that culture and economics are more important than politics and government. In truth, the feminists had not constituted a coherent movement. During the war the militant National Women's party withheld support from Wilson, while the National Women's Suffrage Association supported the war and turned nationalist and jingoist. In the twenties the ranks of the feminist Left divided further over strategic goals for women workers, some urging specific labor legislation to protect working-class women, others urging rejection of all gender categories in the name of universal egalitarian ideals. The paradox had been at the heart of American feminism from its beginning. The rights-based activists, convinced that women were equal to men, argued that they were therefore entitled to equal legal protections guaranteed by the U.S. Constitution. Union organizers maintained that women had particular needs and therefore required special legislation. A third position, taken by the "moralists," held that women were different in the sense that they shared virtues men did not share that would elevate society above the uncouth masculine world. The dilemma facing women was whether they should affirm or deny their womanhood.

In *Concerning Women* (1926) Suzanne LaFollette resisted protective legislation for women on the grounds that similar safety standards must be available to men to avoid employers' discriminating against women, particularly in opportunity for advancement and promotion in industrial jobs. A libertarian as well as a feminist, LaFollette also warned women not to turn to the state for protection of their rights, because what the state grants in one decade it can take away in the next. If government has kept men down, why, asked LaFollette, would it be willing to raise women up? To rely upon government is to compromise individual economic independence and personal autonomy.[54]

In 1927, the year following publication of LaFollette's book, the scattered remnants of the Lyrical Left witnessed with horror the full power of a vengeful government, when the state of Massachusetts executed Nicola Sacco and Bartolomeo Vanzetti, Italian immigrants convicted of murdering a bank official in the course of a holdup. Sentenced to death by a judge who boasted of what he had done to "those anarchist bastards," Sacco and Vanzetti became the single galvanizing political cause of the twenties generation. As the day of execution approached, protesters demonstrated in the streets of Paris, Rome, and New York. Edna St. Vincent Millay and John Dos Passos joined other former Village rebels in walking the picket lines in the hot August sun outside the Charlestown prison. When the signal went out that Sacco and Vanzetti had been executed, American intellectuals were traumatized, shaken by the thought that the state can kill the innocent and force society into class warfare. Dos Passos later captured the shock in his novel *The Big Money* (1936):

> they have clubbed us off the streets   they are stronger
> they are rich
>
> all right you have won   you will kill the brave men
> our friends tonight
>
> America our nation has been beaten by strangers
> who have turned our language inside out who have
> taken the clean words our fathers spoke and made
> them slimy and foul
>
> all right we are two nations[55]

Beginning with the romance of Greenwich Village, America's first Left ended in the despair of the tragedy of the Charlestown prison.

Ben Shahn's *The Passion of Sacco and Vanzetti* commemorates the execution of the two anarchists accused of murder and robbery. The case was a cause célèbre of what little remained of the prewar Left in the 1920s. (Collection of Whitney Museum of American Art, New York)

5

The Old Left

Every time I've encountered the Depression, it has
been used as a barrier and club. It's been a
counter-communication. Older people use it to explain
to me that I can't understand *anything*. I didn't live
through the Depression. They never say to me: We
can't understand you because we didn't live through
the leisure society. All attempts at communication are
totally blocked. All of a sudden there's a generation
gap. It's a frightening thing.

    What they're saying is: For twenty years I've starved
and worked hard. You might fight. It's very
Calvinistic. Work, suffer, have twenty lashes a day, and
you can have a bowl of bean soup.   Diane[1]

Do not let me hear,
Of the wisdom of old men.   T. S. Eliot[2]

But remember, also, young man: you are not the first
person who has ever been alone and alone.
          F. Scott Fitzgerald

In his *History of the Russian Revolution* Trotsky laid down three
conditions necessary for a successful seizure of power: "the ruling
classes, as a result of their practically manifested incapacity to get
the country out of its blind alley, lose confidence in themselves";
the lower classes develop "a bitter hostility to the existing order
and a readiness to venture upon the most heroic efforts and sacrifice in order to bring the country out upon an upward road"; and
"discontent of . . . intermediate layers [roughly the middle
classes], their disappointment with the policy of the ruling class,
their impatience and indignation, their readiness to support a bold
initiative on the part of the proletariat, constitute the third political premise of a revolution."[3]

The Depression and the Image of the Soviet Union

During the Depression, America never came close to meeting these conditions. Amid the panic following the economic crash in the fall of 1929, only the capitalists fulfilled their historical mission by losing faith in themselves and becoming, through their shortsighted economic policies, their own gravediggers. The proletariat failed to show any "bold initiative," while the American middle class remained as timid and conservative as ever. There was much hopeful talk in the left-wing press of "revolution," but those who actually went to the masses found only misery and confusion. The montage that emerges out of the photographic essays of Dorothea Lange, the reportage of James Agee, the novels of John Steinbeck, Horace McCoy, and James T. Farrell, and the microsociology of Helen and Robert Lynd makes a haunting picture of people with blank faces and broken spirits, of human bodies bent over like staring question marks. Watching the bonus marches and bread lines, the starvation of rural migrant workers and the dissolution of urban families, Americans occasionally grew angry and even violent, but just as often they turned their resentment back upon themselves. For most Americans felt the Depression as an individual, not a class, experience, and, since they considered unemployment a sign of personal failure, the idle hands blamed not society but themselves. This was the "invisible scar" that the Depression generation would bear almost the rest of its life.[4] Historically, what was remarkable about the public during the Depression was not the extent of its protest and sense of conflict but the extent of its patience and sense of contrition.

The extent of this psychic wound indicates how much America's working classes had absorbed the values of capitalist individualism. Had there been a viable Left in the 1920s propounding a socialist consciousness among the workers, the story of radicalism in the 1930s might have been different. Nevertheless, although the Depression may have vindicated DeLeon, American intellectuals also felt vindicated as they watched Wall Street collapse like a house of cards. "To the writers and artists of my generation," wrote Edmund Wilson, "who had grown up in the Big Business era and had always resented its barbarism, its crowding-out of everything they cared about, these years were not depressing but stimulating. One couldn't help being exhilarated at the sudden unexpected collapse of that stupid gigantic fraud. It gave us a new sense of freedom; and it gave us a new sense of power to find ourselves still carrying on while the bankers, for a change, were taking a beating."[5]

It is difficult to speak of the Old Left as a single generational entity. The radicals of the thirties differed in age, ideology, social background, cultural sensibility, life-style, and political commitment. Among literary intellectuals alone there were at least three distinct groups. First were the veteran radicals of the 1920s, a disparate band of intellectuals who wrote on a variety of subjects for V. F. Calverton's *Modern Quarterly*. The isolated radical intelligentsia of the 1920s also found a sounding board in the *New Masses*, started in 1926 by its combative editor Mike Gold. A heavy-handed polemicist, Gold loved to affect the unwashed mien of the proletariat, and he relished chomping on foul, three-cent Italian cigars and spitting profusely on the floor while he denounced as "pansies" such writers as T. S. Eliot. A second circle of radical writers rose to prominence in the early 1930s with the publication of *Partisan Review*. Considerably younger than veteran radicals like Calverton and Eastman were such writers as Philip Rahv, William Phillips, Dwight Macdonald, and F. W. Dupee, the brilliant, college-bred intelligentsia of the Depression. Urbane, steeped in modern literature and philosophy, these New York writer intellectuals had no illusions about a proletarian cultural renaissance and refused to cast aside the intellectual heritage of the recent past. A third group of writers who were part of the Old Left were cultural refugees from the 1920s. Novelists and essayists like John Dos Passos and Malcolm Cowley had been survivors of the celebrated lost generation that had expatriated to Europe to flee the emotional and aesthetic sterility of America, "an old bitch gone in the teeth," in Pound's words. Many of these exiles returned with a feeling of guilty relief. In the 1920s they had turned inward and lost themselves either in an abstruse cultivation of literary craft or in a stylized search for personal salvation. Attempting to create new values, some found in Hemingway's stoical characters a code of courage that enabled man to endure a violent and absurd world and confront the nothingness ("nada") of existence. Many emerged from the privatized intellectual life of the twenties with a shameful sense of their egotistical and ineffectual response to the alienation of bourgeois existence. F. Scott Fitzgerald, reflecting with painful honesty upon his own "crack-up," believed that his failure to develop a "political conscience" was partly responsible for his loss of identity ("So there was not an 'I' anymore"). Fitzgerald's conviction that his own nervous breakdown was symptomatic of America's social crisis revealed a strain of guilt, felt by many writers, that their former lives had been shallow and selfish—as the generation of the thirties had judged them. "I think that my happiness, or my talent for self-delusion or what you will, was an exception," confessed Fitzgerald. "It was not the natural thing but the unnatural—unnatural as the Boom; and my recent experience parallels the wave of despair that swept over the nation when the Boom was over."[6]

Fitzgerald's generation looked back upon the twenties as if it had been a joyless quest for beauty by the damned. The fashionable despair of Eliot's *The Waste Land* could not sustain the expatriates, and well before the Depression they began to ache for a positive faith and a new social ethic. In contrast to that of the earlier generation of Marxists, like Calverton and Gold, and the later generation of writers like Rahv and Phillips, the conversion of America's lost generation to radicalism meant the end of a lonely cultural odyssey and the beginning of a new political life. For the Old Left in general, however, the appeals of communism are explained more by the realities of the thirties than by the experience of the twenties. The Depression sensitized intellectuals to life at the lower levels of society. The misery of the unemployed and uprooted, the exploitation of the blacks, and the desperate struggle of workingmen made capitalism all the more atrocious and communism all the more attractive. But the spectacle of human suffering did not in itself account for the widespread radicalization of the American intelligentsia. Injustice and exploitation had existed long before the Depression. The Depression made poverty more visible, but it was communism that made it intolerable.

Central to the appeal of communism was the mighty image of Soviet Russia. In the two years following the Bolshevik Revolution in 1917, the *New York Times* predicted, in ninety-one editorials, the collapse or near-collapse of Soviet communism. With the collapse of Western capitalism a decade later, the image of Russia changed dramatically. As President Hoover seemed to lapse into a funk of indecision, and Stalin celebrated the "success" of his Five-Year Plans, even industrialists like Henry Ford and financiers like Thomas Lamont praised Russia and advocated bestowing on it America's formal diplomatic recognition. To Left intellectuals especially, the young Soviet republic appeared a model of human

A poster by Fred Ellis, American radical artist of the 1930s, depicts "two civilizations"—America *(left)* and the Soviet Union.

brotherhood surrounded by a selfish and aggressive capitalist world. The spectrum of admirers encompassed not only the small American communist Left but the larger liberal Center as well—fellow travelers who supported the idea of communism but did not join the party, and Russian sympathizers who praised Soviet economic achievements but rejected communist ideology. Only a few zealous radicals believed that Soviet communism could be transplanted to America and the Bolshevik Revolution duplicated. What the noncommunist Left wanted to borrow from Russia was the new and bold idea of centralized economic planning. In the liberal *New Republic* and *Nation*, and in the journals of the Left, an image emerged of a dynamic country blazing with smoking factories and churning tractors run by grim-jawed Russian men with enormous biceps and smiling peasant girls with big, honest calves.

The contrast between Russia's highly propagandized economic

The Eternal City, Peter Blume's allegory of fascism. Many saw communism as the only bulwark against the depicted threat of fascism. (Museum of Modern Art, New York)

progress and America's continued economic stagnation was one source of communism's sway over the intellectuals' imagination. Another was the image of communism as the solitary bulwark against fascism. Hitler's accession to power in January 1933 hardly troubled the CP, which accepted the Comintern's judgment that fascism merely signified capitalism's last stage. Yet fascism seemed so barbaric and irrational that most intellectuals could only watch in stunned disbelief as "civilized" Germany succumbed to it. While intellectuals pondered the fate of Western democracy, the communist press claimed that the triumph of the Nazis in Germany exposed the hollowness of liberalism everywhere. Some discerning Marxists, like Sidney Hook and many of the followers of Trotsky, rejected this argument, yet the communist interpretation carried great emotional appeal, for fascism symbolized everything intellectuals hated: political demagogy, capitalist decadence, militarism, and imperialism. Moreover, in analyzing the causes of fascism, some liberal intellectuals found it difficult to admit that the middle classes, previously regarded as the driving force of American progressivism, composed the social backbone of fascist movements. The communist thesis that fascism evolved from "monopoly capitalism" was far more satisfying. But whether intellectuals saw fascism as a plot of industrialists alone or as a popular mass movement, two conclusions could be drawn: that fascism could evolve from capitalism was final proof that capitalism must be abolished; that fascism could eliminate the Left in Europe was final proof that the Left in the United States must organize against it. Organizing against it meant coming to terms with the CP.

A third source of communism's strength in the 1930s was that byzantine organization the CPUSA—the Communist party, U.S.A. In reality, few intellectuals became official party members, because the CP demanded a loyalty that confused discipline with indoctrination, its leaders frequently treated intellectuals with disdain, and its internal doctrinal disputes often took on the arid flavor of medieval scholasticism. Even so, intellectuals had to admit that the CP possessed an effective organization, offered a clear program of action, and enjoyed the blessing of the Soviet Union. The CP's leadership may have been ruthless, but intellectuals saw the ruling classes as much more ruthless and more dangerous. Combating capitalism required more than sweetness and light, and in the early thirties many writers, even those who did not join, found in the CP a source of political strength and comradeship with the mass of workers who possessed the means of overthrowing the existing order. The playwright John Howard Lawson told Dos Passos that though Mike Gold might call him a "bourgeois Hamlet," "my own plan is to work very closely with the communists in the future, to get into some strike activity, and to accept a good deal of discipline in doing so. It seems to me the only course open to people like ourselves." "It is a bad world in which we live, and so even the revolutionary movement is anything but what (poetically and philosophically speaking) it 'ought' to be," Granville Hicks was told in a letter from a communist friend. "It seems nothing but grime and stink and sweat and obscene noises and the language of beasts. But surely this is what *history* is. It is just not made by gentlemen and scholars."[7]

Far more important than the CP was the influence of Marxism upon American thinkers. Actually, most Left intellectuals were only "Marxists of the heart," radicals who sensed that Marxism was right because they knew that capitalism was wrong. But several serious scholars, mainly those who wrote for the short-lived *Marxist Quarterly*, attempted to master Marxism as a philosophy of history and as a theory of economics. In doing so they tried, significantly, to make Marxism compatible with America's intellectual tradition. Hook interpreted Marxism as a "radical humanism" that shared with American pragmatism a common naturalistic theory of knowledge; the historian Louis Hacker reinterpreted the American Revolution as a study in imperialism and the Civil War as a class struggle; and the social scientist Lewis Corey saw parallels in Marx's and Veblen's analysis of class behavior.[8] The attempt to make Marxism the logical extension of traditional progressive values may have set political theory back fifty years. But Marxism did restore meaning and purpose to life by offering a sense of historical direction, a method of class analysis, and an organic vision that dared to be monistic. In an age when all truths seemed relative and fragmentary, Marxism could provide a rare glimpse of the totality of existence, an exciting synthesis that broke down the classical dualisms between self and society, idealism and realism, contemplation and action, art and life.

Ultimately Marxist communism appealed to intellectuals because, as Daniel Aaron has noted, "it seemed a science as well as an ethic, because it explained and foretold as well as inspired."[9] The overwhelming desire of intellectuals to believe that history was on their side also suggests the emotional value of Marxism for the generation of the thirties. For Marxism resolved the contradictory tensions that lay at the heart of the Old Left: professing a pragmatic devotion to William James's pluralistic universe, American radicals devoted themselves to a Marxist worldview that was fixed and predetermined; claiming to have thrown off the sentimental idealism of the past, they embraced a "realistic" doctrine demanding the idealism of sacrifice and commitment; seeing themselves as men of ideas, they admired men of action; believing in truth, they respected power. Clearly it was not the intellectual content of Marxism that converted many American intellectuals to radicalism. "It was not merely the power of ideology that bound one to the Movement," recalled Irving Howe, who had taken to radicalism at the adventurous age of fourteen:

> No, what I think held young people to the Movement was the sense that they had gained, not merely a "purpose" in life but, far more important, a coherent perspective upon everything that was happening to us. And this perspective was something rather different from, a good deal more practical and immediate than, Marxist ideology; it meant the capacity for responding quickly and with a comforting assurance to events. The Movement gave us a language of response and gesture, the security of a set orientation—perhaps impossible to a political tendency that lacked an ideology but not quite to be identified with ideology as such. It felt good "to know." One revelled in the innocence and arrogance of knowledge, for even in our inexpert hands Marxism could be a

powerful analytic tool and we could nurture the feeling that, whether other people realized it or not, we enjoyed a privileged relationship to history. . . .

But there is a more fundamental reason for the appeal of the Movement. Marxism involves a profoundly *dramatic* view of human experience. With its stress upon inevitable conflicts, apocalyptic climaxes, ultimate moments, hours of doom, and shining tomorrows, it appealed deeply to our imaginations. We felt that we were always on the rim of heroism, that the mockery we might suffer at the moment would turn to vindication in the future, that our loyalty to principle would be rewarded by the grateful masses of tomorrow. The principle of classic drama, peripeteia or the sudden reversal of fortune, we stood upon its head quite as Marx was supposed to have done to Hegel; and then it became for us a crux of our political system. The moment would come, our leaders kept assuring us and no doubt themselves, if only we did not flinch, if only we were ready to remain a tiny despised minority, if only we held firm to our sense of destiny. It was this pattern of drama which made each moment of our participation seem so rich with historical meaning.[10]

The Lefts Compared

In contrast to the desperate need for a coherent orientation, the mood of the earlier Left was far less anxious and far more confident. The 1913 Lyrical Left found in history what the Old Left could find only in a visceral ideology. Before the war the exciting rise of socialism in the United States and in Europe enabled the young radicals to issue declarations that rang with the certainty of truth. Moreover, for the most part the Lyrical Left was made up of humanitarians and pacifists, "tender" radicals who knew nothing of the surreal world of totalitarianism and terror that was to emerge in the 1930s. Nor did the earlier radicals witness the decay of European social democracy into petrified party bureaucracies, the bastardization of radical syndicalist ideas into fascist ideologies, and the grotesque betrayals by Stalin. With its vague, quasi-anarchist illusions and festive spirit, the Lyrical Left saw itself standing at the dawn of a new era in which intellectuals at last could live without compromising their devotion to truth, beauty, and justice.

The difference between the Lyrical Left and the Old Left is the difference between innocence and experience. To the radicals of the thirties, the Depression may have first seemed like the beginning of "America's October Revolution." But the unexpected triumph of fascism in Europe caused them to reconsider the resiliency of capitalism and the cunning nature of power. After 1935 few American radicals believed that democratic socialism was the only historical alternative to capitalism. Still more chastening was the choice of comrades: since liberals in America had failed to prevent the revival of corporate capitalism under the New Deal, and since socialists in Europe had failed to prevent the rise of fascism, the Old Left was presented with the cruel alternative of Stalinism or fascism. Even the many writers who refused to accept this myth of the false alternative realized that political choices were not clear and easy. That the choice for and against humanity would involve the trauma of deciding between two forms of totalitarianism, that one would have to choose the bad over the worse, was an experience almost unknown to the Lyrical Left.

The Old Left also differed from its predecessor in respect to social background and intellectual orientation. The major figures of the Lyrical Left, having been brought up in small towns in the Midwest or rural Northeast, found much of their earlier inspiration in the native legacy of cultural radicalism, especially in Thoreau's defiant individualism and Whitman's cosmic collectivism. The Old Left intellectuals, many of Russian Jewish or east European ancestry, born in New York City's ghettos, were more inclined to turn away from American intellectual traditions and look elsewhere for an inspiring radical ideology. Marxism, which seemed uniquely a product of the European mind, emerged as a more natural ideology to the sons and daughters of immigrants. The distinction between the two radical generations can also be seen in the differences between the old *Masses* and the *New Masses.* The former infused the Left with a hearty spirit of adven-

Typical *New Masses* cover, with drawing by William Gropper. (Library of Congress)

ture and innovation; the latter imbued it with an arid strain of dogmatism. Indeed, the *New Masses* attempted to burn out of the American Left every vestige of its bohemian past. Two victims were Eastman (ironically, "anti-bohemian" himself) and Floyd Dell, veterans of the Lyrical Left. Eastman continued to argue that cultural freedom was the quintessence of radicalism, and Dell that radicalism could be a sensual affair as well as a serious struggle. "When you go to Russia," Dell said to a writer, "I hope you will write me about their new sexual conventions in great detail." But the *New Masses* editor Mike Gold dismissed Eastman's concern for artistic freedom as a "Platonic" delusion, and Dell's obsession with sex as that of a sick bourgeois intellectual who "became the historian of the phallic-hunting girls of Greenwich Village." Still the sybarite, Dell later remarked that in the *New Masses* cartoons "the women always had square breasts—which seems to me to denote a puritanical and fanatical hatred of women as the source of pleasure." Gold and Calverton refused to see, said Dell, that sex for him was a "manumission from the bondage of a preoccupation with a Grand Economic Explanation of Everything, which is rigor mortis to the mind."[11]

Even those who tried to establish a bridge between the two Lefts met with frustration. In his *Modern Quarterly* the editor Calverton sought to pursue the themes that had once animated the Greenwich Village rebels: eros, psychoanalysis, birth control, feminism, and, as the title of one of his books put it, *The Bankruptcy of Marriage* (1928). Calverton's writings on the repressive nature of bourgeois institutions in some respects paralleled those of Wilhelm Reich and anticipated those of the later "Frankfurt school" émigrés. The communist *New Masses* and *Daily Worker,* for their part, thought Freudian psychoanalysis would only complicate things when all the revolution needed was a clear-headed proletariat.[12]

Sidney Hook and the Americanization of Marxism

A debate that for several years pitted two former students of John Dewey against each other epitomized the tension that existed between the two Left generations.

In the twenties the Village veteran Max Eastman had tried to persuade the Left that Freudianism could illuminate the inner world of the emotions and of the subconscious that Marx himself had scarcely plumbed. With some prescience Eastman urged the Left to learn from the insights of Freud before the Right could discover for itself the psychic world of myth and symbol and appropriate the irrational for its own ends. But Hook, as a young philosopher on the Left, would have nothing to do with marrying Marx and Freud; he dismissed it as being as hopeless as trying to mix water and oil. Marxism was a science to be tested by empirical methods. Whatever else Freudianism was, its hypothesis about mental processes could not be observed, hence not tested or replicated. What, then, did Hook think of the Marxian dialectic? Did it have to be observed before Marx's philosophy of history could be verified as a rational project?[13]

The challenge of defending Marxism as a science was taken up by Hook, who had received his doctoral degree under Dewey in 1927 at Columbia University. Scrappy, argumentative, unrelenting, Hook lived for controversy as Eastman had lived for beauty— even as a bored pupil in Brooklyn's elementary schools he had struck some of his teachers as a troublemaker because he asked biting questions and rejected bland answers. After studying Marxism in Berlin and Moscow on a Guggenheim fellowship, Hook completed, at the age of thirty-one, *Towards the Understanding of Karl Marx: A Revolutionary Interpretation* (1933). An intricate argument, it was obviously not meant as propaganda for the masses: "Because A presupposes B, it does not follow that B presupposes A; although it is legitimate to argue from non-B to non-A. . . ." Exposing invalid modes of thinking became Hook's passion.[14]

A communist supporter in the early thirties, Hook was America's most original Marxist thinker. From Berlin he wrote to persuade his mentor Dewey that Marxism was not an abstract, dogmatic "system" but a "critique" grounded in historical experience. Like Dewey's own pragmatism, Hook insisted, Marxism rested on the naturalistic principle that there could be no appeal to supernatural, transcendent, or absolute authority. Nor did Marxist determinism guarantee revolution independently of human purpose and effort. The dialectic of Marxism meant not that capitalism was fated to collapse by the weight of its inherent contradictions but that truth arises out of experimental encounters with reality leading to the empirical verification of those encounters. Thus predictions about historical events must either be confirmed in actuality or revised in theory. Hook likened Marx's idea of "praxis"—the notion that to understand the world is to act upon it and thereby, to change it—to James's and Dewey's conviction that truth does not reside in an idea awaiting to be discovered but instead is made to happen in the world of will and action. Both Marxism and pragmatism had their foundations in Darwin's theory of evolution; both urged the philosopher to engage the world of experience; and both regarded mind as a problem-solving instrument whose ideas are either confirmed or invalidated by the consequences they produce.[15]

The historical context of Hook's first writings on Marxism is crucial both politically and philosophically. The CPUSA had yet to claim a major American intellectual; having expelled Will Herberg, Jay Lovestone, and Bertram Wolfe in 1929, the party lost some of the best Marxist theoreticians in the country. Although the CP's leader, Earl Browder, was unhappy with Hook's "reinterpretation" of Marxism and although communists soon attacked him as a "revisionist," the CP tried to recruit him both as a means of getting to Dewey and, to Hook's dismay, to do organizational and propaganda work for Russia—and also, a proposition that left Hook "in a state of panic," to set up a "spy apparatus." A year before his meeting with Browder, Hook signed "Culture and Crisis," a document in which leading American intellectuals endorsed the 1932 communist presidential ticket. But Hook would have nothing to do with the party itself, and thus America became a country with a communist party without a leading Marxist philosopher. The American party lost the battle for cultural hegemony without knowing it.

The theoretical context is also important. Ever since the Second International (1889–1914), Marxism had been regarded as an empirical science in which the laws of history unfolded according to predetermined stages, and hence the transition to socialism had to await economic development. That fatalistic view prevailed until the October Revolution, at which point Lenin broke the spell of theory by seizing power. Subsequently writers like Lukács, Gramsci, and Max Eastman credited Lenin with showing the way to freedom, will, and consciousness. Hook, in contrast, interpreted Marxism itself as a philosophy of freedom as much as of determinism, a philosophy in which human activity could break from mechanical necessity once science was conceived not as the unfolding of laws or as the inexorable realization of ideals but the practical application of intelligence as the agent of social change.

When Hook published *Towards the Understanding of Karl Marx*, he was a revolutionary communist who questioned neither Stalin's silencing of all opposition nor Lenin's principle of the dictatorship of the proletariat. Hook even explained that all other forms of government must be abolished ("Wherever we find a state, there we find a dictatorship") and that there can be no dissent and opposition ("The first task the proletarian dictatorship must accomplish is to crush all actual or incipient counter-revolutionary movements"). Within two years Hook had begun to change his mind about proletarian dictatorship and about the necessity of force and violence. By 1935, in a debate with Will Herberg, he was challenging the principle of party infallibility and the assumption—later expounded by the historian E. H. Carr—that the victory of the Bolsheviks proved their superior grasp of the movement of history and their right to claim that their party alone embodied the interests of the workers. By the time he published *From Hegel to Marx* (1936), Hook had joined the anti-Stalinist opposition in the United States that looked to Leon Trotsky to keep alive the spirit of the October Revolution.[16]

Eastman also had been a Trotskyist and had helped Trotsky deal in exile with American publishers; he had translated Trotsky's monumental *History of the Russian Revolution.* But even though Eastman and Hook sympathized with Trotsky's lonely struggle and though both had Dewey as a mentor, they clashed for years over the proper interpretation of Marxism. In the late twenties Hook wrote a severe critique of Eastman's *Marx and Lenin,* which had, it will be recalled, exposed the residual extent of Hegelianism in Marx's thought, thus rendering the dialectic less a science than a superstition. When Hook published his own studies of Marxism, Eastman was primed to settle the score. A witty rebuttal was issued under the title "What Karl Marx Would Have Thought Had He Been a Student of John Dewey." As a writer who looked to poetry to contemplate reality and to science to change it, Eastman had no patience with any philosophy that confused subject and object, mind and matter, the inner domain of thought and the outer domain that is to be transformed by action. In a forty-seven-page pamphlet, *The Last Stand of Dialectical Materialism,* he challenged both the pragmatic and the Marxist conviction that human activity mirrors the movement of history, dismissing as an "animistic" fetish the attempt to read into the world of reality the unfolding of human desires and purposes. It is only scientists, Eastman held, who cannot claim to know reality because, unlike poets, they reconstruct it and transform it according to their practical purposes. Ironically, Eastman turned on its head Marx's famous eleventh thesis on Feuerbach: only philosophers and poets, at least those who have no urge to change the world, have the potential for providing to their readers the "quality of experience" about the world as it really is. To Eastman, Marxism had to do less with knowledge and truth than with need, desire, and the will to power.[17]

In the late thirties the Eastman-Hook debates stimulated a "doctrinal crisis" in Marxist thought. It is a measure of Hook's intellectual honesty that he ceased to argue with Eastman and began to reconsider some of the once unimpeachable premises of Marxism itself. In the short-lived *Marxist Quarterly* he addressed the subject of "Dialectic and Nature," seeking to expose Engels's creation of a pseudologic of organic totality. All the Hegelian assumptions Engels had read into the processes of nature—the laws of contradiction, the identity of opposites, the transformation of quantity into quality, and the negation of the negation—Hook demonstrated to be pure "mythology" incompatible with scientific method. Engels's dialectical materialism had inspired the communist Left with the conviction that nature, as well as history, progresses through the emergence and dissolution of opposing forces. The communists now saw Hook as the same irrepressible troublemaker his elementary school teachers found him to be at the age of ten.[18]

Hook's and Eastman's different temperaments reflect the distinctions between the Old Left and the earlier Lyrical Left. Both came to have doubts about Hegelian Marxism as a philosophical proposition and both came to condemn Stalin's dictatorship. But Eastman retained his Greenwich Village commitments to passionate cultural issues like literature and feminism, the freedom of writers to interpret life as they see it, and the freedom of women to choose the life they want for themselves. Once the great hope of the Village rebels for the new Soviet state, cultural freedom and women's rights had had their brief day in the sun in the first years of the Russian revolution only to be suppressed under the long nightmare of Stalinist totalitarianism. In *Artists in Uniform* (1933) Eastman described the dire fate of the intelligentsia in the Soviet Union; it was one of several publications to earn him the distinction of being the first American writer Stalin attacked as a "gangster of the pen." In 1935, when Eastman heard of the Kremlin's decree ordering the Russian people to multiply, outlawing birth control and abortion, and raising the cost of divorce and alimony, he no longer could see how it was possible, as Trotsky advised, to defend and support the Soviet system on the one hand while criticizing and attacking Stalin's leadership on the other. The decree abolishing women's rights was "the last straw," Eastman told Calverton, "the ultimate end of a dream."[19]

Eastman and Hook came to admire each other, especially during the cold war, when they opposed America's right-wing resort to religion as a means of saving the world from communism. But their backgrounds, personalities, and passions were wholly opposite. Eastman was born and raised in upper-middle-class comfort by parents he adored for life; Hook grew up in the slum of the Williamsburg section of Brooklyn, a "community of shared poverty," with a mother too busy making ends meet and a father confined to a home for the incurably ill. Eastman's self-centered memoirs are full of romantic encounters with women, the painful breakups as well as the erotic attractions. Hook, in his autobiography, mentions halfway through that he is married; there is no reference to his wedding or his wife. Eastman wrote books on poetry, humor, and the pleasures of friendship; Hook, books on logic, dialectics, and the problems of metaphysics. Eastman lived for the pleasures of life; Hook, for the pleasures of thought. Engels's distortions of philosophy mattered less to Eastman than Stalin's suppression of women.[20]

For the rest of his life Hook sought to save Marx from the Marxists. Unlike many ex-radicals of the thirties, Hook never repudiated Marxism. What he continued to believe to be of enduring relevance was Marx's sense of property as a fundamental category of social relations; his historical and biological materialism, which, like pragmatic naturalism, extirpated dualism so as to see the mind as continuous with nature; and, most important, Marx's "humanism," reflected in "his distrust of overspecialization and excessive division of labor, his concern with human alienation and his view that it can be overcome by creative fulfillments through uncoerced work." The Presidential Medal of Freedom that Ronald Reagan pinned on Sidney Hook was bestowed upon a Marxist.[21]

In the thirties Granville Hicks looked back fondly on Eastman's *Masses.* "It had," he wrote, "the seriousness of strong convictions and the gaiety of great hopes." Eastman's Lyrical Left did make politics a matter for laughter as well as for commitment. With

Hook's Old Left generation the laughter had gone out of American radicalism.[22]

Whereas the Lyrical Left was animated by sensuous emotions, the Old Left was driven by a sodden intensity born of the anxieties and insecurities of the Depression. The strident ideological debates and polemics merely reflected the fratricidal sectarianism of the period. They also suggest a further contrast between the Lyrical Left and the Old Left. To a large extent the former was made up of rebels; the latter, of revolutionaries (or those who, under the spell of Marxism, briefly saw themselves as revolutionaries). The rebel rises as an individual in opposition to all sources of oppression; the revolutionary focuses all his antagonisms upon one object and channels all his energy into one movement. The rebel desires to assault traditional structure and authority; the revolutionary desires to destroy in order to create a specific new social order. The rebel has a quixotic worldview, skeptical of "closed systems"; the revolutionary has an "organically" integrated worldview in which "totality" is everything, in Georg Lukács's words. And the rebel, to borrow Arthur Koestler's useful distinction, has the capacity to change causes; the revolutionary does not.[23] Actually, few radicals in the thirties were true revolutionaries. Nevertheless, communist doctrine did give them the illusion that they were revolutionaries ready to storm the barricades when the hour of truth presented itself. Communism served to constrict the perspectives of radicalism and to confine the intellectual's passion to a single cause. "Individual rebellion has passed out of me," wrote Joseph Freeman, who made the transition from the Lyrical to the Old Left, "and now I would like more than anything else to be a disciplined worker in the movement."[24] The revolutionary movement became the great cause of the Old Left. When it failed, many intellectuals who threw their bodies and souls into it emerged not merely disillusioned, as in the case of the earlier Left, but so bitter, exhausted, and guilt ridden that they abandoned all causes. To comprehend their retreat from radicalism requires a brief sketch of the unhappy history of the Old Left.

The Popular Front

Ideologically, the Old Left encompassed both socialism and communism, and the tensions that had earlier divided the two re-emerged in the thirties. The socialists organized around the older Socialist Labor party and Socialist party and the new American Workers party. In 1934 the AWP was established to forge a radical movement independent of both the SP and the CP. Led by the Dutch-born preacher A. J. Muste, the AWP refrained from dogmatic formulations of economic problems, organized the unemployed in the small industrial towns of the Ohio Valley, and attracted several independent radicals who wanted to avoid repeating socialist and communist tactical mistakes. Meanwhile, the SLP continued to attack the reformism of the democratic socialists and the centralism of the communists, thus remaining true to DeLeon and as isolated as ever from the mainstream of American radicalism. The SP itself could poll only 903,000 votes (2 percent of the total vote) when it ran Norman Thomas for the presidency in 1932. (Debs polled 6 percent in 1912.) Moreover, the party was sick with factionalism. With a membership of roughly 15,000, the SP was made up of older Jewish trade union leaders, a small core of Protestant pacifists, and young students who formed the League for Industrial Democracy. The younger militants often sided with Thomas and challenged the leadership of old-guard socialists like Hillquit. Aside from internal difficulties, the SP faced two new challenges in the thirties: the gradual winning over of workers in the coal mines, steel mills, and clothing factories by the New Deal's labor reforms; and the seductiveness of the wealth-sharing panaceas of Dr. Francis Townsend, Huey Long, and Upton Sinclair.

To the Left intellectuals, democratic socialism seemed stale and timid. "Becoming a socialist right now," wrote Dos Passos in 1932, "would have just about the same effect on anybody as drinking a bottle of near-beer."[25] To intellectuals who wanted a party more audacious than the SP but not quite as centralized as the CP, the

The Socialist party presidential nominee Norman Thomas. (Library of Congress)

only choices were two communist splinter groups whose influence among radical writers was perhaps the one consolation of their lonely isolation. The Lovestonites and the Trotskyists, both expelled from the CP in the 1920s, still regarded themselves as the only genuine communists in America. The former group, led by

Jay Lovestone, Bertram D. Wolfe, and Will Herberg, was often called the CP of the Right Opposition, just as the latter, led by James P. Cannon, James Burnham, and Max Shachtman, called itself the CP of the Left Opposition. After failing to win the Comintern's endorsement in 1929, the Lovestonites continued to stress their conservative thesis of "American exceptionalism," which criticized communists for applying Marxist-Leninist ideas mechanically to the peculiar conditions of America instead of creatively adapting them. Sharing with the Lovestonites an opposition to Stalinism, the Trotskyists claimed that only they represented the true Left and that therefore they, the real Leninist revolutionaries, would soon displace the official CP and reconstitute a new, authentic party and a new Communist International. Although these two opposition factions had together fewer than a thousand members, the Lovestonites' *Workers Age* and the Trotskyists' *New International* gave the Left a variety of refreshing and usually discerning viewpoints. Later in the thirties the Trotskyists won increasing support among several literary intellectuals who could no longer tolerate the Comintern-dominated *Communist* and the CP's *Daily Worker.*

In the early thirties, however, the communists commanded most attention. In 1932 the League of Professional Groups published *Culture and Crisis,* calling upon writers, doctors, scientists, artists, and teachers to vote for Foster and Ford, the candidates of the CP. Those who heaped contempt upon the reformist SP and gave their allegiance to the revolutionary CP included many of America's most notable writers and scholars. What originally attracted intellectuals to communism was the confidence and aggressiveness of the CP, now intoxicated by the "third period" of the international communist movement (the first, 1919–21, witnessed the abortive communist insurrections in Hungary and Bavaria; the second, 1922–28, saw Russia acknowledging the stabilization of world capitalism and making friendly diplomatic overtures to the West). The policy of the third period fitted the mood of the early Depression, for it asserted that the time for a revolutionary offensive had now been reached in the development of world capitalism. This new strategy caused the CP to shift tactics on the labor question. Previously the CP had accepted the Comintern's judgment that the development of a radical consciousness among American workers would be slow. Now the CP reversed itself and made every effort to penetrate and capture the labor movement by taking over strikes wherever possible and, after the economic crash, by setting up unemployment councils and again instructing each of its members to "turn his face to the factory." The CP also launched a policy of dual unionism, under which, as the Depression deepened, rival communist unions or locals were established in the clothing, textile, coal, tool and die, restaurant, shoe, and automobile industries. Later, when John L. Lewis broke from the AFL in 1936 and formed the CIO, communists were able to move in on the ground floor and establish a base in more than a dozen CIO affiliates, including the strategic longshore, maritime, and transport unions.

It is enormously difficult to ascertain the exact influence of the CP in the labor movement during the Depression. The New Left historian Staughton Lynd has recorded the glowing recollections of several CIO veterans praising the organizational efforts of communists. The more thorough research of Theodore Draper, however, suggests the limitations of communist influence on labor in general. The CP, for example, made an all-out effort to win over southern textile workers and miners in the brutal strikes at Gastonia, North Carolina, and in Harlan County, Kentucky. But the failure of these poorly organized, ill-timed strikes was a calamity for the workers, who, always suspicious of the "atheistic" doctrines of communism, became openly hostile to any further efforts at communist infiltration. Nevertheless, communists who entered the South were the first to risk their lives attempting to expose the appalling poverty and working conditions, and they succeeded in gaining the support of a number of important intellectuals, including the novelists Theodore Dreiser and John Dos Passos, who publicized to the nation the desperate plight of the southern workers.[26]

Energy and determination brought success to the communists.

The textile workers' strike in Gastonia, North Carolina, in 1928, was literally heard around the world. (Library of Congress)

The organization men of the American Left, communists were always available to hand out leaflets on bitter-cold mornings, to sit out dreary meetings until they had won their point, never shirking the boring, dirty work of radicalism. Although politically insignificant among the electorate, communists compensated for their lack of power by staging demonstrations and mass parades with fists raised and slogans strident and simple.

Despite its organizational efforts, the CPUSA failed to recruit black Americans. In the election of 1932, the party ran the black Harlem organizer James Ford as its vice-presidential candidate. The soul-stirring Paul Robeson performed at party concerts and benefits. Communists were highly organized in Harlem, where blacks, according to a writer in the *Saturday Evening Post*, could count for help on the party's legal assistant when fired or evicted, or when the gas had been shut off. But out of a total party membership of about fifty thousand in the early thirties, blacks never constituted more than a thousand. Older radical blacks once known to the Lyrical Left stayed clear of the CP. Although McKay, DuBois, and George Padmore had read enough Marx to show their brothers that racial suppression and economic exploitation were related, even during the distress of the Depression they advised blacks to beware of communist indoctrination. They, like Richard Wright, could point to the CP's strategic errors in trying to arouse a mass movement of black workers and intellectuals.

The first such error was the party's formulation of the "Black Belt" doctrine, which, in its attempt to keep the class question separate from the color question, proposed a separate "Negro republic" in the South. The doctrine had been prompted by a position taken by the rival Lovestonites, who were communists but opposed the CP; they held that the industrial revolution would extirpate the remnants of slavery in the agricultural South and "proletarianize the Negro peasantry." The CP, for its part, believed that the struggle for social equality had to continue in the North, where the blacks were in the minority and in the process of cultural assimilation, but that in the deep South, where blacks numerically predominated, the struggle had to aim at self-determination. Its Black Belt doctrine envisioned the overthrow of class rule in the South as integral to the communist war against imperialism. Such a policy failed to respond to the immediate needs of black sharecroppers and other workers, who had evinced little desire, in any case, to separate from the United States.[27]

A second error that alienated the black community was the role of the party in the Scottsboro trials of nine black youths falsely accused of having raped two white women. The NAACP, claiming to be the original defenders of the youths, accused the International Labor Defense, which was a communist front organization, of taking over the case and exploiting it for propaganda purposes, of making martyrs of the nine even at the risk of their conviction.

A third error was the CP's defense of the Soviet Union's policy of supplying petroleum to the Italian army during its invasion of Ethiopia in 1935. Having been told by communists that blacks everywhere in the world could look to Moscow for support and inspiration, American blacks, convinced that they had been betrayed, took to the streets of Harlem in protest.

Even without these errors, communist ideology probably would not have struck deep chords in the hearts of black Americans. Three decades after the Depression, Harold Cruse, in *The Crisis of the Negro Intellectual* (1967), warned the New Left, on the basis of his knowledge of the mistakes made by the Old Left, not to repeat these mistakes. How, he asked, can a black protest movement strive for jobs, housing, and education and at the same time call for the abolition of capitalist property relations? "No foreign ideology can really penetrate the Negro psychology, especially if it is anti-capitalistic to the point of interfering with the desire to 'make good' in the world." Cruse understood communism's own contradictions. What could Marx offer black Americans when he claimed that life had nothing to do with property, wealth, and the pursuit of material happiness?[28]

Communists enjoyed more success with young white Americans. During the Depression almost one-third had not been able to find work, and many from lower-income families left school to take odd jobs to help out at home. Even those who managed to graduate found themselves a "locked-out" generation, an unwanted intelligentsia glad to find work anywhere, even digging ditches on a WPA project. One college newspaper celebrated its graduating class in an "Ode to Higher Education":

> I sing in praise of college
> of M.A.'s and Ph.D.'s
> But in pursuit of knowledge
> We are starving by degrees.[29]

The most important radical youth organizations were the Young Communist League and its campus counterpart the National Student League, which had thriving branches at City College, Brooklyn College, and Hunter College, all in New York City, the University of Chicago and the University of Wisconsin, and, on the West Coast, Berkeley and the University of California, Los Angeles. After visiting campuses, even conservative critics in Congress were forced to admit what most professors knew all along: that YCL members were often the brightest and most articulate students. Young activists fought for academic freedom, raised funds for striking coal miners, rushed to the defense of dismissed radical professors, and, while college presidents fretted over continued support of wealthy benefactors, talked of bringing the class struggle into the classroom. Communists also participated in the upsurge of pacifism among students of the thirties. The greatest display of solidarity occurred on April 13, 1934, when in New York City alone between 15,000 and 25,000 students walked out of their 11:00 A.M. classes in a massive antiwar strike (estimates for the entire country varied between 500,000 and 1,000,000).

For the sensitive young, becoming a communist could mean both a painful and an exhilarating break with parents and relatives. One father, H. Bedford-Jones, published an article in the conservative magazine *Liberty* under the hair-raising title "Will Communists Get Our Girls in College?" claiming he had learned from his daughter how shaggy radicals seduced and subverted innocent coeds. The following week the *New Masses* responded with an article by the daughter of Bedford-Jones, "My Father Is a Liar!" But, on the whole, communists seldom raised the question of gender and, in fact, remained sexist in their assumption that only men could be the revolutionary vanguard.[30]

The CP, which in the twenties had its roots in the immigrant working classes, began reaching out to other sections of American society in the thirties. The results of its recruitment drives were remarkable. Membership rose from 7,500 in 1930 to 55,000 in 1938, with perhaps 30,000 more unregistered members in various youth groups and trade unions.[31] The skill and ability with which communists carried out organizational campaigns is not the only explanation for their success. Equally important was the new strategy of the Popular Front, which replaced the disastrous policies of the third period, described above.

The heady expectations of the third period rested largely on the theory of "social fascism," a notion first developed in the early 1920s by European communists in an effort to undermine the social democrats in Germany and elsewhere. In accordance with this thesis communists were instructed to turn "class against class" so that in the end only two classes (the proletariat and the bourgeoisie) would confront one another in mortal combat. In order to discredit liberals and socialists, the CP took the position that all those who were not communists were class enemies and that liberal-social democracy and fascism were expressions of the same repressive bourgeois state, the only difference being that the former was "masked" and the latter "naked." In Germany, communists thus scorned socialist attempts to oppose Hitler's rise to power, and in the United States communists attacked Norman Thomas and President Roosevelt as "social fascists." The communist strategy presumed that fascism reflected capitalism's "final crisis"; hence, whatever tactic would expedite Hitler's advent to power was a victory for communism ("After Hitler, Our Turn!").[32] But when Hitler consolidated power and made it clear that fascism was anything but a transitory phenomenon, and when Roosevelt seemed able to salvage American capitalism, the theory of social fascism had to be abandoned. Instead of predicting fascism's imminent collapse, communists now described it as an imminent threat. The USSR responded by joining the League of Nations and signing a mutual defense pact with France, and the Comintern announced the new policy of the Popular Front.

The Popular Front of 1935 represented a complete volte-face.

Whereas the CP had previously insisted on class struggle, it now called for collaboration with the bourgeoisie. It had formerly exalted the Soviet system of government; now it extolled the virtues of American democracy. It had once preached internationalism; now it praised nationalism. American communists embraced the new course without so much as a blush of embarrassment, hailing socialists as fellow comrades and praising Roosevelt as an enlightened statesman. Communists now became respectable, and the CP began to seem like an evangelical church that opened its door to all believers. The attempt to make communism into "Twentieth Century Americanism" also meant that the less acrid works of Jefferson, Lincoln, and Paine had to be stressed over Marxist-Leninist writings. At CP meetings the stars and stripes could be seen above the red flag. Patriotism, the refuge of scoundrels, became the haven of Stalinists. Even young communists sounded like clean-cut all-Americans:

> Some people have the idea that a YCLer is politically minded, that nothing outside politics means anything. Gosh no. They have a few simple problems. There is the problem of getting good men on the baseball team, of dating girls, etc. We go to shows, parties, dances, and all that. In short, the YCL and its members are no different from other people except that we believe in dialectical materialism as a solution to all problems.[33]

The Popular Front had immense appeal to many elements of the noncommunist Left, especially to liberals who had always urged a common front against fascism and who found themselves in the midthirties without a viable ideology. By blurring the distinction between Marxism and progressivism and by deemphasizing revolution, the Popular Front also gave liberals the impression that they had persuaded communists to come to their collective senses. Speaking of CP members, Upton Sinclair boasted, "I do not mean to be egotistical and imply that they have taken my advice, but it is a fact that they are now saying and doing what I urged them for many years to say and do: to support and cooperate with the democratic peoples."[34]

The Spanish Civil War and the Moscow Trials

Caught up in the spirit of the Popular Front, much of the American Left accepted the Stalinist interpretation of two momentous events that began in 1936: the Spanish civil war and the Moscow purge trials.

Approximately thirty-two hundred Americans joined the Abraham Lincoln Battalion to fight for the imperiled Spanish republic. Arriving in Barcelona under the aegis of the Comintern, the volunteers were required to accept the political and military leadership of the Spanish Communist party. Some, of course, were communists themselves, but the majority were antifascist liberals and socialists convinced that they had personally to do what their government had refused to do—halt the spread of fascism. Mussolini and Hitler were sending troops and tanks to support Generalissimo Franco, and the Soviet Union was sending supplies to the Loyalists; the American, French, and British governments refused to intervene to save a democratically elected government in Spain. The United States cited the Neutrality Act of 1936, passed in response to the Ethiopian War, which placed a munitions embargo on all belligerent powers.

The largest number of American volunteers were public school teachers and college professors. Many were Jewish alarmed by the anti-Semitic virus of nazism; about a hundred were blacks, some seeking revenge against Mussolini in Madrid for his earlier aggressions in Abyssinia. Years later, looking back and recognizing that neither anarchists nor communists in Spain wanted a constitutional republic, some writers concluded that the civil war was no death struggle of the Left against the Right, of democracy against fascism. Still, at the time, the war appeared essential to stop the oppressions of the privileged classes against the masses and the intolerance of the Catholic church. It was the sentiment of democratic idealism, not cynical power politics, that motivated the American volunteers. "Young non-communist liberals who went to Spain," the historian Robert Rosenstone has written,

Guernica, Picasso's famous expression of the anguish of his homeland under Franco during the Spanish civil war. (Copyright 1991 ARS, N.Y./SPADEM.)

"were the same people who in another era would be going on freedom rides, registering Negro voters in Mississippi, or demonstrating against the Vietnam war."[35]

The Spanish civil war became a test for the moral convictions of the Left everywhere in the Western world. In the international brigades came the English novelist George Orwell and poet John Cornford; in the Garibaldi Battalion came the Italian *fuorusciti,* exiles from Il Duce's dictatorship. The French writer André Malraux organized the international brigades' air squadron. The American writers Ernest Hemingway, John Dos Passos, and Archibald MacLeish went to Spain to report on the war and shoot the prorepublic propaganda film *The Spanish Earth.*

The use of the name Abraham Lincoln Battalion was not a mere example of Popular Front propaganda. The Lincoln Battalion was instructed that its first duty was to preserve the republic in Spain, not to turn the civil war into a social revolution, just as Lincoln had believed that his first duty was to hold the Union together even if it meant permitting slavery. At the same time, the real forces of the Left in Spain were the Trotskyists (POUM), and especially the more numerous anarchists, whose experiments in collective farms and workers' councils attempted to transform Spain's social and political structure. But the Comintern, possibly fearing that a revolutionary Spain would arouse the wrath of Western nations, ordered Spanish communists to put down a popular uprising in Barcelona and to liquidate several anarchist leaders. In the United States only a handful of anti-Stalinists publicized the repression. Dos Passos was particularly upset when Hemingway, his old companion, first tried to dismiss as rumor the disappearance of José Robles Pazos, a professor at Johns Hopkins University and longtime friend of Dos Passos. When the murder of Pazos was confirmed, Dos Passos broke with Hemingway and declared that a crime is a crime whether committed by the Left or the Right.[36]

By the time he wrote *For Whom the Bell Tolls* (1940), Hemingway knew he had to acknowledge the murderous activities of Stalinist leaders, as Dos Passos had done in his lesser-known *Ad-*

ventures of a Young Man (1939) and George Orwell in his better-known *Homage to Catalonia* (1938). The internecine struggle between anarchists and communists was almost as exhausting as the fight against fascism, although few wanted to admit it. The outcome of of the Spanish civil war left many writers with intellectual and moral, as well as physical, wounds. But Hemingway could never admit defeat, even if Franco's victory in 1940 chastened the Left everywhere. Once confident that history was on its side, the Left knew the meaning of tragedy as a lost cause that must, but refuses to, die. "It was in Spain," Albert Camus wrote in 1946, "that men learned that one can be right and yet be beaten, that force can defeat spirit, that there are times when courage is not its own reward. It is this, no doubt, which explains why so many men, the world over, feel the Spanish drama as a personal tragedy."[37]

While news from Spain upset a few radical intellectuals, reports from Moscow convulsed the entire Left. Stalin's systematic purge of thousands of former Bolshevik leaders, some of them heroes in the eyes of American radicals, remains one of the most enigmatic episodes in the twentieth century. Branded as traitors or fascist agents, the accused often confessed in open court to crimes they could not possibly have committed. They did so knowing a firing squad awaited them no matter how they pleaded. From 1936 to 1938 the American Left was stunned by the eerie proceedings. Most socialists, suspicious as ever of Stalin, denounced the trials; and the Trotskyists, fearing a bloodbath against anti-Stalinists everywhere, sought to expose the farce. Trotskyists in America, led by Hook and supported by the anarchist Carlo Tresca and also by the libertarian feminist Suzanne LaFollette, succeeded in persuading John Dewey to head a commission of inquiry that went to Mexico for testimony from the exiled Trotsky for a "countertrial" outside the USSR. That Dewey could both disagree with and defend Trotsky represented the spirit of the American Left at its democratic best.

The Dewey-Trotsky Debates:
"A Veritable Pharos" as "A Fearful Monument"

The Trotsky inquiry of 1937 preceded by a year an exchange with John Dewey in the party journal *New International.* Trotsky had assailed the "banalities" of liberal sensibilities in an article, "Their Morals and Ours"; Dewey responded with a reflective theoretical statement entitled "Means and Ends." The conflict between democracy and revolutionary socialism had been troubling Dewey for years, and in Mexico he questioned Trotsky's own version of democracy-in-action:

Dewey: Was there any organized, recognized method by which, aside from criticism and discussion, the worker could control the committees, the different branches of the Party?

Trotsky: Of the Party or of the Soviet?

Dewey: Of the Party.

Trotsky: It was the right only of Party members to change the Party and to control the Party. In the soviets, it was the right also of non-Party members—the Constitution assured to the workers and peasants the right to remove at any time their representatives to the soviet and to elect new ones.

Dewey: I was not referring to the soviets. I was referring to the governing bodies of the Party.

Trotsky: The bodies of the Party were elected only by the Party members and submitted only to the Party Congress.

Dewey: Under these circumstances, how can you say that it was democratic?

Trotsky: I didn't say it was democratic in the absolute sense. I consider democracy not as a mathematical abstraction, but as a living experience of the people. It was a great step to democracy from the old regime, but this democracy in its formal expression was limited to the necessities of the revolutionary dictatorship.

Dewey did not press Trotsky on the issue of democracy. The following year he did reply to Trotsky's stirring and controversial article "Their Morals and Ours," which was to do much to divide the American Left. Trotsky had charged anarchists and democrats with shirking the harsh realities of class struggle and with succumbing to "absolute" principles of ethics, to vague "moral effluvia" preached to revolutionaries but not to their persecutors. Ridiculing the "theory of eternal morals," Trotsky noted that even utilitarian philosophers insisted that the ends justified the means, whereas the Jesuits, "more consistent and courageous," taught that a means is condoned or condemned depending on the specific end it serves. Since Marxist morality is governed by the imperative of revolution, "all means are possible which genuinely lead to mankind's emancipation." But the dialectic of means and ends is such that only certain means can lead to that end, only those means that instill "solidarity and unity" to revolutionary workers and imbue them with the "courage" and "consciousness" necessary to carry out their "historic tasks." Addressing himself to American Marxists, Trotsky drew upon episodes in American history to demonstrate that posterity would judge his views in the same light:

> Lincoln's significance lies in his not hesitating before the most severe means, once they were found to be necessary, in achieving a great historic aim posed by the development of a young nation. The question lies not even in which of the warring camps caused or itself suffered the greatest number of victims. History has different yardsticks for the cruelty of the Northerners and the cruelty of the Southerners in the Civil War. A slave-owner who through cunning and violence shackles a slave in chains, and a slave who through cunning or violence breaks the chains—let not the contemptible eunuchs tell us that they are equals before a court of morality!

Could Dewey have a convincing answer to Trotsky's argument? His instrumentalist philosophy, too, rejected ethics based on rule-bound principles rather than on pragmatic consequences, and hence both the liberal and the revolutionary denied the efficacy of

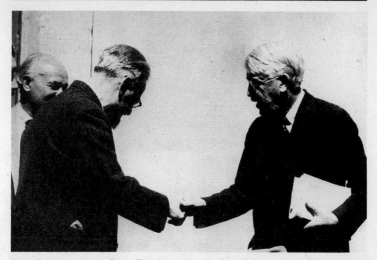

John Dewey greeting Leon Trotsky before the latter's "countertrial" on charges of disloyalty to the Soviet Union, Mexico City, April 13, 1937. (Wide World Photos)

transcendent moral judgments in history. Nevertheless, Dewey questioned, during the trial itself, the factual accuracy of the charges Moscow had made against Trotsky. The philosopher's attention to the canons of jurisprudence impressed even Trotsky, who had first thought that Dewey, then seventy-eight, would fall asleep during the hearings. At the conclusion of the trial Trotsky passionately and eloquently presented his case. The countertrial, he exclaimed to the hushed audience,

> has not only not destroyed my faith in the clear, bright future of mankind, but, on the contrary, has given it an indestructible temper. This faith in reason, in truth, in human solidarity, which at the age of eighteen I took with me into the workers quarters of the provincial Russian town of Nikolaiev—this faith I have preserved fully and completely. It has become more mature, but not less ardent.
>
> In the very fact of your Commission's formation—in the fact that, at its head, is a man of unshakable moral authority, a man [who] by virtue of his age should have the right to remain outside

the skirmishes in the political arena—in this fact I see a new and truly magnificent reinforcement of the revolutionary optimism which constitutes the fundamental elements of my life.

After hearing the stirring peroration, the audience broke into applause when Trotsky expressed his "profound respect" for Dewey, "the educator, philosopher and personification of genuine American idealism." "Anything I can say," remarked Dewey when he pronounced the hearings closed, "will be an anti-climax."[38]

Shortly after the countertrial cleared Trotsky of the charges, he became the object of a different one, first raised by Dwight Macdonald. As leader of the Red Army, Trotsky had presided over the suppression of anarchist sailors in the Kronstadt uprising of 1921. Had Trotsky succeeded Lenin, would the course of Russian history have been different? Once the whisper of Kronstadt was circulated, many American writers expressed doubts that Trotsky himself would have shrunk from establishing a ruthless dictatorship. But throughout most of the thirties Trotsky stood in the American Left's imagination as "a fearful monument," whose ideas of permanent revolutionary struggle burned brighter with each defeat of the working class. Even Eastman, who forever reproached Trotsky for refusing to move against Stalin upon Lenin's death, believed he represented a curious combination of diffidence and arrogance, an absence of ego and an excess of confidence. And even though Eastman blamed Trotsky for the failure of the Bolshevik Revolution, he was struck by his "Mephistophelian character," the "black art" of causing "an oratorical opponent to shrivel in the air with the single shaft of sarcastic logic."[39]

No doubt writers like Eastman also identified with Trotsky as a fellow writer eking out a precarious livelihood. Eastman translated several of Trotsky's works, helped him find American publishers, and explored the possibility of producing a "talking film" on the Russian revolution. Trotsky knew that publishers required profits; hence the irony of expecting the worst and wanting the best. Any hope for the coming of revolution in America depended upon further economic deterioration in the Depression years; yet any prospect of a publisher's advance, Trotsky informed Eastman, hinged on whether the New York Stock Exchange picked up "a bit of spunk."[40] For their dissemination Trotsky's revolutionary ideas, he knew, depended upon Wall Street's performance.

In some respects Trotsky was to the anti-Stalinist Old Left of the thirties what Lenin had been to the Lyrical Left of the First World War years. Eastman, Reed, and other Greenwich Village radicals saw in Lenin the glorious identity of history and will; he was the revolutionist whose daring conquest of power in 1917 seemed to symbolize the fulfillment of both the idea and the deed of Marxism. Trotsky enjoyed a similar heroic image, but for the generation of the thirties it took on a different character—the purity of an idea whose essence had been tainted by Stalin. He emerged as the "prophet outcast" who in losing power had saved the conscience of the revolution. To Irving Howe, Trotsky was "an embodiment of past grandeur, a voice of corrosive honesty attacking the terror and corruption of Stalin, a thinker in the great Marxist tradition, a revolutionist of exemplary fearlessness." To the literary critic F. W. Dupee, Trotsky was the Thucydides of the Russian revolution. Even to the sardonic Dwight Macdonald, not given to hero worship, Trotsky's career "showed that intellectuals, too, could make history." Trotsky could scarcely satisfy the intellectuals' thirst for power—a latent impulse more likely fulfilled by identifying with Stalin and the Soviet state. If some radical intellectuals saw Stalin as the only answer to Hitler, others saw Trotsky as the only answer to Stalin, the last hope that the meaning of the October Revolution would not be lost in what Isaac Deutscher called the "hell-black night" of totalitarianism. In the gloomy political atmosphere of the thirties, when writers felt the urgent necessity of choosing the bad against the worst, Trotsky and Trotskyism held out the possibility that one could choose better than the bad and defy the grotesque fallacy of the false alternative.

Edmund Wilson best expressed this desperate hope of his generation:

We who of recent years have seen the State that Trotsky helped to build in a phase combining the butcheries of the Robespierre Terror with the corruption and reaction of the Directory, and Trotsky himself figuring dramatically in the role of Gracchus Babeuf, may be tempted to endow him with qualities which actually he does not possess and with principles which he has expressly repudiated. We have seen the successor of Lenin undertake a fabulous rewriting of the whole history of the Revolution in order to cancel out Trotsky's part; pursue Trotsky from country to country, persecuting even his children and hounding them to their deaths; and at last, in faked trials and confessions more degrading to the human spirit than the frank fiendishness of Iván the Terrible, try to pin upon Trotsky the blame for all the mutinies, mistakes and disasters that have harassed his administration—till he has made the world conscious of Trotsky as the accuser of Stalin's own bad conscience, as if the Soviet careerists of the thirties were unable to deny the socialist ideal without trying to annihilate the moral authority of this one homeless and haunted man. It is not Trotsky alone who has created his role: his enemies have given it a reality that no mere self-dramatization could have compassed. And as the fires of the Revolution have died down in the Soviet Union at a time when the systems of thought of the West were already in an advanced state of decadence, he has shone forth like a veritable pharos, rotating a long shaft of light on the seas and the reefs all around.[41]

But the image of Trotsky, though it could fire the literary imagination, haunted the Stalinists and even the liberals. When the countertrial commission defended Trotsky and published the book *Not Guilty*, a storm of controversy erupted. Immediately 150 "American Progressives" signed a statement supporting the Moscow trials. Although motives were complex and varied, those intellectuals who condoned the trials generally feared the collapse of the Popular Front. In their minds Trotsky preached world revolution, class struggle, and opposition to democracy; hence it was Stalin's enemies who played into the hands of the fascists, undermined the strength of the Soviet Union, and thereby endangered a united front on the Left. But even those communists who opposed the Popular Front justified the purges by appealing to the goddess of history. Citing the political trials that occurred during the French Revolution, Jay Lovestone concluded, "In effect, we practically ignore the charges, refutations and counter-charges, and ask ourselves: *Which tendency was carrying forward the interests of the revolution and which was obstructing it?* Some may be shocked at this utterly 'unmoral' approach but it seems to be the approach of history!"[42]

After a Stalinist agent in Mexico killed the heavily guarded Trotsky with an ice ax, embittered American Trotskyists accused other radicals of supporting Stalin because he had power while Trotsky had only the most brilliant mind of the century. Had radical intellectuals admitted the monstrous hoax of the show trials, they would have had to question the moral distinction between communism and fascism and admit that truth was no longer the virtue of the Left. "One of the worst drawbacks of being a Stalinist at the present time," wrote Edmund Wilson in 1937, "is that you have to defend so many falsehoods." But in the same year Malcolm Cowley assured Dewey in a private letter that Trotsky was "touched with paranoia, with delusions of persecution and grandeur." Waldo Frank scarcely knew whom to trust. "It is difficult for me to believe that you entered an alliance with fascism," he complained to Trotsky, "but it is equally difficult for me to believe that Stalin carried out such horrible frame-ups." To concede the terror of the trials required an admission of one's own naïveté for having believed that Marxism would somehow solve the problem of human aggression. With excruciating self-analysis, Frank later asked, "Could the vision within Marxism not be deepened? Not be made true? This was my hope, and my strategy. In my journal of those days I wrote: 'I collaborate with the revolutionists not expecting them to understand me: the bad logic of their dogmatic empiricism prevents that. But I must serve and understand them; and part of my service is to let them exploit me.' " Years afterwards some Left intellectuals would justify their support of Stalin on the grounds that Hitler was the greater threat and Stalin the only ruler willing and able to crush the Third Reich. Even so, those who remained silent emerged from the decade with a conscience as pained as it was penitential. Reflecting on the private doubts, which he confided to a notebook rather than publish, Cowley confessed, "That failure to publish led me into false situations, and later I would suffer for it—deservedly, I say to myself in private reckonings. When I add together these various sins of silence, self-protectiveness, inadequacy, and something close to moral cowardice, there appears to be reason for my feeling a sense of guilt about the second half of the decade."[43]

Thus the Moscow trials created a crisis of conscience for the American Left. Although many could not bear the burden of truth, a number of important writers broke with the Popular Front and publicly condemned the Soviet government. Anti-Stalinist intellectuals formed the Congress for Cultural Freedom to protest the suppression of civil liberty in Russia as well as in Germany. While scholars began to apply the new term "totalitarian" to Russia along with Germany, Trotskyists debated whether Stalin's Russia could in any sense be considered a "workers' state" and, if not, whether they were obligated to defend it in case of war or adopt a policy of "revolutionary defeatism."[44] Stalin himself resolved the issue when the Soviet Union, on August 24, 1939, announced a neutrality and nonaggression pact with Nazi Germany. To wavering fellow travelers, the pact came as the final blow. Even communists, who might view the expedient maneuver as Stalin's answer to the Munich settlement, were shocked when they realized the Kremlin had given no hint of the negotiations. Thousands of members now left the CP, shaken by the thought that communism no less than fascism meant the end of morality in politics. During the height of the Popular Front, Russian stood for all that was good, rational, and progressive, and Germany for all that was evil, barbaric, and reactionary. The Nazi-Soviet pact killed that dream and, as W. H. Auden expressed it, "the clever hopes expired of a low dishonest decade." Granville Hicks, an influential critic and literary editor of the *New Masses*, received a letter from a young woman protesting his resignation from the CP shortly after the pact:

So it all comes to this: that your whole life previous to this time, all you underwent for the party, all the privations you seem willingly to have suffered when you could have had any post you wanted anywhere in the country, all this has gone up in a puff of smoke and lost its meaning. What for? You might just as well have taken it nice and easy and saved yourself the trouble. It might just as well never have happened. What a pity, to find one's life without meaning. What is left for you now?[45]

The Critique of Marxism: Legacy of the Old Left

Finding their lives emptied of meaning, some radicals of the 1930s felt an overriding urge to come to grips with their past. A few intellectuals wrote novels or autobiographies in the hope that political truth might be generalized from personal experience. Most writers began to reexamine the faiths that had nourished and sustained their radicalism. In the process, Old Left intellectuals subjected Marxism to a critique in every area of human knowledge, and from their reconsiderations arose a new outlook on the nature of American society and the nature of man.

SOCIOLOGY: FROM MARX TO TOCQUEVILLE   In the 1920s American intellectuals condemned capitalism on moral grounds. The despair with which many writers fled America's business culture merely revealed that few questioned the efficacy and durability of the free-enterprise system. In the thirties, however, capitalism was attacked not primarily because it was immoral but because it was irrational. Influenced by the Marxist theory of the inevitable clash of social classes, many writers believed they were witnessing the death agony of the old order as described in *Das Kapital.* Capitalists, in a frenzy of irrational competition, introduce labor-saving machinery and reduce further the workers' wages and buying power. As profits continue to shrink, unemployment rises, underconsumption spreads, small businesses go under, and, while the few remaining industrialists blindly continue to produce, the middle class realizes who its enemy is as it descends "gradually into the proletariat." After a series of worsening crises, "centralization of the means of production and socialization of labor at last reach a point where they become incompatible with their capitalist integument. This integument bursts asunder. The knell of capitalist private property sounds. The expropriators are expropriated."[46]

The idea that capitalism was prey to its own "contradictions" led Marxists to engage in an unrelieved dialogue on "inevitability." The dialogue was questioned when the collapse of capitalism failed to destroy the bourgeoisie and produce a polarization of classes in America. In *The Crisis of the Middle Class* (1935), the Marxist Lewis Corey perceptively described the condition of the "petite bourgeoisie"; but as Corey would later admit, the old bourgeois stratum of small, victimized entrepreneurs declined only to be replaced by a "new middle class" of industrial technicians and middle-management employees. Corey wanted the Left to reach out to the new middle class. But gradually intellectuals began to sense that the "objective" concept of class, which viewed the worker only in relation to the means of production, must be modified by an analysis of the worker's self-image in relation to his social and professional role. Anxieties about status helped explain why the "new middle class" would remain conservative and why the déclassé citizen could never bring himself to identify with the proletariat, as Marx had assumed. Moreover, when America failed to polarize into two warring camps, Left intellectuals began to analyze the historical sources of America's peculiar social structure and value system in a search for the factors that had prevented the development of class consciousness. The key appeared to be in the writings of Alexis de Tocqueville, who a century earlier had described America as a homogenized and integrated social order where "equality of condition" was both an ideal and a reality. After the Second World War, ex-Marxist sociologists like Max Lerner and Seymour Martin Lipset would describe America as an "open class society" that was dynamic and mobile, bound together by common beliefs and values rooted in economic individualism and social conformity. This new outlook on American society marked a dramatic shift from Marx's theory of class struggle and economic oppression imposed from above to Tocqueville's theory of class diffusion and self-imposed social repression. In American sociology the concepts of status and consensus replaced those of class and conflict.[47]

ECONOMICS: FROM MARX TO KEYNES   If American society confounded Marxism, so did Franklin D. Roosevelt. It was the New Deal that gave hope to the American middle class and rescued capitalism from the cyclical manifestation of its death instinct. Roosevelt's programs failed to relieve the massive unemployment and revive the shaky economy—only the Second World War would bring about the huge government spending that restored stability—but the New Deal, with its social security measures and its recognition of labor's right to collective bargaining, eased the discontent of the lower and middle working classes. To the Left, the New Deal at first appeared a futile and chaotic experiment in class collaboration. The idea that a government could rise above the interests of the ruling class and respond to the pressures of organized labor and the majority of citizens (if not to the needs of the unorganized poor and forgotten minorities) was alien to the communist concept of the state. The Left also feared that the Roosevelt administration would be dominated by monopoly capitalists who would gradually transform America into a fascist corporate state. But Roosevelt's ability to steer a middle course between capitalist exploitation and socialist expropriation, while at the same time preserving traditional democratic institutions, seemed more attractive to disillusioned radicals who found a new respect for the politics of moderation as they watched the politics of extremism in Germany and Russia.

During the Second World War, moreover, even anticapitalist intellectuals were impressed by the great productive capacity of American enterprise, now being harnessed to destroy the awesome industrial might of the Krupp works and the Third Reich. After the war no one could speak of America's economy as irrational or contradictory in the realm of production. Yet, instead of going beyond Marxism to a moral criticism of capitalism, some ex-radicals became fascinated by the government-spending policies of Keynesian economics and all but mesmerized by the magic of industrial growth. They now believed that the old socialist goal of equality could be ignored, since wealth no longer had to be redistributed but merely expanded. "There are no problems on the side of depression with which the American economy and polity cannot, if it must, contend," wrote John Kenneth Galbraith in 1952. "This change in western political life," wrote Lipset in reference to the "end of ideology," which supposedly accompanied the advent of abundance, "reflects the fact that the fundamental political problems of the industrial revolution have been solved." The idea that a progressive increase in aggregate income would lessen the harsh contrast between rich and poor is a doctrine as old as Daniel Webster. Postwar intellectuals understood that an obsession with gross national product had conservative implications, and many liberal Keynesians called for structural and social reforms. Yet it was hard to deny that the spectacle of affluence had replaced the specter of scarcity, making consumption the new opiate of the people. Werner Sombart's "melancholy" predictions at the turn of the century, made in his book *Why Is There No Socialism in the United States?* seemed to be coming true: "On the reefs of roast beef and apple pie socialistic utopias of every society are sent to their doom."[48]

POLITICAL SCIENCE: FROM MARX TO MADISON   The Old Left believed communism would resolve not only the problem of justice and equality but also the problem of power. The idea of a classless society implied that political power would be democratized as economic power was collectivized. But in Russia, the state, which Marx once called "the executive committee of the ruling class," failed to "wither away" even though the ruling classes had long been destroyed. The reemergence of despotic power under Stalin puzzled the Old Left, and younger radicals, especially the Trotskyists, felt the need to go beyond orthodox

Marxism to reconsider the elusive character of political power and to study the unanticipated phenomenon of postrevolutionary bureaucracy. The earlier writings of Italian elitist theorists like Vilfredo Pareto and Gaetano Mosca and the gloomy meditations of Max Weber haunted American intellectuals as they considered the prospect that oligarchy could emerge in all forms of modern society. Drawing upon these sources, James Burnham claimed to demonstrate the impossibility of democracy and the inevitability of a ruling class. The new ruling class, he argued, would be not the capitalists but the managerialists—the technicians and administrators who, by virtue of their essential skills, had assumed control over the means of production.[49]

To a large extent the deradicalization of intellectuals was a result of the impact of European totalitarianism upon American political thought. Stalinism was the mystery and the terror of the Old Left. In contrast to fascism, Stalinism could not be explained as a product of either monopoly capital or middle-class decadence. Unlike Hitler, Stalin was not the creator but the creation of a political system no one had foreseen. In the face of Soviet totalitarianism, American intellectuals began to reconsider the classical conservative argument against the monolithic state. Former radical students of politics like Martin Diamond and John P. Roche soon rejected Marx's theory of class conflict and rediscovered Madison's theory of factional conflict. The notion that democracy could be sustained only by a conflict among counter-vailing interest groups came to be known as liberal pluralism in the 1950s.

If Stalinism made former radicals fearful of centralization, fascism made them fearful of rampant egalitarianism. The paradox of fascism was that the more elitist and ruthless the regime became, the more popular it was in the eyes of the nation. As political scientists studied Mussolini's Italy and Hitler's Germany they began to sense that popular consent itself was inadequate to preserve democracy. Eventually a suspicion of mass movements in general developed, perhaps best expressed in Eric Hoffer's widely acclaimed *The True Believer* (1951) and in Walter Lippmann's *The Public Philosophy* (1955). A few political sociologists, like the former radical Lipset, even began to explore the forbidden subject of "working class authoritarianism." Having lost faith in the masses as the carriers of democratic values, social scientists in the 1950s could speak frankly of the positive benefits of public apathy. Mass involvement in politics and democratic participation in decision making became suspect to writers like Burnham, who believed that freedom must rest upon institutional foundations. Later in the fifties the Yale political scientist Robert Dahl developed a theory of democracy that did not require mass mobilization or even active citizen participation. More suspect still was the role of theory in politics. The reaction against the revolutionary ideologies of communism and fascism became a reaction against normative theory in general. The foundations of pluralism, Daniel Bell declared in explaining the failure of American socialism, rest on the "separation of ethics and politics." Those who tried to infuse politics with morality in order to transcend pluralism failed to heed Weber's dictum: "He who seeks the salvation of souls, his own as well as others, should not seek it along the avenue of politics."[50]

THEOLOGY: FROM MARX TO KIERKEGAARD After the Second World War, conscience politics did survive in one area—theology. Yet even here one finds a retreat from radicalism and a rejection of Marxism for the psychology of the soul. Former radicals like Reinhold Niebuhr and Will Herberg came to the conclusion that Marxism failed because it could not transcend the limitations of bourgeois culture. Marxism arose as a reaction to nineteenth-century liberalism, but it also absorbed liberalism's illusions about human rationality, the cult of technology, and the progressive nature of history. A millennialistic philosophy, Marxism placed the Kingdom of God in history and thereby falsely lifted the spiritual burden of freedom from the conscience of mankind. "History cannot solve our problems," wrote Herberg; "history is *itself* the problem." Above all, Marxism had rendered the Left oblivious to the ambiguities and corruptions of power. Private property is not the root of all evil; property is "not the cause but the instrument of human egotism," maintained Niebuhr. The human drive for power, as Hawthorne had pointed out a century earlier, is deeply rooted in the contradictory nature of man.[51]

The horrors of totalitarianism and the fallacies of liberalism drove theologians like Niebuhr and Herberg to develop a new theory of freedom that rejected Marx's world of social action for Kierkegaard's world of moral "inwardness." "Anxiety," declared Kierkegaard, "is the dizziness of freedom." In the inner dialogue of private conscience, freedom means anxiety because freedom requires making decisions in which all choices are finite, tragic, and guilt ridden. In the teeth of liberal relativism and Marxist determinism, this existential definition of the authentically free person makes the individual the source of moral will and value judgment. Yet the tense strain of paradox and irony in Niebuhr's and Herberg's Christian and Judaic existentialism undermined the utopian, millennialistic ethos of Marxism and deprived the Left of its worldly quest for paradise regained. Man had a moral duty to struggle for social justice but, fallen, could never escape the stain of sin and achieve self-transcendence. Significantly, the theologians' view of human nature led to the same political conclusions reached by the pluralists in social science. Both stressed the negative concept of freedom that called for restraints upon man's egotism. Thus the most democracy could achieve, given the dual nature of man, was balanced conflict and equilibrated power. "Man's capacity for justice makes democracy possible," observed Niebuhr; "but man's inclination to injustice makes democracy necessary." By tempering radical hopes with conservative fears, ex-Marxists like Niebuhr and Herberg gave America a theology of crisis that strengthened the fiber of American liberalism and strangled the millennialistic myths of American radicalism.[52]

LITERATURE: FROM MARX TO MELVILLE The controversy over proletarian realism in the thirties divided party Marxists from learned humanists and classicists and eventually demoralized the literary Left. Briefly, Marxists argued that all literature is a reflection of socioeconomic relations, and, since the class struggle is the core of human existence, the life of the proletariat is the proper subject of art. Maintaining that most literature of the past represented an escape into bourgeois sentimentality or philosophical pessimism, the Marxists insisted that literature must lead to action rather than contemplation. Ignoring the fact that neither Marx nor Engels dared to lay down canons of literary theory, and ignoring Trotsky's observation that the proletariat was too "temporary and transient" to create its own culture, some American Marxists imposed formulas that reduced literature to a branch of sociology and made art into a crude class weapon. The result was a hack literature, mechanical in flow and metallic in flavor.

Most independent radical writers eventually rejected the monotony of proletarian realism. The tension between literary creativity and political dedication troubled learned *Partisan Review* critics like Phillips and Rahv, who refused to treat art as propaganda and to confine the literary imagination to political orthodoxy.[53] One result of the Old Left's repudiation of proletarian literature was a rediscovery of the value and integrity of American literature. In the 1920s writers had tended to look beyond provincial America for subject matter; and in the 1930s, Marxism reinforced the writers' conviction that the answer to America's social and cultural problems could be found only in Europe. The ideologies of Stalinism and fascism, however, discredited the appeal of European ideas, and the relativism of Marxism and Freudianism, which rendered absolute value judgments untenable, seemed to leave humanist intellectuals without solid principles on which to make a moral stand against Hitler. With the outbreak of the war, moreover, and with the influx of Europe's intellectual refugees, American writers came to feel that somehow their own fate and that of the rest of the world were inseparable from America's experience and destiny. No longer able to look to Europe as a cultural sanctuary or as a fount of political wisdom, literary critics now believed they could find a new, deeper strength and higher awareness in the classical works of Hawthorne, Whitman, Henry James, T. S. Eliot, and, above all, Melville—"the most plumbed and 'prophetic' of American writers," observed Louis Kronenberger.

A widespread impression holds that the Old Left abandoned its radical sentiments during the cold war when the anticommunist hysteria of McCarthyism led certain American writers to become self-serving patriots. The notion that the Left forsook its past out of fear and shame is historically inaccurate, for the reappraisal of America's heritage had been inaugurated by literary intellectuals long before the McCarthy era. Actually the curious pattern of radical exhaustion and nationalistic celebration had been foreshadowed ten years earlier in Alfred Kazin's *On Native Grounds* (1942) which marked the beginning of the Left's return home. The final chapter, "America! America!" opens with a remark by Abigail Adams to John Adams: "Do you know that European birds have not half the melody of ours?"[54]

AMERICAN HISTORY: FROM MARX TO LOCKE The study of the American past followed somewhat the same pattern. American historians like Hacker also abandoned European Marxism in order to rediscover America. Unlike literary critics, however, historical scholars could scracely return to the writings of classical American historians, none of whom, with the exception of Henry Adams, had envisioned the terrors of the twentieth century. Indeed, postwar historians even felt impelled to reject recent progressive historiography, which had depicted the American experience as a moral battleground between the forces of industrialism and agrarianism, capitalism and democracy, realism and idealism. Whereas literary intellectuals found in Melville and James a rich and complex vision of reality, historians found in Charles Beard and Vernon L. Parrington a simplistic and stilted theory of conflict. If economic conflict was the key to history, how did the United States survive a world depression and a world war with its institutions and values intact? After the war three prominent historians, Richard Hofstadter, Daniel J. Boorstin, and Louis Hartz, addressed themselves to this question of American uniqueness and exceptionalism. Significantly, all three had come of political age during the thirties; all had been influenced by Marxism, by what Boorstin called "the materialist interpretation of history." They never completely abandoned that perspective. For although they departed from European Marxism in denying class conflict in America, they also departed from progressive historiography in denying moral conflict. What resulted was something of a Marxist description without a Marxist solution. Minimizing the role of democratic and ethical ideals, they still stressed the driving forces of economics, environment, and social structure.

Hofstadter discovered "a kind of mute organic consistency" in the ideologies of all major statemen from Jefferson to Hoover, a philosophy of economic individualism that bound Americans to the values of competitive capitalism and made America "a democracy of cupidity rather than a democracy of fraternity." In a critique similar to Marx's attack on nineteenth-century liberalism, Hofstadter observed that the American Constitution had dehumanized man by sanctifying property and by codifying a Hobbesian view of unchanging human nature. "Modern humanistic thinkers who seek for a means by which society may transcend eternal conflict and rigid adherence to property" would find no answer in the philosophy of the founding fathers.[55]

Whereas Hofstadter located America's political values in the repugnant "cupidity" of bourgeois liberalism, Boorstin located them in the resplendent spaciousness of the American environment. Since Americans believed that values arose not from mind but from nature, Boorstin found the American "genius" in the mindless activity of a Paul Bunyan rather than in the heightened consciousness of a William James, in the "unpredicted whispering of environment" rather than in the theoretical and moral intellect. Louis Hartz also realized that the American political mind had little capacity for moral vision, but while Boorstin celebrated the discovery, Hart, like Hofstadter, deplored it. In a brilliant analysis of the relationship between social structure and ideology, Hartz maintained that the absence of a feudal heritage in America led naturally to the development of middle-class, Lockean liberalism, which made the acquisition of property tantamount to the "pursuit of happiness." Because America did not experience a real social revolution in 1776, America was "born free" (Tocqueville's phrase). Lacking an ancien régime to resist radical change, America also lacked a mass socialist movement struggling *for* radical change. The absence of an entrenched, anti-industrial Right in America deprived the Left of an identifiable enemy against which a hostile class consciousness might have developed. Since there was neither a landed aristocracy to destroy nor a landless mob to denounce, liberalism absorbed America.[56]

The historiography of consensus and continuity that emerged in the 1950s is fraught with irony. So placid and homogenized did the image of the American past become that many historians began to argue whether there was anything to argue about. Moreover, the description of Americans as a homely people whose mental horizons had been bounded by common political attitudes and economic values began more and more to seem like the false consciousness of "one-dimensional man" that Herbert Marcus popularized the following decade. Indeed, Boorstin and Marcuse could agree, albeit for different reasons, that Americans lacked a radical ideology and a theoretical vision enabling them to transcend the "given" values of capitalism. But the final irony is that Hartz himself anticipated a way out for radicals who could find no inspiration in a consensualized American past. More than any other historian, Hartz realized that America's "irrational Lockianism" had become "one of the most powerful absolutisms in the world," and he knew that America would be incapable of sympathizing with the need for radical change at home and revolutions abroad. "Can a people 'born equal' ever understand peoples elsewhere that have to become so? Can it ever understand itself?" Unlike most literary scholars and historians of the fifties, Hartz was one of the few writers who perceived that America's intellectual heritage could provide no answers to the troubling dilemmas of modern political life. "Instead of recapturing our past, we have got to transcend it. . . . There is no going home again for America." In contrast to Boorstin, who was convinced that the outside world had nothing to teach America, Hartz maintained that "America must look to its contact with other nations to provide that spark of philosophy, that grain of relative insight that its own history has denied it." The New Left of the 1960s would scarcely be aware of how it had followed Hartz's advice when it found in the third world a flash of radical insight that the American past had denied it.[57]

Sidney Hook, logician of the Old Left in the 1930s, who became critical of many of its theoretical foundations. (Pictorial Parade)

PHILOSOPHY: FROM MARX TO JAMES   American historians could use a truncated Marxist mode of analysis to explain the "uniqueness" of America, but few intellectuals could accept the philosophical propositions upon which the entire structure of Marxist thought depends. The premises of historical materialism led to a battery of unresolved questions: To what extent do the ideas of human beings react upon the environment? Do changes in material circumstances effect real changes in mind? If mankind is governed by laws "independent of human will, consciousness, and intelligence," can individuals influence the course of history? These issues were thrashed out in learned journals like the *Marxist Quarterly* and *Modern Monthly*. Hook's effort to Americanize Marxism by demonstrating that the Marxist theory of knowledge as praxis could be found in the "epistemological activism" of James and Dewey puzzled the Left. Hook's erudite essays on Marxism, pondered by students and young radicals, were circulated "like the reports of the great theologians' disputes in the Middle Ages," recalled Lewis Feuer. "Copies of the *Symposium* and *Modern Monthly* articles were passed among impecunious undergraduate hands. Soon, however, a warning spread through the left-wing grapevine: Hook is a revisionist."[58] Communists regarded the combative Hook as subversive because, aside from his political independence, he dared to question the mystique of dialectical materialism and its corollary of historical inevitability. The dialectic is the fountainhead of Marxist optimism. That all history is class conflict, that capitalism and socialism are absolute polar opposites precluding all other alternatives, and that revolution will negate all the existential contradictions in man's social life are convictions deeply rooted in the dialectic. Basically an illuminating concept of change involving the contradiction and reconciliation of a triadic thesis, antithesis, and synthesis, the dialectic became a vessel into which any idea could be poured. To Marxists the triad suggested feudalism, capitalism, and socialism; but to Christians it could mean the creation, the fall, and the redemption, and to Freudians, instinct, repression, and sublimation. All along, many academic philosophers had doubted the validity of the dialectic, and in 1940 three important books appeared that repudiated it as either religious myth, pseudologic, or even a Pythagorean allusion suggesting the insurgent power of a phallic symbol: Max Eastman's *Marxism, Is It Science?* Hook's *Reason, Social Myths and Democracy,* and Edmund Wilson's *To the Finland Station.* Three years later Hook went even further and challenged the whole Marxist approach to historical understanding in *The Hero in History.* Maintaining that great "event-making" personalities like Lenin had decisively influenced the course of history, Hook returned to William James's classical protest against absolute determinism.

The crisis in philosophical Marxism resulted in large part from the inability of Marxists to predict the failure of the proletariat and the triumph of Hitler and Stalin. Instead of an experimental guide to action, Marxist philosophy now appeared an ironclad system of laws that gave intellectuals what James had once derided as the "sumptuosity of security." Some philosophers, like Hook and Roy Wood Sellars, salvaged from Marxism its brilliant epistemological insights and its materialist analysis of social change. Others abandoned Marxism completely for humanism or existentialism. What was curious about the discussion of Marxism in the late thirties and early forties was the absence of any mention of "alienation." The "God that failed" the Old Left was the cold, thundering prophet of scientific laws and historical doom. The Old Left was not aware of the younger Marx of the "Economic and Philosophic Manuscripts" (1844), where one finds the first conceptualization of alienation as rooted in the monotony of industrial work. It is in this document that the New Left of the 1960s found a vital ethical consciousness in Marxism. Henceforth Marx could no longer be treated simply as the demon of the dialectic. When Marxism emerged again in American radical thought in the New Left of the sixties, it was not as a crude science of prediction but as a penetrating, humanist critique of the sickness of modern society. And the dialectic would arise again from the dead in Hegel's redemptive concept of "negation."

A Tenuous Continuity

Many of the New Left did not start out as Marxists or even as socialists. The first organizers of the student Left drew on Dewey and other native writers, just as Martin Luther King, Jr., had drawn on Thoreau and Niebuhr, as well as on Gandhi, to forge the civil rights movement. These early doctrinal differences suggest a deep ideological break between the Old Left and the New. Yet Maurice Isserman, a New Left scholar, has recently insisted that there is more continuity than discontinuity between the two generations of American radicals, hence that the New Left was not born de novo, and was no aberration or mutation, but rather had inherited ties to the Old Left.[59] It is true that several splinters of what remained of the Old Left in the post-Second World War era rejected the critique of Marxism discussed above; and, of course, other dissident doctrines and moods—specifically anarchism, pacifism, and bohemianism—did not need to rely on the status of Marxism for survival. But the argument for historical continuity with the past is only one side of a complex story of two generations. The student radicalism of the sixties seemed to come out of nowhere, and no one was more surprised than many of the older radicals themselves. Its sudden eruption in the sixties could very well indicate that the American Left is the history of what never happens twice.

One link between the remnants of the Old Left and the birth of the New was Michael Harrington. Born into the Irish-American middle class, educated by Jesuits at Holy Cross, Harrington maintained that knowledge must have an ethical content and politics must respond to religious values. In 1950 he joined the Catholic Worker, an organization founded during the Depression by Dorothy Day, a saintly veteran of the earlier Lyrical Left. Boyish and affectionate, a talented writer and an effective speaker, Harrington was a tender radical who refused to acknowledge that Marx had made the critique of religion the basis of all criticism. A Catholic with a bad conscience and a good heart, a graduate student in English troubled by the literature of fate and tragedy, he made attending to the plight of the poor his spiritual vocation. Harrington's now famous book on poverty, *The Other America*, would shake up the complacency of college campuses and political circles in the early sixties. As a leader of the Young Socialists League, Harrington became a self-appointed adviser to the budding New Left, only to find his own loyalties divided along generational lines.[60]

In the midfifties Harrington identified with the views of Irving Howe's *Dissent*, a sophisticated quarterly devoted to saving democratic socialism from sectarian squabbles, and to subjecting American society of the complacent Eisenhower years to scornful cri-

THE INSTITUTE FOR DEMOCRATIC SOCIALISM

Michael Harrington, author of the influential *The Other America* and powerful orator who inspired the New Left. (Democratic Socialists of America)

tiques. A brilliant writer who was comfortable both with his working-class background and with the highest reaches of culture, Howe thought the theoretical problems of socialism through with such rigor that he often questioned his own answers. For much of his intellectual life he returned again and again to the writings of the Italian novelist Ignazio Silone to recall the meaning of socialism as moral example. What mattered to both writers was not ideological verbiage but simple acts of kindness to others and loyalty to ideals. Howe had little patience with radical clichés. When the New Left came along, he dismissed it as a politics of style without substance.[61]

Both Harrington and Howe were protégés of Max Shachtman, a fearless, spellbinding debater and college dropout, who could demolish communist opponents and leave Trotskyists roaring with laughter. Shachtman became a friend of Trotsky and sometimes accompanied the old Bolshevik abroad, carrying a revolver as protection in case of an assassination attempt. At the end of the thirties Shachtman and James Burnham started the journal *New International* to announce their break with Trotsky and to formulate a new definition of the Soviet Union to counter Trotsky's description of a degenerate workers' state that should, nonetheless, be defended as embodying the progressive forces of history. Shachtman and Burnham saw the Soviet Union as an entirely new form of "bureaucratic collectivism" and "managerial state" that rendered impossible Trotsky's dream that the glories of the October Revolution could be revived through a Fourth International. In Russia the private means of production had been abolished only to allow bureaucrats and technicians to control the means of administration. An unswerving Marxist, Trotsky saw property as inextricably bound up with exploitation. What he failed to see was that Soviet communism eliminated the former only to leave Russian people in perpetual bondage to the latter.[62]

Burnham moved rapidly to the right after the Second World War; Shachtman first tried to salvage the Left and work with the Socialist Youth League. For a while he looked nostalgically on the Bolshevik Revolution and on Lenin's theory of party organization

Irving Howe, a Trotskyist, as a teenager in the 1930s; he became a democratic socialist and, as editor of *Dissent*, the calm voice of reflection and integrity. (Harvard University Press)

even while recognizing they were no model for America. He toyed with the idea of an alliance of ex-Trotskyists and communists but never at the price of forgetting Stalinism's atrocities. In 1951 he debated the CP leader Earl Browder, reciting a list of Stalin's European victims, then turning to his shaken opponent and, pointing an accusing finger, thundered, "There but for an accident of geography sits a corpse."[63] In the fifties young Shacht-manites like Howe thrilled to the words of their wily leader, who had inherited Trotsky's art of annihilation by aspersion. But by the end of the decade Shachtman's followers began to argue among themselves as the New Left was starting to take its bearings. Ironically, his undying anti-Stalinism made him deeply suspicious of revolutionary movements modeled after the Leninist tactics he had once admired. Thus he turned against Castro's revolution and supported America's intervention in Vietnam. During the height of the sixties, Shachtman, then living in Long Island surrounded by his collection of African art, wryly remarked to this writer than he would consider going into Manhattan to debate the New Left only under the protection of bodyguards. He died in 1973.[64]

Of American Trotskyism it would be just as valid to argue that a continuity can be traced not only from the Old Left to the New Left but from the Old Left to the New Right as well. Ex-Trotskyists like Shachtman, Burnham, and Eastman became conservative cold warriors in the fifties (so did a number of ex-Lovestonites). Three decades later, in the "neoconservative" eighties, several social democrats who had once sat at Shachtman's feet emerged in the Reagan administration to give advice on foreign affairs. "Max's boys" remained, like Shachtman, loyal to organized labor at home and hostile to left-wing dictatorships abroad. Some of Trotsky's American "orphans" found an adoption home in a White House that entertained the same illusions that had once given hope to a Fourth International: as a degenerate totalitarian state that has suppressed democracy, the Soviet Union as "the evil empire" is destined to collapse from its own internal contradictions.[65]

Writers who contributed to *Politics,* a short-lived but lively magazine, entertained no such illusions. Its editor, the ex-Trotskyist anarchist Dwight Macdonald, managed to publish this journal on his own from 1944 to 1949. Educated at Phillips Exeter Academy and Yale, Macdonald animated the Left with fresh ideas as well as comic relief. His irreverent, anarcho-cynical disposition led some to characterize him as a "thinker on the run," forever jumping from Trotsky to Orwell to Gandhi, and from politics to mass culture. Although he was brusque as a polemicist, Macdonald was actually, as many Old Left memoirists attest, a kind and gentle person grieved by the sight of misery and persecution. In *Politics* he often carried European voices of unswerving integrity: Simone Weil on the problem of suffering and affliction; Hannah Arendt on the eclipse of classical virtue and the dark night of totalitarianism; Albert Camus on the duties of the disinherited; Nicola Chiaromonte on the humility of mind before the imponderables of history; George Orwell on the imperatives of truth and decency before politics and expediency.

Macdonald's personal manifesto, "The Root Is Man," attempted to rescue radical thought from the sins of scientism. In 1917 Randolph Bourne had tried to do much the same for Dewey's pragmatism, and in 1940, again during a war crisis, Lewis Mumford undertook a similar rescue of liberal progressivism. Macdonald came to recognize, as did Niebuhr, that Marxism simply extended the liberal illusion that reason, progress, and morality would issue forth from the triumphs of modern science. Such faith in history, Macdonald contended, could not be sustained in the face of the Holocaust, or of Hiroshima, or of totalitarianism, or of other horrors of modern politics that dramatized the depersonalization of society and the disappearance of moral responsibility. The great error of Marxism and progressivism was to trust history to redeem the world. The true radical, Macdonald insisted, places the human individual at the center of events where conscience both determines and is accountable for the choices it makes.[66]

Like Eastman and Bourne in 1917, Macdonald in 1945 observed that war turns the liberating forces of production into new enslavers of humankind. But if war is the health of the herd instinct as well as of the state, peace is no less suffocating. After the war Macdonald studied the inanities of popular culture in order to ponder the collective stupor of mass society. Bereft of faith in history and in the working class, and always suspicious of the welfare state as an instrument of control rather than of compassion, Macdonald had no practical solution to offer the Left. His call to establish anarchist communes based upon pacifism struck

Marxists of the forties as historically irrelevant, an anarcho-individualist escape from power and collective action.

But two decades later Macdonald and a few other former *Politics* contributors, most notably the anarchist Paul Goodman, expressed sympathy with the early New Left. Contributors to *Politics* and subscribers to the Students for a Democratic Society's Port Huron Statement protested the tyranny of bigness, the passivity of the working class, and the abuses of science and technology and looked to small groups as the agencies of change. Macdonald would upbraid the New Left for ignoring the lessons of history whenever it supported communist dictatorships. But he shared the New Left students' opposition to the Vietnam War and supported their demonstrations and sit-ins. In the early sixties it was Macdonald who retrieved from public inattention Harrington's study of poverty in America with a powerful review, "Our Invisible Poor," in the *New Yorker*. Although skeptical of Marxism as a philosophy, and of workers' class consciousness as a reality, Macdonald had two qualities essential to the American Left: he was cynical about power and merciful toward suffering.[67]

Macdonald was a well-known figure in the War Resisters League, a pacifist organization started after the First World War. The conscientious objectors of the Second World War had received little sympathy from a country fighting the most popular war in its history. But pacifism enjoyed a rebirth in the fifties when A. J. Muste, Norman Thomas, and David Dellinger published the new monthly *Liberation*. During the Vietnam War the league drew inspiration from Old Left pacifists, like Muste and Thomas; some undergraduates went back to the Lyrical Left to read Bourne's antiwar essays. Macdonald esteemed the nonviolent Gandhi as the last political leader in the Western world to deal with people face-to-face; Martin Luther King, Jr., experienced an epiphany when he heard a lecture on Gandhi's idea of satyagraha, the persuasive power of truth that lies in love and nonviolence. Toward the end of the decade antiwar activists organized around the National Committee for a Sane Nuclear Policy (SANE), with 130 chapters and about 75,000 members.

The pacifist inheritance became a component of the New Left in its opposition to the Vietnam War. But whether this constitutes a "thread" of continuity with older radical generations is doubtful. In any case, by the midsixties much of the New Left was ridiculing Martin Luther King's tactic of peaceful civil disobedience as naive, and by the end of the decade the Maoist Weatherman faction was making bombs and taking to streets in violent, bloody "guerrilla" warfare. "In a sense the Days of Rage would be the Weatherman's act of Satyagraha," concluded the New Left historian Maurice Isserman.[68] It was a far cry from Gandhi's concept of the term, and King's, which meant winning over one's opponent by the "truth force" of moral example, by persuasion, not violence.

Many historians of the sixties suggest that the rebellion of the young had its antecedent in the previous decade in the discontent of the beatniks. Possibly there are many parallels between the New Left and the earlier poets and novelists who wanted to shock the country with their beards, sandals, and outrageous utterances. One notes the same restless movement back and forth across the country to make a virtue out of vagrancy; the same rejection of reason and intellect for emotion and instinct; and the same quest for mind expansion through music, drugs, and sex. Some New Leftists resonated to Allen Ginsberg's poem "Howl," which inaugurated the "San Francisco Renaissance" in 1955, denouncing America as a madhouse that drove the young to seek "an angry fix." In the sixties Ginsberg became a hero to the New Left as an antiwar protester. Two decades earlier the poet Kenneth Rexroth had arrived in San Francisco seeking the traces of the romantic radicalism of the early Wobblies and Jack London. During the war he remained a pacifist and identified with Macdonald's *Politics*. But many San Francisco writers aspired to higher truths that could not readily be translated into politics. The gifted poet Gary Snyder, after work on the docks, enrolled at Berkely to study Chinese and Japanese and later went to the Orient to practice Buddhism. Gregory Corso spent his late teens in prison for robbery and later dedicated one of his poems to his incarceration as a period of "illumination." The poetry of Michael McClure was all passion and rage; that of Brother Antonius, a Franciscan, tender and sacred. Charles Olson, Robert Duncan, Jack Spicer, and Philip Whalen saw themselves as prophetic bards announcing the coming apocalypse of a dehumanized, bomb-shadowed, consumer-obsessed technocratic civilization. Some of these manic-inspired poets had more in common with the hippies and their sixties counterculture. Although a few showed up at New Left protest rallies in San Francisco, they seemed more interested in sniffing the leaves of grass in Golden Gate Park than in striking an alliance with the working class. Whether the bohemian's quest for Dionysian ecstasy could be turned toward political responsibility was a question the New Left never resolved.[69]

As teenagers in the late fifties and college students in the sixties, some New Leftists recalled Jack Kerouac's *On the Road* (1955) as offering in fiction their first exciting escape from bourgeois society. The novel savors America's wide-open spaces, depicting youths adrift, prowling midnight streets and bars in search of themselves. A few book reviewers saw an analogue in Hemingway's lost generation; others saw the scenes of sex, booze, and drugs as radically subversive. Always haunted by a Catholic sense of guilt and sin, Kerouac took to alcohol and sank into passivity and fits of paranoia. He died in 1969, watching TV, sipping scotch, sitting in a rocking chair with a stack of copies of William F. Buckley's *National Review*. In his last interview Kerouac was asked if he had identified with the hippies and the New Left. After scolding the students using acid drugs like LSD, he sought to set the record straight: "I wasn't trying to create any kind of new consciousness or anything like that. We didn't have a whole lot of heavy abstract thoughts. We were just a bunch of guys who were out trying to get laid."[70]

What would Max Shachtman have said?

Marxism, Modernism, McCarthyism:
The New York Intellectuals

In 1959 Ginsberg returned to Columbia University, from which he had been expelled around 1950 for writing obscenities on a dormitory wall, to give a poetry recital. The event failed to impress the academy, and soon America's leading literary critics were dismissing the beats as "know-nothing bohemians," as writers who were shrill rather than subtle, apocalyptic instead of ironic, striving for purity when they should settle for paradox.[71]

The critics came to be called "the New York intellectuals," to use Irving Howe's expression. Seldom had America witnessed a generation of intellectuals so absorbed in the life of the mind. For the most part they were Old Left veterans still in search of a cause, still taking to ideas with the "analytic exuberance" that had characterized the passionate Trotskyist years. If intellectuals are "minds devoted to mind" in Paul Valéry's words, the New York intellectuals seemed more prone to demolition than to devotion. The art critic Harold Rosenberg called them "a herd of independent minds" to suggest the endless internecine quarrels. Later the philosopher William Barrett labeled them "the truants," theoreticians who postponed facing the harsher practical world. Hook looked back on some of them as "radical comedians," armchair revolutionaries who played at politics. And William Phillips described his colleagues as a "charmed circle," only to add that they were also capable of "a super-rationalism, a competitiveness, an intellectual hardness, and an indifference to loyalty that was humanly destructive." The New York intellectuals thrived on controversy, as though they could discover their own ideas only by repudiating the thoughts of others. Gramsci's dream of the solidarity of the "organic intellectuals" would have been hopeless with this tribe of superb egotists.[72]

When Norman Podhoretz, editor of *Commentary*, referred to the New York intellectuals as "the family,"[73] he had in mind the enormous array of Jewish talent: Diana and Lionel Trilling, Hannah Arendt, Daniel Bell, Saul Bellow, Leslie Fiedler, Paul Goodman, Clement Greenberg, Robert Heilbroner, Irving Howe, Sidney Hook, Alfred Kazin, Norman Mailer, Philip Rahv, Philip Roth, Harold Rosenberg, Meyer Schapiro, Delmore Schwartz, Susan Sontag, and Robert Warshow. To qualify as a member of the family one had either to edit, write for, or read *Partisan Review,* especially, and to a lesser extent the socialist *Dissent,* the anarchist *Politics,* or the American Jewish Committee's *Commentary.* But there were also eminent non-Jews (Edmund Wilson, Dwight Macdonald, Arthur M. Schlesinger, Jr.), sin-struck Christians (W. H. Auden, R. P. Blackmur), Catholics both loyal (James Agee) and lapsed (William Barrett, James T. Farrell, Michael Harrington, Mary McCarthy), blacks (James Baldwin, Ralph Ellison, the early Richard Wright), classical liberals (Jacques Barzun), and even conservatives (Wallace Stevens), especially southern (John Crowe Ransom, Allen Tate, Robert Penn Warren). Yet the real inner circle consisted of those who had gone to the City College of New York, who engaged in fierce debates about Trotsky in the college alcoves, and who in the post–Second World War years hung out in Greenwich Village bars and engaged in equally fierce discussions about the art of abstract expressionism.

In the fifties *PR* writers defended artists like Robert Motherwell and Willem de Kooning, but the defense of modernism actually began in the late thirties when *PR* quarreled with Marxists over literary formula. Championing contemporary artists and authors also meant breaking with some veterans of the early Lyrical Left. Max Eastman, for example, favored Millay over the self-conscious innovators Pound and Eliot. Accusing them of turning "indoors" to escape life for literature, Eastman had no patience with their intense, stylized expressions perfected by the "mental blur" of ambivalence and ambiguity. Literary critics of the Old Left, on the other hand, refused to repudiate what Eastman dismissed as "the cult of unintelligibility." On the contrary, they wanted to explain why modern art and literature required obscurity rather than clarity, intimation rather than representation, the complexity of experience even at the expense of its comprehension.[74]

The modernist convictions about the limits of human cognition and the impossibility of an accurate representation of reality did not sit well with the Marxists of the thirties, particularly the "vulgar" types who remained certain about the power of their own intellects to discern the course of history. Later, in the sixties, Marxists would view modernism as a product of the conditions of "late capitalism," wherein private subjectivity remains the alleged illusion of bourgeois society. But reality and its representations became a serious problem to Old Left intellectuals who wanted to embrace the latest developments in modern thought, from Einstein to Freud and Joyce. Critics like Rahv and Trilling valued the modernist sensibility of introspection, fragmentation, and discontinuity. Where Marxists saw inevitability everywhere, they were determined to see indeterminacy somewhere.

Yet an awkward problem had to be faced. The more innovative the modern poet and novelist was stylistically, the more conservative he tended to be politically. *PR* contributors knew that William Butler Yeats had flirted with Irish fascism, that Pound had combined anti-Semitism with paeans to Mussolini, that Eliot chose royalism over democracy, that William Faulkner was a southern racist and Wallace Stevens a white supremacist (at least, during the Ethiopian War.) Nevertheless, Rahv accepted Dostoevsky as both a reactionary and a genius, a daring novelist who could yearn for order and at the same time radically subvert it because he "discovered inversions and dissociations in human feeling and consciousness which literature has to this day only imperfectly assimilated." In the same fashion, Trilling preferred the conservative Henry James to the progressive Theodore Dreiser; although Dreiser had a simpleminded grasp of reality as wholly external and reducible to the material, James, though "politically useless," understood reality as rich, various, problematic, subject to almost infinite interpretation. The poetry of Eliot, once dismissed as "fascist" in *PR*, could challenge Old Left intellectuals to separate politics from literary judgment. The communist critic Granville Hicks thought poetry should be analyzed as a reflective social document; many New York intellectuals wanted to appreciate it as a self-referential work of art. Deeming aesthetics as important as didactics, *PR* writers rejoiced in the precision, intricacy, and perception that derived from the compositional process of modern verse.[75]

The Old Left's defense of modernism suggests another way in which there was no continuity with the New Left. Many of the Old Left New York intellectuals were Jewish, and their identification with the higher culture of modern art and literature reflected their preference for cosmopolitanism over parochialism. The conservative Dostoevsky as well as the radical Silone spoke to the Old Left because they conveyed universal insights into the human condition. Esteeming the classics as it did the moderns, the Old Left saw itself as part of the rich heritage of Western civilization. Marx was as much a cosmopolitan as any other wandering Jew. Did he not insist that the workers have no country and that they must be liberated from the "idiocy" of provincial life?

With the New Left, Western civilization itself became the problem as more and more students identified with the third world. Now race, gender, and ethnicity, instead of being provincial hindrances that one must escape in order to free the mind, were social categories that one must embrace to discover the self. Somehow the categories that once were used to discriminate and keep people oppressed came to be seen as forces for change and freedom. The Lyrical Left and the Old Left wanted to eliminate racism and sexism; the New Left wanted to see minorities and women empowered.

The Old Left's attitude toward its native country also distinguished it from the New Left. Although Dos Passos's three-volume *USA* had provided a bitter portrait from the period of the First World War to the Depression, the novelist volunteered in Spain and returned to embrace America as "the chosen country." When, in the late sixties, some New Left activists traveled to Cuba or Vietnam, they returned to denounce "Amerika" as though Hitler himself were residing in the White House. True, the early New Left drew on native intellectual sources in composing its stance. But the shameful Vietnam War brought forth an anti-Americanism that depicted the country as a chamber of horrors, and many radicalized students, hating their own homeland, desecretated its patriotic symbols.

The Korean War had produced no such outburst among the remnants of the Old Left. On the contrary, in 1952 *PR* ran a symposium called "Our Country, Our Culture," in which intellectuals were asked if their attitudes had changed toward America and its institutions. Most said that they had reconciled themselves to their native country (an exception was Mailer, who derided the whole idea of a symposium). Had the veterans of the Lyrical Left been asked the same question after the First World War, they would most likely have followed the lost generation in abandoning a politically bankrupt America for a culturally rich Europe. But, after the Second World War—with its totalitarianism, its death camps, and the postwar cold war; all caused by European "ideology"—*PR* contributors believed it was no disgrace, no shallow philistinism, to accept, even to admire, America. Some expressed disdain for mass society and its vulgarities; others agreed with the editors about the need to sustain "a critical non-conformism." They remained committed to cosmopolitan values, yet were content to accept the support of a capitalist society while they continued to ponder the eternal questions.[76]

But in the fifties an issue arose that split the Old Left, McCarthyism. In 1932 Edmund Wilson had called upon intellectuals to take communism away from the communists; now, twenty years later, intellectuals wondered how they could take anticommunism away from anticommunists like Senator Joseph McCarthy. Contrary to later arguments of certain New Left scholars, the Old Left's anticommunist zeal was not occasioned by fear of McCarthy's witch-hunts, for the case against the Moscow-dominated CP had been made long before the Wisconsin senator poisoned American politics with his wild accusations. The interna-

tional Congress for Cultural Freedom, whose values were anticommunist, had been organized before the Second World War,
with intellectuals like Raymond Aron, Arthur Koestler, and Ig-
nacio Silone; and after the war former Trotskyists, among them
Hook, Macdonald, Eastman, and Burnham, organized the American Committee for Cultural Freedom. Anti-Stalinist liberals—
Arthur M. Schlesinger, Jr., Reinhold Niebuhr, and others—
launched Americans for Democratic Action. In the election of
1948 the ADA criticized Henry Wallace for what it regarded as
his pro-Soviet position and for not preventing communists from
penetrating his presidential campaign as head of the new Progressive party. McCarthyism stimulated both the ACCF and the ADA
to take a public stand on such issues as faculty loyalty oaths,
"un-American activities" investigating committees, the espionage
trials of Alger Hiss and Ethel and Julius Rosenberg, and the security cases of fellow intellectuals like the nuclear physicist Robert
Oppenheimer.

For the most part the New York intellectuals opposed the loyalty oaths and investigating committees, and they bitterly criticized McCarthy for turning anticommunism into a farce, misleading the public to believe, as Rahv put it, that communism was a
threat *in* America rather than *to* America. Hook supported the
right of teachers to teach even communism, but he demanded
that college faculties judge the "professional ethics" of CP members who used the classroom to promulgate the Moscow line—
"heresy, yes; conspiracy, no!" Not a little guilty themselves, the
New York intellectuals defended Oppenheimer, who repented his
radical past, and they argued about the innocence or guilt of Hiss
and the Rosenberg, who remained silent about the past. By 1955
several writers had concluded that anticommunism had more to
do with politics than with cultural freedom, and they resigned
from the ACCF. McCarthy was through by then. Others, Burnham, Eastman, and the young Irving Kristol among them, insisted
that McCarthyism posed no more danger to civil liberties than did
the Soviet Union. Burnham and Eastman resigned and moved in

the opposite political direction, becoming the brain power of William Buckley's cold war Right, where anticommunism would live on as a sacred cause.[77]

Between the Old Left of the 1930s and the New Left of the 1960s would lie a gulf of hostility. Younger students rejected the critique of Marxism that older radicals tried to pass along. This generational denial was unfortunate, for the existentialism that some ex-Marxists espoused after the Second World War was not completely incompatible with radicalism, as Jean-Paul Sartre would demonstrate. Also, Burnham's theory of bureaucratic and technological power could be critically applied to the elitist structure of American society, as C. Wright Mills would demonstrate. So, too, the Judeo-Christian sense of tragedy, which Niebuhr and Herberg rediscovered, could be elevated to a higher anguish of social guilt and political responsibility, as Michael Harrington and Martin Luther King would demonstrate in their actions as well as in their writings; and the historian's theory of consensus, first developed by Hartz and Hofstadter, could be used to explain the "one-dimensional" character of middle-class America, as Antonio Gramsci himself had already shown in his earlier formulation of his theory of "hegemony."

Ultimately, what discredited the Old Left and caused it to lose moral authority in the eyes of a younger generation was the cold war and its anticommunist legacy. After Stalinism and the Soviet occupation of Eastern Europe, the Old Left became convinced that democratic freedom and one-party dictatorships are incompatible. Unable to believe in social revolution abroad and radical change at home, veteran Leftists could no longer sustain their vital spirit, their will to believe that existing reality can be negated and transformed, that ideals can be realized despite the dark record of historical experience.

A change of temper came over the radical intellectuals as they moved into the 1950s and out of politics, addressing themselves in *Partisan Review* to cultural criticism and the problem of mass society. Even in the politically conscious *Dissent*, writers felt deeply the loss of innocence and good hope. The simple faiths of former Trotskyists like Howe gave way to a feeling for the moral complexities of political action and the structural complexities of political power. Thus when the nearly defunct Old Left saw familiar radical mythologies reemerging in the 1960s, the only counsel it could impart was the counsel of failure. "Ours, a 'twice born' generation," wrote Daniel Bell, "finds its wisdom in pessimism, evil, tragedy, and despair. So we are both old and young before our time." The New Left of the 1960s rejected the tragic mood of ambiguity and irony that hung over the collective memory of older radicals. The Old Left could only offer the lessons of experience, which to a subsequent generation must always seem like wisdom without power and knowledge without action. The cry that went up in the 1960s for "relevance" became a cry not for truth itself but for a truth that could be made politically useful. The Old Left could not respond to this demand. Having tasted power and having seen the future, the "twice born" generation rejected both. Hofstadter poignantly summed up the pathos of his generation of the thirties: "The war, the bomb, the death camps wrote finis to an era of human sensibility, and many writers of the recent past were immolated in the ashes, caught up like the people of Pompeii in the midst of life, some of them in curious postures of unconsummated rebellion."[78]

6

The New Left

Communism? Who the hell knows from Communism?
We never lived through Stalin. We read about it, but it
doesn't affect us emotionally. Our emotional reaction to
Communism is Fidel marching into Havana in 1959.

Jerry Rubin

Nothing is clearer to a later generation than the
naivety of an earlier one, just as nothing is clearer to
the earlier one than the naivety of the later.

Stephen Spender

From Alienation to Activism

In 1960, in Greensboro, North Carolina, four black students
stepped up to a segregated Woolworth's lunch counter and quietly
asked to be served. Three years later four black children died in
the dynamiting of the Sixteenth Street Baptist Church in Birmingham, Alabama. In 1961 Robert Moses, a northern student
steeped in Camus, trekked alone into the deepest and most violent
parts of the South to register black voters. Three years later the
bodies of the slain civil rights workers James Chaney, Andrew
Goodman, and Michael Schwerner were found in an earthen dam
in Mississippi.

The radicalism of the 1960s was as much deed as doctrine. The action began in the South, America's moral looking glass and embarrassing mirror image. The antisegregation protests soon spread to northern cities, where young whites and blacks engaged in peaceful sit-in demonstrations against job discrimination. The 1964 Berkeley free-speech movement was a galvanizing experience after which the college campus would become the scene of bitter confrontations and escalating radical demands. As the 1960s unfolded, the New Left moved backwards into the 1930s. Starting with nonideological reformist goals, it ended by issuing heavily doctrinaire ultimatums. The Old Left began with a whoop of revolution and sank into a whimper of reconciliation—thanks to Russia; the New Left started in a spirit of moderation and ended calling for nothing less than revolution—thanks to America.

The New Left was one of the great political surprises of the midtwentieth century. It arose suddenly, in the wake of the quiescent conformism of the politically silent generation of the fifties. Something of a historical mutation, its appearance defied the expectations of sociologists, who depicted American youths as "other-directed" personalities and the corporation men of the future. It defied opinion surveyors, who found students conservative and politically apathetic. And it defied the Old Left, which had declared America the graveyard of radicalism. In order to begin to understand the phenomenon of the New Left, or perhaps not to misunderstand it, it is necessary to discuss briefly three interrelated developments that provided its historical setting: the economic context of affluence and guilt, the political context of disillusionment and powerlessness, and the cultural context of alienation and anxiety.

Young radicals of the sixties were mainly the children of parents who had grown up in the thirties and forties. Rushed into adulthood after having survived the privations of depression and war, their parents embarked upon a frenzy of spending and building. Systematically they bulldozed the American landscape, filling it with shopping centers and ticky-tacky housing developments until the monotony of the environment began to resemble the drab uniformity of a Second World War army camp. While showering the children with the good things in life that had been denied them, the parents were too busy getting ahead to conceive life in any terms deeper than those of economic security and material comfort. Frozen at the level of material existence, American society became an antiseptic wasteland of stucco and plastic; echoing Henry Miller, the beat poets of the fifties called it "an air-conditioned nightmare."

Jaded by affluence, estranged from parents who so valued this affluence, young radicals began to sense that their middle-class alienation had something in common with lower-class exploitation. The key social document for the early sixties was Harrington's *The Other America.* Here high school seniors and college freshmen first read about the desperate "invisible poor," who had been hidden from America by a mental wall of suburban content. The discovery of the existence of poverty and racism in the ghettos of the North as well as the South brought forth what Jack

Typical uniformity and regimentation in a huge suburban housing division.

Newfield described as "a kind of mass vomit against the hypocrisy of segregation." At first middle-class youths, nurtured by their parents' part-time liberalism, found some hope for change in the Kennedy administration. But as the New Frontier turned out to be more style than substance, young activists thirsted all the more for a new politics of personal witness and moral confrontation. According to Tom Hayden, those who worked on voter registration in the South experienced "schizoid or ambivalent feelings" toward the White House, which "might" support their efforts only "when push came to shove." When Kennedy was assassinated, on November 22, 1963, ambivalence turned to anguish as young people felt more politically alone than ever. "For me this one act," a student told his professor, "has made all other acts irrelevant and trivial; it has displaced time with paranoia, good with evil, relative simplicity with incomprehensibility, and an ideal with dirt."[1]

The same sense of personal loss and political distrust grew also out of the diplomatic developments of the sixties. The young, who had inherited the nuclear bombs as a child inherits an incurable disease, originally looked to Kennedy as an idealist without illusions. The new president refrained from attacking neutralism, established the Peace Corps as a means of helping underdeveloped countries, and allowed his ambassador to the United Nations, the urbane Adlai Stevenson, to speak of the need to "make the world safe for diversity." But any hope that there would be a reexamination of America's cold war policies was soon shattered by the Bay of Pigs invasion, which indicated to many that the president had rejected the old strategy of the threat of massive nuclear retaliation only to adopt the covert strategy of counterinsurgency. Young radicals, now beginning to identify with the political and economic destiny of the third world, embraced Cuba as the embodiment of a "new humanist socialism" while attacking the faceless, bureaucratic "socialism" of Eastern Europe.[2]

With Kennedy's death, American militarism, always latent in his administration, grew to seem malignant. Thereafter America's increasing involvement in the Vietnam War dramatized to young antiwar dissenters the powerlessness of idealism. Hopes for an end to the interminable war were aroused in the 1968 democratic primaries, when Senators Eugene McCarthy and Robert Kennedy challenged President Lyndon Johnson's renomination. But McCarthy's following was confined to young white liberals; and an assassin's bullet tragically cut short the promising career of the young Kennedy, the only major candidate who appealed to the blacks and Chicanos as well as to many whites—perhaps the only one who might have been able to put together a "rainbow coalition." As Kennedy's body lay in state in Saint Patrick's Cathedral, the activist Tom Hayden was seen sitting in the rear, crying quietly and holding in his hand a guerrilla beret given to him by Castro.

Ideological Origins

Although the American public did not take much notice of the New Left until the midsixties, its ideological foundations had been put in place several years earlier. The movement should be judged not simply by what it became in its final days of rage but also by what it was in its first moments of reflection. Before the New Left decided that state power must be fought with street power, its leaders believed in the possibility of change fostered by ideas, especially critical ideas that would make society the object of consciousness. Efforts to lay an intellectual basis for the New Left came from two groups, both centered, curiously, in the heart of the Midwest. The first group organized around the journal *Studies on the Left*, started in Madison in 1959 by students at the University of Wisconsin; the second, Students for a Democratic Society (SDS), was founded in Ann Arbor, Michigan, in 1961.

Editors and contributors to *Studies on the Left* sought a way out of the impasse the Old Left had faced after the Soviet leader Nikita Khrushchev denounced "the crimes of Stalin" in his Twentieth Party Congress address of 1956. Events that followed the address—the Hungarian uprising put down by Soviet tanks in the bloodbath of Budapest—discredited the CPUSA and, at the same time, confirmed the anticommunist stance of the Old Left. Some

Studies group members had earlier belonged to the CP's Labor Youth League; many more had been radicalized by the populist-progressive traditions of Wisconsin politics. As graduate students about to enter the academic world, they wanted models to define the political role of the radical scholar so that they could espouse personal involvement rather than objective detachment. They disdained the New York intellectuals for, as they saw it, succumbing to McCarthyism and to the arms race, preaching consensus instead of conflict, and celebrating America's miracles rather than exposing its maladies. In their search for ideological guidance, the young Wisconsin students turned to a pious midwesterner and a sardonic Texan, the historian William Appleman Williams and the sociologist C. Wright Mills.

Williams offered a fresh perspective on the cold war. Educated at the U.S. Naval Academy, in Annapolis, Williams had left the service after the war and gone on to earn a Ph.D. in history from Wisconsin in 1950. In *The Contours of American History* (1961) and *The Tragedy of American Diplomacy* (1959), Williams attributed the East-West confrontation to imperial America's drive toward overseas expansion and domination. But in contrast to Marxists, he believed it possible to reform America, once its people could understand that the days of frontier expansion were long over and hence face up to the nation's problems rather than externalizing them. Williams's call to return to forgotten American traditions had deep appeal to Wisconsin students dedicated to democratic ideals. One way to restore old values was to recapture the vision of "the Christian Commonwealth" that had been lost sight of in the United States, with its commitment to private property and competitive individualism. Williams's assignment to America of responsibility for the cold war had a good deal to do with a Calvinist sense of guilt and his own search for a communal America purged of the sins of individualism. He had no patience with a factual account of the cold war's origins in Eastern Europe. His political views in the sixties were bewilderingly inconsistent. One of his heroes was former President Herbert Hoover, who detested radicalism and admired Mussolini's dictatorship; another was Fidel Castro, whose Cuba looked less like an old Christian commonwealth than like a godless brave new world.[3]

The writings of the sociologist C. Wright Mills also inspired the Wisconsin radicals. A burly Texan who rode to his classes at Columbia University on his motorcycle, a notorious fringe figure of the Old Left New York intellectuals, Mills could never conform to what he regarded as the complacencies of cold war orthodoxy. In the war years Mills had suggested the title for *Politics*, whose editor Dwight Macdonald had planned to use "New Left," the very term Mills himself would borrow from a British journal in his much discussed "Letter to the New Left," published in *Studies* in 1960. Madison activists were ecstatic to find an older radical proposing that the political future of America must lie with students, "the young intelligentsia." A half century earlier a similar proposition spirited the Greenwich Village radicals.

Like Bourne and Reed, Mills died relatively young (in 1962, at the age of forty-five), and he also drew many of his ideas from two heroes of the Lyrical Left, Veblen and Dewey.[4] Mills shared Veblen's conviction that Marx had erred in looking to the working class to redeem the world. The idea of class consciousness, Mills contended, was part of Marx's nineteenth-century Victorian "labor metaphysic." With Veblen he believed that society remains almost passive, while the ruling class, by virtue of its capacity both to wield power and to shape opinion, dominates from the top down. Hence Marx's emphasis upon the base rather than the superstructure required reversal. Mills, however, could never sustain Veblen's hope that science would penetrate and expose as irrational the "pecuniary interests" and the ceremonial institutions of the leisure class. In his postwar view of America, scientists, engineers, and technicians, the very heroes of Veblen, worked with finance capitalists, military leaders, and top government bureaucrats to constitute the essential core of the "power elite."[5]

As a graduate student at the University of Texas in 1938, Mills had acknowledged the pragmatic philosophers Dewey, George Herbert Mead, and Charles Sanders Peirce as his "intellectual

C. Wright Mills, skeptic and scholar who came of political age with the Old Left. Mills is one of the few survivors of the political thirties who gave intellectual direction to the emerging Left of the sixties. (Pictorial Parade)

godfathers." From the pragmatists Mills learned that consciousness was not a fixed entity but part of the process of social interaction. From Dewey, in particular, he learned that truth had more to do with practical consequences than with theoretical correspondence or cohernce, that the purpose of social inquiry was political

225

change, and that action, therefore, was the consummation of thought. He remained critical of Dewey for failing to see why scientific intelligence could serve bureaucratic ends, why a public philosophy of active citizens had little chance in a capitalist society of passive consumers, and why no harmony of interests could emerge in the presence of the inequities of power and wealth. Rejecting the liberal assumption of consensus, Mills sought to awaken America to the specter of elite domination.[6]

In such works as *The Power Elite* (1959) and *The Sociological Imagination* (1968), Mills emerged in the eyes of the New Left as the best kind of scholar, a skeptic who never lost passion or vision, a radical without illusions. Reading Mills, students learned of the ideological hegemony of the ruling class, the myth of objective empirical research, and the need to formulate a theory of sociology that would confront human relations directly and morally.

What seemed simple and direct to young New Left scholars seemed more subtle and complex to veteran Old Leftists. Theodore Draper researched and analyzed the image of Castro's Cuba that Williams and Mills had implanted in the New Left—of the Cuban revolution as a peasant-proletarian struggle against yanqui imperialism and for Caribbean communism. Draper showed that Castro's July 26 movement had actually been forged by the Cuban middle class in an effort to overthrow the Batista dictatorship and to establish liberal social democracy. According to Draper, Castro had betrayed the revolution. The New Left continued, nevertheless, to believe that Cuba, unlike the totalitarian regimes of Eastern Europe, offered the possibility of "socialism with a human face."[7]

The Old Left sociologist Daniel Bell took on Mills's power-elite thesis. In *The End of Ideology* (1960), Bell sought to show that no clear community of interest existed among the upper classes, that those who ran the institutions of power could hardly conspire, since they could seldom agree, and that on major decisions or policies—like those regarding the Korean War or the welfare state—Wall Street, the military, and the federal government were often at cross-purposes. Not surprisingly, Bell's analysis failed to impress the New Left as to the complex dimensions of power. However power was defined, New Leftists regarded it as illegitimate since they had no experience in exercising it.[8]

How to establish a power base in order to achieve social change became the central concern of the second midwestern organization to lay the intellectual foundation of the New Left, Students for a Democratic Society. Many of its early members had been active in campus politics at Michigan, Oberlin, Swarthmore, and elsewhere. Some had taken part in civil rights demonstrations in the South; others had protested the House Un-American Activities Committee; a few had walked the picket lines in support of Detroit's auto workers. SDS itself grew out of the older Student League for Industrial Democracy, an organization that had roots in the Lyrical Left and illustrious graduates like Lippmann and Reed. But the sixties activists saw SLID emerging from the thirties Old Left as timid and ineffectual, too ready to compromise and fall back on empty slogans. The leader who decided it was time to make a break and form SDS was Al Haber, a talented organizer who exhorted students to forsake the pessimism and cynicism born of the atomic age and commit themselves to a politics of clear thinking and direct action.

Such a politics had already been adopted on the Ann Arbor campus by Tom Hayden, the James Dean of the New Left. Shy, sensitive, a sloppy dresser and serious thinker, Thomas Emmett Hayden (the FBI file title) grew up in a Detroit suburb, an only child raised by an abandoned mother who made ends meet the Irish way—with meals of mashed potatoes. A teenage athlete, Hayden became politicized as a student at the University of Michigan, where he protested the restrictions of dormitory life and the arbitrary power wielded by campus administrators. After reading Jack Kerouac's *On the Road*, he hitchhiked across country to Berkeley, where students had been protesting sorority and fraternity racial discrimination, violations of free speech, and compulsory ROTC (Reserve Officers Training Corps) classes. The speeches and actions of Martin Luther King, Jr., inspired him to

join the "freedom ride" South and take part in sit-ins. So did those
of Sandra Cason, a philosophy graduate student at the University
of Texas who set an example for Hayden, who later married her,
by translating slogans into acts of moral courage in the racially
segregated South. For Hayden such acts amounted to an existential commitment to justice as an immediate ethical imperative.
His reading of the French philosophers Camus and Jacques Mari-
tain reinforced his conviction that ideals are born of struggle,
suffering, and sacrifice. At the age of twenty-one Hayden was in
the Deep South putting his body on the line, demanding that a
racial society change its ways in order to save its soul. In October
1961, in McComb, Mississippi, he was dragged from a car and
beaten over the head by an assailant before an audience of approv-
ing whites.[9]

In the summer of 1962, fifty-nine SDSers showed up for a
conference at Port Huron, Michigan, an education camp run by
the United Auto Workers. Some were liberals, others socialists,
and a few converts to politics out of deep religious convictions.
Hayden had been working on a draft of an "agenda for a generation" to be discussed at the conference. The passages critical of
anticommunism and references to the cold war and to America's
"military aggressiveness," as well as the sneering description of
trade unions as having "sold out" the rank and file, offended
Harrington and Norman Thomas. His advice ignored, Harrington
attacked the SDS and left the conference in high dudgeon. SDS
voted, in a decision that would be crucial, not to exclude communists from membership.

The Port Huron Statement, as it was called, that emerged from
the conference was the first manifesto in the history of the twentieth-century American Left to focus primarily on the problem of
ethical existence. Values like "fraternity," "honesty," "vision,"
and "love" were invoked to overcome the "estrangement" of modern man. It was also the first such document to focus on the
university as an institution not of cultural transmission but of
social change. From the college campus students "must consciously build a base for their assault upon the loci of power." It

was also the first such document not to identify the fate of the American Left with the Soviet Union, yet it dismissed anticommunism as irrational and rejected the assumption that the Soviet Union constituted a threat to the nation's security. Only America's "paranoia" about the Soviet Union, it said, prevented the two countries from giving serious attention to disarmament. SDS may have been right about security but wrong about disarmament. Premier Khrushchev's rejection of the Eisenhower administration's demand for on-site arms control inspections was motivated by fear that the United States might discover how far behind Russia remained in the missile race. But the Port Huron theoreticians had little patience with the political realities of superpower rivalry.[10]

Declaring "Our work is guided by the sense that we may be the last generation in the experiment with living," SDS attacked the deterrence theory of the cold war, the welfare state, the military-industrial complex, and the public's "crust of apathy." In 1963 SDS issued a second manifesto, "America and the New Era," criticizing the Kennedy administration as a "corporate liberal" political elite. SDS also applied the same criticisms to the undemocratic structure of world communist parties, and it rejected Mills's "labor metaphysic"—the illusion that the working class would fulfill its Marxist-conferred mission of transforming capitalism into socialism. Instead of a workers' revolt, SDS called for a "democracy of individual participation" in which all people would share in the social decisions determining the quality of their lives. With the ethic of "participation" elevated to a political mystique, and with a small grant of $5,000 from the United Auto Workers, SDS set up the Economic Research and Action Project to organize the ghetto poor and develop neighborhood programs.

Off to a brave start, SDS would have to live with the theoretical confusions inherent in its own conception. The group that sponsored *Studies on the Left* had been weakened by rigorous debate on a number of issues. Was theoretical reflection and writing on the campus more important than political action in the community? (Marx changed the world without leaving the British Museum.)

Could students forge a Left without labor? Were America's problems institutional and structural or existentialist and spiritual? Should the New Left march to the future or, as the young historian Staughton Lynd exhorted, return to 1776 and complete the unfinished work of the American Revolution? Division over such issues eventually led to the demise of *Studies on the Left*; it ceased publication in 1966.[11]

By comparison with *Studies on the Left*, SDS was more practical than theoretical, more determined to prove in action what could not be resolved in thought. Its central concept was "participatory democracy," which Hayden derived from his Michigan philosophy teacher, Arnold Kaufman. The notion that active political participation was essential to civic education goes back to Aristotle and the Greek city-state ideal of the polis; thinkers as diverse as Arendt and Dewey believed in its possibility even in modern America. The idea of mass political activity may have seemed disturbing to those of an earlier generation. Did not Mussolini and Hitler mobilize Italians and Germans in the name of ideals higher than those of parliamentary government and representative democracy? Hayden was aware of such dangers and knew that totalitarian movements satisfied the human longing for solidarity and transcendence. Even so, he and Kaufman remained convinced that participatory democracy was the answer to alienation because it provided the only means of overcoming powerlessness. Still, its meaning in practice was never clarified. No doubt it was meant to activate the apathetic, to achieve face-to-face trust in the community, to test the limits of normal electoral politics, to challenge the structure of hierarchy and power, and to involve people in decisions that would affect their lives through discussion and achievement of consensus. With no place for authority and leadership, SDS members often sat through meetings that dragged on for hours—once to decide whether or not to take a Saturday afternoon off to go swimming. No wonder many sixties radicals later became college professors with a seemingly endless capacity for boring committee meetings.

In a way SDS was a misnomer. If by "democracy" is meant the

interests and needs of the majority, the many as opposed to the few, SDS did not respect but rather disdained the contented majority of middle-class Americans and also was insensitive to the demographic majority of the population itself, namely, American women. Feminism had yet to emerge to become part of the "agenda for a generation." Also, although its socialist predilections led SDS to assume it could speak for the working class, like previous Lefts, it could never speak to workers in terms that a carpenter or auto mechanic could understand. It courageously struggled for civil rights in behalf of a distinct racial minority, and did so on the grounds that equality demanded an end to discrimination. One recalls that Tocqueville supported egalitarianism not because it promoted liberty and excellence but rather because it answered to his own aristocratic passion for justice—"and therein lies its beauty." Perhaps a more apt title would have been SJS, Students for a Just Society.

The Lefts Compared

Comparing the New Left to its predecessors, one is struck more by geography than by ideology. The Lyrical Left and Old Left flourished in New York City, worrying ideology in Greenwich Village bars, displaying art and posters in Greene Street galleries. The New Left emerged in Madison, Ann Arbor, and Berkeley. And even though many radical students had come to Wisconsin and Michigan from East Coast Jewish backgrounds, they chose not to return East with the excitement of a John Reed arriving in Manhattan from Oregon. Instead of looking farther east to Russia for revolutionary inspiration, they headed to either the rural South or the West Coast to start changing the world.

The New Left was also unique as a student phenomenon. In the period of the Lyrical Left it would have been almost unimaginable. In 1919, when revolution seemed to be breaking out all over the world, some Harvard students left Harvard Yard to help Governor Calvin Coolidge put down Boston's general strike. A half century later American students everywhere in the country were on the opposite side of the barricades. By the thirties and the Depression many students were radicalized, but even those who identified with the Old Left kept their politics separate from culture and education; radicals of the thirties wore the jacket and tie required in campus dining halls, obeyed campus rules and regulations, and seldom thought of demanding direct involvement in the governance of academic institutions. The New Left changed both clothes and curriculum, sporting guerrilla field jackets and long hair, and demanding to study only its "own thing." The sixties generation also succeeded in becoming part of the administrative structure of the university by gaining seats on academic committees, thereby proving, if not its knowledge of power, its capacity for bureaucracy. The New Left even converted a few faculty members to its cause, particularly those who felt helpless about the Vietnam War.

But the New Left could never convert the Old Left, whose experience with revolution rendered its members bereft of revolutionary hope. The New Left's main charge against the old radicals was the *"trahison des clercs,"* the intellectual cop-out of ex-Troyskyists like Howe and Macdonald, who supposedly compromised their Leftism by their anticommunism, and of leaders like Harrington and Bayard Rustin, older labor movement radicals who chose to work through the system. Advocating coalition politics and reformist programs, the Old Left seemed to young radicals to have committed the sins of their fathers by becoming "establishment liberals."[12]

But the real difference between the two generations of radicals is a matter more of context than of tactics. The historical context of the Old Left was the abundance of poverty; that of the New Left, the poverty of abundance. The Depression led older radicals to believe that history would do for them what they could not do for themselves. Assuming that the masses would be radicalized as America went from bad to worse, they could find reassurance in the Trotskyist adage "The worse the better." The children of affluence, however, confronted the other side of the proposition, and thus for them a change of consciousness had to precede, or at least accompany, a change of conditions. Their hope was that a socialist consciousness would develop as the victims of society liberated themselves through autonomous community action. The Old Left, educated on the realistic determinism of Marx and Lenin, remained skeptical of the noble dream that participatory democracy would engage the needs and interests of impoverished minority groups. The New Left, brought up on the psychological optimism of neo-Freudians like Erich Fromm and the communitarian ideals of progressive educationists, enjoyed endless visions of human possibility.

"As for old socialists," wrote the young novelist Jeremy Larner, "their limitations as people seem disastrous, and frustrate me insofar as they are my own. They appear to be tedious, tired of themselves, full of self-hate, and chained to an idealism so abstract that it precludes all love of life." The New Left claimed to be chained neither to doctrine nor to history. "The old Marxist Left was intensely ideological," stated the young organizer Clark Kissinger. "They could rattle off the cause of *any* war as capitalism, imperialism, fight for free markets: one two three. We are characterized primarily by skepticism. Not having all the answers, we don't pretend to." The New Left relied "more on feel than theory," explained Hayden. From the perspective of this new antinomianism, the unpardonable sin of the Old Left was less the inadequacy of its formal ideology than its loss of passion. "When they proclaim the end of ideology," stated Kissinger, "it's like an old man proclaiming the end of sex. Because he doesn't feel it anymore, he thinks it has disappeared." Yet if the young radicals could not tolerate the veteran's dried-up dogmatism, neither could the latter comprehend the youth's renascent mysticism, which seemed more symptomatic of a religious revival than of a social revolution. "We went in for Talmudic exegesis," stated Leslie Fiedler to an audience of students; "you go in for holy rolling."[13]

In spirit, the New Left was originally closer to the 1913 rebels than to the Marxists of the thirties. For one thing, both generations saw themselves as self-conscious youth movements. Bourne's description of youth as the "rich rush and flood of energy" and his attacks on the "medievalism" of college education had their echo in the New Left's quest for original innocence and in its attacks on the "multiversity." Reed's and Dell's reflections on "Life at Thirty" indicated that the New Left was not the first generation to become obsessed with that age as the point at which self-trust turns to doubt. And Walter Weyl, in his postmortem on the "tired radicals" of the First World War, perceived that the Left's greatest enemy was age itself, a biological fact that has haunted both generations: "Adolescence is the true day of revolt, the day when obscure forces, as mysterious as growth, push us, trembling out of our narrow lives into the wide throbbing life beyond self."[14]

In its élan and anarchist bravado the New Left also resembled the Lyrical rebels. The parallel was particularly apparent with respect to the yippies, whose calculated strategy of sensation and shock seemed designed less to take power than to liquidate it by laughter. The impish antics of Reed and Dell, whose outlandish behavior offended party socialists, were carried on by Abbie Hoffman and Jerry Rubin, who believed that "confusion is mightier than the sword," that ideology was the "brain disease" of the Left, and that a "Be In" was a prelude to revolution. Women's rights, which would emerge from the New Left, had also been a passionate concern of the Lyrical rebels. Max and Crystal Eastman championed female suffrage and the emancipation of the housewife from the drudgery of domesticity; and Emma Goldman's demand for complete sexual parity made her one of the founding sisters of the women's liberation movement. As for the sexual revolution itself, doubtless the New Left went much further. Dell and Eastman would have been bewildered by those youths of the 1960s who saw Freud as an oppressor of women ("Freud is a fink"), an aphrodisiac as the answer to alienation, and the orgasm of the body as the proper oblivion of the mind. The Lyrical Left had to struggle seriously against government censorship and the moral repression of society. The dilemma of the New Left was that government and society had become so permissive about sex that it found itself in a vacuum of nonresistance. Eventually, the underground culture had to escalate the flaunting of

Cuba's Fidel Castro, leader of its revolution, esteemed by many of the New Left. (Marc Riboud/Magnum)

erotocism, from sex to nudity and ultimately to pornography, hoping to meet opposition so that it could expose American society as sick and repressed. But as the popular success of the musical *Hair* indicated, the American middle class was not outraged but titillated by private pleasures made public. Although the counterculture continued to believe that nakedness would liberate the mind from its "ego-defenses," the New Left wanted to make the revolution with its working clothes on.[15]

Cultural differences aside, the New Left almost echoed the Old Left in political rhetoric. Comparing the *New Masses* and *Modern Monthly* of the 1930s with *Ramparts* and *Liberation* of the 1960s,

Mao Zedong, Chinese revolutionary leader and a focus of adulation by the PLP. (Wide World Photos)

one finds the same view of America as a "corporate state" bent on imperialistic war, the same equation of liberalism and fascism, and the same attack on the liberal Center in order to "shorten the birth pangs of history." Nor did the New Left disabuse itself of the older Stalinist cult of the iron-willed hero. The adulation of Chairman Mao allowed young radicals to dismiss the terrorism of the Red Guard with the same naïveté that older radicals had shown in dismissing the Moscow trials. The will to mythologize also remained characteristic. Despite Castro's own admission that Cuba had failed to advance workers' self-management through nonmaterial incentives, the New Left still looked to Cuba's campesinos as models of participatory democracy, just as the Old Left once looked to Russia's peasant collectives as models of grass-roots democracy.

The Cuban revolution succeeded in eliminating poverty, racism, and illiteracy along with corruption, gambling, and prostitution. What about freedom? C. Wright Mills told the "Yankees" that destruction of capitalism came first. "Without the destruction of these interests—both Latin and North American—no real economic changes can reasonably be expected, certainly not at a sufficiently rapid rate. And without such structural economic changes, 'democracy' will remain what it is now in most of the continent: A farce, a fraud, a ceremony." Susan Sontag tried to warn *Ramparts* readers against mistaking the passionate energies emanating from the Cuban revolution, all directed against overcoming underdevelopment, for the energies the New Left was directing against their own, overdeveloped society of abundance and middle-class complacency. But readers of *Liberation* and other New Left journals learned a simpler and more exciting message about Cuba: that it was a "humane society" that had conquered the curse of money and "bourgeois legality." Faith in Castro as a charismatic caudillo mesmerized much of the New Left. Young, bearded, defiant, Castro became the symbol of rebellious young Americans in search of a John Wayne of the Left, a guerrilla who could shoot his way to power and at the same time remain virtuously uncorrupted by the temptations of power:

He looked vigorous, trim, brimful of energy. And there is unquestionably an aura of nobility—of majesty, for that matter—in the atmosphere of his presence. Those are dangerous words to use, I know, because they come down to us from old times, especially feudal times, and thus may be taken to mean that the person so described is separated by divine right from the mass. The quality of mythical hero which in my opinion belongs to the personage of Fidel partakes, however, of two elements: He seems extraordinary and ordinary at the same time, he seems both historical and current, both what is and what might be. Perhaps it will muddy things further to say that he appears to move within the general

Revolution and in his own individual Revolution, emblematic of the continuing resolution of the contradictions formed and re-formed in these distinct but related organisms.[16]

Although the New Left started out as an open, democratic, and nonideological movement, by the end of the sixties much of the New Left had reverted to the clichés of economic Marxism; it succumbed to the fury of sectarianism and even to the "cult of personality." Like the Old Left, it would find itself isolated from the political arena.

The Civil Rights Movement and the Antiwar Resistance

The Old Left died when communist Russia failed to fulfill its prophecies; the New Left was born when democratic America failed to keep its promises. The first stirrings of the postwar Left originated in the civil rights movement. Led by respectable, mid-dle-class black students, the southern antisegregation campaign was basically a moral protest entirely within the spirit of the law. For a century the South had been able to circumvent the Four-teenth and Fifteenth amendments, which guaranteed voting rights and equal protection of the law to black Americans; and for almost a decade the South had managed to sabotage the 1954 Supreme Court decision that ordered the immediate desegrega-tion of public schools. Thus when the protests began in the South, there was no call for social revolution. The tactics of civil disobedi-ence and passive resistance reflected the Christian principles of love and justice, values that had lived on in a land where the black Baptist church had instilled an ethic of stoic suffering. Visiting Amite, Mississippi, Jack Newfield observed that "a meeting in a broken-down shack called a church approaches Gandhian *agape* with the singing of religious hymns and the preachments of love thy neighbor." White students who risked their lives as freedom riders in 1961, and those who participated in the 1964 Mississippi summer project, discovered in the deep South "simple people liv-

ing lives of relative peace, love, honor, courage, and humor."
Their crusade became a "back to the people" movement in which
youths could struggle in interracial solidarity to overcome their
isolated existence. "We seek a community," said one activist, "in
which man can realize the full meaning of the self which demands open relationships with others."[17]

The same quest for intimate community and selfhood inspired
students in the North who were outraged by the cossack-like police charge against the Birmingham civil rights demonstrators in
late spring 1963. Many students, women especially, as Sara Evans
has recalled, feared for their lives in making the decision to go
South. Some were recruited by Casey Hayden, Tom Hayden's
wife; others were inspired by the oratory of Martin Luther King
("I have a dream") or by the ballads of Joan Baez ("We Shall
Overcome"). In the South they joined forces with the Congress of
Racial Equality (CORE) and the Student Nonviolent Coordinat-
ing Committee (SNCC) in voter registration projects and "free-

The 1963 civil rights demonstration in Washington, D.C. The size was estimated
at over 200,000. Attorney General Robert F. Kennedy addresses demonstrators
in front of the Justice Department. (UPI/Bettmann)

dom schools," where young blacks were taught remedial courses along with math and the history of their people. White women had to endure many harassing phone calls; men and women, black and white, the possibility of arrest and occasionally a narrow escape out of town on a back road racing at high speed in a pickup truck. In 1965 a dozen murders related to civil rights activities were recorded in the South. Several years later northern audiences watching the film *Easy Rider* felt the wrath of the redneck white racist and knew why he would rather kill than listen.[18]

After the midsixties the New Left directed most of its energies to ending the Vietnam War. In the 1964 election most students supported Lyndon B. Johnson as the peace candidate against Barry Goldwater, the conservative Arizona senator who promised to use nuclear weapons in Asia as a quick remedy. After the election SDS members debated whether to become fully involved in the growing antiwar resistance. Some feared that focusing on the war effort would compromise the possibility of a multi-issue movement, thereby sacrificing domestic concerns like poverty and racism to foreign policy matters that diplomacy might need to resolve. The possibility that SDS would be tainted with procommunism by identifying too closely with the resistance also worried some leaders. But Johnson's securing the Tonkin Gulf resolution in February 1965, and the systematic bombardment of North Vietnam that followed, forced SDS to take a stand. In April between twenty and twenty-five thousand resisters demonstrated in front of the Washington Monument in the District of Columbia, in the largest peace march in American history. In an impassioned speech the SDS leader Paul Potter called upon the audience to "name that system" that was causing the war as the first step in stopping it. Although Potter did not intend it, the speech made it tempting for others to identify "corporate liberalism," "capitalism," and "imperialism" as the ingredients of "that system" that must be brought down before the war could end.

Tom Hayden in 1966 accompanied the pacifist Staughton Lynd and the communist Herbert Aptheker on a trip to Hanoi. Impressed by the mobilization in the countryside, he praised the courage and heroism of the communist guerrillas and their "socialism of the heart." Back home he wrote and lectured on the new "rice-roots democracy" and likened peasant village politics to "colonial American town meetings," an attitude closer to that of the Old Left toward proletarian Soviets than to the skeptical spirit of Port Huron. The actress Jane Fonda (whom Hayden would marry) made a similar voyage of innocence later and was photographed waving and smiling, in front of a Vietcong artillery installation. In the "Tom and Jane show" the Left surrendered to the call of the moment and confirmed Max Weber's point that one of the "deadliest sins" of modern politics is "vanity," the need to stand in the foreground close to the "glorious semblance of power."[19]

The American class system the New Left assaulted actually worked in behalf of students, who, unlike most GIs, could afford to attend college and enjoy draft deferments. But opposition to the war, motivated by both a sense of guilt about what was happening to the Vietnamese people and a desire for self-protection, spread across the country to campuses everywhere. At Stanford University the student body president David Harris, who would marry Joan Baez, led the resistance. In Chicago a "We Won't Go" conference was held in 1966, and in New York a "Spring Mobilization" gathered in Central Park. Students debated whether to burn their draft cards publicly. Risking arrest, activists mobilized campuses and staged demonstrations at draft boards. The tactic was aimed at inundating the court system, overcrowding jails, depriving the army of body power, and thereby pressuring the government to end the war. The great majority of students hesitated, knowing full well that the only thing keeping them out of a foxhole was their draft card. Some of those who did torch their cards sought asylum in Canada.[20]

The failure of the resistance was a blow to SDS from which it never recovered. Frustration begat factionalism. When the attorney general announced that SDS would be investigated because of the involvement of communist sympathizers in antiwar activities, SDS's national secretary issued a public statement trying to clarify its role, a move that upset chapter members, who had not been consulted. Before long, women would express resentment at the male-dominated infrastructure of SDS, and feminist elements broke away to become part of the women's liberation movement. Black radicals would also deride SDS as ineffective. Communists would penetrate the organization and eventually take it over. The spirit of Port Huron, based on the sentiments of "fraternity" and "solidarity," collapsed in sectarian rancor.

The Counterculture

In 1967 the historian Arnold Toynbee, on a walk through San Francisco's Haight-Ashbury neighborhood, thought he perceived a genuine religious revival and "a red warning light for the American way of life." A Protestant bishop marveled at the Jesus-like gentleness of the youths on the streets. A Democratic politician asked, "Who are these outrageous young people?" "I suggest to you," wrote Daniel P. Moynihan, "that they are Christians arrived on the scene of Second Century Rome." Will Herberg, ex-communist turned Jewish theologian, saw them as "Adamites," an anarcho-nudist sect of the early Christian church. A sociologist called them "the Freudian proletariat," a liberated libido of continuous orgiastic ecstasy. A writer likened them to Diogenes and to the ancient Cynics, also bearded, unkempt, and unimpressed by reason and logic. They were the hippies, the "flower children" of the sixties who lived on herbs and hashish, denied evil, and loved love.[21]

The hippie phenomenon sprouted across the country, from New York's East Village to Oregon's rural communes. The most concentrated spectacle was in Haight-Ashbury, which a *Newsweek* reporter described as a "slow motion circus." No single message was suggested by the style of male hippies: army field jackets, naval uniforms with big colorful buttons, cowboy hats, tall stovepipes, sombreros, serapes, denims, threadbare tuxedo jackets, football jerseys, boots, bare feet. Women seemed to want to return to frontier days: ankle-length prairie dresses, overalls, home-sewn moccasins, Indian paint instead of cosmetics. Hippie food emphasized a diet of the organic and macrobiotic: sprouts, turnips, rice, cabbage, cereal, bean curd, natural springwater. The growing demand for special garments and food led to a proliferation of used-clothing outlets, natural food restaurants and stores, and eventually profits, expansion, and creeping cuisine capitalism.

"Turn on, tune in, drop out," advised Dr. Timothy Leary after he had dropped out of teaching science at Harvard. Turning on to drugs, a forbidden addiction once confined to the underworld, became a liberation for middle-class white youths in search of a "high" from peyote, marijuana, hashish, and, for the more daring, psychedelic LSD. In San Francisco alone in 1967 ten thousand youths sought help for drug abuse at the city's health clinics. But the counterculture spread, and in the process it turned some hippies into amateur chemists who wanted to make their own drugs or gardeners who took pride in growing them. "Tripping" on hallucinogenic drugs promised heightened perception and aesthetic vision as a means of self-discovery. In 1967 one East Coast hippie had a "funeral" for his former self.

Sex also took on mystical overtones for hippies. Willing female "groupies" followed rock musicians everywhere; communes experimented with free love and group sex; and eastern tantra offered the possibility of spiritual bliss as the mind supposedly overcame the body and the sperm reversed its natural direction and headed upward toward the godhead—at least until the doctor informed the hippiette she was pregnant. Promiscuity had other rude consequences: hepatitis, vaginitis, herpes. But in the fantastic world of hippiedom fearing reality and its consequences was the only sin. The drop-outs of the sixties seemed to be on a magic carpet searching for a land where, as one musician put, no one dies and no one cries.

Much of the New Left disdained the hippies, with their childlike fascination with beads and flowers, exotic dress, mind-withdrawing drugs, and erotic freedom. But the two movements had the same anxieties. The culture of the young, especially their rock and folk music, reflected their growing mood of frustration and powerlessness. Contrapuntal notes of joy and sadness, love and loneliness, fantasy and dread reverberated in the lyrics of the Beatles, Jimi Hendrix, the Jefferson Airplane, and Bob Dylan. The optimistic call for revolt was often accompanied by a fatalistic sense of political impotence and an acute conviction that filial love was a snare and the "American Dream" a fraud. Hence the Jefferson Airplane:

> War's a good business, so give your son . . .
> And I'd rather have my country die for me . . .
> Sell your mother for a Hershey bar
> Grow up looking like a car.

The demon of technology also emerged as a rock theme. The young felt that a technological culture denied man's autonomy and the reality of values like beauty and love, mystery and imagination. And behind the cult of the machine lurked the imminence of holocaust, as the poet Dylan prophesied:

> This wheel's on fire
> Rolling down the road
> Just notify my next of kin
> This wheel shall explode.

Toward the end of the 1960s America witnessed a series of Dionysiac folk-rock festivals—huge, organized "happenings" celebrating passion, experience, and fulfillment, instead of the old Western culture of reason, knowledge, and achievement. "Every period which abounded in folk songs has, by the same token, been deeply stirred by Dionysiac currents," wrote Nietzsche a century ago.[22]

At a festival at Woodstock, in upstate New York, in August 1969, four hundred thousand youths showed up to hear the world's greatest rock musicians and to create a "new nation" based on love and goodness as opposed to power and selfish interests. Woodstock amazed the public, which had expected the worst and was relieved to hear there were no mishaps and that hippies befriended neighboring farmers. Four months later, however, a festival at Altamont outside of San Francisco turned into a nightmare of fear and terror. The Rolling Stones had hired the Hell's Angels as security guards—the same bikers who had frequently disrupted anti–Vietnam War demonstrations. At Altamont the Angels kept order by cracking hippies over the head with pool clubs. By nightfall panic came when word spread that an Angel had knifed and killed a black youth. But not even the Hell's Angels of death could bring hippies to believe in the realty of evil. Altamont was dismissed as bad vibes and bad karma.

While most Hippies told each other, "Do your own thing," one element of the flower children did have a social conscience. In San Francisco a group calling themselves the Diggers opened up stores where they gave away food and clothes; they provided shelter for the down-and-out, and returned runaway children to their parents. Named after a seventeenth-century English society of benevolent growers, the Diggers came to be known in Haight-Ashbury for their good works and gentle ways. But the press focused on such episodes as San Francisco's "Human Be-In" in Golden Gate Park, where the poet Allen Ginsberg chanted "Hare Krishna" amid the aroma of pot and incense, the scream of electronic rock music, and the evidence of open sex under the pine trees.

Although the hippie phenomenon puzzled mainstream America, in many ways it had been predicted by the German philosopher Max Weber at the turn of the century. The incessant social changes of modernity, he observed, will result in "the disenchantment of the world," the eclipse of faith, feeling, and the sacred as the triumph of science and technology brings mechanization, routinization, and bureaucratization. This process of "rationalization" renders life flat, drab, predictable, and thus undramatic and uninteresting. Neither Marx, Veblen, nor Dewey anticipated this consequence of rationalization, because of their faith in science and industry. Weber feared its inevitability but did glimpse the possibility of a human revolt against the "iron cage" that would represent a return to spontaneity, mystery, charismatic personality, and other preconscious impulses.[23]

The industrial forces Weber described had been characteristic for a century. Generations of Americans, especially those of the thirties and forties, had lived under the shadow of depression and war, in periods of scarcity and deprivation; and even teenagers of the postwar era were reminded by their parents of the hardships of the past. But middle-class parents of the fifties enjoyed unprecedented prosperity and abundance, and their children grew up to take for granted endless material satisfaction and remained innocent of the very notion of scarcity, whether of money, jobs, housing, or other comforts that previous generations had to earn. Accepting as given what others had to strive for, the children of the sixties were the first generation to feel free to move beyond the yoke of necessity.

During the sixties parallels were made between the hippies and the beats of the previous decades. But whereas the beats were pagan, earthy, and angry, the hippies were ethereal, spiritual, and happy. The beats also took on the challenge of creativity and originality, which meant living with doubt and tension. The hippies exalted creativity, but they remained poets without a written page, artists without a painted canvas, philosophers without knowledge that knowledge may be a problem. Beat music was cooly cerebral and subtle and was often played by black jazz musicians. Hippie rock music was anything but subtle and complex, and its electronic cacophony required vast audiences to look more than to listen.

Comparisons of the hippies to the poet-philosopher Henry David Thoreau could also be misleading. The pre–Civil War author of Walden Pond showed Americans what they needed to know in order to know what they do not need. Hippies, too, wanted to reduce life to its essentials. But there were many things hippies were unwilling to give up, especially sex, music, drugs, and "happenings" involving huge crowds. Thoreau preached simplicity, silence, solitude.

Like the New Left, the hippies died out with the end of the sixties. Viewing the two phenomena together, it may be more important to note what the hippies renounced than what they espoused.

The cultural alienation of the young signified an increasing rejection of the values of the industrial way of life: work, duty, rationality, and mastery of the environment. More and more middle-class youths began to turn against these Protestant values in order to recapture nature and feeling. The romantic pastoralism was most pronounced in the hippie phenomenon. The children of the new ethereal culture appeared to have moved beyond not only capitalism but materialism itself. Their communal life-style suggested a sustained willingness to share all one's possessions so that the body might be dispossessed and the "soul" freed. In search of new, nonrational sources of wisdom, hippies turned to intuition, telepathy, and the occult; and in their quest for moral purification and self-expression they displayed a remarkable indifference to organizational failure. Their only fear was the institutionalized boredom of their parents—what the earlier Puritans used to call deadness of heart. Some hippies took up Zen, Lao-tzu, and tantric Yoga, desiring, in the spirit of Thoreau, to transcend physical reality; others became disciples of Wilhelm Reich and Norman O. Brown, desiring, in the spirit of Whitman, to immerse themselves in the pleasures of the body and embrace the holiness of sin.

The emergence of what Theodore Roszak called a "counterculture" accounted for the unusual degree of personalism and humanism in the early New Left. Young radicals shared the hippies' desire to restore warmth to human relationships, to translate social problems into dialogues of conscience that would lead to moral action. Originally a psychoethical rather than a doctrinal movement, the New Left also felt the need to achieve "authenticity." Yet, before long, the hippies' antipolitics of solipsism and ecstasy became unacceptable to many New Left activists. For one thing, the old epistemological problem divided the hippies from the activists in much the same way it had divided the nineteenth-century transcendentalists from the abolitionists. If feeling determines reality, as the hippies maintained, then the poor and oppressed were merely those who felt poor and oppressed. Salvation lay not in changing conditions but in changing perceptions—and the door to perception was not politics but psychedelia ("Imagination is Revolution!"). Moreover, when the hippies spoke of peace and love, they were talking about an ethic of passivity, a creative quietism that seemed dangerously innocent to experienced activists. Hippies may not have been going through the "technological obsolescence of masculinity," as Leslie Fiedler charged when he described the tight pants and long hair of males who saw themselves as "more seduced than seducing," but no doubt there was a tenderness to their life-style that transformed the traditionally aggressive male into a political cipher. Power grows out of the barrel of a gun, the New Left was convinced, not from the bud of a flower.[24]

Hippies may have been irrelevant politically but they were precious culturally. Although they were not true followers of Thoreau, their impulses would have been familiar to the transcendentalists. The outlandish youth of the sixties also turned to nature as a religion, denied original sin, rejected action in favor of meditation, and regarded conformity as death to the "oversoul." Hippies had no desire to take over the institutions of society, obtain a formal education, save the world, or regenerate humanity through political means. If their communal life-style departed from Emerson's principle of "self-reliance," they did agree with his political dictum: "Power ceases in an instant of repose."

1968: A Year That Shook the World

In the history of the American Left strife and violence have focused on the labor struggles of the late nineteenth and early twentieth centuries, as militant and bloody as any early industrial strikes in Manchester, Paris, Hamburg, or Turin. But the New Left introduced a novel form of radical violence: the campus confrontation. The strategy of confrontationism all but paralyzed the academic world from 1964 to the end of the decade. The television networks replayed the pitched battles on the evening news, creating the impression that New Left activists made up the majority of students on a campus. "Who's in charge of the zoo?" demanded a California legislator. Some conservative politicians, including a future president of the United States, benefited from the radicalization of the campus by promising to restore law and order. But the New Left also benefited, for the college campus was the one place where it could claim a record of successful conquests. In the early sixties students demonstrated outside administration buildings; by the late sixties they were inside the president's office, rifling his files, smoking his cigars, and, with feet up on his desk, placing long-distance calls to Paris announcing that the "revolution" had begun.

The first campus to explode was the University of California at Berkeley, then the only free public university to rank with the top three schools of the elite eastern Ivy League. Tensions at Berkeley had been building over strict dormitory regulations, compulsory ROTC, impersonal bureaucratic procedures, in which students were treated like IBM cards ("Do not fold, bend, or mutilate"), and restrictions against on-campus political activity. When the administration prevented students from setting up pamphlet tables at Sather Gate in the fall of 1964, the free-speech movement (FSM) organized to rally students to the cause of the First Amendment and the right to collect funds and engage in political advocacy on behalf of civil rights and César Chávez and his United Farm Workers. In the beginning FSM had the support of many elements, including conservative libertarians who believed in free-market economics. The Berkeley administration made some concessions, allowing students to espouse political causes without recruiting or raising funds. Too few concessions for the FSM leader Mario Savio, who headed a march on Sproul Hall. After occupying the building, the crowd, then about two thousand strong, left to surround a police car that had been holding an arrested student. The drama continued for thirty hours with TV cameras highlighting the standoff. The crowd dispersed after the administration agreed to drop charges. But before long FSM activists sensed betrayal when the administration vacillated and a local district attorney hinted at prosecution. In December three thousand students took over Sproul Hall and Governor Edmund Brown ordered six hundred police to the campus to arrest those who refused to leave. FSM called for a general strike to close the entire university. The "On Strike, Shut It Down!" tactic proved only partly effective at first, but later, with the rise of the antiwar movement, FSM succeeded in turning Berkeley into a bedlam of barricades, with rock-throwing students on one side and club-wielding police on the other.[25]

Across the Bay at San Francisco State the carnival of confrontation and coercion became a predictable, daily ritual. Here the original issue was the right to teach Negro history, demanded by black activists on their own terms and with their own appointed instructors. Soon other minorities got into the act as the administration agreed to start various ethnic studies programs. But when the chancellor of the state college system suspended a black student leader, his followers responded with ten "nonnegotiable" demands, from open admissions to all minorities to the promotion of black teachers to full professorships.

One day in October 1968 the author, who taught at SFS during the time of troubles, unlocked his office door and opened it. Inside, staring at him were seven leather-jacketed, armed giants from the San Francisco police's "tactical squad," slapping nightsticks against their palms, smiling sadistically and waiting like NFL linebackers, ready to pounce on students entering the building to disrupt classes. SFS became an armed camp. One black student injured his hands trying to plant a bomb. Faculty who continued to teach were labeled "white oppressors." Some received threatening phone calls; a few had their tires slashed; one had his office raided by men in stocking masks; an administrator narrowly escaped from his firebombed house. Black Panthers (of whom more later) came over from Oakland and spoke of "taking out" uncooperative faculty leaders. But they and other intimidators met their match in S. I. Hayakawa, the newly appointed president, who had a zest for confrontation, even to the point of pulling the plug on the strikers' public address system and admitting to the press that he was exhilarated at the sight of cops routing the troublemakers. Hayakawa became an instant hero across the nation.

Was there any solution short of police force? Hardly.[26] When the administration made concessions, striking militants escalated their demands. Perhaps the only solution that remained for those teachers who did not want to fight fascism with fascism was to hold classes early in the morning, for the strikers' hate rally did not start until noontime and the school would not shut down, if it did, until around two or three. At SFS the "revolution" would have to wait until the revolutionaries had a good night's sleep, the morning ocean fog had lifted, and the TV cameras had arrived.

The strike that erupted at Columbia University in April 1968 seemed for a while like a scene from a Mack Sennett film comedy. The immediate issues were the school's releasing class rankings to the draft board, its sponsoring of classified war research, and black students' protest of a proposal to build a gymnasium on an adjacent block that would, they claimed, deprive Harlem dwellers of scarce housing resources. The black students protested with decorum and discipline. But Columbia's SDS branch had come under the leadership of Mark Rudd, a lanky white combatant who had recently returned from Cuba convinced he could get a greater "high" from direct-action confrontation than hippies could get from a toke of pot. "Up against the wall, motherfucker; this is a stick up," announced Rudd in a message to President Grayson Kirk as students gathered to storm the citadel of learning. Several buildings were occupied and declared "liberated zones." When the police arrived, the occupants jumped out of the president's first-floor window; but when the police headed for other buildings, students climbed back in as mounted police chased bystanders across the lawns. The faculty, though opposed to the war, was upset by the president's decision to call in the police but even more outraged at the students' Luddite antics. Columbia had been the sanctuary of the New York intellectuals, some of them veterans of the Old Left, notably Daniel Bell and Lionel Trilling. When the faculty tried to mediate, SDS's attitude was summed up in Rudd's response: "Bullshit!"[27]

The events at Columbia looked like children's war games compared with the showdown at Cornell University in December 1968. There black students, angered by a cross burning on campus, seized a building, ejected the occupants, armed themselves with rifles, demanded a black studies program and the firing of "racist" professors, and promised violence if their ultimatum was not met. The administration fired no professors but capitulated on other issues, and the black students walked out of the building victoriously. Already suffering from a bad conscience about the Vietnam War, some faculty members also felt guilty about the behavior of their own institution. A few recalled the cowardly submission of German universities to Hitler's dictatorship.

Feeling the lust for power, New Left students went after professional associations and pressured their executive committees to take a position on the Vietnam War and to denounce "imperialist" America. The Modern Language Association elected as president a young associate professor, Louis Kampf, who advised students how to respect New York's Lincoln Center: "Not a performance should go by without disruption. The fountains should be dried with calcium chloride, the statuary pissed on, the walls smeared with shit." At an Organization of American Historians convention the New Left ran as presidential candidate a graduate student (no one remembers his name) against one of the country's greatest historians, Richard Hofstadter. Some professors, like John Searle of Berkeley, who had originally supported the student revolt turned against it when the New Left refused to reason and compromise. Who could be trusted? While some administrators promised amnesty to strike leaders, others called for prosecution. While some New Left activists championed free speech, others did not hesitate to prevent Robert Kennedy from speaking in the Bay Area. The struggle for the control of the university embraced faculty appointments, curricula, reading lists, and the creation of new minority studies programs. Many professors who had been involved a decade earlier with *Studies on the Left* went along with the students' assault on the ivory tower. A courageous exception was the Marxist historian Eugene Genovese, who warned the American Historical Association of the threat to intellectual freedom posed by "the pseudo-revolutionary middle-class totalitarians."[28]

The year 1968 was to the New Left what 1919 was to the Lyrical Left, a year of insurrection, assassination, the collapse of regimes, and the birth of revolutions that turned out to be still-born. In each year the symbols of hope and change had been struck down by assassins—Rosa Luxemburg and Karl Liebknecht in 1919, Robert Kennedy and Martin Luther King, Jr., in 1968. But the Left was on the march everywhere. In Paris students led by the romantic anarchist Daniel Cohn-Bendit took over the Latin Quarter, joined forces with factory workers to paralyze the economy, and brought down the de Gaulle government. In Czechoslovakia students of the "Prague Spring" revolted in an effort to win the political freedoms the American New Left took for granted or dismissed as "repressive tolerance"—only to be crushed by Soviet tanks. The near-assassination of the West German student leader Rudi Dutschke set off furious riots at Berlin's Free University. In Britain students seized the London School of Economics and demonstrated their solidarity with the French Left by hanging red-and-black flags from classroom windows. Student uprisings in Bologna and Milan planted the seeds of Italy's Red Brigades. In Mexico City students engaged in bloody clashes with the police to dramatize to a world about to watch the Olympic Games the miserable conditions of the working classes. In Japan student strikes closed Tokyo University for six months before riot police stormed the buildings with hoses and tear gas.[29]

The revolt of the young around the world created a seemingly novel paradox: a revolutionary vanguard crying, "All power to the people," and, at the same time, a people too content, at least in the industrial affluent world, to seek a revolution. Older radicals who had survived the thirties with their isolated integrity intact could not help wondering why the rebellious young refused to accept the relative powerlessness that is the fate of any Left without a proletariat. Irving Howe and the German social democrat Richard Lowenthal believed that the young were trying to realize through politics certain kinds of meaning and transcendence that have more to do with religion than with politics. Here the prophet seemed to be Dostoevsky, who foresaw alienated man as incapable of living with the "dizziness" of freedom and the agony of choice. Freud could also be cited, as he was by the ex-radical Lewis Feuer, to give the worldwide New Left phenomenon a generational interpretation that had students in an "oedipal" struggle with older symbols of authority and hence stuck in a "prolonged adolescence." Parallels could also be drawn with students in Weimar Germany who had been similarly contemptuous of liberalism and parliamentary politics. Some became Hitler's children and donned the brownshirt. Could there be such a creature as "Left-fascism," or were the young closer to Marx's nemesis, the ghost of Mikhail Bakunin? Daniel Cohn-Bendit offered a curious compound of negations: anticommunist, anticapitalist, antiliberal. The graffiti on the walls of the Sorbonne would have frightened Kremlin apparatchiks perhaps more than Wall Street brokers: *"Pour tout ce qui est Contre. Contre tout ce qui est Pour."* One slogan said it all: "It is forbidden to forbid."[30]

Whatever the motivation of Parisian students, by 1968 America's New Left had made the brutal and prolonged war in Viet-

The "days of rage" at the Chicago Democratic convention in 1968. (Warder Collection)

nam its own war at home. The entry of Robert Kennedy and Eugene McCarthy into the Democratic primaries had offered a glimmer of hope, and some SDS activists shaved their beards and put on coats and ties to work for McCarthy ("Be clean for Gene"). Kennedy had the support of a number of New Leftists willing to give the "system" one last chance. But Kennedy's assassination and the certainty of the liberal senator Hubert Humphrey's nomination at the convention drove the New Left into a frenzy of frustration. Various elements planned to converge on the Democratic convention, in Chicago in sweltering August, and obstruct its proceedings. The yippies set out to provoke street violence. Hayden had lost hope for reform and, according to the pacifist David Dellinger, the SDS leader's "eyes would light up at the prospect" of "violent resistance and armed struggle." But the New Left brought no guns or bombs to Chicago. Against Mayor Richard Daley's well-armed 12,000-man police force, and the 6,000 army troops and 5,000 national guardsmen standing by, the New Left had only, at best, blood, guts, and tears, and, at worst, rocks, bottles, and taunts ("Fuck pigs, oink, oink!").[31]

In Chicago during "the days of rage" the New Left had its moment at the center of the stage as television brought the specter of Byron's "fearful monument" into family living rooms. While America watched, Chicago reeled. Smoke, sirens, flying rocks, tear gas, tanks, cracking bullet sounds (cops firing into the air), Hayden moving about in disguise, Daly lashing out at eastern liberals ("Go home, you Jew bastards"), the TV man Dan Rather roughed up by Daley's security goons, McCarthy sulking in his hotel room, street freaks trashing police car windows, demonstrators lowering the flag at Lincoln Park, police moving in with clubs swinging, at night a silent candlelight parade by peace delegates, the next day police chasing students into the Hilton Hotel lobby, bloody faces, troops with gas masks moving menacingly like upright praying mantises, kids staggering, gagging from gas and mace . . . "We were awash in the purity of the we-versus-them feeling on the streets, the crazy battlefield sense that all of life was concentrated right here, forever," recalled Todd Gitlin two decades later. Hayden remained undaunted. "The coming of repression will speed up time," he wrote at the time, "making a revolutionary situation . . . more likely." The same fantasy that revolution follows repression had sustained the faith of German Communists when Hitler came to power. Neither the German Old Left nor the American New Left had learned the political lesson of radical life in modern industrial society: Don't mess with the middle class.[32]

Factionalism and Suicidal Extremism

More than any other organization, SDS shaped the tone and spirit of the early New Left. Generally from upper-middle-class white families, SDS members included gifted graduate students and sophomore dropouts, Christian pacifists and militant activists, weekend potheads and midnight mystics. Its Port Huron Statement remains an impressive document, even if it did not foresee that participatory democracy could degenerate into guerrilla violence and produce a Hobbesian reaction among the mainstream middle class. Two thoughtful historians of SDS, Tod Gitlin and James Miller, have registered their anguish about the fate of a movement that set out to bring America to a moral accounting of its lost soul. The same cannot be said of other elements in the New Left.

Compared with the generous, if vague, existential humanism of SDS, the doctrines of the Progressive Labor party were depressingly familiar. PL was formed in 1962, when it broke with the CP and sided with the Red Chinese during the Sino-Soviet rift. Maoist in inspiration, Leninist in organization, PL opposed the emotional anarchy and spontaneity of SDS. It subscribed to violence, believed armed struggle probable, cited Marxist-Leninist doctrine as gospel, and dredged up old terms like "exploitation" as the last word in social analysis. Intellectually PL was a throwback to the worst aspects of the Old Left. Offended by hippie sensuality, uptight about drugs, critical of countercultural heroes like Bob Dylan and Allen Ginsberg, PL seemed a parody of the grim radicalism that characterized the worst aspects of the Old Left.

Two other important organizations of the early New Left were the Young Socialist Alliance and the DuBois Clubs of America. The former represented the Trotskyist youth branch of the old Socialist Workers party. The Trotskyists, keeping the faith of their namesake, continued to insist that only the working class could carry on the struggle against Soviet bureaucracy as well as against American capitalism. Although numbering only a few hundred members at its birth, YSA picked up support in the late sixties. The DuBois Clubs defied all generalizations about generational revolt, for they were started by the children of former communists. Organized in 1964, the DuBois Clubs had roughly one thousand members concentrated in Berkeley, San Francisco, and New York. Like the post-Stalinist and conservative CP, the young communists advocated working with labor unions and supporting, when necessary, the liberal wing of the Democratic party. In contrast to SDS, DuBois members believed in the enduring viability of Marxist theory; but in contrast to the Maoist fanaticism of PL, they feared the threat of a new McCarthyism and the possibility of native fascism more than they hated American liberalism.

Originally SDS believed in the miracle of community organization, PL in the might of violent revolutionary struggle, YSA in the mystique of proletarian consciousness, and the DuBois Clubs in the method of coalition politics. Not surprisingly, SDS regarded PL as dangerously adventuristic, while the latter accused the former of "bourgeois romanticism": YSA criticized DuBois members for betraying the working class, and they in turn suspected young Trotskyists of ideological paranoia. Beyond the familiar polemics, the history of the Left in the sixties is the story of the demise of SDS and the rising influence of PL.

Two developments accounted for this shift from participatory socialism to revolutionary Maoism. First of all, the Vietnam War undermined SDS's argument that it was possible to work within the system. SDS was slow to recognize the mounting hostility to the war. Concentrating on slum neighborhood projects, SDSers felt that the war was not directly related to the lives of the poor.

SDS took an active part in draft resistance and campus confrontations with military recruiters and the Dow Chemical Company (manufacturer of napalm), and it helped organize the 1965 March on Washington against the Vietnam War. But it was PL, invoking Lenin's First World War thesis on mobilizing the masses against capitalism and turning a national war into a class war, that could claim to have the "correct analysis" of the crisis. As more and more radicals came to regard the war in Vietnam as one of imperialistic aggression, PL's classical Marxism appeared to offer a solution.

Moreover, the growing militancy in the black civil rights movement meant the Left could no longer be the exclusive province of middle-class whites. In 1964 Stokely Carmichael emerged in a fury of eloquent black rage, determined to liberate his people from internal "colonialism." That summer the Mississippi Freedom Democratic party challenged the Democratic convention for representation on the all-white Mississippi delegation. After long, bitter negotiations MFDP was granted two token seats, and militants came away convinced more than ever that "black power" was more important than civil rights. At first the black power movement, possibly emboldened by the riots in Watts in 1965 and in Newark in 1967, repudiated its white supporters. During the 1967 Chicago convention of the National Conference for a New Politics—organized to promote the black leader Dr. Martin Luther King and the white antiwar spokesman Dr. Benjamin Spock on a presidential ticket—African-robed black radicals dictated inordinate demands on voting rights, seating arrangements, and resolutions, humiliating white participants, who groaned of "flagellating our white conscience" and of being "castrated." The following year, after the tragic assassination of Dr. King, the Black Panthers emerged as the most flamboyant force of Afro-American militancy.[33]

Unlike previous generations of black radicals, who listened to Claude McKay, Paul Robeson, and Richard Wright, the Panthers had little genuine interest in the Soviet Union, and they remained indifferent to the rich legacy of W. E. B. DuBois, who had made

POLITICAL PRISONERS
OF USA FASCISM

The Black Panther leaders Bobby Seale and Huey Newton. (Library of Congress)

the historical American Negro problem a challenge of radical
scholarly research. Thus the Panthers had no intellectual ties with
earlier American Lefts; instead, they identified with Chairman
Mao, Che Guevara, Ho Chi Minh, and Frantz Fanon, the Algerian
theorist of national liberation and spokesman for "the wretched of
the earth." Some Panthers also identified with the Palestine ter-
rorist organization al-Fatah, and a few were so anti-Israel that
they justified Sirhan Sirhan's assassination of Robert Kennedy.[34]

The Black Panther party had been formed in Oakland, California, in 1966 by Huey Newton and Bobby Seale. Originally the Panthers seemed just another small band of black nationalists, although better known than most because of their armed neighborhood patrols. Then Panther chapters sprang up in the ghettos of a dozen large cities, and their membership rose to about five thousand in 1968. At the same time the Panthers broadened their ideology. Inspired by third world illuminati, the Panthers adopted a "Marxist-Leninist" amalgam that succeeded in combining nationalism with socialism, preaching self-determination along with class struggle. Unlike other black nationalist groups, the Panthers became convinced that a social revolution against racism and capitalism could be made only by a coalition of whites and blacks. Accordingly they entered an alliance with the white-based Peace and Freedom party, which ran the black writer Eldridge Cleaver for president in the 1968 election. Some white radical groups welcomed this ideological turn, but SDS could not accept the Panthers' claim that they alone constituted the vanguard of the revolution. In July 1969, at a National Conference for a United Front against Fascism in Oakland, Seale warned "those little bourgeois, snooty nose . . . SDS's" that if anyone "gets out of order" they can expect "disciplinary actions from the Black Panther Party."[35]

By 1970 the New Left was in disarray. Pressured on one side by Panther machismo and embarrassed on the other by yippie freakout, it could no longer sustain an impelling vision or offer a viable program of action. Without a unified, broad-based organization, without a leader who could inspire more than a small band of faithful adherents, the New Left remained what it always had been—a mood in search of a movement.

The fate of the antiwar resistance had ironic implications, for the more American adults turned against the war, the less the New Left had to offer American youth. Opposition to the war first expressed itself in petitions, peaceful marches, and campus forums. By spring 1967 the antiwar movement had assumed a new, militant posture. Demonstrations now became massive, with participation by as many as 400,000 people (the April 1967 "mobilization" in New York and San Francisco); organized draft resistance penetrated several military camps, where servicemen risked being tried for mutiny by publicly protesting the war; and dozens of campuses exploded in a spasm of violent protests over issues like ROTC and on-campus military recruiting and classified war research. Yet the New Left could never successfully organize the discontent that the war had spawned. Even more serious, after accurately predicting the inevitable expansion of the war, the New Left found itself powerless to prevent what it had predicted. The moment of truth came in May 1970, when President Nixon announced his decision to invade Cambodia. America reeled in a torrent of student protest as white puffs of tear gas rose across the skies of campuses throughout the country. Students succeeded in closing down or impairing the operations of about 425 colleges, but at a tragic price. In New York City "hard hat" construction workers waded into a crowd of student demonstrators while police looked the other way; at Kent State, in Ohio, four students were fatally shot by national guardsmen. Some revolutionists tried to escalate the confrontation on the campuses, but by the time the smoke had cleared, a widespread revulsion against violence had developed. Many students who had been quickly radicalized by the events decided to go off campus in an attempt to "communicate" with middle America, to explain their opposition to the war, to organize support for peace candidates, and to take "the long walk through existing institutions." The following year, when the 1971 May Day mobilization was held, the antiwar movement belonged more to students and the public in general than to the New Left. "Peace has become respectable," shouted Jerry Rubin in disgust.[36]

Among the reasons given for the failure of the New Left, government repression is often cited by contemporary radical scholars. The earlier Lyrical Left had felt the crushing force of the state in the Red Scare of 1919 and the Old Left the harassment of McCarthyism. When one considers the resiliency of the European Left, however, actions taken by the American government seem

mild by comparison. In Italy, France, and Germany the Left survived both fascist dictatorships and military defeat. In several
European countries communist and socialist parties, enjoying the
heroic honor of the resistance, emerged from the Second World
War as strong as ever. Nevertheless, although repression may be
inadequate to account for the demise of the New Left, several
radical activists were on the run from arrest warrants, and others
who did not flee fast enough stood trial for conspiracy or rioting.
With the FBI taking the offensive and often planting its own
agents, the New Left's earlier bravado gave way to fear, suspicion,
and recrimination.

Under the Johnson and Nixon administrations the Department
of Justice first targeted SDS as the prime culprit of social unrest.
Seeking information in order to prosecute, government agents
investigated the personal lives of SDS members and broke into its
offices and stole files. The government pressured colleges and
universities to take severe punitive measures against activists or
risk losing federal funds. Later in the sixties FBI Director J. Edgar
Hoover described the Black Panthers as "the greatest threat to the
internal security of the country." Panthers had been involved in
shoot-outs with the Oakland police. In 1969, eight Panthers were
arrested in New Haven, Connecticut, and charged with murdering a fellow member who the police claimed was an informer.
Charged with homicide, the famous writer Eldridge Cleaver fled
to Algeria. In hiding, he told the CBS reporter Mike Wallace that
one aim of the Panthers was to storm their way into the Senate,
take off the head of Senator John McClellan (a right-wing anticommunist), and shoot their way out. Another Panther promised
to "kill" President Nixon. With such statements the Panthers
made Hoover into a prophet, and the extreme end of the New Left
invited its own repression.[37]

Confrontation politics worked well on the campus, where the
New Left could force professors who identified with their antiwar
goals to capitulate to ever-increasing demands and could effectively exploit the television medium to create the impression that
it spoke for the majority of students. Outside the sanctuary of the

campus, however, confrontation brought a backlash of repression. The nasty awakening came during the Democratic convention of June 1968, when the Left discovered the brute power of Mayor Daley's police force. Every opinion poll indicated that the substantial majority of the public supported Daley's inept, merciless treatment of the screaming demonstrators. The presidential candidate Richard Nixon, playing to the fears of middle America, made "law and order" the catchword of his campaign. With the crackdown on campus disorders, the increase in school expulsions, and the stepped-up war on drugs, the era of tolerance had ended.

No longer could the Left organize demonstrations without fear of indictment, mount the barricades without fear of the National Guard, abuse the symbols of America without fear of the hard hats. There was no doubt now that the government would have the full support of the majority of the citizenry should it resort to even the severest measures to suppress the Left. Significantly, the Black Panthers, the most harassed of all radical groups, were among the first to realize that the game of confrontation politics was over. In May 1970, when a rally was held in New Haven in support of the imprisoned Bobby Seale, the Panthers tried to tone down the demonstration for fear of government reprisal. After the Cambodia crisis, American campuses lapsed into a strange mood of quiet frustration and fatigue—what one administrator called an "eerie tranquility."

Like all Lefts, the New Left acted out the dismal pattern of faction and fission. Even the tightly organized Panthers divided into rival sects that accused one another of being police informers or male chauvinists. But the dissolution of SDS had repercussions for the entire Left. In the early 1960s PL had set up the May 2 movement in an attempt to compete with the more popular and more youthful SDS. But in 1965 PL dissolved this branch and entered SDS. Once inside, PL charged SDS with student elitism and middle-class condescension toward American workers. As a result, SDS split wide open at its 1969 convention, with a majority going over to the Maoist PL. At the same time radicals began to look beyond the campus and the ghetto in order to end the isolation of the academic intelligentsia from the mass of workers. The attempt to forge a "worker-student alliance" (WSA) was prompted in part by the dramatic May 1968 uprising of what radicals saw as a coalition of French industrial workers and Parisian students. The newly formed WSA accepted PL's thesis that only the working class possessed the leverage crucial to achieving radical change in America. But the students' attempt to infiltrate the factories and support workers' causes met with little success. In November 1970 some 750 members of the now decimated SDS turned out in Detroit to demonstrate before the General Motors Building and join the automotive strikers. According to reporters, not a factory worker was in sight.[38]

Meanwhile, another faction had been developing within SDS—the Revolutionary Youth movement. Skeptical of the potential of students and workers alike, RYM maintained that it was a mistake to try to make a revolution in one country when in reality it had already begun in Vietnam, Cuba, and the rest of the third world. The role of the Left was thus to align itself with the international revolution abroad by engaging in irregular warfare behind enemy lines, thereby undermining the overextended power of America's imperialistic war machine. Out of this new strategy came the Weathermen, an underground guerrilla cadre who believed that the core of the "Red Army" could be built in the streets of America through the symbolic power of violence. This American version of the nineteenth-century Russian *narodniki* (terrorists) staged its first encounter in Chicago in October 1969. Dressed in helmets and blue denims, trained in karate, the Weathermen went on a three-day "trashing" rampage until the police arrested 290 of its 300 members. While radical critics accused the Weathermen of suicidal "Custerism," several fugitives escaped to New York City and plotted to intensify their campaign through the use of well-placed bombs. In March 1970 three members accidentally killed themselves while preparing explosives in a Greenwich Village town house.

The mangled bodies found in the basement in Greenwich Village—spiritual home of the first Lyrical rebels—dramatized the tragic desperation and exhaustion of the New Left. During the early civil rights movement radical youths tried to work through the liberal state. In the midsixties some experimented with counterinstitutions. Toward the close of the decade PL steered a course to orthodox Marxism and presumably to the unawakened power of the working class. The unrelieved failure of all these strategies culminated in terrorism, the ego politics of karma, or, perhaps more charitably, the last act of a lost cause.[39]

Failures and Achievements

Repression, factionalism, extremism—such considerations scarcely account for the failure of the New Left. The charge that the New Left lacked a coherent, unified movement seems less an explanation of its defeat than a definition of its essence. Opposing bureaucracy, it relied upon spontaneous activity, and its suspicion of the hierarchical tendencies of organizational structures precluded the possibility that a sense of leadership could emerge with a single voice. The actual reason for its failure was the assumption that it stood for more than itself. History did not come through for the New Left, because the missing ingredient of radical mythology never appeared—the agency of change. The central dilemma that has faced all three Lefts in twentieth-century America is the inability to find a social force that would adopt a commitment of active opposition to the existing order. SDS originally hoped that at least some sections of the labor movement could be radicalized. But the American worker proved indifferent to the New Left and hostile to its libertarian life-style. Spurned by trade unionists, young radicals later flirted with the idea of a "new working class" emerging among the frustrated, increasingly displaced technological intelligentsia. But under pressure from dogmatic Marxists who scorned this new outlook as "petit bourgeois revisionism," SDS dropped the notion of a white-collar working class. What remained for the noncommunist Left were those groups that originally aroused the sympathy of young activists, the poor and the oppressed minorities, supposedly the last remnant of unco-opted virtue in America. Out of a population of 205 million, there were about 25 million "poor" in the United States. According to the 1970 census this category included about 34 percent of the black people and about 10 percent of the white, roughly 7.5 million blacks out of a population of 23 million, and 16 million whites out of 168 million. The remaining poor were Puerto Ricans and Mexican-Americans—1.5 million and 500,000, respectively—and Indians and others. In the radical sense of the term, the poor scarcely constituted a solidified "social class" of the racially oppressed, since one-third of the nonwhite families in America had an income of more than $8,000 per year. Even more serious, since the poor of all colors represented a small minority (about 13 percent of the total population), it was no longer possible, as it was in the nineteenth century of Debs and Marx, to claim that the oppressed had on their side the power of numbers.

In the beginning, the New Left was not blind to these realities. The original strategies of participatory democracy, community action, and self-determination implied that radical change had to be generated from among small minorities. SDS's ERAP projects had aimed to reallocate power at the neighborhood level by making it possible for welfare recipients to have more control over social policy. In Cleveland SDS had had some success with black women on welfare, but in Chicago efforts to organize the white poor failed, and almost everywhere else unemployed youths felt nothing but hostility toward the better-off college students. What sustained hope was a widely shared radical conviction that a recession was just around the corner and that, when it hit, stagnation would swell the ranks of the unemployed and bring about radical change. The Old Left knew that no such radicalization of American workers happened even during the Depression, but the New Left was more interested in making history than in understanding it.

If practice confirms theory, one must judge SDS's strategy as flawed from the start. The noble efforts to establish health clinics, garbage collection, and nursery schools helped mitigate the suffering of the poor but did little to affect real social change. Community control could offer only control over poverty itself. Participatory democracy was the naïve ideal of a generation that had been reared to believe that goodwill and "togetherness" could bring instant change. Innocent of the realities of power and the slow pace of historical change, lacking personal experience with the psychology of poverty, young radicals were unable to cope with setbacks and defeats.

Ironically, despite its tactical and strategic failures, the New Left had achieved one success that had eluded all other Lefts: politically and morally it made a difference. The 1913 radicals were powerless to oppose the First World War, the anti-Bolshevik hysteria of 1919, and the politics of "normalcy" in the 1920s; and the Old Left was prostrate in the face of McCarthyism and the cold war consensus politics of the 1950s. Although the New Left did not stop the war in Vietnam, it did much to foster sentiment against escalation and to publicize the complicity of industry and the academic community. Indeed, the publication of the Pentagon Papers vindicated the New Left's skepticism about the official version of the war. The downfall of Lyndon Johnson, and President Nixon's pledge to withdraw all American troops from Vietnam by the end of 1972, also indicated that the antiwar forces could no longer be ignored. Even though those forces moved from the streets into the halls of Congress, it was the New Left that first set them in motion. There can be no doubt that the New Left, through sustained dissent and resistance, did much to pressure a government into changing its course from escalation to withdrawal in the midst of an inconclusive war. This historically unprecedented achievement was, curiously enough, in the nature of one of the great hopes of the Lyrical Left. "Nothing could be more awkward for a 'democratic' President than to be faced with this cold, startling skepticism of youth, in the prosecution of his war," wrote Randolph Bourne in 1917. Bourne saw in "the non-mobilization of the younger intelligentsia" an "idealism" that could not "be hurt by taunts of cowardice and slacking or kindled by the slogans of capitalist democracy." In the legacy and the lesson the New Left bequeathed to America lay the fulfillment of Bourne's prophecy:

> If the country submissively pours month after month its wealth of life and resources into the work of annihilation . . . bitterness will spread out like a stain over the younger generation. If the enterprise goes on endlessly, the work, so blithely undertaken for the defense of democracy, will have crushed out the only genuinely precious thing in a nation, the hope and ardent idealism of its youth.[40]

The New Left had been no less prescient in anticipating the domestic crises that would convulse America. Many programs enunciated by SDS in 1962 were later articulated by congressmen and senators who criticized excessive military budgets and demanded that the government address itself to social priorities. Thus, by forcing critical issues like racism and poverty into the center of public debate, the New Left made those issues politically safe. Moreover, by making America aware that youth was a growing political force to be reckoned with, it was instrumental in lowering the voting age to eighteen; and by exposing America's worship of technology, it helped make Americans more aware of the peril to the environment. Although much of the theoretical criticism of American society had been articulated by liberals like John Kenneth Galbraith, it was the young radicals who challenged by deeds the subtle methods of bureaucratic control, the ubiquitous manipulation by advertisement, the deadly chambers of corporate life, and the winking hypocrisy of conventional sexual morality. The New Left, together with the hippies and the counterculture, effectively called into question the whole quality of American life by invoking a "new consciousness."

The "New Consciousness" and Herbert Marcuse

"The young men were born with knives in their brain, a tendency to introversion, self-dissection, anatomizing of motives," wrote

Herbert Marcuse, scholarly critic of the Protestant ethic and celebrant of sensual liberation, is a leading philosopher of the New Left. (Pictorial Parade)

Emerson of the 1830s. "The key to the period appeared to be that the mind had become aware of itself. Men grew reflective and intellectual. There was a new consciousness."[41] Almost every generational rebellion trumpets itself as the bright dawn of a "new consciousness." Young radicals of the 1960s grew up to discover that consciousness was dead in America and that Americans had lost their freedom without knowing it. This arrogant conviction could be traced through the ideas of some of the intellectual heroes and instant gurus of the era. As we noted earlier, the New Left's first major inspiration came from C. Wright Mills, the gruff Texan and Columbia University professor who told students that it was the task of the sociological imagination to find political solutions to personal problems and to beware of "the power elite" and the "great American celebration." Two other intellectuals also shaped the awakening radical mind of the sixties. Paul Goodman exposed the idiocy of urban government and the absurdity of programmed adolescence while defending his Gestaltist faith in the spontaneous emotions of the young. Erich Fromm gave a pseudo-scientific legitimacy to old-fashioned ideas like "love" and "goodness" and started students searching for the self by developing a capacity for "relatedness." European existentialism also had a liberating role. From reading Sartre, American students learned that ultimate freedom is the ability to resist, to say no. From reading Camus's *The Stranger*—assigned reading for many entering college freshmen—they learned the difference between legal moralism and personal morality.

As more and more students sensed the emptiness of everyday existence, their search for meaning led to at least three new avenues of awareness. The tender-minded, having ascended from J. D. Salinger to the supernatural speculations of Hermann Hesse and the cosmic consciousness of Aldous Huxley, began exploring the deeper recesses of mind. The jaded, graduating from *Mad* comics to the entropic world of Joseph Heller and Ken Kesey, decided that to survive the rationalization of an irrational society, one might feign insanity. The radically oriented, taking Mills's advice, translated personal or philosophical problems into social causes. The first option led to hippieland: Haight-Ashbury, Timothy Leary, tripping, and acid; and later, organic foods, fasting, Lao-tzu, Hare Krishna, and Jesus Freaks. The second led to the Pop Left: pornopolitics, Lenny Bruce, the Merry Pranksters, the San Francisco Mime Troupe, yippies, redemptive genitality, and Reichian orgone. The third led to the New Left: praxis and commitment, conflict and struggle as the test of manhood and self, radicalization as conversion, and Fanon's "identity won in action." But what the New Left needed to justify its course of action to all other disaffected youth was a philosophy that explained the causes of alienation and offered a solution to it. Herbert Marcuse provided both.

A scholarly philosopher then close to seventy years of age, Marcuse looked like a gentle, deflated Santa Claus and thought like an angry Prometheus. His role in contemporary American thought is remarkable, for he succeeded in revolutionizing what Americans assumed they had safely domesticated—the ideas of Hegel and Freud. In nineteenth-century America, Hegelianism had become a philosophy of celebration (Whitman) or a theology of reconciliation (Josiah Royce). And in the twentieth century Freudianism became a progressive psychology of cooperation and adjustment (Harry Stack Sullivan) or a heroic philosophy of stoicism and tragedy (Philip Rieff). In addition, both these systems of thought had been discredited when some Americans erroneously identified them with fascist absolutism and irrationalism, and the Old Left, as we saw, had rejected the dialectic as a species of German mysticism.

In reviving Hegelianism, Marcuse restored the respectability of dialectical reasoning, which illuminates the tension between the "is" and the "ought," between what is given and what is potential, between immediate appearance and ultimate reality. Hegel's concept of the dialectic, Marcuse first pointed out in *Reason and Revolution* (1940), denies predominance to anything by showing that everything changes.

In earlier studies in Germany, Marcuse drew on the philosophy of Martin Heidegger to show how being is grounded in the given structures of existence; and he drew on Marx's recently discovered 1844 manuscripts to show how human praxis can free man from all ontological and historical determinants by reconceiving him as reflexively self-creative and capable of rising to consciousness through action. But human existence in advanced industrial society, Marcuse discovered in America, remains passive and acquiescent and unaware of its own alienated condition. Hence the role of the intellectual is to adhere to Hegel's concept of reason as the only higher standard against which society must be assessed. This adherence to the abstract propositions of philosophy, and at the same time seeing philosophy as a concrete product of history that begets its own "negation," would come to be what the Academic Left called "critical theory."

In the United States, Marcuse addressed the status of psychology as well as philosophy. After writing on Hegel and Marx, he revised Freud's central dictum that civilization requires the repression of man's instincts. Basic repression of harmful biological drives may be necessary for survival, Marcuse said, but "surplus repression" is a contrived social phenomenon based upon capitalist domination. Thus he drew a distinction between Freud's "pleasure principle" and the "reality principle." Historically it was necessary to defer immediate gratification and sublimate drives into productive work because of the economic reality of scarcity. With the advent of abundance, however, man no longer needed to repress himself by performing joyless acts of labor. The contradiction of modern society is that it perpetuates the traditional "performance" ethos instead of transforming work into play and redeeming sexual pleasure, and thereby reunifying man's nature.

The abolition of repression is improbable in the Soviet Union and impossible in the United States. In America, especially, technological rationality has created a status quo that "defies all transcendence," wrote Marcuse in *One Dimensional Man* (1964). Every improvement in the quantity of comfort "militates against qualitative change," for the "people recognize themselves in their commodities; they find their soul in their automobile, hi-fi set, split level home, kitchen equipment." Even the sexual revolution, Marcuse believed, serves only to "desublimate" repressed tensions, to pacify the potentially discontented; *Playboy* magazine supports the existing social order by creating the illusion of fulfillment. American society can absorb all possible opposition, tolerating moral deviance and political dissent but allowing no real resistance. Unable to think dialectically, Americans have become "one-dimensional," conditioned to accept the incomplete state of existence as the highest possible state of being. The "is" has become the "ought," the actual the possible. The "given" can be neither negated nor transformed.

What, then, are the prospects for radical change in America? Marcuse had never been entirely clear on this question. But in *An Essay on Liberation* (1968) his earlier pessimism gave way to a glimmer of optimism. Now it became clear that the Marcusean revolution will begin aesthetically, arising from the beautiful untouchables, the young, deracinated intelligentsia and dropouts who have cultivated "the sensuousness of long hair, of the body unsoiled by plastic cleanliness." Only they are blessed with the "new sensibility of praxis," an aesthetic vision that descends from high culture "in desublimated 'lower,' and destructive forms, where the hatred of the young bursts into laughter and song, mixing the barricades and the dance floor, love play and heroism. And the young also attack the *esprit de sérieux* in the socialist camp: miniskirts against the *apparatchiks,* rock 'n' roll against Soviet Realism." With this mythopoeic image of revolution, with this invocation of eros, song, dance, play, and the beauty of festive youth, we are back with the Lyrical Left. Curiously, like the rebels of 1913, Marcuse relied less on Marxism than on "Aesthetic Form" as the subversive medium of "the Great Refusal—the protest against that which is." Marcuse speculated, as had the poets of 1913, that man may be endowed with a capacity to make "the primary distinction between the beautiful and ugly, good and bad." With the lyrical radicals he also maintained that the task of overcoming repression "involves the demonstration of the inner connection between pleasure, sensuousness, beauty, truth, art, and freedom," all of which presupposes an "aesthetic ethos" that makes the "imagination" the liberating faculty of man. The "rebellion of the young intelligentsia," advised Marcuse, indicates that the "right and the truth of imagination [may] become the demands of political action" and the spark of social change. Finally, just as the Lyrical Left rejected all dualisms between science and fact and art and value, Marcuse insisted that "the historical achievement of science and technology has rendered possible the *translation of values into technical tasks."* Despite his heavy Teutonic prose and Hegelian logic, Marcuse was a poet who shared the Lyrical Left's conviction that political issues can be given aesthetic dimensions and that freedom is the realization of beauty as well as justice.

But Max Eastman, the patron spirit of the Lyrical Left who wrote on beauty, love, and the pleasures of visual perception, might have reminded Marcuse that art is more an interpretive than a transitive activity that, like science, requires the presence of objects to be acted upon and transformed. For all his passion for lyrical aesthetics, Eastman believed, as did Dewey, Veblen, Hook, and Marx himself, that science would supplant literature in providing knowledge of the world. Marcuse's idea of art as creativity could extend the Marxist-pragmatist thesis that knowing is making, but such a stance is not necessarily peculiar to the Left; capitalists are just as convinced that they understand what they make and produce. Moreover, the notion that political change could be brought about as a kind of poetic production signified a desperate departure from the meaning of the Left. Historically the Left had remained faithful to the concept of class struggle and the plight of the working class. Marcuse departed from this tradition. The proletariat is a phantom and even the working class "is no longer qualitatively different from any other class and hence no longer capable of creating a qualitatively different society," he wrote in 1965. Yet Marcuse also maintained that the student Left could scarcely be a revolutionary force by itself. At most it "can articulate the needs and aspirations of the silent masses" and possibly "induce radical change" as militant students later "take their places as political and social forces in the society." After *"les événements"* in France in 1968, Marcuse was asked,

> Do you believe in the possibility of revolution in the United
>   States?
>
> *Absolutely not.*
>
> Why not?
>
> *Because there is no collaboration between the students and the
>   workers, not even on the level on which it occurred in France.
>   . . . I cannot imagine . . . a revolution without the working class.*[42]

Oracular, ponderous, erudite, Marcuse gave the New Left a philosophical dimension that promised the dominance of the dialectic. It was a measure of his integrity and pessimism that he did not go indiscriminately whoring after the young—as did some who spoke in his name. Yet Marcus's assessment of the political situation in America was nothing more than a restatement of the predicament that had confronted the American Left at the turn of the century. Once again we have a young radical intelligentsia without a radical proletariat. Although he recognized the profound cultural cleavage between radical students and the workers, Marcuse still insisted the two must collaborate. In the past the Left at least enjoyed the comfort of an illusion. In the late nineteenth century, socialist intellectuals could look forward to the growth of a revolutionary working class because, in Marxist terms, the proletariat was the absolute antithesis of the bourgeois order. Before the First World War, as we have seen, the question was whether the intellectuals could become a genuine revolutionary class. Today this question has been transmuted.

If radicalism means "going to the root," then the most radical elements in Marcuse's America were the hippies and their counterculture, for it was the hippies who questioned the ultimate rationality of industrial society and the ultimate meaning of Christian civilization. Yet it was highly doubtful that these mystical mutants would become a force of the Left, as Marcuse assumed. The counterculture was not the affirmation of Marxism but its repudiation. The affluent children of technology represented a challenge not only to capitalism but to the basic philosophical and political assumptions of historical Marxism: the validity of material reality, the imperative of organized, collective action, and the inalienable quality of work as the highest source of life's meaning and value. Countercultural radicalism moved far beyond New Left radicalism, for it sought a new consciousness not so much to realize as to obliterate the Western industrial idea of consciousness.

Both the New Left and the counterculture died out as the social unrest of the sixties subsided in the early seventies. Some hippies retreated to the woods and to farms to start communes and grow grass. Several radical activists went curious ways: Rennie Davis converted to Hare Krishna; Mario Savio survived a bout with drugs to return to graduate school; Mark Rudd went underground to escape arrest and later emerged to become, after criminal charges were dropped, a high school teacher in Arizona; Tom Hayden entered politics and represents Santa Monica in the California legislature; Joan Baez started a retreat for contemplation before returning to singing; a few SDS members became Reagan Republicans as either cold warriors or free-market capitalists; David Horowitz, having written against "the American Colossus," writes against those who write against it; Jerry Rubin found fulfillment on Wall Street; Eldridge Cleaver found Jesus in Paris.

But in the late seventies and eighties a substantial number of former New Left students found themselves comfortably inside the very institution they had once assaulted as part of the corrupt "system" that must be destroyed—the college and university of the "higher learning." Here Marcuse's idea of "critical theory" would flourish, as would a development he failed to anticipate, the women's revolution, perhaps the single most important social movement to emerge from the sixties. Here, too, Marxism would take another stand under the guise of a new terminology. Although the Academic Left of the eighties represented several diverse groups, all had a common desire to solve the problem that had seemed very simple in the sixties—the problem of power.

Three

ANOMALY

7

The Academic Left

Can you imagine anything more horrible than
government by professors!

Georges Sorel, 1908

Post-Vietnam America

In the early seventies more than two-thirds of the American people opposed the war in Vietnam, the longest war in the Republic's
history. Some opposed it because it was immoral, others because it
was unwinnable, and still others because it was draining the economy and weakening America's position in the rest of the world.
The Republican administration of Richard Nixon continued
Johnson's early assumption that the war must be fought in order
to demonstrate America's commitment to intervention wherever
and whenever the "free world" was threatened by communist
aggression. Ironically, the longer the United States was bogged

down in Vietnam, the more noninterventionist and even isolationist the American people became.

Even more ironic was an assumption shared by the Left and the Right—that the war was about communism. Many radicals who opposed the war believed that America as a capitalist system would have to be transformed and its "imperialistic" impulses extirpated before the war could end and communism could prevail in Vietnam. Many conservatives who supported the war believed that a withdrawal without victory would result in communism's overrunning all of Southeast Asia. Yet when Nixon withdrew all American troops in 1973—prompted as much by such embarrassments as the publication of the Pentagon Papers and the Watergate scandal as by the hopelessness of the situation in Saigon—Wall Street applauded and the American economy failed to experience the severe recession the Marxist Left had predicted. The Right's predictions also proved ill founded. The "dominoes," instead of falling, stood as communist regimes in Vietnam and Cambodia, and elsewhere fought each other more fiercely than they had their class enemies from the West. Having dismissed as false the deep-rooted sentiment of patriotism, the New Left and the U.S. government both became obsessed with communism and almost oblivious to the divisive forces of nationalism in Asia.[1]

What remained of the New Left could take little satisfaction from the events that followed the war overseas. The mass atrocities of Cambodia's Khmer Rouge under Pol Pot made Kampuchea an evil imitation of Auschwitz. The fate of the Asian "boat people" fleeing the tyranny of the Vietcong put a cruel end to Tom Hayden's promise that Hanoi's communism meant "rice-roots democracy." No less disillusioning was the mystique of "the third world," which collapsed with the Iranian "revolution" of 1979. Having overthrown the Westernizing Reza Shah Pahlavi, the ayatollah Khomeini and his Islamic fundamentalists put Marxists behind bars and women back behind veils.

America's cultural radicalism also had its sinister surprises. The mass murder in Hollywood by the Charles Manson "family" sent

Gdansk, Poland, May 4, 1988. Solidarity leader Lech Walesa and striking ship-yard workers raise the victory sign during Walesa's address. (Bettmann Archive)

a chill through the counterculture, for his psychopathic savior complex and apocalyptic harangues had once been regarded on Haight-Ashbury as the harmless mumblings of a healthy dropout. Even more ghastly was the mass suicide of hundreds of adults and children at the People's Temple in Guyana in 1978. The temple had been organized in San Francisco by the "reverend" Jim Jones, a hysterical paranoid schizophrenic who so appealed to his desperate, salvation-seeking followers that he persuaded them to drink Kool-Aid laced with cyanide to escape the injustices of the world. Radical experiments with communes seemed to increase the possibility of evil even in the name of "love."[2]

Perhaps the most confounding of all developments for the New Left was the positive emergence at the end of the seventies of the Polish Solidarity movement. Solidarity also caught the American Right by surprise, particularly neoconservatives who had insisted that right-wing dictatorships were preferable to communist totalitarian systems since the former are potentially changeable and the latter inexorably irreversible. True, the New Left never had any sympathy for East European communism. But the Polish workers who struck at Gdansk and the Warsaw *intelektualista* who joined them represented that synthesis of a proletariat and an intelligentsia that had always been the elusive dream of the American Left. Ironically, Solidarity was struggling to free itself from the Bolshevik legacy that earlier Lefts in America had once championed.

The learned New Left journal *Telos,* which had been inspired in the sixties by the rediscovery of the writings of the Hungarian philosopher Georg Lukács, offered thoughtful responses to events in Eastern Europe. Solidarity enjoyed close coverage in the *Nation. Dissent* and the *New Leader* had all along promoted the cause of freedom behind the Iron Curtain, but these publications represented the lingering democratic socialist sentiments of the Old Left. A small remnant of the New Left, attracted by the editors Harrington and Howe, went over to *Dissent,* a quarterly that best reflects the Left's capacity to endure defeat with dignity instead of despair. Several contributors to *Telos* started what came to be called the "redemption debate," which divided those who continued to espouse familiar grandiose plans to transform the world and those who sympathized with Solidarity's demands for formal political freedom and a revolution that would be "self-limiting." Although no contributor mentioned it, the debate over whether the world should be redeemed or reformed resembled Daniel Bell's and Reinhold Niebuhr's earlier criticisms of radical politics as eschatological. A particularly thoughtful essay was Murray Bookchin's "Were We Wrong?" The anarcho-libertarian asked *Telos*'s readers to consider the possibility that the whole Marxist apparatus had led the sixties generation astray.[3]

While *Telos* was more antistate than anticapital, other Left journals like *Radical America* were antiliberal as well as anticapital, and not a few veteran New Leftists remained fixated on Gramsci's call for total hegemonic unification; at the same time Solidarity was demanding the diversification and pluralization of all aspects of political, social, and cultural life. Freedom, in effect, required not unanimity and hegemony but autonomy and heterogeneity. In the sixties the New Left had regarded such pluralistic tendencies as the original sin of American liberalism. Two authors most influential among contemporary Polish intellectuals were Robert Nozick, an American libertarian philosopher, and Friedrich von Hayek, a refugee free-market economist. Much of the New Left regarded capitalism as moribund and dialectically fated to self-destruct, the fitting end to a decadent social order. But the Poles might well have revised Lincoln Steffens's advice: "We have seen the future, and it doesn't work."

It is interesting to consider the response of the French New Left to these post-Vietnam historical developments. Many of the *barricadistes* of May 1968 had been militant Maoists, yet news of Kampuchea and other atrocities shocked Parisian intellectuals who had once looked to Vietnamese communism as the proper answer to French colonialism. The publication of Alexander Solzhenitsyn's *The Gulag Archipelago*, an exposé of Russia's brutal labor camps, seared the conscience of French Leftists, many of whom had earlier accepted Jean-Paul Sartre's claim that no such camps existed and his later advice that America should be attacked for its "war crimes" in Asia. During the war period Sartre refused to speak to his old friend the philosopher Raymond Aron, a critic of the Soviet Union and defender of Western liberalism. After Kampuchea and the Gulag, Sartre's reputation suffered and Aron's gained even among the Left, especially among "les Nouveaux Philosophies," former incendiaries of May 1968 who had turned against Marxist doctrines. One of them, André Glucksmann, a student of both Sartre and Aron, succeeded in bringing his two mentors together for a meeting of French intellectuals to raise funds in behalf of the boat people. Glucksmann also wrote *Les Maîtres Penseurs* (1977), in which he argued that Left intellectuals had succumbed to German philosophical idealism and become bewitched by Hegel's dialectic. Curiously, the thesis that Soviet totalitarianism could be traced not only to Stalin, Lenin, and Marx but all the way back to Hegel was the argument Max Eastman had put forth in his debates with Sidney Hook forty years earlier.[4]

In the United States no similar reexamination of philosophy and politics occurred among remnants of the New Left. The activists of the sixties knew that history had left them behind and reduced a once mass student movement to isolated sects without an institutional base. Anguished by the senseless brutality of the new rulers in Southeast Asia, Joan Baez and several former antiwar activists issued "An Appeal to the Conscience of Vietnam," but, unlike its counterpart in France, the dwindling New Left in the United States scarcely heard the appeal. The actress Jane Fonda refused to condemn communist repressions, and *Liberation* even praised the Vietnam government for its "moderation." The Soviet invasion of Afghanistan and the spectacle of the Marxist Ethiopian government's allowing its own people to starve brought no strong denunciations from the New Left. In 1982, when Susan Sontag, once a communist sympathizer who penned a classic piece of fellow traveling, "Trip to Hanoi" (1968), spoke at a Town Hall meeting in New York in honor of Solidarity declaring, "Communism is fascism," she was roundly jeered by many New Leftists in the audience and attacked in the *Nation* and the *Village Voice*. In 1987 two ex-radicals, Peter Collier and David Horowitz, organized a "Second Thoughts" conference in Washington, D.C. Collier and Horowitz had become pro-Reaganites and supporters of the Contras, the guerrilla opposition to the Marxist Sandinista government in Nicaragua. Martin Peretz, the *New Republic* editor, expatiated on his radical positions in the sixties and enthusiastically endorsed the conference. The historian Ronald Radosh, once a radical critic of America who later was shocked to discover that certain Old Leftists admitted to knowing what was going on in Stalin's Russia, also backed the Contras. Todd Gitlin, in contrast, could admit his past illusions and misguided hopes and still have "third thoughts" about embracing the Contras. Most veteran activists like Gitlin would acknowledge what he called "the abominations" of communist regimes without feeling the need to follow the example of the Old Left and take up anticommunism as a noble cause.[5]

The 1980s witnessed something of a counterrevolution when the Reagan administration set out to dismantle the welfare state. Reductions in health, education, and other social services were matched by increased military expenditures. Workers saw their incomes lose ground, and many midwestern farmers watched in despair as banks repossessed their land. While "supply-side economics" benefited the upper classes, the New Left clung to James O'Connor's thesis—spelled out in his earlier *The Fiscal Crisis of the State* (1973)—that there would be an inevitable clash between the government's need to assure continuing capital accumulation for Wall Street and its need, at the same time, to sustain its own legitimacy by assuring substantial income redistribution for the people. Yet even the frantic days of the stock market crash, in fall 1987, led many Americans to blame the greed of individual brokers, especially the yuppies, and not necessarily the "system" itself.[6]

While the New Left and the American people had different attitudes toward Wall Street, they shared a curious distrust of the federal government. To the New Left government meant deceit and manipulation, the draft and the CIA, the military-industrial complex and the arms race, and an imperialist foreign policy. To many middle-class Americans government meant high taxes, enforced school desegregation, the protection of constitutional rights at the expense of community sentiment, and welfare cheats picking up their checks in a Cadillac. At times the New Left seemed to come close to agreeing with neoconservatives that the welfare state was a bureaucratic form of power, a mode of legitimization and domination in the guise of Social Security and other dispensations that did less to reduce poverty and more to increase dependency.

With faith in the national government shaken in the seventies, both middle America and the New Left, each for its own reasons, advocated decentralization of power and the return of authority to the people. The idea of local government and community control had always been an article of faith to the New Left. Yet, when the idea was put into practice, it failed to overcome citizen apathy, and in New York, Chicago, and certain other cities, some of the decentralized educational systems succumbed to corruption, others to political weakness, in the eighties. Some school boards became the "personal fiefdoms" of officials who took payoffs, engaged in nepotism, some even in drug dealing, and who bestowed teaching and administrative positions in response to a phone call from a local politician. School decentralization was meant to give America's children a better chance to escape the ghetto; it did more to provide equal opportunity for the opportunist.[7]

The young activists of the sixties saw themselves, self-righteously, as the chosen generation, the first to think radically and act rebelliously to bring about unborn ideals. It told older Americans that they were the problem; no one over thirty could be trusted! Identifying truth and morality with the heyday of life, the New Left inadvertently made growing old the test of radicalism in the same way as time is the thief of youth.

But did the New Left enable the sixties generation to defy its rendezvous with middle age? According to a 1988 *Rolling Stone* survey, not very well at all. The survey covered persons between eighteen and forty-four, those who had experienced in their youth the tumultuous and idealistic sixties, the self-indulgent "me generation" of the seventies, or the proudly ambitious yuppie phenomenon of the eighties. The respondents regarded the civil rights movement and the Vietnam War as the most important events to influence their lives in the sixties, and they still had fond memories of JFK and Martin Luther King, Jr., as generational heroes. Scoffing at Rambo machismo, they retained the antiwar sentiment of the sixties. The great majority of the men, roughly 70 to 80 percent, would be unwilling to enlist for military service, whether to protect American interests in the Persian Gulf, or to save a third world country from falling to communism, or even to come to the aid of a democratic ally like England. More isolationist than pacifist, the sentiment seemed to have to do more with geography than with morality. In the event that war broke out on the North American continent, 73 percent of the men would fight for their country. Post-Vietnam isolationism remained consistent. On domestic issues, however, the survey revealed considerable change and even a glaring paradox.

Americans between the ages of eighteen and forty-four, the group polled, constituted America's largest voting bloc in the eighties yet many had inherited from the sixties a distrust of institutions. While looking to government to address social problems and stimulate the economy, they remained suspicious of almost anything that emanated from Washington. Thus while 29 percent of the respondents thought that the next president's high priority should be providing food and shelter for the homeless, 46 percent thought it more important to stop people from abusing the welfare system. Only 14 percent thought that supporting equal rights for women should be on the president's agenda, and only 8 percent believed it important to "promote general social concern/less materialism in young people."

The group portrait that emerges from the survey must be disheartening for the remaining New Left that had once envisioned itself as a rebellious movement arising from the idealistic passions of the young. It turned out that much of the youth of the eighties supported Reagan, and even the no longer young who had come of age in the late sixties and seventies had lost interest in politics as civic responsibility. The generation that had bravely dropped out and turned on had now found itself "tuned out" and "turned off," as William Grider put it. Their sentiments also defy conventional Left-Right categories. With liberals and the Left it gave priority to cultural tolerance, a clean environment, civil rights, and day care for children with working mothers. With conservatives and the Right it emphasized safe neighborhoods, reduced inflation, protection of American jobs from foreign competition, and less bureaucracy. How can child care centers be started without the creation of new government agencies? Can there be safe neighborhoods without some risk to civil liberties? In the face of such questions the old incantation of "participatory democracy" was nowhere to be heard.[8]

From this survey one might conclude that the New Left disappeared like an extinct ideological species. Actually it did thrive in the post-Vietnam era but not in American politics—rather, in the "higher" spheres of intellectual life. Having been spawned on the American campus, the New Left would return to its natural habitat and live comfortably ever after. It remains a strange anomaly, a radical enclave in a conservative environment—an influential, if gradually dwindling, school of Marxists and ex-Marxist scholars who assign students books by authors who write of the "transition" from the "commodity world" of capitalism to the "moral economy" of socialism to be read at a time when the world is moving in the opposite direction.

The Left Academy

Although the New Left saw itself as the victim of history, in at least one respect it became its beneficiary. In the sixties and early seventies American higher education expanded enormously. University enrollments increased and new campuses opened on the East and the West coasts to accommodate the postwar baby boom children now reaching college age. Consisting to a large extent of graduate students, the New Left entered the academic profession en masse and found respectable positions at virtually every distinguished university except Chicago. Appointed at a time of expansion, the "tenured Left" survived the budget-cutting contractions of the early Reagan years. With no new massive hiring expected in the immediate future, the remnants of the New Left are the most significant ideological presence on the American campus today and most likely will continue to be so well into the next century.

The New Left's finding an afterlife in the academic world is replete with ironies. It will be recalled that at the turn of the century Daniel DeLeon and other socialist theoreticians worried about the implications of a radical intelligentsia whose interest may not coincide with that of the proletariat. With the dreams of the New Left shattered in the seventies, no one had to worry about whether the Academic Left could articulate the needs and aspirations of an American proletariat, since that creature had no existence. With no constituency in the real world, the New Left had no choice but to ascend to the ivory towers of theory. Yet the move into the groves of academe is surprising in many ways. No one who had watched campus demonstrations in the sixties could have anticipated the eagerness with which former protesting graduate students later accepted positions at the very institutions they said were responsible for racism, imperialism, fascism, sexism, and other evils of "liberalism." At Berkeley, Columbia, San Francisco State, and several other campuses in the sixties there seemed to be two incompatible worlds—academic gentility and revolutionary fury. Inside the university building was the faculty member: nicely dressed, family photo on office desk, surrounded by books, polite and patient, wondering when the troubles would end so that the sacred serenity of the library might again be enjoyed. On the outside the graduate student: with ragged army jacket and beard, fist raised, noisy, rude, impatient with explanations. Facts are fictions. Scholarship is for squares. The system sucks. Fuck you, faculty; you're either for us or against us.

And so it went for half a dozen years. But in the end the

majority of New Left graduate students, after repeating again and again that they would never allow themselves to be "co-opted," did so without so much as a blush. Once inside academe, the New Left gave up all pretense of reaching "the people," to whom "all power" was supposed to belong. Unlike veterans of the Lyrical Left and Old Left, or true public intellectuals who carried on as editors or journalists for widely circulating magazines, New Left veterans regrouped as a professoriate and wrote primarily for each other in small, arcane academic journals. The decline of "the last intellectuals," to use Russell Jacoby's apt description, had many implications for the status of the Left in America. Traditionally the Left had been sustained by urban bohemian culture or aroused by political crises like war, depression, or foreign revolution. Today the Left's life-support system is the university, which has produced a "new class" credentialed with advanced degrees and enjoying elite status, what Thorstein Veblen—whose *Higher Learning in America* bears the subtitle "A Study in Total Depravity"—would probably have called "The Leisure of the Theory Class." With the ambition of yuppies, many veteran New Leftists turn out the same kind of dense scholarly verbiage as other professors in a competitive effort to climb the greasy pole of promotion. The short walk from the barricades to the bureaucracy simply called for a shift in "discourse," from confrontation to publication.[9]

Although a fraction of New Left academics drifted away from radicalism, the majority continued to espouse the causes of the sixties. The extent to which the Left predominated in the American university became a controversy in the journals of the Left and of the Right in the late eighties. Seeing itself as a beleaguered, marginal voice existing on campuses of quiet contentment, the Left pointed to the Right's influence at the University of Chicago, the rise of free-market economics as a discipline, and the number of wealthy foundations supporting neoconservative think tanks. But the Left could hardly deny the plethora of radical journals in college bookstores; the proliferation of radical courses, the development of new programs like black studies, women's studies, and critical legal studies; the preponderance of panels at professional conventions on such subjects as "hegemony," "oppression," and "domination"; the heckling on campus of conservative speakers like Defense Secretary Caspar Weinberger and UN Ambassador Jeane Kirkpatrick; and the continual hiring of young scholars whose dissertations were scrutinized for liberal heresies. In the field of American history, for example, a liberal Ph.D. who subscribed to consensus instead of class conflict, or a white male conservative who admired Madison more than Marx, had about as much chance of getting hired on some faculty as Woody Allen of starting as point guard for the Knicks.[10]

The New Left had once marched under the banner of Students for a Democratic Society. But the controversies that arose in the seventies and eighties over affirmative action and admissions quotas had little to do with society or democracy. The Academic Left supported preferential treatment for women and minorities as victims of sexism and racism. Such programs received mixed reactions on the campus and encountered bitter opposition from much of the public as a resort to "reverse discrimination." Operating apart from society, the Academic Left lectured on egalitarianism while practicing elitism. The Left could still claim to identify with the masses and call for studying history from "the bottom up," but any implementation of affirmative action would have to come from the top down; and, in the view of some, it would be carried out by a power elite consisting of organized faculty activists working through the administration, the very "system" against which the New Left had once inveighed. In the sixties SDS participated in a civil rights movement that, rooted in southern black churches, drew its strength from culture, community, song, ritual, memory, honor, pride, and vision. Such sentiments rejected all discrimination on the grounds of race. Twenty years later the Left settled for racial percentages.

In the late eighties, when controversy arose over the teaching of required courses in Western civilization, the public became aware of the existence of an Academic Left. "Hey, hey, ho, ho, Western culture's got to go," shouted radical black and white students at Stanford. At Duke and other universities the whole idea of a "canon," a body of literature recognizes as authoritative, came to be challenged by younger faculty members. Student activists also demanded "equal time" to read minority, women, and non-Western authors in place of, or along with, Plato, Saint Augustine, John Stuart Mill, Rousseau, T. S. Eliot, and Freud. Several inseparable issues prompted this battle of the books: turmoils within specific academic disciplines that left the curriculum in disarray; interest politics of minorities to hire more minorities to cover more minority subjects; and a genuine feeling that the contributions of Arabic, Islamic, Indian, and Asian cultures had been ignored on American campuses. But much of the Academic Left was also convinced that Western civilization was morally bankrupt and responsible for third world poverty. Radical professors of literature believed that the university must reject an elitist approach to high culture, specifically Matthew Arnold's dictum about teaching "the best that has been thought and done in the world," and instead have students read whatever uncovers the darker secrets of class, race, and gender. Thus the authority of excellence, greatness, truth, and morality must give way to the realities of power, the experience of oppression, the lives of the common, average, and ordinary.[11]

Curiously, Randolph Bourne and the Lyrical Left had also been critical of Matthew Arnold's idea of education as the authoritative appreciation and transmission of high culture. But the earlier Greenwich Village critics were less crude and blatantly ideological. Whereas the contemporary Academic Left insists that the canon must go in order to awaken students to oppression and domination, Bourne's criticism of classical education was less political than aesthetic. To focus solely on the "best," Bourne advised, may lead students simply to imitate and even to worship the remote. What the young need is not truth as recitation but beauty as perception:

> For as long as you humbly follow the best, you have no eyes for the vital. If you are using your energy to cajole your appreciations, you

have none left for unforced aesthetic emotion. If your training has been to learn and appreciate the best that has been taught and done in the world, it has not been to discriminate between the significant and the irrelevant that the experience of every day is flinging up in your face. Civilized life is really one aesthetic challenge after another, and no training in appreciation of art is worth anything unless one has become able to react to forms and settings. The mere callousness with which we confront our ragbag city streets is evidence enough of the futility of the Arnold ideal. To have learned to appreciate a Mantegna and a Japanese print, and Dante and Debussy, and not to have learned nausea at Main Street, means an art education which is not merely worthless but destructive.[12]

But the Academic Left's quarrel was with Wall Street rather than with Main Street. To sustain that quarrel meant keeping the Marxist faith and speaking the language of negation and contradiction. Years earlier in the fifties, when William F. Buckley, Jr., wrote *God and Man at Yale* and Marcuse wrote *One Dimensional Man* and other works aimed at overcoming "false consciousness," which both identified as liberalism, with its commitment to openness, tolerance, skepticism, neither saw any harm in using education for political purposes, whether for God and capitalism or for Marx and socialism. A text of the Academic Left, *Studies in Socialist Pedagogy* (1978), made it clear that a good dose of indoctrination would enable students to see the "best" that has been thought and done on the basis of a new canon:

> The task for a Marxist teacher, then, is not only to develop the best possible Marxist analysis but to find ways to communicate his material in a manner that takes into account a Marxist analysis of the classroom situation, namely, the role of the teacher and student . . . and the false consciousness of many students that will decrease their receptiveness to revolutionary ideas.[13]

The Academic Left is not as dogmatic as that mindless statement suggests or as monolithic as its critics insist. Many radical professors teach Freud, Tocqueville, and Edmund Burke along with Marx. As president of the Organization of American Historians, the Marxist Eugene Genovese called upon the profession to hire young conservative scholars, and he himself went so far as to cross class lines and write for Buckley's *National Review.* His own journal of the seventies, *Marxist Perspectives,* began with a triumphant flourish and folded within two years as a result of disputes on the editorial board, but before its demise *Marxist Perspectives* was praised by the *Wall Street Journal* for its "entrepreneurial skills." Like love affairs, radical journals are easier to start than to sustain.[14]

What is striking about the Academic Left is its persistence despite historical developments and political realities. The intellectual staying power of the Left in the United States is matched by that in only one other European country, England, where Marxism retains some hold on the academic mind. Curiously, where communist parties have traditionally been strong, as in France and Italy, Marxism fell on hard times in the eighties, but where communism as a political force has been weak, as in England and the United States, Marxism as an ideology survives with some strength in the cloistered world of the academy. Perhaps this disparity only highlights the insights of Max Weber about the demise of movements and the inevitability of institutions. As an intellectual movement promoting itself in protests and publications, the Left had to compete on the open market; as an academic phenomenon presiding over a university, the tenured Left has less need to compete to survive, and it now has an ally in bureaucracy and its drive to expand. If Wall Street depends upon capital accumulation, the Academic Left depends upon cohort accumulation.

Most members of the Academic Left came from comfortable middle-class backgrounds. Many teach about the working class, but probably few know it as a concrete personal reality. Unlike previous Lefts, present-day Academic radicals seek to reach primarily students, not workers, a new focus on middle-class—and even upper-class—youths that is a departure from orthodox

Marxist theory with its emphasis on workers as society's economic base. More than any other thinker, as was discussed earlier, the Italian Marxist Antonio Gramsci freed radical thinkers from obsession with the bottom group in society. Convinced that the "superstructure" was more important than the structural base because it is the former's "hegemony" that binds the masses, Gramsci advised intellectuals to seek power by undermining the dominant cultural authority. America's Academic Left embraced Gramsci as endowing the intellectual with a revolutionary role. The challenge was to persuade students of the power and truth of Marxism in class lectures and scholarly publications. Now it no longer mattered that the working class remained resistant to radical ideas. Marxism itself was to become hegemonic and cease to be marginal and adversarial:

> A Marxist cultural revolution is taking place today in American universities. More and more students and faculty are being introduced to Marx's interpretation of how capitalism works (for whom it works better, for whom worse), how it arose, and where it is a peaceful and democratic revolution, fought chiefly with books and lectures, with most of the action taking place on the fringes of the established disciplines. Paradoxically, few of the participants on either side are aware of the extent of this struggle of positions that have already changed hands. The general public knows even less. Yet, its initial results are evident throughout the academy.[15]

So announced Bertell Ollman and Edward Vernoff in the opening page of *The Left Academy: Marxist Scholarship on American Campuses* (1982), a three-volume compilation of studies in almost every discipline in the college catalog—except music, mathematics, and physics, where tonal chords and invariant laws may have nothing to do with dialectical materialism. The philosopher Ollman was certainly the right person to teach how capitalism works and for whom; he himself put together a game, modeled after Monopoly, and called it The Class Struggle. It sold like hotcakes at Saks Fifth Avenue and made Ollman a pocketful of money, which is fine and indeed enviable except that in a scholarly book he informed readers that money is the "alienating medium" of mankind.[16]

The Left Academy came close to being all encompassing. In the social and behavioral disciplines efforts were made to bring back to life what the Old Left had buried: in sociology, the "logic" of class conflict; in economics, the division of labor and the "profit squeeze"; in political science, the theory of the state and the promise of "Eurocommunism"; in anthropology, the origins of property and colonization and "dependency theory"; in geography, environment, space, and population growth ("classquake"); and in psychology, therapy as social control, race prejudice as class behavior, and what to do with Freud.

The humanities also registered the impact of radicalism; in history, exposure of the claims of value-free scholarship and the myth of the individual; in literary study, the mystique of the autonomous text and the imperative of dialectical criticism; in art history, the social determinants of production; in classical antiquity, slave society and the status of women; and in philosophy, self-externalization, reification, mystification, and other tendencies resulting in alienation. Education, too, took on a Marxist cast as conventional learning came to be seen as reproducing the social order. Biology was the only science covered, primarily to point out the dangers of genetic engineering, sociobiology, and reductionism.

In job-related disciplines, the influence was consistent with the emphasis on human beings as victims of power structures; criminology scrutinized the judicial system and peniteniary discipline; public health and medicine instructed readers in how to understand the corporization of hospitals and the struggle over expenditures; social work offered the potential of inducing the determining power of people rather than of prescribing regulations for the poor; and communications research revealed how advertising structures the social relations of consumption.

Some of these radical approaches to traditional disciplines would have been familiar to previous Lefts. Ethnic studies, however, as separate disciplines was entirely new in the academy. Black scholarship explored slave resistance and the problem of reconciling a class analysis with race, gender, and nationalism. Mexican-American and Puerto Rican studies discussed the political economy of migration in and out of the barrio. And Asian-American scholars addressed the question of ethnic and political identity on the part of a people almost entirely neglected in prior Marxist literature.

As the decade of the nineties got under way, some remaining Academic Leftists took up the cause of multiculturalism, a new orthodoxy on the campus that the press described as "PC" (politically correct). To be PC was to denounce Western culture from the top down until one found enclaves of third world ethnics in the ghettos of industrial society. Identifying with every color but white, multiculturists attacked racism, sexism, and DWEMism— partiality to dead, white, European males who wrote most of the books on a course's reading list. The non-WASP students demanded that education enhance their self-esteem and cultural identity, and faculty members who offended their sensibilities were often savaged for political incorrectness.

The spectacle of PC had no parallel in previous Lefts, whose heroes (Marx, Trotsky, Gramsci) believed in the value of classical education and the future of Western civilization. In the thirties, it will be recalled, intense debates broke out over cultural modernism and its relation to radicalism. What settled the debate was the profundity, not the politics, of a given author or painter. The battles that the *Partisan Review* had won half a century earlier appear to be almost lost on the contemporary campus, where PC has become a new loyalty test reminiscent of McCarthyism.

The politicization of the campus in the late eighties and nineties has puzzled those who wonder why American colleges seem to be radical while the rest of the world has turned more and more conservative. The Academic Left represents only a partial explanation, since some of its members, especially those associated with *Dissent*, have challenged the cult of multiculturalism as simply a drive toward domination in the name of education. But the assault on Western civilization began in the sixties, and hence the puzzlement. To the extent that the ideas of the New Left of the sixties have been discredited in world events in the last two decades, why are they now reemerging in the academic world? The answer seems to be structural. At present New Left veterans are tenured professors within the system and now have the means of expounding their ideas to a captive college audience. The New Left is an idea whose time has passed and whose power has come.

The phenomenon of the Feminist Left also lends itself to a structural explanation. How American women of the sixties generation came to liberate themselves and later enter the academy is one of the best success stories of the twentieth century. Its explanation can hardly be found in the writings of Marx and Engels, who forecast no advance in women's status as long as capitalist exchange values persisted; or in those of Gramsci, whose advice to the radical was to cease being rootless and return to one's native environment as an "organic intellectual." For American feminists there would be no going back, no return to traditional home and hearth.

The Feminist Left

The success of the women's movement that came out of the sixties may not seem so surprising when one considers that it did not have its initial impulse specifically in idealism or altruism, or in any sentiment that gives highest priority to the well-being of others. While SDS men were, in general, hopelessly trying to help the poor, homeless, jobless, and street youth, women in the organization were coming to feel that their first goal might be to help themselves. And with good reason. Although SDS had rejected authority, leadership, and hierarchies of all kinds, a silent gender discrimination mocked its egalitarian pretensions. Too often women's assignments consisted in little more than handing out coffee and doughnuts, stuffing envelopes, and taking dictation at the typewriter. Many SDS men showed sympathy for blacks and Vietnamese but ignored their own women except when they wanted to get laid or get fed. Women debated whether chauvinism antedated capitalism and whether women's real subordination would, therefore, continue despite the political outcome of their struggles. One SDS female recognized why women must have their way: "Our own comrades oppress us."[17]

The male-dominated SDS infrastructure became more pronounced when its members joined the civil rights movement and worked with SNCC. The black leader Stokely Carmichael provided the ultimate insult: "The only position for women in SNCC is prone." Women demanded that SDS clean up its sexism. When some males admitted their chauvinism but made no effort to amend their ways, a number of women concluded that such gender issues necessitated a break with SDS and the start of a new, autonomous struggle with its own goals. The decision to split occurred in 1967. Given the dismal future of a SDS having to contend with the Black Panthers and the communists, it could well have been the wisest political decision of the sixties generation.[18]

Much of the feminist ferment of the sixties followed from the publication of a literary bombshell, Betty Friedan's *The Feminine Mystique* (1963). Exploring "the problem that has no name," the restless unhappiness of middle-class housewives who supposedly had everything in the affluent fifties, Friedan brought to light the utter dullness and triviality of kitchen chores and the frustrations of being a dutiful parent while desiring, at the same time, a challenging career. The book made millions of women who felt similar stirrings feel less lonely, relieved their unspoken guilt, and restored their sense of self-worth. Soon new magazines like *Ms.* hit the newsstands, and a few women made the headlines by burning their bras in public. Suddenly all sexual conventions and traditional social roles seemed unbearable as women opened up to each other in small evening discussion groups while their husbands baby-sat the children and, noticing how late it was, made themselves a nightcap and went to bed alone. Before long America was asking itself the question Freud had pondered half a century earlier: "What does woman want?"[19]

Many women responding to Friedan's message were married, older, relatively well off; some with professional jobs had experienced the tension between work and family. More interested in women's rights than in radical causes that aimed to transform the "system," and somewhat like the earlier suffragettes, they believed constitutional reforms would give women the status and opportunities men enjoyed outside the home. They organized to pass an equal rights amendment (ERA) designed to ban sexual discrimination in employment, education, property settlements, exclusive men's clubs, and other areas that prevented their entry and advancement. The National Organization for Women (NOW) advocated easier access to contraceptives and the personal right to abortion, to maternity leaves without jeopardizing job security or seniority, tax deductions for child-care expenses, and job training programs for poor women. With the exception of the ERA, most of NOW's goals have been enacted into law.

Feminists marching on New York's Fifth Avenue to protest sexual discrimination and to demand "51 percent of everything." August 1977. (Bettmann Archive)

The Feminist Left, on the other hand, was more involved in women's personal liberation than in rights-based action. The younger liberationists emerged from the New Left and carried on the dissident style of sixties politics. At first less interested in public policy than in personal transformation, liberationists aimed at "consciousness raising" for men as well as for women. The Left feminists formed "rap groups" to share their grievances and to try to figure out how and why they had become, in Simone de Beauvoir's telling phrase, "the second sex," and found themselves confronting, in the words of the title of Elizabeth Janeway's book, "man's world, woman's place." Thus began the search for a feminist ideology, and many liberationists went to graduate school and entered the academic profession and the ministry to try to find it.[20]

The attempt to develop an ideology generated arguments that would continue to be debated and remain unresolved. Although most male New Leftists were convinced that Marx had the last word on the origins of human alienation, not all feminists were sure that he or Engels had a satisfactory explanation of the origins of women's oppression. Women may have been regarded in primitive society as species of property to be possessed, but why among some tribes and not others? Was women's subordinate status due to economics or to culture? Aside from theoretical issues involving the past, feminists debated whether socialism was a prerequisite for women's liberation. Some militants insisted that only the abolition of the nuclear family would free women; others believed the family could be structurally modified with more duties for men and more freedom and opportunities for women. A small faction of feminists opted for lesbianism and argued that all intimacy with men had to cease before male domination could be overcome. Liberationists were propelled into a debate over whether to exclude lesbians from the movement on the grounds that their life-style would endanger the movement's credibility with the public. The majority of liberationists stood behind the lesbians and affirmed the solidarity of all women victims of sex discrimination.

Other controversies waxed over issues of prostitution and pornography as evidence of women's exploitation as sexual objects.
The Moral Right regarded both as sinful temptations, the Feminist Left as realities that depended on capitalism. Women against
Pornography (WAP) insisted that *Playboy* and *Hustler* magazines
drove their readers to violence and rape and that male sexual
desire amounted to predatory aggression, advocated legal censorship of all pornography, and denied that pornography could be
distinguished from erotica. Other feminists saw censorship as a
threat to free speech and argued that taboos against sexual expression were traditionally used to suppress women. Max Eastman, an
early champion of feminism, may have well wondered what
would be the point of a Left without lust.[21]

The role of the academy in the survival of the Left is best
illustrated in the case of women radicals. Many women's rights
advocates entered professions like law and publishing; many
women's liberationists entered higher education as young assistant professors. Gaining tenure in a few years, a number won
fellowships and book awards and went on to become notable
scholars in their fields. Here arises one of the great ironies of the
Feminist Academic Left. Its success was made possible not by any
ideas emanating specifically from radical doctrines but instead
from conservative institutions relatively immune from the vicissitudes of public opinion. Although the hiring of women became
accepted in the sixties, in the long run it was not the "masses" but
the judicial system that pressured universities into establishing
equal opportunity policies and affirmative action programs. Indeed, the courts and the Civil Rights Commission engaged in the
very activity that the Left had always protested: social control by
means of close monitoring. Yet even though feminist academics
benefited from more rigorous implementation of the equal protection clause, few would go on to teach the importance of the Constitution or any institution or idea that had to do with liberalism
or conservatism. The Feminist Left had its own agenda.

Their first objective was to reclaim women's history by studying the plight of mothers, factory workers and secretaries, immi-

grant daughters and peasant wives, reformers and feminists. Less attention was given to the ideas held by outstanding women intellectuals; they were often considered a "social type" preoccupied with the single issue of gender. Women writers and intellectuals of the past are not depicted as searching for the meaning of existence but as protesting their powerlessness in a male-dominated world. Such a characterization may describe Simone de Beauvoir, Charlotte Gilman, and Jane Addams but not necessarily Simone Weil, Hannah Arendt, and Emily Dickinson.

Each feminist discipline had its own objectives. In political science, it was the investigation of women's voting behavior and a close tab on job discrimination in business, the military, and the academy. In philosophy, it was logical arguments for the right of abortion and an analysis of language as gendered discourse; in English, the "crises of male desire" in Freud, Thomas Mann, Robert Musil, and Shakespeare. The most researched discipline was history, especially social history. Here scholars studied the family, child rearing, marriage customs, and inheritance; premarital sexual practices; patriarchy, reproduction, and the sexual division of labor; the gender differences between preindustrial and industrial work; the impact of the typewriter; the separation of spheres. American historians, in particular debated whether it was more important to study political demands that had advanced the status of women, or cultural attitudes that retarded it and thus must be changed. Twentieth-century social science concepts like "networks" and "support systems" demonstrated how women found themselves united by shared experiences and turned to each other for emotional sustenance.[22]

The quest to find a "sisterhood" in history often led to a rarely perceived conflict between the aspirations of feminism and the presuppositions of socialism. If there was one thing feminists wanted to deny about women in the past, it was passivity. In Marx's theory of alienation, however, under conditions of private property and exchange value, history moved "behind the backs" of people who remained not so much inactive as unaware and therefore incapable of rising to consciousness. Some feminist scholars wanted to see women in the past, even sixteenth-century peasant women, as they saw themselves—fully aware and actively taking control of their lives. Women scholars seemed unable to decide whether their historical subjects were primarily passive victims or active agents. If passive, feminist claims to sisterhood consciousness were in doubt; if active, women's innocence was in doubt. How could women be depicted as consciously shaping their own lives without being in any way responsible for their subordinate status? Marx, it should be noted, saw nothing but oppression and alienation in the past and advised radicals to draw their "poetry" from the future. The sixties generation—and this characterized male historians as well—could look backward and still sing "We Shall Overcome!"

But certain theoretical problems failed to be overcome in practice. Nowhere was the dilemma better dramatized than in the "Sears case," a lawsuit filed by the government's Equal Employment Opportunity Commission against Sears, Roebuck and Company, which occasioned bitter academic controversy in the mid-eighties. The government's commission charged that statistics showing few women in commission-sales jobs constituted evidence of gender discrimination. Testifying for Sears, the historian Rosalind Rosenberg held that women traditionally preferred jobs less stressful than commission selling. In a countertestimony, the historian Alice Kessler-Harris reasserted the government's argument that women had always been available for such jobs and that their present absence could only mark "the essence of discrimination." A number of women scholars sided with Kessler-Harris and accused Rosenberg of betraying the cause of feminism. Yet in her own historical writings, which were cited in court, Kessler-Harris was closer to Rosenberg, depicting women as resenting "competitive" work and having to "rationalize their activities in terms of familiar humane and nurturing values"; only in her testimony did she agree with the commission that women have job preferences identical to men's.[23] In order to win such a case, must feminist scholars deny any difference between men and women in the name of equality? In order to show women workers in the past as resistant to capitalism, must they affirm differences to endow their subjects with a special identity? An awkward situation.

Theoretical dilemmas aside, the Feminist Left that came of age in the late sixties proved remarkable for its staying power. No other nonacademic Left in American history had lasted more than a decade. The women's movement survived even the conservative Reagan years of the eighties. Two explanations may account for this extraordinary achievement. First, the liberationists of the sixties avoided repeating the mistake of previous feminist movements by refusing to identify themselves with other ideological causes. Women reformers of the 1840s became caught up in the abolitionist movement, and the feminists of the Lyrical Left hitched their wagon to the star of socialism. Women activists of the sixties retained a commitment to civil rights and opposition to the Vietnam War, but the outcome of either cause would not determine the future of feminism. Liberationists wanted a movement of women, by women, for women. Moreover, they saw the handwriting on the wall sooner than did the male-oriented SDS. Instead of complaining about institutions and denouncing government, they decided to infiltrate institutions and work with government. Instead of carrying on the futility of a participatory democracy with the underclass, radicalized women went straight for what one called "the power grab." Whereas student demonstrators of the sixties threw their bodies against the bureaucratic structures of modern life, women activists later created their own bureaucracies and, with Title 9 of a 1972 federal law, established state boards of equal opportunity and enacted administrative codes to be supervised by feminist public office holders.[24]

In nineteenth-century Victorian America, most upper-middle-class women shunned politics as sordid with corruption and the stench of cigars. To the feminists of the later twentieth century, politics posed no threat to virtue or perfume. The "system women" took to politics like an army of *apparatchiks*. Publishing newsletters, lobbying elected officials, they issued resolutions, committee reports, and press releases, while holding annual conventions, rotating committee chairpersons, and seeking wealthy heiresses for contributions. If it could be said that feminist political activists made a revolution, it was through an elaborate system of rules and regulations that they bent to their own purposes.

Thus the feminist movement that emerged belatedly from the New Left of the sixties represents a curious exception. The beneficiaries of bureaucracy, women knew where to find power and how to use it in their own institutions. Another anomaly of the contemporary Left is that its feminist wing had found a home within the system.

The male counterparts in the Academic Left were not exactly innocent of the power realities of modern American life. When it came to writing about the American past, however, power and oppression seemed to have disappeared, as virtue and community emerged to ward off the evils of capitalism and liberal individualism. This strange reinterpretation of American history demands close scrutiny.

8

Poetry of the Past: The Rewriting of American History

> A teacher must either treat history as a catalogue, a record, a romance, or as an evolution. . . . He makes of his scholars either priests or atheists, plutocrats or socialists, judges or anarchists, almost in spite of himself. In essence incoherent and immoral, history had either to be taught as such—or falsified.
>
> Henry Adams, 1906

The Old and the New in New Left Historiography

Of all the academic disciplines influenced by New Left scholarship, the study of American history registered the greatest impact. Young radical professors had good reason to boast that "Marxism is the mainstream."[1] Several senior scholars elected as president of the Organization of American Historians represented Marxist, feminist, or radical dissident backgrounds. One was William Appleman Williams, whose works were discussed in chapter 6. Although highly influential, the genre of diplomatic history that Williams continued to write was scarcely original. In diplomatic history there was little that was "new" in New Left historiogra-

A former CP member as a youth, Theodore Draper became a historian critical of communism and other ideologies that distort the past. (Anthony Barnum)

phy. The critique of American expansionism and imperialism goes back to Charles Beard and the progressive school of history that had its heyday in the First World War era, and in the thirties progressives and Marxists depicted FDR's diplomacy as an instrument of Wall Street. Williams, Gabriel Kolko, and other New Left historians extended the progressive-Marxist line of reasoning to the cold war, interpreting the East-West confrontation as a struggle between "capitalism" and "socialism."

Three other subjects in American history were treated by New Left scholars in a manner not only new but bold and even bizarre: the history of the CP as an independent organization, the institution of slavery as a paternalistic community, and the American working class as a "class conscious" movement. The first subject deserves brief discussion; the latter two, involving theoretical issues in radical political thought, more extended examination.

When New Left historians reviewed each other's books on the history of the CP, praising one another and in a few instances claiming that a particular work was "the best" thing written on the subject, the praise was more than generational conceit, for young radical scholars had either to get around or to put down a truly superior senior former Old Left historian—Theodore Draper, the nemesis of anyone who had his facts wrong.

As a college student in the thirties Draper had belonged to the "front" organization the National Student League. During the era of the Popular Front he was foreign editor for the *New Masses*, and remained unshaken by the nonaggression pact of 1939, explaining it as "ruthless Soviet *Realpolitik.*" But with France reeling, Draper decided that the pact was no longer useful and that the Soviet Union had to disabuse itself of the illusion that Hitler would not turn eastward. When Moscow refused to concede that France's swift collapse posed a crisis, Draper fell out with the CP and was warned "that was the way Trotsky and all the renegades had gone." He served in the U.S. Army during the war and never forgot what his involvement with the CP had meant. "The lesson, I told myself, was to think for myself and never again get caught in the coils of a party line. Never again was I able to join a party or even a group of any kind."[2]

In the Eisenhower fifties Draper went through the files of every available document related to the history of the American Communist party. He was the first to examine its nineteenth-century socialist-anarchist background, the "riddle" of Reed's relation to the Comintern, and the CP's succumbing to Stalinism and to manipulation by Moscow in the late twenties. His two magisterial volumes *The Roots of American Communism* (1957) and *American Communism and Soviet Russia* (1960) were favorably reviewed and praised for their scholarly objectivity.

Two decades later young radical scholars gave the Academic Left's version of the history of the CP in a series of monographs. The new version, which Draper would challenge in a devastating critique in the *New York Review of Books,* asks that the CP be understood primarily as a "distinctively American" organization, one whose members took their own initiative on political matters involving their own "social struggles," not necessarily related to Moscow's directives. The new version sought to deemphasize the institutional nature of the CP, which would have to be acknowledged as authoritarian and subservient to the Kremlin, and focused instead on "social history" in order to highlight the daily lives of the rank and file. Whether intentionally or inadvertently, this new perspective also meant a new definition of what constitutes the Left. Previously the term implied rebellion, risk, romance—Reed riding with Villa, Eastman smuggling Lenin's testament out of Russia, Dos Passos serving with the Loyalists in Spain, Dewey defending Trotsky in Mexico, Savio marching on Sproul Hall, Hayden evading the cops in Chicago. With academics turning the idea of the Left into a social species, the new scholarship romanticized CP members as solid, hardworking Americans who remained faithful to the cause no matter what the new party line. The hero as obedient functionary![5]

That some CP members became heroes to some on the Academic Left is perhaps not surprising. What *is* is the way in which certain people in the American past who were victims of injustice have reemerged in the new scholarship as moral heroes possessed of special virtues. Specifically, this reorientation involved the study of slaves and workers. More broadly, it called into question the legacy of certain Old Left scholars who had come to the conclusion, in the forties and fifties, that America was a liberal society shaped by a Lockean mentality. One of the ironies is that the Academic Left drew upon the writings of two European philosophers, Hegel and Gramsci, in an effort to counter the history of America's liberal heritage. Yet Hegel and Gramsci themselves

Antonio Gramsci, important Marxist theoretician, the first to explain the role of the intellectuals in forming counterhegemonic "blocs" to win over the minds of the masses. Relatively unknown at the time of his death in 1937, he became one of the most influential thinkers for America's Academic Left.

saw American liberalism as real, the natural result of a frontier society without an aristocracy ("viscous parasitic sedimentations") or a peasantry, but with an environment of material abundance, restless mobility, and other activist and acquisitive tendencies that prevented the young nation from becoming conscious of its identity. The historiography of the Academic Left attempted to give America a new ideological identity. In doing so, veterans of the New Left could compensate for their political frustrations. Having failed to transform contemporary America by reaching the working class, they could rewrite history to speak for an older working class. Having failed to secure an alliance with black Americans to rescue them from racism, they could rewrite the history of slavery to save blacks from capitalism.

Historians of the Academic Left could hardly deny that liberalism prevailed in contemporary American culture. But a number drew on Gramsci's idea of "hegemony," convinced that society's prevalent values are part of the "false consciousness" that must be extirpated by winning over the hearts and minds of the populace. Ironically many American social historians believed that history should be studied from the bottom depths, whereas, as we noted above, Gramsci believed it more important to study history from the top down to penetrate such superstructural phenomena as education, art, and philosophy, in addition to popular culture. Whereas historians became, as we shall see, preoccupied with the language of politics, Gramsci insisted that people's real conception of the world is found not in their verbal affirmations but in their practical activity. And whereas American historians would claim that workers in the past had the potential for breaking the spell of hegemony, Gramsci had seen no such possibility in Italy's history. He believed that Italy's past failures at transforming consciousness could be overcome in the future if the nation's intellectuals abandoned their cosmopolitan aloofness and merged with the masses as "organic intellectuals." The American historians' answer to Gramsci was simply to enter the academic profession and rewrite the past.[4]

Let us follow Gramsci's advice and begin with the superstructure, that is, the ideological "problem" of America as perceived by generations of American intellectuals.

The conservative philosopher George Santayana used to console himself with the notion that America would find its soul only when it had lost its mind. More bemused than exasperated, Santayana believed the American mind had come to be dominated by two deeply ingrained but vaguely understood ideas: liberalism and Protestantism. Liberalism had given the American male the inalienable right to be free, become rich, and escape his marital vows, while Calvinism ensured that he could do none of these without experiencing guilt.[5]

Santayana was not the only American theorist troubled by the thought that liberalism as the pursuit of self-interest is both the essential principle of America and its essential problem. John Adams and the framers of the Constitution worried that political man might be motivated by "avarice" and "self-love." Tocqueville and Thoreau saw in the American character an "egoism" that refused to "simplify" its desires, and Veblen concluded that "pecuniary" norms of waste and consumption were eroding the older ideas of work and production. Contemporary radical scholars complain of the "possessive individualism" and "culture of narcissism" said to be the dominant traits of liberal capitalist society. Santayana would have agreed with these radical assessments, if not their causal assumptions. His response to liberal America was to seek refuge in an Italian convent, where he spent many of his remaining years wondering how self-government could teach man to govern the self.[6]

We can hardly be surprised by the contemporary lamentations of the Left. In an earlier chapter we saw how an older generation of historians spent much of their academic careers pondering the dilemmas of liberal America. Richard Hofstadter's *The American Political Tradition* (1948) might be regarded as the first statement of the "consensus" theory of American historiography, founded on an ideology of economic individualism that bound Americans to the values of competitive capitalism and made America "a democracy of cupidity rather than a democracy of fraternity." This essentially "Lockean ethos," as Louis Hartz cogently argued, also created what the Old Left called "American exceptionalism," the conviction that America was unique and could not be comprehended by categories found in European political philosophies, or at least not by philosophies that replaced property with class and economic interests with political ideals.[7]

The conception of a liberal "synthesis" was challenged in the 1960s and 1970s by a new generation of scholars, among them Marxists and republicans. These two groups had little in common save the conviction that America is not unique and that liberalism does not explain America's historical development. Whether drawing on the processes of class formation or the principles of classical traditions, both Marxists and republicans used European ideas to challenge the liberal consensus and propose new ways of interpreting American history. As a means of questioning the conventional view that America has been permeated by capitalist values, Marxists imported the idea of social class and republicans the idea of civic virtue. The Marxist perspective suggested that America had an aristocracy capable of resisting capitalism and a working class capable of achieving "class consciousness." Republicans proposed that America absorbed Old World classical republicanism and its conflicting juxtaposition of "virtue" and "commerce."

Ignoring Tocqueville, the first theorist of "American exceptionalism," New Left scholars drew on Marx and Engels, Gramsci, and Hegel for their analytical tools. Playing down Locke, who made Americans "intelligent without poetry" (Emerson), republicans drew on Montesquieu, James Harrington, and Machiavelli, who gave Italians "intelligence without property" (Edmund Burke).[8] The new postliberal generation of historians also operated from entirely new presuppositions about human nature that would have astonished Marx and the *Federalist* authors alike. Marxists and republicanists both assumed that ideas and culture are more important than interests and power as determinants of action. They both suggested, moreover, that such ideas can best be appreciated by understanding what the subjects of their studies were protesting. Marxists emphasize protests against economic exploitation; republicans, the protests against political corruption.[9] Marxists and republicans similarly joined together in arguing that the new way to write social and intellectual history is to pay close attention to "language," whether the language of labor or the language of politics. Finally Marxists and republicans were both pleased to discover in early American history a moral culture of wholesome comrades and active citizens whose sense of solidarity and community helped resist the supposedly corrosive effects of liberal capitalism. Thus they somehow found what Tocqueville and Orestes A. Brownson, Emerson and Thoreau, James Fenimore Cooper and Melville, Veblen and Henry Adams, Beard and Lippmann, and almost all other American intellectuals, including expatriates like Santayana and even émigrés like Arendt and Marcuse, so consistently failed to find in America. How was this accomplished? Their discovery, the Marxists claimed, comes from doing history "from the bottom up." Let us begin, then, with those at the very bottom, the American slaves, or the world according to Eugene D. Genovese, where we get to the bottom by way of the top, the planter aristocracy.

Hegel's "Lordship and Bondage"

Genovese's bold scholarship touched off an extensive debate over the nature of the antebellum South. Older historians like Hofstadter and Hartz viewed the South as subject to the ubiquitous forces of liberal capitalism, but Genovese insisted that we give credence to the claims of southern culture to be more than a mirror image of the North. Offering what might be called his own version of "southern exceptionalism," Genovese depicted the South as a genuine aristocracy consisting of a stable, hierarchical social structure guided by the sentiments of paternalism and benevolence.[10] His thesis was challenged in its details,[11] but it is the doctrine that inspired the thesis that needs to be questioned. For Marx no theory had any value beyond its efficacy in transforming the world, and the watchwords of Marxism are not stability, hierarchy, and order but conflict, progress, reason, and liberation. Where, then, do we see the Marxist ambition of changing the

Eugene Genovese, the historian who brought Marx, Hegel, and Gramsci to bear upon American history. (Andrew Doyle)

world by interpreting it more correctly through a privileged ideological perspective? We see it not so much in Genovese's Marxism as in his use of Hegel and Gramsci.

In his long-awaited and prizewinning book *Roll, Jordan, Roll,* Genovese set out to challenge the view that the plantation system utterly destroyed the slaves' culture and reduced them to a state of helpless dependency. That view had been put forth in the fifties by Stanley M. Elkins,[12] but Genovese's work even questioned, at least by implication, the conventional interpretation of slavery as

the tragedy of American liberalism. The "whole commerce between master and slave," confessed Jefferson, "is a perpetual exercise in the most boisterous passions, the most unremitting despo-
tism on the one part and degrading submission on the other."[13]
Although one would not expect to find a Marxist scholar helping
liberals assuage their propensity to feelings of guilt, Genovese
provided some relief, if not exculpation, by asking us to view
slavery as irony as well as tragedy. Thus he questioned whether it
was theoretically possible to impose absolute obedience on slaves
and at the same time expect them to be responsible and productive in their daily lives. The entire edifice of his argument derives
from the dubious thesis—first spelled out in Hegel's discourse
"Lordship and Bondage"—that masters want and desperately
need recognition from their subjects. This need, Genovese argued,
mitigated the brutal conditions of slavery, forcing plantation owners to be paternalistic in their concern for the affections of their
own slaves, who in turn could manipulate the conditions of mutual dependency. "To the idea of reciprocal duties they added
their own doctrine of reciprocal rights," Genovese claimed. "To
the tendency to make them creatures of another's will they coun-
terposed a tendency to assert themselves as autonomous human
beings." The case for the viability of slave culture rests on the
Hegelian premise that in order to be recognized one must recognize the other in return and that man's highest aim is to refuse to
live by a will other than his own. "The slaves," Genovese wrote,
"proved themselves good Hegelians."[14]

Genovese's thesis influenced some eminent American historians, most notably David Brion Davis. In *The Problem of Slavery
in the Age of Revolution*, Davis claimed that Hegel's account of
master-slave relations offers "the most profound analysis of slavery ever written." It might be mentioned that Hegel's "Lordship
and Bondage" is not about slavery as such or about the objective
conflict in master-slave relations. "Lordship and Bondage" is
about the inner processes of the reflective mind trying to free
itself from its "doubleness" and the subjective conflict within the
alienated self that requires recognition for its identity. For Hegel

the question was whether the self could constitute itself in the act of observing its own estrangement, a feat that implies that self-consciousness is introspectively discoverable.[15] But the deeper problem is how philosophical speculation can be verified historically. Like Genovese, Davis found himself absorbed in the "intricate dialectic of dependence and independence," a process that results from the master's need to have his identity acknowledged in the eyes of the slave. In the struggle for recognition, the slave possesses the genuine potential for freedom, while the master becomes dependent on the slave as the mirror of his self-affirmation. Both Genovese and Davis were also convinced that a slave could, in theory, win his freedom through the self-actualizing feats of human labor. "Unlike the master," wrote Davis, "the slave is not a consumer who looks upon 'things' as merely a means of satisfying desires. The products he creates become an objective reality that validates the emerging consciousness of his subjective human reality." By locating consciousness in labor, Genovese and Davis were able to turn the theories of both Hegel and Marx to their purpose and arrive at a solution to the problem of slavery that is profoundly consoling. For in the beginning the master possesses knowledge, and the slave submits to the master's status by working for him. Through his labor the slave reshapes the world and acquires knowledge in the process, whereas the master begins to lose knowledge because he no longer puts it to productive use. In the end the master has only his possessions, while the slave has now acquired the knowledge that will liberate him from bondage. Thus it "is not fanciful," concluded Davis, ". . . to see in Hegel's thoughts a message to slaves and the powerless."[16]

The problem with this philosophical solution to servitude is that the exact opposite seems to have happened in history, at least in American history as closely observed by such writers on nineteenth-century society as Tocqueville, Melville, and Thoreau. In *Democracy in America*, Tocqueville offered the disturbing perception that work actually limits rather than liberates those engaged in toil, because the division of labor renders workers less resourceful and more dependent.

At the same time that industrial science constantly lowers the standing of the working class, it raises that of the masters. While the workman confines his intelligence more and more to studying one single detail, the master daily embraces a vast field of vision, and his mind expands as fast as the other's contracts. Soon the latter will need no more than bodily strength without intelligence, while to succeed the former needs science and almost genius. The former becomes more and more like the administrator of a huge empire, and the latter more like a brute.[17]

How is it possible to know that the American slave deferred to his master because he possessed knowledge, as opposed to power, and that the master in turn depended on the slave's recognition for his identity as a social being? To understand master-slave relations as a concrete historical phenomenon, and not simply as a deduction from the dialectic, we would need numerous angles of insight. We would need to know, first, the world as the slave saw it and the world as the master saw it; we would also need to know the world as the slave thought the master saw it and the world as the master thought the slave saw it; and then we would need to know what the slave assumed that the master assumed about what he, the slave, was actually thinking apart from his behavior. Melville attempted to explore this solipsistic nightmare in "Benito Cereno," a short story that in some respects presages Ralph Ellison's *Invisible Man.* The story's hero, the "benevolent" and "charitable" Captain Delano, possesses all the virtues Genovese attributed to aristocracy, yet Delano's genteel moral qualities render him incapable of penetrating the slave's mentality. "Benito Cereno" is a cautionary tale about the ethical attitudes—one is tempted to say "false consciousness"—of the ruling classes, who continually fail to understand that between truth and its perception stands the sin of pride.[18]

Caution is needed not only in using Hegel but also in using Gramsci. As originally conceived by the Italian Marxist, "hegemony" refers to the process by which a ruling class projects its values on lower classes in order to influence them to see the world as it does and to accept that worldview as natural. And Gramsci specifically cited Fordism and Taylorism as examples of how an industrial elite gains legitimacy and domination by disseminating its own morality and social philosophy. Can the concept of hegemony be made to explain the presumed social-psychological bond between master and slave in an aristocratic culture? Hegemony is based on consent, however false; slavery, on coercion, however benign. Hegemony exemplifies the deliberate permeation of lower-class consciousness with ruling-class convictions; aristocracy recognizes distinct class divisions with each class having its own peculiar values. Hegemony describes the standardization, uniformity, and homogeneity of a bourgeois culture coming to be dominated by "Puritanical" efficiency;[19] aristocracy prides itself on the differences, gradations, and hierarchies of a life of ease and refinement. Hegemony enables the ruling class to impose its power by imparting its culture to all others; aristocracy rules by maintaining a separate culture that is not meant to be imitated by others. Surely plantation owners had no interest in having slaves take on their worldview and emulate their life-styles. On the contrary, masters wanted their slaves to do precisely what they themselves refused to do—labor with their hands.

Marxists assume that labor is not only the source of value but also the means by which man overcomes his alienated condition. Strange, then, that they seem to give so little attention to the fate of a race of people who were taught to believe that work was not a spur to human development but the rightful burden of an inferior class. The different attitudes toward work that prevailed in the South and the North impressed Tocqueville. "On the left bank of the Ohio work is connected with the idea of slavery; but on the right with well being and progress; on the one side it is degrading, but on the other honorable." Tocqueville knew a good deal about aristocracies, and he could see the vices as well as the virtues of the plantation master. "The Southerner loves greatness, luxury, renown, excitement, enjoyment, and, above all, idleness; nothing forces him to make an effort in order to live, and having no necessary work, he slumbers, not even attempting to do anything useful."[20] Genovese, in contrast, seemed to see only the southerner's virtues, and he asked us to believe that the slaves also saw them. "They by no means deceived themselves about the brutal and seamy side of their masters' lives. But when they expressed admiration for the aristocratic features of southern life, they set a high standard for themselves. They noted that the more patriarchal masters could display grace, dignity, courtesy, and coolness under fire. Why should the slaves not have admired these qualities?"[21] Perhaps because, as Emerson might have replied, slavery, like poverty, makes aristocratic virtues "a luxury . . . at a market almost too high for humanity."[22] Grace, courtesy, and other such modes of conduct represented a leisure-class culture that would not stoop to labor, and those qualities reflected a relaxed life-style that may only have served to confirm in the slaves' minds that their own field and housework was irksome, unworthy, and disgraceful, thus reinforcing compulsions of submission by a culture of shame. The distinct roles that plantation owners wanted to sustain excluded the slave from much hope of changing his status. Nor can those roles be easily mediated by Hegelian negations and transformations, for Hegel insisted that only subjects who faced death by risking their lives could liberate themselves—small comfort to those who knew from experience how heavy and how crushing the chains of oppression really were. In denying black slaves what free white workers could enjoy under the real "hegemony" of northern capitalism—the possibility of individual gain by means of productive activity—the plantation system denied American slaves the vital sentiments of emulation and self-esteem, emotions stimulated by the comparative self-evaluations of free men and women in a society of opportunity and potential reward.[23]

The thesis that master and slave shared a culture because each required the other's recognition fails to consider that slaves were not free subjects, and one can only wonder what value lay in recognition by a slave whose response might have been more feigned than felt. The thesis also ignores the possibility that plantation owners sought confirmation from those above or equal to their status. Francis J. Grund, an Austrian who spent ten years in the United States and studied closely what passed for aristocracy in America, perceived a sang-froid indifference toward the lower orders:

> In all countries in which there exists an hereditary, wealthy nobility, there exists a sort of good-will towards the inferior classes which leads to the relation of patron and client, and through which many an apparent injustice is smoothed over by liberality and kindness; but the mere moneyed aristocracy which is establishing itself in this country, however you may disguise the fact by cunning and soft speeches, or an hyperbolical affectation for republicanism, *hates* the industrious masses over whom it strives to elevate itself. . . .
>
> Your aristocracy, therefore, has not the power of dazzling the lower classes with that air of self-possession and dignity by which gentlemen of rank are at once recognized in Europe. On the contrary, the manners of your rich people in their intercourse with the less successful aspirants to fortune are markedly coarse and vulgar, in order, I believe, to give the latter to understand that they are sufficiently *independent*—that, I think, is the word—not to *care* for their opinion.[24]

Grund did see plantation owners treating slaves with "humanity and kindness," though not from any conscious need for external recognition and identity.[25] In Frederick Law Olmsted's *The Cotton Kingdom*, we grasp why this was so and why masters and slaves inhabited two different mental worlds. Olmsted visited southern plantations to confirm for himself that the "advantages accruing from slavery" could be easily assumed because slaves were "forced into intercourse with a superior race and made subject to its example." But he found that his assumption was wrong—yet so deep-seated that he would not reconsider it until after a year's observation and reflection. His doubts began when he examined "the home of a large and virtuous white family" but saw there little "association" between black slaves and white owners. Indeed, the overseer had no close acquaintance with slaves, and the owner often did not know their names and occasionally could not even tell if the "chattels" he met on the road belonged to him or his neighbors. Olmsted commented on the slaves' religion and work habits, but he saw that their "religious exercises are almost the only habitual recreation not purely sensual, from steady dull labor, in which the negroes are permitted to indulge, and generally all other forms of mental enjoyment are discouraged." Although slaves may have acquired the "shibboleths of Christianity" from their masters, "much less did the slaves have an opportunity to cultivate their minds by intercourse with other white people." Olmsted's discovery that slavery had deprived black people of "all the usual influences which tend to nourish the moral and develop the intellectual faculties"—the opposite of his original belief—was, he wrote, "unexpected and painful" to him.[26]

Little of the dismay experienced by Grund, Olmsted, Tocqueville, and others appears in the works of those contemporary historians who approach the problem of servitude and authority by asking us to believe in the qualities of a leisure class whose pretensions offended many nineteenth-century writers. At times Genovese could even grow rhapsodic about his gentry planters, as though we should forget all that Emerson told us about the corruptions of aristocratic idleness and luxury. "If we blind ourselves to everything noble, virtuous, honest, decent, and selfless in a ruling class," Genovese asked, "how do we account for its hegemony?"[27] Paine believed Burke's glorification of the British aristocracy was merely a product of his own imagination. "He pities the plumage, but forgets the dying bird," Paine said of Burke, and he "kisses the aristocratical hand that hath purloined him from himself."[28] When Jefferson asked Adams whether America could produce a "natural" aristocracy based on "virtue" and "talent," Adams replied that all aristocracies are only one-tenth talent and nine-tenths tinsel.[29] The antifederalists also distrusted the "wellborn" and "able," as did the Jacksonians and other democratic elements.[30] Presumably Marxist historians want to save the slave from capitalism by consigning him to the better, kinder world of an aristocracy whose power is not subjected to critical analysis but is treated as legitimate authority because of its purported superior moral qualities. But one can only wonder whether the slave endowed the planter class with the right to govern or whether he submitted because he feared the consequences of not submitting. Hegel's wonderful dialectic on the presumed reversal of relations between master and slave does nothing to relieve us of Simone Weil's deeper and more painful insights into the real meaning of oppression.[31]

In Marxian analysis political ideas derive from the structure of the economic system, which in turn is determined by labor relations and the mode of production. Whether or not the economic structure created an aristocratic culture in the South is an issue that historians will continue to debate, and Genovese's stimulating scholarship established the agenda for that debate. Yet there remains another side of the southern mind that drew its ideas not from economic conditions but from political philosophy, not from an aristocratic hegemony but from a Jeffersonian heritage. Louis Hartz brilliantly anatomized the schizoid thinking of John C. Calhoun and other southern intellects. When defending slavery, Calhoun proclaimed the South an "organic" society rich with feudal solidarity and paternalism. When defending the right of nullification and secession, he cited Locke's argument that society is a "compact," invoked the Declaration of Independence on the right of revolution, and even concocted the mechanical devices of a "concurrent majority" in order to demand that interests be given greater representation than people.[32] If we blind ourselves to all that was desperately liberal in the southern mind, how do we explain its agony?

The same liberal provenance is found in the northern antislavery movement. Abolitionism evolved from political and religious convictions rooted in the Declaration and the Puritan jeremiad. Yet these deep currents of liberalism and Calvinism are scarcely acknowledged in Eric Foner's *Free Soil, Free Labor, Free Men.* Here we have another text that, while excellent in its own right, is written by a Marxist who cannot write Marxist history in a way that establishes the validity of Marxism. Indeed, the popular concept of "free labor" and "free soil" was part of the American

Lockean sentiment, which held that because man "mixes" his labor with the materials of the earth he is entitled to the fruits of his toil and access to nature.[33] Foner conceded that the antislavery cause expressed "the middle class goal of economic independence."[34] Had Foner probed more closely his central concept of "free labor" as expounded by its most influential spokesman, Abraham Lincoln, the historian of northern antislavery might have been able to inform the historian of southern slavery why aristocracies exploit and oppress. The Lockean-Calvinist conviction that "the Fall" condemned man to work gave Lincoln an answer to a problem that even Marx was unable to resolve.[35] "When . . . in consequence of the first transgression, *labor* was imposed on the race, as a *penalty*—a curse—we find the first born man—the first heir of the curse—was a 'tiller of the ground.' " For Lincoln the religious origins of human toil, and not man's alienation from the means of production, explain why man has no love for labor and why he imposes it on others, however "decent" and "selfless" he may see himself. "As labor is the common *burthen* of our race, so the effort of *some* to shift their share of the burthen on to the shoulder of *others* is the great, durable curse of the race. Originally a curse for transgression upon the whole race, when, as by slavery, it is conceived on a part only, it becomes the double-refined curse of God upon his creatures." While seeing slavery as "sin," Lincoln nevertheless believed, along with Locke and the Puritans, that it was labor that gave meaning to life and dignity to the worker. "I want everyman to have a chance—and I believe a black man is entitled to it—in which he can better his condition—when he may look forward and hope to be a hired laborer this year and the next, work for himself afterwards, and finally to hire men to work for him. This is the true system."[36]

To the Marxist, of course, Lincoln's "true system"—otherwise known as capitalism—is simply part of the problem. Yet Lincoln wanted to evoke in American slaves the deepest value at the core of all his convictions, the very idea that the virtuous and noble southern aristocracy denied black Americans—ambition.[37]

The New Labor History

The values of ambition, enterprise, and opportunity are precisely the values that the new labor historians refuse to ascribe to the American working class. What is denied is not so much the presence of these values in the early-nineteenth-century work force as their indigenous origin in the workers' own desires. Workers are born free, it would seem, but everywhere they become victims of "social control." Having been told that slaves were actually more free than we or they had reason to believe, we are now told that workers were less free than they themselves were aware. Education, religion, and other agencies of culture instilled in workers the new industrial habits of discipline and obedience, thereby deflecting their potential for radical resistance. Such controlling institutions were "not a capitalist plot," we are told, but simply the outcome of "new relations of production." If aristocratic society was benign, industrial society is bewitching.[38]

The new labor historians who came to prominence in the Academic Left were determined to refute the liberal interpretation that drew both on Tocqueville's insights about the individualistic nature of American society and on the John Commons-Selig Perlman interpretation of the conservative nature of the American working class. Studying workers in relation to their union's place in the labor market, Commons and Perlman concluded that workers' consciousness would evolve no further than "economism," an immediate, practical concern for "wage and job control." But if this is what the worker may want, what he needs, according to the "intellectual," is socialism. In his famous debate with Samuel Gompers, it will be recalled, Morris Hillquit refused to specify an "end" or "ultimate goal" of socialism other than to say that the socialists' demands went "further" and "higher" than those of rival workers' organizations. The basic difference was, Hillquit declared, "a quantitative one—that the Socialist Party wants more than the American Federation of Labor."[39] More of what?

Herbert G. Gutman's *Work, Culture, and Society* was hailed by

Herbert Gutman, the influential historian who pioneered the turn to the new labor history. (Arthur Wang)

David Montgomery and many others as offering a compelling answer to the Commons-Perlman thesis. Gutman has "provided thick descriptions, where others had offered ideological formulas," acclaimed Montgomery.[40] These descriptions reveal workers actively shaping their own destinies by engaging in political struggles, using native religious ideas and symbols to protest injustices, and nourishing their own "preindustrial" values—rooted in ethnic and kinship networks—to resist the new compulsions of time and work imposed by the modern culture of industrial capitalism.[41] Gutman's scholarship is seminal, but is it radical? He told us that American workers feared "dependency and centralization," ridiculed Andrew Carnegie's "Gospel of Wealth," and invoked the Jeffersonian values of the Declaration. Thus history "from the bottom up" has seemingly brought forth a Vernon L. Parrington in overalls. Gutman credited the labor leader Joseph McDonnell for forging progressive reforms and anticipating the twentieth-century welfare state. To which one must say, "Welcome to 'the vital center.' " A liberal historian can hardly be surprised to discover the Social Gospel being invoked to condemn capitalist greed. What would come as a surprise would be to discover that resistance to new industrial work routines represented a conscious rejection of capitalism on the part of the working class, and not simply a reluctance to undergo the painful ordeal of change. "Thick descriptions" are no substitute for searching analyses of workers' motives and aspirations. Whereas Commons and Perlman determined—like Veblen and Werner Sombart—what workers wanted, Gutman dramatized what workers did, as though their "preindustrial" values blessed them with an autonomous culture.[42] But let us be truly radical and go to the root of things and ask whether the new social historians have anything new to say about the problem of class.

Avoiding that difficult issue, Gutman seemed to assume, like many American labor historians, that E. P. Thompson definitively resolved the issue of class in his monumental *The Making of the English Working Class.* In his preface Thompson insisted that class is a "relationship" that develops, not a "thing" that can be defined and analyzed as a static phenomenon. "For I am convinced that we cannot understand class unless we see it as a social and cultural formation, arising from the processes which can only be studied as they work themselves out over a considerable period."[43] But to insist that something can be explained only in relation to something else, and that it has the essential character of a "process," is elusive wordplay that misleads us into thinking that if we simply watch something develop we shall understand it. Now, obviously Thompson meant that we should study workers in the context of their ongoing activities. But one wonders why the term "class" is more useful than, say, "group" or "faction." To argue that class is a "process" experiencing its "formation" is merely to say that something is happening to it without saying what it happening or why, or what exactly it is that experiences what is happening when it is being formed. "Where there is a process," R. G. Collingwood observed, "there is something which undergoes the process; and it is often possible to know what it is that can undergo a certain process even without knowing what the process is."[44] What does the working class undergo when it undergoes a process?

A new generation of young, able American social historians adopted Thompson's idiom in order to try to move beyond the liberal consensus theory and to prove that the American working class held values and attitudes considerably different from the dominant capitalist ideology. In Michael H. Frisch and Daniel J. Walkowitz's recent anthology, *Working-Class America*, we encounter the terms "class formation," "moral economy," "social transformation," "work culture," "linguistic socialization," "defensive insularity," "artisan rituals," "plebeian culture," "class conflict," "class solidarity," and other expressions that supposedly prove that this generation of scholars has overcome the "narrower scope" of the Commons-Perlman school by viewing "class as a set of changing historical relationships and not as a fixed group stratification—as a process, not as a series of results."[45] All the essays were written with intelligence, compassion, and a sense of the complexity of workers' attitudes. The real question is whether the authors, inspired by Thompson's talismanic vocabulary, faced directly the old dilemma that led many liberal scholars to become sadder but wiser historians of consensus—America is a class society without class consciousness.

The fifties generation eschewed the concept of class, seeing it as part of the baggage of Marx's "labor metaphysic," to use C. Wright Mills's dismissive term.[46] To reject Marx's idea of class, however, is by no means to suggest that class conflict does not exist. Indeed, it is incorporated into the very structure of the Constitution, which was designed to function precisely by virtue of competing factions all pursuing similar material interests, factions themselves originating in unequal property relations. Marx, however, distinguished "contradiction" (*Widerspruch*) from other related terms such as "conflict" and "antagonism" to insist that, among other things, industrial workers would someday reach a stage of consciousness that ultimately involves the antithesis, and hence the "negation," of bourgeois society.[47] Engels, writing on the English working class, believed he saw this happening before his very eyes. "The bourgeoisie has more in common with every other nation of the earth than with the workers in whose midst it lives. The workers speak other dialects, have other thoughts and ideals, other customs and moral principles, a different religion and other politics than those of the bourgeoisie."[48] The new American social historians may well argue that the working class took the common political and religious values of the middle class and turned them to different ends. To make that argument convincing, however, they would have to demonstrate that different uses of the same values resulted in different qualities of consciousness, that such transformed values offered not only a complaint against capitalism but also a "contradiction" of it, that the American worker wanted, in short, something other than what the middle class had, and that he therefore escaped the obsession that Marxists regard as liberalism's curse on humanity—"possessive individualism."[49]

All that we really find in *Working-Class America*, however, is that the individual's needs are expressed collectively through organized power. Thus female department store workers struggled to achieve some measure of decision making in the workplace; the Knights of Labor considered turning to the political state; Pittsburgh workers found an outlet for their frustrations in mass entertainments; the American Federation of Labor engaged briefly in "trade union evangelism"; Sidney Hillmann prepared the Amalgamated Clothing Workers for the New Deal; and New York's Irish-American transportation workers had support from both the Communist party and veterans of the Irish Republican Army in their effort to react "to their plight not as isolated individuals but as part of a self-conscious, structured movement." Although we are told that workers were neither passive, individualistic, nor materialistic, we still wonder whether they expressed what Engels called "other thoughts and ideals" distinct from those of the middle class. One of the demands of Irish-American motormen was that workers not "be discriminated against when they take off special holidays such as May 1, St. Patrick's Day, etc."[50] I'll drink to that.

The new social historians assume that American workers wanted a noncompetitive society, where class solidarity would protect them from the pernicious influence of liberalism. In fact, it is some of the historians who yearn for such a society. Sean Wilentz, one of the historians brave enough to take on the problem of class consciousness, believed he found a key to understanding the deepest aspirations of American workers by turning to the advice given by a historian of modern France. Wilentz argued that we can use William Sewell's methodology, "the language of labor," to discover how workers employed a rhetoric that offered "a complete counter system to industrial capitalism,' one that would honor labor rather than property, useful work rather than social privilege, fraternity rather than selfish competition." Wilentz found New York's union journeymen in the Jacksonian era offering a similar counterideology based "on older ideals of harmony and fraternity but containing a thorough critique of the inequities of capitalism. . . . Furthermore, the class consciousness of the most active entrepreneurs was not some fixed liberal 'bourgeois' outlook; in defense of the emerging order, the entrepreneurs also wished to vindicate commonwealth, virtue, and independence."[51]

The difficulty with the "language of labor" analysis is the assumption that political language explains political conduct. That assumption was rejected by the farmers, and, by the time of the Jacksonian era when "class consciousness" was supposedly being reformulated, Tocqueville concluded that the *Federalist* authors were right to believe that no group or faction, whether capital or labor, could be counted on to pursue disinterested political ideas, especially the ideas of classical republicanism that American historians have embraced. In particular, Americans did not think that "virtue" and "commerce" were in conflict. "No longer do ideas, but interests only, form the links between men, and it would seem that human opinions were no more than a sort of mental dust open to the wind on every side and unable to come together and take shape."[52] Wilentz, however, concluded that American workers remained untouched by the "fixed, liberal, 'bourgeois' outlook" simply because they talked of harmony and solidarity. Focusing solely on speech, language, and rhetoric, he discovered that both the American worker and the entrepreneur were at heart republican humanists dedicated to "commonwealth, virtue, and independence." Assuming that language reveals motive and intent, Wilentz observed, "As they spoke of independence, the artisans also shied away from endorsing the pursuit of self-interest for its own sake."[53] Should we not expect to do so when speaking on such patriotic holidays as the Fourth of July? When we ask for evidence of what workers wanted, and not simply for accounts of the patriotic rhetoric they used, we find that their behavior contradicted their language. For it appears that workers did not, in fact, consistently practice republicanism and subordinate their private interests to the public good, the "commonwealth." The New York journeymen insisted "that they be paid," as Wilentz acknowledged, "the full value of their labor—a price they alone, and not the market, could fix."[54] However high-minded the language, it seems that workers shared with capitalists the desire to control markets and fix prices. So much for "virtue."

Thus far these American labor historians have taken us three steps backward. Unable to show that workers are radical, such historians try to prove that their behavior is ethical (E. P. Thompson's "moral economy").[55] Unable to find a proletariat, these historians then depict workers as patriotic. Unable to document the Marxist idea of class consciousness, they have now adopted Machiavelli's and Montesquieu's idea of classical republicanism without seeming to understand that the idea of civic virtue had little to do with labor as the source of value (Marx), the origin of property (Locke), or the will of God (Calvin). As for the "language of labor," we should ask the same question that John Adams asked about Machiavelli's and Montesquieu's discourses on the language of classical politics: Are political ideas causes that determine conduct? The question is merely to remind social historians that political language may offer little more than what Marxists themselves call "mystifications" and the Old Left literary critic Kenneth Burke has called "eulogistic coverings." Political rhetoric may only be a verbal strategy for dealing with situations in which conflicting interests must be addressed in language that does not admit the ingredients of motivation. "And the very important thing among these 'contexts of situations,' " Burke observed, is "the kinds of factors considered by Bentham, Marx, and Veblen, the material interests (of private or class structure) that you symbolically defend or symbolically appropriate or symbolically align yourself with in the course of making your assertions."[56] The rhetoric and symbols of idealism can be appropriated to defend the interests of either capital or labor, but the activity of language itself tells us little about what is going on independently of the way in which words are used, particularly if they are used as rhetorical strategies. That both Whigs and Jacksonians could appropriate republican ideology and accuse their opponents of "corruption" and "tyranny" while claiming for themselves "virtue" and "liberty" should caution us about the limits of language in explaining historical reality and human motivation.[57] To resort to language to account for behavior implies that political discourse and public speech have revelatory value, which would be possible only if there existed precise rules governing the use of language. Without such rules, we must remain skeptical of the recent marriage of Marxism and classical republicanism. For we should remember that "virtue" in the classical sense implies the existence of standards external to those who claim it simply by uttering its language—critical, objective standards whereby the claims can be scrutinized in light of the "commonwealth" and *res publica.* Marxist historians, however, seem reluctant to assess such claims critically, and thus we are led to believe that both the nineteenth-century southern aristocracy and the northern working class were genuinely "virtuous" and beyond the sins of materialism. But the question remains whether there really is an alternative to the Lockean idea of consensus, whether Machiavelli and Montesquieu can replace Locke, Tocqueville, and Lincoln and do for American history what Hegel, Marx, and Gramsci were supposed to do—liberate us from liberalism.

Alexis de Tocqueville, whose classic study *Democracy in America* depicted the Republic as a new experiment in liberal individualism. (Bettmann Archive)

Tocqueville's Shadow

It should be noted that previous radical generations doubted that the American past offered much guidance or inspiration. In the thirties Old Left scholars criticized the liberal historian Parrington, author of the three-volume *Main Currents in American Thought*, for offering the Jeffersonian heritage as a solution to an emergent corporate capitalism. A decade earlier neither Beard nor Veblen had seen much to be gained by invoking the American past, except perhaps to debunk its heroes and ideals. W. E. B. DuBois, who studied Hegel at Harvard, never once entertained the notion that the philosopher's meditation on lordship and bondage could be interpreted to mean that the future belonged to the slave. The Lyrical Left essayist Randolph Bourne wrote "The Doctrine of the Rights of Man as Formulated by Thomas Paine" in an attempt to clarify the differences between liberalism and radicalism. As Bourne saw it, the eighteenth-century ideas of Paine and of Rousseau rested on the false assumption that society could be rearranged to harmonize with human nature without considering the economic forces that needed to be brought under control. After explaining the requirements of socialism, Bourne observed,

> How different is this attitude from the constant assumption of Paine and his fellow reformers that society is composed of units which can be combined and separated like marbles in a box! and from their childlike innocence of the infinite complexity of the social fabric with its interweavings of personal ambition with class antagonisms and variety of cultural and traditional influences. Modern Socialism recognizes society as a process, determined by economic forces; Paine thought of it as a state, determined by the agreement of individuals.[58]

In contrast to previous Lefts, the Academic Left that evolved from the shambles of the New Left seeks to appropriate curious figures from the American past, and often without acknowledging any possible ideological difficulty. Thus the distinguished historians Foner and Wilentz have written persuasively about the influence of Paine on American workers in the eighteenth and nineteenth centuries. One would never learn from their writings why the conservative Ronald Reagan invoked Tom Paine in his first presidential inaugural address. In this instance Reagan seemed to be shrewder than Theodore Roosevelt, who called Paine "a filthy atheist." Actually Paine was a deist, but his appeal to all American classes lies mostly in his hatred for the one class that failed to establish itself in the early Republic—an aristocracy whose chivalric pretensions to nobility only revealed its actual "no-ability" and its desire for an indulgent, leisure-class life-style. If Paine became a hero to generations of American workers, it was not because workers possessed proto-socialist sentiments but rather because Paine himself stood for emergent-middle-class values like industry, opportunity, and entrepreneurial ambition. In embracing Paine, the Academic Left stretches its capacity for anomaly to the point of embracing the patron saint of the bourgeoisie.[59]

One of the curiosities about the historiography of the Academic Left is the new attitude toward American patriotism. When constituted as the New Left of the sixties, graduate student activists deplored patriotism as responsible for the Vietnam War and for perpetuating a racist and elitist society. In this instance the sixties carried on the critique of patriotism first voiced by the Lyrical Left in the pre–First World War years. Eastman, Bourne, and other Greenwich Village rebels denounced patriotism as the "herd-instinct" of the brain-dead, and for writers of the lost generation like Hemingway and Pound, words that invoked glory, God, and country could only be the lies of a "botched civilization" that sent its youths to slaughter. The New Left shared such sentiments until certain of its members felt the need to rewrite history. Some Left labor historians now had no trouble identifying with patriotism of the past and regarding its utterances as expressions of genuine idealism. Students were assigned books with such titles as "Workingmen's Democracy," "Liberty under Siege," and "Working-Class Americanism." Not only did radical historians use Paine and Jefferson, whose individualist values made American capitalism possible; they also invoked classical republicanism to argue that American workers wanted to escape dependency on their masters in order to become virtuous, independent citizens devoted to the ideals of the public good. The assumption seemed to be that private interest disappears when it puts on a patriotic face. Thus historians have investigated public rituals and patriotic holidays with all the skills of a cultural anthropologist. But just how the festivities and pieties of a Fourth of July celebration help us see evidence for civic virtue and class consciousness remains unclear. Observing the same celebrations taking place in Jacksonian America, Tocqueville asked us to consider the possibility that "patriotism . . . is most often an extension of individual egoism."[60] No doubt American workers, even immigrant workers, could wax patriotic on holidays. But a radical consciousness depends upon class hatred growing out of the conditions of misery and not upon love of homeland springing from expectations of opportunity.

The reorientation of attitudes toward patriotism reflects a more telling reorientation of attitudes toward the working class. In the sixties Michael Harrington grew hoarse trying to convince student radicals that they should engage in coalition politics and ally with the Democratic party and the working class, which he regarded as the largest and most crucial element in the American electorate. But SDS and other activists rejected Harrington's advice and suspected workers of being conservative if not reactionary and racist as well as chauvinist—a suspicion that seemed confirmed when "hard hat" construction workers attacked student antiwar demonstrators on the streets of New York City. Years later, when student radicals became professors of history, workers were either forgiven or forgotten. In book after book they were now depicted as potentially radical, free of racism and chauvinism, and so virtuous that one would never think that a worker might drink heavily, abuse his children, and take out his frustrations by belting his wife around the kitchen. Having felt the blows of the hard hats of the sixties, the New Left rewrote nineteenth-century American labor history and found only soft hearts.[61]

New Left historiography rested on the assumption that a rediscovery of socialist and republican antecedents would encourage the hope that America enjoyed a genuine radical heritage. But the categories of socialism and republicanism are precisely the concepts that Tocqueville believed to be of little use in explaining America. Something other than class feelings and classical ideals had emerged in the New World.

Unlike many American intellectuals, Tocqueville was untroubled by America's intense egoism and individualism, those private sentiments so destructive to classical republicanism and to socialism alike. For America was different, unique, a modern liberal society whose "exceptionalism" meant that it did not require two European ideas for its interpretation. America did not require socialism, which focuses on class formations, and it did not require republicanism, which focuses on political institutions. What then explained America?

One common assumption holds that Tocqueville became an advocate of individualism and that the methodological implications of that idea blinded him to the class realities of America. Yet Tocqueville denied that society can be logically explained by the conscious motives of individuals. "I do not speak of individuals who do not effect the essential phenomenon of history," Tocqueville advised. "I speak of classes, which alone should concern the historian." America, however, lacked an ancien régime. What precluded the development of "proletarian" class consciousness, therefore, was not only the absence of huge concentrations of wealth and poverty characteristic of the Old World but also the absence of an entrenched aristocracy, which meant there was no class in America to denigrate the value of labor, deny the principle of equality, and resist the forces of social change. In America, where "every honest calling is honorable," the work ethic found universal recognition (at least outside the South), and the people grew increasingly alike in their attitudes because there was no distinct separate class whose aristocratic arrogance provoked opposing class mentalities based on genuinely different interests and ideals. In Europe both the middle class and the working class found their identity in struggling against the ancien régime, which preached the virtues of paternalism when confronted by the rights of labor. In America the middle class and the working class faced each other and, lacking a class enemy, became increasingly indistinguishable or, to use a more contemporary expression, one-dimensional.[62]

In America classical republicanism suffered the same fate as class consciousness. "The Americans are not a virtuous people, and nevertheless they are free," reflected Tocqueville, struck by the thought that the long historical connection between liberty and virtue had collapsed in America. Tocqueville wrote *Democracy in America* with the Machiavellian legacy in mind and seemingly with Montesquieu looking over his shoulder. "We must not take Montesquieu's idea in a narrow sense," Tocqueville wrote elsewhere. "What he understands by virtue is the moral power which each individual exercises over himself and which prevents him from violating the rights of others." The American people lack that moral quality, for "it is not disinterestedness that is great, it is interest that is taken for granted." The result may be the same, but in "America it is not that virtue is great, but temptation that is small." Small? The framers assumed that people of all classes were prone to "vex and oppress" others, and their Calvinist suspicions led them to adopt republican solutions. But Tocqueville saw, as did Henry Adams, that the solutions were illusions. "I have always considered what is called a mixed government to be a mere chimera. There is in truth no such thing as a mixed government (in the sense usually given to the words), since in any society one finds in the end some principle of action that dominates all others." Those thinkers who had looked to eighteenth-century England as a model were mistaken. "The mistake is due to those who, constantly seeing the interests of the great in conflict with those of the people, have thought only about the struggle and have not paid attention to the result thereof, which was more important. When a society really does have a mixed government, that is to say, one equally shared between contrary principles, either a revolution breaks out or that society breaks up."[63]

Tocqueville departed boldly from classical traditions in order to provide an extrapolitical focus that enables the historian to see a long-hidden truth: the nature of society explains the stability of government. Thus freedom in America would be preserved not by the forms and structures of political institutions but by the peculiar habits, attitudes, and values of a people, by the *moeurs* that have been conditioned by society itself. Even the idea of a republic had to be redefined. "What is meant by a 'republic' in the United States is the slow and quiet action of a society upon itself." By emphasizing society and social relations over government and political institutions, Tocqueville draws our attention to the "principle of action" that explains America. Of the seemingly diverse, restless American character, he asked, "What makes of them a people? *Interest.* That's the secret. Individual interest which sticks through at each instant, *interest* which, moreover, comes out in the open and calls itself a social theory." He knew his discovery was "a long way" from classical republicanism, and he tried to convince his French contemporaries that acquisitive individualism could be elevated into something approximating "a sort of refined and intelligent selfishness," or "enlightened self-interest," or possibly even a "virtuous materialism."[64]

Tocqueville did for American thought what David Hume had done for British political theory; he brought the whole legacy of classical politics based on the conflict between public "virtue" and private "interests" to a nonpolitical denouement.[65] His perception that Americans shared the same material concerns, and that worker and capitalist would legitimate their pursuits in the language of republicanism, does much to explain why class consciousness could not develop in a country that lacked the class structure to produce it. Had America been truly a class society, as the framers assumed when they tried to organize the divisions of government to balance its presumably conflicting constituencies, America would either have broken out in revolution or broken up as a political unit. Tocqueville was no celebrator of "consensus," which he would have regarded as a form of majoritarian "tyranny." His genius was in his ability to uphold simultaneously contradictory political values and, in doing so, to penetrate the essential truths of America. A thinker of aristocratic sensibilities, he saw in the idea of equality a striving for conformity that rendered life drab and dreary. "The sight of such universal uniformity saddens and chills me, and I am tempted to regret that state of society which has ceased to be." Yet Tocqueville was also a man of genuine democratic sympathies, and, rather than succumbing to illusions about the old order, he concluded his study with a Lincolnesque affirmation of American ideals. Equality promotes "not the particular prosperity of the few, but the greater well-being of all. . . . Equality may be less elevated, but it is more just; and in its justice lies its greatness and beauty."[66]

Tocqueville saw through the pretenses of aristocratic "paternalism," discerned in middle-class *moeurs* the meaning of the latterday concept of "hegemony," demonstrated how social forces had superseded political institutions to render classical republicanism irrelevant to America, and expounded, as did Lincoln, the priority of land and labor to politics and virtue. In Old World republicanism property was regarded as an object of right and a precondition of virtue to the extent that ownership gives man the independence to resist the corruptions of ministerial politics. Yet property had no necessary connection to labor and the dignity and value of work. Edmund Burke's observation that Machiavelli was "intelligence without property" suggests the flaw of classical republicanism. In placing civic virtue ahead of man's means of subsistence and freedom, Machiavelli violated a sentiment that would be shared not only by Lincoln and Tocqueville but also by thinkers as diverse as Dostoevsky, Emerson, Locke, Marx, Veblen, and Tolstoy. First give people land so that they can feed themselves and overcome their alienation through labor and workmanship; then ask them to be virtuous. Therein lies the liberal synthesis.[67]

9

Power, Freedom, and the Failure of Theory

The beginning student of politics, the beginning
student of philosophy, will explain at once the
impossibility of ever seeing the object as it really is.
... But the limitations of men exist in varying degrees;
surely it is not the limitation itself but the worship of
limitation which is degrading.   Lionel Trilling, 1939

When you are running out of gas, you begin to study
things theoretically.   Barbara Rose, 1990

Hegemony, Critical Theory, Deconstruction

Someone once described characters in Hemingway's novels as
people to whom things happen. In studying the American past,
historians of the Academic Left tended to depict workers and even
slaves as people who make things happen, not passive objects but
active subjects engaged in organizing an industrial strike or forming a community dedicated to "moral economy." Yet when the
Academic Left studies not the past but the present an entirely
different picture emerges, one in which nearly all possibility of
human freedom and morality is gone. To the student of intellec-

tual history this contemporary eclipse of freedom and virtue seems ironic in several respects.

First of all, as a product of the sixties, the Academic Left represented something like the second life of the New Left, the audacious movement of rebellious youth who demanded "freedom now," whether free speech, free choice, free love, or free pot. It was the sixties generation that felt free to challenge the political system, defy authority, and experiment with new life-styles. Yet, when as young faculty members that generation freely and willingly entered the universities it had once set out to bring down, the emergent Academic Left concluded that there existed no authentic freedom and no genuine act of conscious choice. People in the past might be praised for acting; people in the present are acted on as humankind disappears into the "structures" of domination and discourse. Whether the Academic Left was studying the latest European ideas of critical theory, poststructuralism, or deconstruction, power rather than freedom became the object of inquiry.

Another irony about power is that it lost its oppressive, coercive, and arbitrary connotations and became silent, invisible, and so systematically omnipresent as to be almost indistinguishable from the routines of everyday life. The French philosopher Michel Foucault likened power to a "capillary" phenomenon, not something suddenly imposed downward but slowly insinuating itself outward and adhering to whatever it touches.[1] Power also came to be regarded as tied up with how things are seen and perceived, attitudes not necessarily consciously submitted to but unconsciously subscribed to in daily practices. This notion of "false consciousness" received its most influential articulation in the idea of "hegemony" developed by Antonio Gramsci.

Although virtually unknown outside Italy in the twenties and thirties, Gramsci, who died in a fascist prison in 1937, became after the Second World War the single most important Marxist thinker in the Western world. In part the sudden recognition in the postwar era resulted from political developments that made his ideas more relevant than ever. Gramsci's rediscovery seems all the more ironic in that it occurred in the midst of a cold war that signified to many former Marxists and ex-radicals "the end of ideology."

With the convulsions created by the Soviet Union's Twentieth Party Congress, in 1956, and shortly afterwards the upheavals in Poland and Hungary, a need arose to find a new path to the democratic goals of Marx that would avoid the tragic disasters of Stalinism. What impressed anti-Stalinist Left writers, and also Hannah Arendt, a scholar with a nostalgia for the polis of ancient Greece, was the emergence in Eastern Europe of "workers' councils," spontaneous organs of the laboring classes that aimed to topple the totalitarian state and its party apparatus. Gramsci's earlier ideas about "factory councils" as vehicles of revolutionary education and strategy, developed in the journal *Ordine Nuovo* in 1919 and 1920, now shone like a beacon of hope. Later in some circles Gramsci's example of turning to Italy's nationalist traditions came to be regarded as the seeds of "polycentralism" and subsequently Eurocommunism.

But the real Gramscian moment came in May 1968, when Parisian students took to the streets to join factory workers in massive demonstrations that brought down the de Gaulle government. This novel class alignment of educated elite and labor unions appeared to fulfill Gramsci's glorious dream of "organic intellectuals" acting as a revolutionary vanguard. Student followers of the Frankfurt scholars, who had no hope in a working class mesmerized by middle-class comforts, could look to Gramsci for advice on counterhegemony tactics to wean the masses away from the enticing deceptions of bourgeois culture. Even students who had no stomach for revolution could take to heart Gramsci's call for a return to politics in the classical sense, not Marx's "sphere of domination" but the means by which humankind overcomes its alienated condition through democratic participation in the noble life of civic culture. Offering something for everyone on the Left, Gramsci became a man for all seasons, or so it seemed.

Although Gramsci's reputation in Europe has been somewhat

eclipsed in recent years, in the United States, where Marxism enjoys its own hegemony among college faculty hired from the sixties generation, his influence remains almost paradigmatic. One might even speak of the "Italian turn" in the study and reinterpretation of American history. In the last two decades Gramsci's concept of hegemony has been used to explain not only planter-slave relations in the old South but also the following: consumer society and the fetishism of commodities; Puritanism, Americanism, Fordism, and Taylorism as reigning ideologies; popular media like cinema and television as instruments of cultural domination; and new methodologies in literary studies such as critical theory and deconstruction. The idea of hegemony contains an integrating mystique that incorporates all facets of life: economy, politics, money, labor, law, language, religion, education—all the stuff of American studies. Above all, Gramsci's concept appears to provide the final answer to the question that Werner Sombart raised at the turn of the century: "Why is there no socialism in America?"

It is commonly agreed by scholars that Gramsci's greatest contribution to modern social theory is his concept of hegemony. Latent in his post–First World War writings, hegemony became crucial to explaining the failure of revolutionary socialism and the triumph of reactionary fascism. Why did the Italian masses adhere to old ways and, under Mussolini's dictatorship, lose what little freedom they had had under parliamentary government? Gramsci's idea of hegemony suggested that the ruling class is capable of exercising "moral direction" and that its power is more cultural and ideological than economic and political. Hegemony presupposed consent, but not in the political sense of a contract between the ruler and the ruled in which government is founded upon the deliberate will of the people it represents. Instead, consent, whether consciously or unconsciously rendered, represents a social-psychological deference on the part of the "subaltern" strata toward the attitudes of the upper classes. Hegemony meant consent as opposed to coercion, authority as opposed to power, the hidden subtleties of submission in contrast to the more visible and harsher realities of oppression. Most Gramsci scholars have emphasized the way in which hegemony signifies a shift in Marxist theory from base to superstructure, from the economic foundations of society to its cultural configurations, from structure to agency, and from the mode of production to the means of communication.

Gramsci's emphasis upon hegemony appealed enormously to radical intellectuals for several reasons. First, hegemony meant the struggle toward socialism would take place not necessarily in the factories and fields but in such cultural institutions as the schoolhouse and the popular theater. The Gramscian message was not to wait until new historical developments changed the the mode of production but to capture the hearts and minds of the people by means of persuasion and propaganda. This cultural task meant that the intellectual has a role in history, especially the "organic intellectual" who identified with local, ascending social classes in an effort to enable the unaware, those "who do not know," to overcome their hegemonic confinement. Moreover, Gramsci's idea of praxis, the idea that knowledge arises from concrete action, also appealed to American Leftists who shared pragmatism's conviction that the point of philosophy is not to contemplate truth but to experiment and act upon the environment in order to introduce change.[2]

In turning toward such ideas as hegemony, critical theory, and deconstruction, the Academic Left was expressing its exhaustion with orthodox Marxism, which had once made the "point of production" the focus of inquiry, labor and class relations the field of investigation, and the proletariat the flame of inspiration. The Lyrical Left and the Old Left, disillusioned with Marxism and its unfulfilled promises, and having given up hope that the proletariat would carry out its historical mission, set out to find new grounds for freedom and the truths that promised to make man free. Some veterans of the Left embraced free-market economics; others converted to religion; still others returned to historical doctrines like natural law. Here comes another irony. For the Academic Left no liberating truths were to be found in the past.

Social historians may have consoled themselves by describing the warm intimacy of peasant and working-class communities. But in intellectual history the past itself was precisely the problem, the setting in which illusions and false reasoning first distorted the whole course of Western culture and imposed on modern life barely visible forms of power, domination, surveillance, and control. Thus, unlike previous Lefts, the Academic Left was more interested in probing the structures of power than in finding the basis of freedom. Whereas older radicals like Max Eastman and James Burnham had searched for principles with which to preserve political liberty, many members of the still underadicalized Academic Left wanted to expose the forces that dominated social life.

The Academic Left's preoccupation with power and domination derived from the earlier influence of the German refugee scholars and their idea of "critical theory." Marcuse was perhaps the most notable exponent of the Frankfurt school, with his notions of "repressive tolerance" and liberation through aesthetic expression. But two other figures, Theodor Adorno and Max Horkheimer, did more to provide the theoretical foundations of critical theory. In contrast to traditional theory, which claims to be objectively progressive by virtue of standing above politics and social relations, critical theory reflects on its own historical and social context in an effort to see existing situations from the perspective of their potential transformation. The aim of the critical theorist is to demystify the mechanisms that rule people's lives under the guise of accepted necessities.[3]

Because of the influence of critical theory, the Academic Left was the first Left in American or European history to distrust the eighteenth-century Enlightenment. Whereas Marx and other revolutionary thinkers valued the Enlightenment for having eliminated feudal remnants and made possible the spread of knowledge and science, Adorno and Horkheimer viewed the Enlightenment as an intellectual disaster for turning nature into "mere objectivity." In seeking to conquer the forces of the environment, man alienated himself from them to the extent that he had to exercise his own power as experimenter and manipulater. The Enlightenment believed that the domination of nature would bring forth the knowledge to master the impersonal forces of history, and Marx also assumed that increasing man's control over the environment would lessen his control over his fellow men. Adorno and Horkheimer, however, insisted that the domination of nature by alienated human beings, whose cognition is reduced to repetition and whose idea of the moral is simply the factual, would only increase the domination of man by man.[4]

With Hegel critical theorists hoped that reason and enlightened thought could liberate man from his alienated condition. But Adorno and Horkheimer were closer to Weber in seeing rationality replace reason as instrumental and technological forms of organization render society efficient, comfortable, and intellectually dormant. Although they valued the philosopher Kant for having emphasized human autonomy, they were also critical of him for having failed to see all the conditions that prevented the exercise of freedom without compulsion. Marx viewed history as developing according to patterns in which individual conduct need not be subjected to moral judgment. Kant gave man both choice and culpability "by saddling him in freedom's name with a guilt that would be no guilt if there were total determination." The critical theorist sought to reason dialectically to show how propositions upon close examination turn into their opposites—how, for example, freedom becomes unfreedom when man is told he is free, the better to command his obedience.[5]

The themes of authority and domination appealed to those members of the Academic Left who shared the critical theorists' conviction that all aspects of modern life—the family, education, popular entertainment, the media—must be probed to uncover the hidden modes of power and control. This meant that the radical scholar could inch away from Marxism and leave behind political economy, the activity of labor, the mode of production, and economic scarcity and work as necessity. In modern society, in a predominantly service economy run by computers and supported by data banks, men and women no longer work upon things to produce products. Access to knowledge and its transmission renders the "mode of information" the crucial institution of postindustrial society. It will be recalled that the New Left's first major protest, in Berkeley in 1964, had Mario Savio exhorting students to "put our bodies against . . . the wheels and machines, and make the machine stop until we're free." A quarter century later, members of the Academic Left found themselves sitting behind the machinery of computers and word processors as they pondered the problem of power not as the brute whack of a cop's club but as the benign communication of print and screen. This shift from economics to epistemology, from the structure of organization and distribution to the superstructure of representation and communication, explains in part why some academic Leftists could make the transition from German critical theory to French poststructuralism.[6] Having failed to transform society, the Academic Left now felt that its task was not so much to strive toward freedom as to explore the subtle modes of domination. The earlier New Left saw the problem of history as the problem of alienation and the meaning of existence; the later Academic Left saw domination and hegemony everywhere and wondered how subjugated humanity had lost its freedom without knowing it. The challenge was to unmask concealed power wherever it could be spotted. The challenge was to spread suspicion.

In many ways that challenge was inspired by the emergence of Michel Foucault as one of the most eminent, provocative, and daring philosophers in postwar France, and also one of the most discussed and debated in a variety of disciplines in American universities. Foucault's primary concern was to show how historical periods were governed not by economic laws but by "discourses" and the rules and classifications that permit some phenomena to be seen as true, rational, and normal and others as false, deviant, and immoral. Foucault also wanted to show how all elements in and of changes in the *episteme* that shapes discursive shifts are arbitrary rather than rational, disruptive rather than progressive, and often productive of unforeseen and paradoxical consequences. Thus hospital and welfare agencies set out to help

Michel Foucault, the French philosopher who had enormous influence on some members of the academic Left with his theories of power and structural domination. (Jerry Bauer)

people but end by exercising power over them by defining health practices and need requirements.

In the middle of his illustrious career Foucault described his studies as a form of "archaeology" in which the languages and practices of other ages are seen to be determined by silent structures rather than by conscious human voices. In his most extreme observation Foucault depicted the human subject as disappearing from history altogether, for the idea of a rational man comprising a constant human nature could no longer be identified. Even the struggle to oppose power merely produces newer forms of power as history changes direction only to reconstitute itself as the force it always was. The eclipse of man meant the death of humanism, which traditionally implied some external standard of reason from which the meaning and direction of history could be explained. For Foucault knowledge cannot penetrate power, because what comes to be accepted as truth is itself a product of the relentless activity of power. The idea of rational man in control of his destiny will soon fade away, Foucault chillingly observed, like a human image on the sand erased by the incoming tide.[7]

Although much of the Academic Left enthusiastically adopted Foucault, he himself was more of a skeptical anarchist than a revolutionary Marxist, more interested in the fate of those who futilely struggle to resist domination than in those who call for a new system of domination in the name of liberation. Foucault also rejected the Marxist idea that sexual repression and the incarceration of the insane were the necessary outcomes of a rising bourgeois economy. Some neoconservatives in America appreciated Foucault's treatment of the welfare state and mental institutions as bureaucratic power structures exercising control and surveillance in the name of philanthrophy and compassion. Even radicals who read the hippie Ken Kesey's *One Flew over the Cuckoo's Nest* and applauded the film version agreed with Foucault and the American historian Christopher Lasch that the "helping professions" did more to harm patients than to heal them. The debunking of humanitarianism as coercion has a long tradition in American intellectual history, broad enough to include even conservative writers like Nathaniel Hawthorne and H. L. Mencken.[8]

The specifically radical thrust in Foucault's brilliant writings was the Nietzschean critique of Christianity. In his last interview just before his death in 1984, Foucault answered a question with the remark "I can only respond by saying I am simply Nietzschean." Like the German philosopher, Foucault saw the will to power as the essential constant of human history. He, too, could perceive in religion an institution in which certain types of power-driven people seek to exercise authority over others by moral reprimand, shame, and guilt. This Foucauldian analysis resembles nothing so much as Randolph Bourne's essay "The Puritan's Will to Power" (1917). "The true Puritan is at once the most unselfish and the most self-righteous of men," Bourne warned the Lyrical Left. "To the true Puritan the beauty of unselfishness lies in his being able to enforce it on others. He loves virtue not so much for its own sake as for its being an instrument of terror." Like Foucault, Bourne was a Nietzschean, and he, too, was intrigued by the abnormal and deviant and once praised the "superb modern healthiness" of Dostoevsky for drawing no dividing line "between the sane and insane."[9]

Bourne's writings on Nietzsche, Burnham's on the "new Machiavellians," Lasch's on the "helping professions," and Foucault's on the *philosophes* and other thinkers cover the ground of twentieth-century radical thought from the Lyrical Left to the Academic Left. All writers provided critiques not simply of society but of power as intellectual in nature—that is, power emanating from specific ideas and doctrines whose proponents claim superior knowledge and seek authority by securing their acceptance and compliance. Insofar as the critique of intellectual power applies to Marxist ideology and its claims to a privileged political consciousness, it remains to be seen whether the Academic Left will renounce its Gramscian urge to aspire to hegemonic heights.[10]

But the most disturbing aspect of Foucault's treatment of power is that it emerges as an effect without a cause. In much of post-structuralist thought narrative description replaces analytical explanation and power moves without a human agent or rational purpose. The idea that people can be oppressed when the philosopher cannot specify an oppressor is surely a novel thought in the annals of radicalism. If there is only domination without a dominator, how can the Left help liberate humankind?

In some respects the writings of another French philosopher, Jacques Derrida, may be even more disturbing to the Left, for the Marxist conviction that human activity expressed in labor is as important as the inexorable laws of historical development disappears in Derrida's subtle and richly playful poststructural analysis. With Derrida it is in language, not labor, that inquiry begins and ends. To go outside of the text is as futile as swimming against a riptide, for we cannot communicate without word-bound inscriptions or utterances and we cannot think except through a linguistic medium. Language itself, along with paintings, institutions, and other human artifacts, is neither consciously conceived nor expressed by men but instead by structures that may be the fragmented results of human actions but that are indifferent to human intentions. So intent was Derrida on denying authorial intention that he came up with ingenious distinctions in the expression *différence* to suggest, among other things, the opposite meanings of "to differ" and "to defer" that had gone unnoticed in philosophical discourse. This momentous discovery that it was impossible to end the differing and deferral of meaning in language allowed him to argue that there is no such thing as the present, since anything is "always already" behind us when we think about it, and once we commit it to writing there remain only marks on the page, traces that indicate the presence of the author's absence. The "metaphysics of presence" Derrida regarded as an illusion, the conceit of "logocentrism" in Western philosophy that assumes a rational consciousness in pursuit of truths that are externally verifiable or introspectively discoverable. Instead of regarding knowledge as present to the mind, Derrida recognizes only writing and texts that generate interpretations, and interpretations of interpretations, in which the author as subject disappears without a trace, supposedly having lost control of the meaning and intent of the words he or she wrote.[11]

Derrida's reputation, and his highly original manner of thinking, hit America's literary Academic Left like lightning, but some of his philosophical thoughts had been anticipated by earlier American thinkers. Like Foucault, Derrida had been influenced by ·Martin Heidegger's discovery that beyond language there is only the "abyss" of nothingness, no presence of anything but the inner awareness of the angst of death's approach. William James, who also sensed anxiety about death and the annihilation of the self, coined the phrase "the specious present" to show that the movement of time defies consciousness and linguistic representation. But ideas in the mind must be "representational," George Herbert Mead pointed out, for "while they are in the present, they refer to that which is not in the present." Melville made us aware that truth and reality, the "inscrutable," surpass comprehension by words. And Thoreau and Eastern philosophers of Lao-tzu knew that *presence* eludes will as well as intellect and is "always already" absent—the moment one tries to hold on to it, presence slips away and the unenlightened find themselves holding nothing.[12]

Initially Derrida's message appealed to the Academic Left, whose literary scholars were searching for a critique of the New Criticism, supposedly a suffocating and reactionary theory of reading texts purely for their aesthetic qualities independently of political and social considerations. The French thesis that texts are structurally determined, that their meaning may come from the outside in systems of discourse, arrived from Paris as a methodological deliverance. Equally exciting was Derrida's concept of "deconstruction," the process of uncovering sustained incoherences within a text, rhetorical devices, marginal metaphors, sudden contradictions, and other surprising betrayals that suggest unacknowledged tensions within Western philosophical thought. Derrida attempted to deconstruct metaphysics by demonstrating that traditional binary oppositions—mind/body, presence/absence, existence/essence, male/female, good/evil, knowledge/power—were false dualisms sanctioned by social practice.

Feminists and Marxists alike found much that was useful in Derrida, as well as in Foucault, Jacques Lacan, Julia Kristeva, and other poststructuralists who wanted to "unread" old texts to put new meaning into them. The notion that structures and language systems can either determine or repress consciousness and privi-

lege male over female helped explain the prevalence of patriarchal authority. And with the critique of logocentrism, the assumption that the object of knowledge resides in the mind, it was
tempting to replace cognitive rationality with feminist-based subjectivity in order to "engender" the subject of gender by exploring
why women have been omitted from Western Cartesian and Platonic thought. Not surprisingly, deconstruction became an important methodology in feminist studies. In the field of labor history,
however, some women scholars remained convinced that language only expresses, and does not determine, social structures
and class relations, and they questioned a methodology that hy-
postatized discourse to the point where human agency and historical change went unexplained. Other feminists were also uneasy
with the poststructuralists' determination to see the subject,
whether men or women, as having no other basis than the arbitrary constructions of language, the representations in which the
subject has been described and from which he or she can, in
theory, disappear—the same way God disappears when one ceases
to believe in the Bible because its words simply refer to other
words and not to demonstrable proofs of "His" or "Her" existence.
Feminists had struggled too long to find their identity to be told
that who they are turns on the vicissitudes of textual representation. The philosopher Seyla Benhabib doubted that poststructuralism could be emancipatory. "While Foucault celebrates the disappearance of man, feminists have just discovered 'woman.' Are
they ready to bid her farewell too?"[13]

Marxist literary critics could use deconstruction to read texts
with the aim of illuminating the purported fissures and conflicts
inherent in capitalist society. But how could a Marxist go all the
way with deconstruction? It was not only true that distinguished
literary scholars like Frank Lentricchia, Terry Eagleton, and
Frederick Jameson wanted to see less attention devoted to the
formal properties of a text and more to its social determinants.
The greater danger, it seems to me, is that the writings of Marx
himself could be deconstructed. In a way, Old Left figures like
Edmund Wilson and Max Eastman already had done this when

they exposed the "dialectic" as a religious metaphor disguised as science. The Academic Left faced an even broader threat to the entire edifice of Marxism. What becomes of the conflict between labor and capital if no binary opposition has an ontological status? What becomes of the "contradictions" of capitalism if all differences cancel each other in the realm of discourse?[14]

Yet deconstruction had enormous value to New Left literary academics. Having lost the confrontation on the streets in the sixties, they could later, as English professors in the eighties, continue it in the classroom. A new nemesis haunted the Left. Everything wrong with modern society would be explained no longer by the mode of production but by the mode of discourse. All aspects of existence, even the self struggling to know itself, are linguistic constructions. The autonomous structures of language imprison the human mind in its own productions, like a spider unknowingly caught in the web that it instinctively continues to spin out of itself. If words control reality by virtue of misrepresenting it, what's to be done? As Irving Howe wryly noted, the task of the deconstructionist is to change not the world but the literature department. All power to the professors! The New Left in its academic phase remains campus bound in its struggle to establish its own hegemony. Since there is no world outside the text, the point is not to interpret the world but to capture the canon. Language isn't everything; it's the only thing.[15]

The World Turned Upside Down, 1989–1990

The influence French poststructuralism enjoyed in American academic life was more than a trendy fad; indeed, it answered a deep need, if only the need to rationalize failure. In 1968 both the French and the American New Lefts felt something like eschatological exhilaration in storming the streets and taunting the symbols of authority. But when the illusion of revolutionary cataclysm passed and the backlash came down, the generation of '68 began to feel confused, suddenly impotent, and not a little betrayed by its own misplaced hopes. Entering the academic world,

New Leftists would find in various poststructuralist theories ready-made answers to their defeat and disillusionment. Unlike the veterans of the earlier Lyrical Left, they did not look to familiar older villains—Puritanism, capitalism, nativism—and unlike Old Left survivors, they did not so much turn away from Marxism as go beyond it for new explanations of their failure and frustration. French poststructuralism, which seemed so elegantly intricate, provided such comprehensive explanations with its emphasis on structures and systems, the reified constraints residing outside human agents whose actions may only reproduce them. With the conscious "subject" gone from history, the poststructuralist knew a good deal about the mechanisms of domination and repression but little about the human mentality of desperation and aspiration. In a mode of inquiry that saw thought as imprisoned in interpretation and action resulting in the replication of power structures, freedom was not supposed to happen.

It would be unfair to indict only the poststructuralists for clinging to a theory that bore no relation to the simple desires of people living under oppressive regimes. Neoconservative theorists and foreign policy advisers, for example, regarded communist regimes as frozen totalitarian systems impermeable to change. No American, including this one, had been prepared for what would happen in 1989–90. But those who suspected power everywhere failed to suspect the unexpected.

The unexpected erupted in May 1989, when Chinese students began to gather in Beijing's Tiananmen Square to protest the CP's bureaucracy, corruption, and repression of political freedom. The momentous confrontation had been precipitated by two events that had little to do with systems or structures: the death of a reformist Chinese leader sympathetic to the students' grievances, and the visit of the Soviet premier, Mikhail Gorbachev, welcomed by Chinese students as a symbol of hope and change. Students in Tiananmen Square told reporters that they had studied the civil rights movement in the United States as well as the long history of student protest movements in China. Marching and chanting, students attracted some workers to their cause; a few staged poi-

Chinese students taking inspiration from the statue of liberty dubbed the "Goddess of Democracy," in Beijing's Tiananmen Square. (Wide World Photos)

gnant hunger strikes. As a stunned world watched on television, the eighty-four-year-old Deng Xiaoping, refusing to engage in a dialogue with students, called out the "People's Liberation Army" and surrounded the square with tanks. For weeks a tense standoff led to speculation that the CP had lost control and that if the army refused to move, China and its 1.1 billion people would escape a regime that had lost all legitimacy. But after seven weeks of daily demonstrations, soldiers and tanks moved into Tiananmen Square, firing away at panicked mobs and wreaking a bloodbath before the eyes of the world.

The statue of Lenin, "godlike" hero of the Lyrical Left, being dismantled by Romanian workers, 1990. See Max Eastman's poem on Lenin, page 109. (Bettmann Archive)

In California, a conservative legislator was denouncing the Chinese massacre when a liberal colleague interrupted to ask, "What about Kent State?" Assemblyman Tom Hayden quickly jumped in, denying the analogy between the tragic fate of Chinese students and the situation of New Left activists who went on trial for disrupting the Democratic convention in Chicago in 1968. "Chicago was a pacifist tea party compared with Tiananmen Square, where there was probably more brutality inflicted on students than anywhere in the history of the world." (No one knows how many died; the soldiers quickly cremated the bodies.) Joshua Muravchik, a former sixties radical converted to neoconservatism, chastised the administration of George Bush for restraining criticism in order to keep up friendly relations with "the butchers of Beijing."[16]

In May, when students were parading in the square with flowers and songs, former secretary of state Henry Kissinger, who had earlier been awarded a Noble Peace Prize while he was escalating the air war in Vietnam, insisted that the United States side with Deng and the CP against the students. Why? No government, he told reporters, could "tolerate" such demonstrations in its own capital city.[17] No sooner had Kissinger uttered such gerontological advice than demonstrations began to break out in every capital city in Eastern Europe. Events erupted like a revelation. Daily news coverage created a strange impression, as though a movie of Reed's *Ten Days That Shook the World* were running backwards, with the story culminating in the toppling of communism instead of its triumph, and the bust of Lenin being shattered to the ground instead of radiating like an icon in the sky.

The first victory over Stalin's legacy occurred in Poland, where Solidarity defeated the CP in a landslide election in June 1989. Months later the Hungarians proclaimed a republic; Romanians ousted and executed the dreaded chief Nicolae Ceausescu; Czechs staged strikes until the CP capitulated; Bulgarians forced their long-term communist leader to relinquish power; and East and West Germans embraced one another and toasted one another with champagne on top of the Berlin wall soon to be torn down. Once Gorbachev made it clear that the Soviet Union would no longer prop up communist satellite regimes, it was only a matter of time before they collapsed from their inner rottenness. Except for a few diehard American CP members, no one harbored illusions that the satellite countries had any popular support or that "workers' states" actually worked. More surprising was the bitter repudiation of communism as an ideology as well as a form of government. In Czechoslovakia students succeeded in ending the compulsory study of Marxism-Leninism. "It was beaten into us at every turn," said one student of the past. "Even though we complained to our professors and told them that a person has to be exposed to all kinds of theories and ideas, we couldn't succeed in changing the way things were taught."[18]

How did the remaining Left in America respond to events in China and Eastern Europe? For the most part with eager enthusiasm and praise for Gorbachev's encouraging change and reform in Russia. Predictably the few Communist publications condemned the Chinese student demonstrations as "reactionary." A radical Berkeley paper hailed the end of "false" communism and the birth of the "true" thing. The *Nation* saw no reason why the overturning of communism spelled the death of socialism as well. A few writers believed that Chinese students had allowed themselves to espouse American ideas by quoting Jefferson, Paine, and Lincoln because incipient economic reforms had tempted them with consumerism and careerism. Thus the Left applauded the struggle for political freedom but grew a little glum at the thought that *glasnost* ("openness") and *perestroika* ("restructuring") might mean the emergence of free-market economics in formerly communist countries.[19]

Many people of the Soviet Union and Eastern Europe, especially workers, remained ambivalent about capitalism; much as they desired its consumer products, they feared that unregulated prices would benefit only an emergent entrepreneurial class. A certain ambivalence must also confront those in America who identify themselves as social democrats: historically people who enjoyed sovereignty voted not to install socialism but, mainly, for welfare measures like social security and public medical care. Such theoretical problems faced the Left in the new decade of the nineties. A conference at the University of Massachusetts on the topic "Rethinking Marxism" was expected to draw about 150 professors. Instead, 1,500 showed up to hear, among other things, how genuine socialism had been "perverted" in various communist countries. The Marxist professor Anatole Antin told reporters, "The old model of statist, authoritarian socialism really had been dealt a blow. That sweeps the slate clean and asks intellectuals to think about the meaning of democratic socialism." Ironically, and perhaps understandably, interest in Marxism remained stronger in the United States than in Eastern Europe, where it had become a squalid incantation. Antin advised American Marxists how to keep the faith: "The slogan I came up with is: Socialism is dead. Long live Socialism!"[20]

Whatever the future of socialism, theories like Marxism, structuralism, poststructuralism, and others that accord little role to the individual could hardly explain the revolutions in Eastern Europe. The deconstructionist may have declared the "death of man" and showed students why the subject must now be seen as the object of history rather than its originator, but the chain of events in Eastern Europe took place because Gorbachev desired to initiate change rather than impeding it. To use the categories of Sidney Hook's *The Hero in History*, Gorbachev was both the "event-making" and the "eventful" leader of exceptional capacities whose actions decisively influenced the direction of history, thereby refuting the theory of historical determinism. Structures and systems, whether deriving from class relations or from mental constructions, scarcely illuminated developments in China and Eastern Europe. Except for Poland, where workers originally formed the backbone of Solidarity, elsewhere in the communist world demonstrations were spearheaded by courageous intellectuals and students who could no longer stomach the lies and repressions their parents had to endure. In Prague, students from Charles University were clubbed by police; in Bucharest, adults cried for youths who had lost their lives fighting Ceausescu's security forces—even after the overthrow of Ceausescu, remaining communist officials called out workers and miners to put down student demonstrators in order to eliminate opposition parties. Upheavals in East Germany and elsewhere were also triggered by impatient youths who braved bullets to win freedom. The generational revolt of the young seemed to defy all assumptions about the unalterable conditioning processes of domination and subordination. No doubt the rising up of the young and the emergence of the Polish *intelektualista* along with Solidarity would have delighted Gramsci, even though he went to his grave convinced that the role of the "organic intellectual" was to usher in communism, not to lead it out to the garbage dump of history.

To the extent that the Academic Left partook of various structuralist theories, reality eluded its vocabulary. Such terms as "power and hegemony" and "domination and discourse" marked a shift from labor to language in which text, speech, and other forms of communication came to be seen as more refined systems of control, with power ubiquitous and anonymous. Much of the Academic Left assumed that language and communication reinforced the omnipresence of power in unseen "structures" more sensed than understood. Yet in 1989–90 language and communication turned out to be liberating rather than repressing. Television news of events in China and Eastern Europe was beamed from satellite transmitters. The shout of the demonstrators at the Chicago convention in 1968, "The whole world is watching," became a fulfilled prophecy two decades later. The visual and verbal media, rather than being a form of exclusion and repression, became the tools of freedom. Chinese students communicated to the world with computers and fax machines. In Eastern Europe the movement against totalitarianism originated among poets, novelists, historians, musicians, actors, and playwrights. Writers, composers, and performers who use language to speak truth to power know whereof they speak. The modernist, antihumanist dictum, however, declares that the subject has disappeared from history; therefore, knowledge can have no object, because the act of thinking cannot transcend its own discursive practices to get at the truth of things in the real world and thereby help change conditions in that world. No wonder those who had lived under the conditions of totalitarianism had no patience with poststructuralism. The Czech leader and playwright Václav Havel spoke of "the miracle of human speech" as emancipatory. Knowing full well that knowledge requires a linguistic medium, Havel nevertheless insisted on "the power of words to change history." If the human subject died in Paris, it remained alive in Prague, where language served spirit rather than structure.[21]

From Poststructuralism to Pragmatism

The possibility that language and communication could be the basis for leftist politics had been offered by Jürgen Habermas and Richard Rorty more than a decade before the events of 1989–90. Significantly both philosophers sought to return political theory to American pragmatism. America's one original contribution to philosophy seemed to provide a way out of the dilemmas of post-structuralism. Both Habermas and Rorty believed that universal truths about nature and reality cannot be known; nevertheless, knowledge itself can still be emancipatory. "Truth" will not make us free, because whatever it is it cannot be accurately represented in language on the assumption that words directly mirror things. But cognitive linguistic activity can help inform people about society so that its members can reach agreement about what is to be done. The Parisian poststructuralists dismissed "reason" as an eighteenth-century illusion; Habermas set out to demonstrate that a saving rationality resides in communication as dialogue and discourse.

The German philosopher Habermas became a key figure to the Academic Left because he was in the vanguard of its theoretical inquiries. A former student of the Frankfurt school, Habermas sought to use critical theory to do two things: update Marxism in light of historical developments, and rescue modern philosophy from the seeming nihilism and relativism left by various expressions of poststructuralist thought.

Habermas agreed with the earlier Frankfurt scholars that in advanced industrial society the working class had become thoroughly integrated, and he acknowledged that modern capitalism would no longer be subjected to the crises, contradictions, and class conflicts predicted by Marxists in the pre–First World War era. In the sixties and seventies Habermas even defended Western capitalism as progressive and not necessarily predatory, as radical partisans of the third world argued. But he did foresee democratic capitalism's experiencing a "legitimation crisis" to the extent that inevitable technological changes would undermine the status and values of older groups and perhaps provoke the rising expectations of newer elements. Environmentalists and religious fundamentalists, for example, would possibly see their values threatened by technological advances, while feminists would welcome the latest birth control devices. The new crisis would be more political than economic as groups made conflicting demands on the state.[22]

But Habermas was concerned less with political possibilities than with deeper philosophical dilemmas. The writings of Foucault and Derrida seemed to undermine the possibility of radical opposition to the existing order, and scholars on the Left were never clear as to how to apply to social institutions deconstructive methods designed for literary and philosophical texts. A nineteenth-century philosophy like Marxism scarcely anticipated that in the following century science would come to seen as domination, knowledge as power, truth as coercion, and thought as interpretation. The challenge was not to interpret a text but to change the world! It was the genius of Habermas to attempt to overcome the nightmare of poststructuralist thought that left philosophy without a rational subject or a real foundation. One way out of the impasse, Habermas proposed, was to redirect philosophical investigation away from the origins and foundations of knowledge and toward the manner in which knowledge is used.

Whereas Marcuse had been almost obsessed with repression, Habermas advised critical theorists to consider reflection, especially hermeneutical reflection, that is, the self-awareness that all understanding takes place within a context that involves interpretation, not just of texts but of human utterances. To put it rather crudely, the point of philosophy is not to try to possess truth but to pursue knowledge where the action is—in the world of "intersubjective" communication. Habermas saw a certain integrity in linguistic action, for whenever human agents orient themselves toward "reaching an understanding," they implicity hold themselves accountable to one another. Should the validity of a comment be challenged, the commentator is obliged to provide the grounds for his truth claims and hence for his sincerity. Whereas deconstructionists saw written language as elusive and duplicitous, Habermas believed that in "communicative action" legitimacy could be established according to rules of "practical discourse." Habermas's hope to work out the conditions for "an ideal speech situation" in which a "consensus" could be reached on the basis of "the force of the better argument" may seem a little fanciful. But the important feature of his theory in respect to the American Left is that some of his ideas came from American pragmatic philosophers like Charles Sanders Peirce and George Herbert Mead. Peirce, too, believed that the point of philosophical inquiry was not to reach ultimate truth and reality but to "settle an opinion." In the New Left journal *Continuum,* Habermas quoted Mead: "Universal discourse is the formal idea of communication. If communication can be carried through and made perfect, then there would exist the kind of democracy . . . in which each individual could carry just the response in himself that knows he calls out in the community. That is what makes communication in the significant sense the organizing process in the community."[23]

The philosopher who showed the relevance of European poststructuralist thought to America, or vice versa, was Richard Rorty. In several widely discussed books and articles published in the seventies, Rorty argued that Dewey must be ranked with Heidegger and Wittgenstein as among the first to perceive that the world could no longer be grasped as it actually is through philosophy as traditionally conceived. The mind should not be seen as a "mirror" upon which we gaze to see the world reflected accurately. According to Rorty, Dewey showed us why the mind should be abandoned as a transcendental subject and truth as correspondence to reality. Philosophy as representational had to be abandoned because the known and the activity of knowing could not be separated. Like European poststructuralists, Rorty concluded that philosophy is not about origins and first principles, the foun-

Richard Rorty, the American philosopher who has attempted to reinvigorate the liberal Left by assimilating Dewey's pragmatism with French poststructuralism.

dations on which all thoughts supposedly rest, but about meanings and interpretations in which things and events are described. He also insisted that there is no way to arrive at judgments outside the language and beliefs we already accept. Ultimately Rorty's target was "foundationalism," the assumption that inquiry arrives at true knowledge only when it reaches something antecedently existent, a presence present prior to its discovery.[24]

Rorty was less theory oriented than Habermas, less concerned to insist that modern society must look to the criterion of "communicative competence" as a means of finding common grounds for unifying different interests as well as the unique spheres of science, morality, and art. The American philosopher believed that a consensus arising from a context of communication can provide no independent criterion for judging that context itself. Instead, he argued that modern society can live with differences and that philosophical problems will resolve themselves in the daily practices of science and politics. Rorty would forsake the quest for knowledge, which presumes one knows what knowledge is before one searches for it, and rest content with practical questions and arguments that lead people to hold or change an opinion about a given issue. Participation and communication take up where classical philosophy left off as human beings encounter in daily life situations new experiences that require them to change and grow. Thus philosophy needs to be not representational or foundational but edifying and expanding. "The point of edifying philosophy is to keep the conversation going rather than to find the objective truth." With Dewey, Rorty would agree that one cannot know truth and reality directly but that one can, by keeping intelligence active, cope with experience.[25]

One way Rorty proposed that the political activist keep the conversation going is by means of description, or more precisely, "redescription." With the "linguistic turn" in modern thought it was assumed that one cannot derive knowledge from what thinkers know, for many thinkers do not know that they cannot know anything about "foundational" questions—the traditional philosophical attempt to ground ideas in universal truths that transcend historical context and social conventions. Instead, one can know and make use of what thinkers say and write by analyzing the "genealogy" of their texts, that is, understanding the conditions under which their ideas are generated and used to justify beliefs. Rorty also advocated that philosophers and intellectual historians adopt the methods of the anthropologist and observe the social practices of particular people acting in specific historical situations. Such discursive practices can be known because they are products of human action. Thus while access to objective, discoverable truths may be impossible, we can understand our actions and linguistic conventions because we ourselves have created them.

In *Contingency, Irony, Solidarity* (1989), Rorty wanted to see the Left, together with liberals, turn to the political possibilities of language. He called upon writers to follow the example of George Orwell and describe the world of suffering, cruelty, and humiliation. The Left's idea of "solidarity" can also be written about as an act of the moral imagination. "Socialization," Rorty declared, "goes all the way down." What people are is a result of social conditioning and historical circumstance, a result of "contingency" rather than the necessity of any essential human nature or national character. The world itself is simply a matter of vocabularies. We are what we say. Rorty would agree with Santayana's observation that "discourse is a language, not a mirror," and that the "truth which discourse can achieve is truth in its own terms, appropriate description." To describe is to narrate and tell a story. Thus Rorty convinced himself that "solidarity" could be created by redescribing the world as we want it to be. It would be a matter not of inquiry but of imagination. "This process or coming to see other human beings as 'one of us' rather than as 'them' is a matter of detailed description of what unfamiliar people are like and of redescription of what we ourselves are like."[26]

Ironically what Rorty was advocating at the end of the eighties had already been carried out by New Left historians two decades earlier. In the field of labor history especially, the Academic Left redescribed the American past in ways that satisfied the emotional needs of the present in order to tell us "what we ourselves are like." Nineteenth-century American workers appeared in history texts as endowed with class consciousness, community, and a commitment to the solidarity of "moral economy." Marx must have been wrong when he wrote in the preface to *Capital,* "We suffer not only from the living but from the dead. *Le mort saisit le vif!*" The radical historian reverses the dictum: the living can make the dead say what they want to hear. Both Marx and Dewey felt there is nothing to be done about the past, because it cannot be changed. But the radical historian can refashion the past to the requirements of the contemporary imagination. In the act of textualization lies the will to believe and redescribe. The world can be changed by writing about it—a fitting formula for the Academic Left.

Rorty's attempt to provide some theoretical guidance to the Left is both appropriate and in keeping with the spirit of American radicalism. His father, James Rorty, was a Trotskyist in the thirties and a close friend of Sidney Hook, "a man upon whose knees," Richard Rorty recalled, he "was bounced as a baby." Just before Hook's death in 1987, Rorty debated with him over the proper legacy of Dewey's ideas. Hook continued to hold that Dewey's pragmatism meant science and the scientific method, while Rorty contended that pragmatism should become more poststructuralist and reconceive philosophy as a language activity, a continuous discourse for a democratic society of free inquiry and open encounters that requires only procedures of knowing rather than the possession of truth. Rorty believed that the Left should cease regarding America as a "prison-house" of structures and come to terms with the nation's liberal heritage and its "opportunities for self-criticism and reform."[27] The Left could also do well to reconsider its erroneous critique of the Enlightenment. Suspicion of power, after all, hardly began with the French poststructuralists.

Power and Suspicion:
The Enduring Relevance of the Enlightenment

With Habermas and Rorty the study of the American Left ends where it began, with American pragmatism as a philosophical call to engage life as a continuous experiment. The writings of James and Dewey animated the Lyrical Left when Bourne instructed Greenwich Village rebels with advice that resembles Rorty's: "The mind is not a looking-glass, reflecting the world for its private contemplation, not a logic-machine for building up truth, but a tool by which we adjust ourselves to the situation in which life puts us. Reason is not a divinely appointed guide to eternal truth, but a practical instrument by which we solve problems."[28] Pragmatism also influenced Hook to demonstrate to the Old Left that Marx and Dewey shared a basic disposition toward practice over theory. And Hayden and the early New Left drew on Dewey for principles of community and participatory democracy. But pragmatism has also made Marxists uneasy.

Today some Marxists of the Academic Left suspect Rorty's synthesis of pragmatism and poststructuralism. The proposal to accept an open-ended, multivoiced cultural conversation seems to them simply an older version of pluralism and liberal tolerance. The literary Marxist Frank Lentricchia argues that conversation is perhaps already "decisively co-opted by late capitalist economy."[29] A deconstructionist could do no less than to point out the power realities in what passes as normal conversation and discourse. For while Habermas and Rorty advocated reaching consensus through communication and conversation, Foucault and Derrida claimed that the norms society accepts are produced by ignoring the dissident voices of poets, madmen, prophets, women, and bohemians. Such exclusionary strategies suggest that even democratic dialogues may restrict knowledge rather than expand it.

Pragmatism and poststructuralism may share a distrust of philosophy as representational, but when we consider Dewey and Veblen and Derrida and Foucault we are in two different worlds. In the early twentieth century the Left could attack capitalism as anarchic and backward, and Dewey and Veblen could juxtapose the logic of science and technology to the irrationalities of business and the profit system. In modern thought capitalism appears too rational, driven by bureaucratic impulses and governed by inherent structural imperatives. Bourne's reference to reason as a "practical instrument" could be seen, in modern thought, as "instrumental rationality" as science itself came to be regarded as a mode of domination instead of liberation. Similarly with language. Dewey saw language as essential to promoting social interaction and sustaining the democratic spirit. "Democracy begins in conversation," he remarked on his ninetieth birthday.[30] Poststructuralists see discourse and language systems as arbitrary, repressive, an activity in which nothing can be said to begin and almost everything becomes an infinite play of dissemination and indeterminate interpretation.

It could be said that pragmatism, Marxism, and some features of poststructuralism share a conviction that the abstractions of theory and philosophy must give way to the concrete realities of practice. Dewey and the neopragmatists, together with some deconstructionists, insist that all thought arises from a specific context, perhaps a "problematic situation," and thus practice cannot be guided by an idea or position above or outside a given situation. How, then, is practice to be evaluated? Dewey insisted that experience would verify the success or failure of practice, but a deconstructionist might add that the results of experience are themselves subjected to the contingencies of interpretation. It is also worth considering whether experience can be the basis of useful knowledge. For experience must be experienced before we know it, and afterwards we may not rely upon what we know if it is true that no two situations ever replicate one another. To Derrida's "always already," one might add "never again."[31]

In the synthesis of pragmatism and poststructuralism the problem of power is perhaps even more politically relevant than the problem of knowledge. In Dewey's pragmatism the distinction between power and authority is difficult to maintain. In his debates with Bourne, Dewey distinguished legitimate "force" from uncontrolled "violence," and, in his later debates with Trotsky, Dewey, now more a pacifist, insisted that only peaceful, democratic means could be used to realize a just democratic society. Nevertheless, as a pragmatist Dewey held that ideas are not to be judged by any intrinsic principles or external standards; instead, they are to be assessed by their efficacy at producing effects, their consequences in the world of practice and action. In this respect all ideas require the use of power for their realization. In poststructuralist thought power not only is essential in realizing ends but moves without a subject. Whereas pragmatism looks to power to control the environment, poststructuralism, as we noted above, sees power activating itself with no human agent consciously involved. All that can be perceived are endless contexts of domination that develop on their own, and the authority of truth is powerless to resist such developments, since there is no rational subject to render it.

With the humanist tradition weakened in modern thought, the Left also loses its sting. As was pointed out in the opening pages of this book, historically the Left has stood for what Leszek Kolakowski termed "negation," the relentless intellectual assault on the existing order in the name of "unborn ideals." The original concept of the Left presupposed a real world apart from mystifying linguistic discourses, and history was seen as rational, logical, and progressive. In much of modern poststructuralist thought history becomes a succession of events determined by power and interests and incapable of intelligible interpretation. Freedom was once regarded as either the capacity to resist oppression in the name of liberty or the ability to be aware of history and its contingencies as the precondition of being free by virtue of understanding what is happening. With Foucault and Derrida freedom is an illusion as human beings undertake actions that either reproduce existing structures of power or create new ones independent of their intentions. The free are slaves trying to escape their bondage by walking up a descending escalator or writers looking for truth and finding only words. Formerly the Left set out to comprehend the world in order to change it and to speak truth to power. The contemporary Academic Left can barely grapple with the "undecidability" of texts.

The critique of the Enlightenment may be the most burdensome legacy that critical theory imposed on the Academic Left. In the eighteenth century communication and education were forces for change and progress, and the distinction between freedom and tyranny was clear to the bourgeois citizen as well as the indentured servant and slave. The political ideas and values of the

Enlightenment are also vitally relevant today in countries of Eastern Europe and Asia, whose inhabitants know the meaning of
power not as a text but a tank. Ironically in Western countries and
in the United States, where formal freedom prevails in existing
political institutions, freedom is denigrated as the repetition of
coercion; in Eastern Europe it is valued as a real weapon in the
struggle for change and transformation. Much of modern thought
draws no distinction between force and persuasion, the exercise of
power and the acceptance of legitimate authority; or between
manipulation and communication, the control of "signs" and symbols and the transmission of genuine information. Yet having
repudiated the Enlightenment, the critical theorist has elevated
the idea of power to a pre-enlightenment status of absolute sovereignty, an autonomous force, whether divine, dialectical, or discursive, accountable to no one.

When one thinks of American history together with critical
theory, today's Academic Left seems divided against itself. Radical American historians, it will be recalled, are encouraged to find
workers in the nineteenth century citing the Declaration of Independence to defend their rights. While such recourses may have
more to do with liberalism than with Marxism, it cannot be denied that the Declaration was vital to the abolitionists and sacred
to Lincoln. But one wonders what deconstructionists would do to
such a document. How could God and nature endow us with
inalienable natural rights when God and nature are regarded as
inventions of human subjectivity? How can the Declaration be
interpreted when every interpretation is only another misinter-
pretation of a text whose authorial intent cannot be recovered?

In the nineteenth century Lord Byron saw how those rebels
who had made themselves "a fearful monument" set out to
"wreck old opinions / But good with evil they also overthrew" as
"they mistook their prey." Today the Academic Left may no longer be "a fearful monument," but from the university's ivory
towers it still wants to "wreck" old ideas and institutions even
while realizing, as did Byron for different reasons, that the forms
and structures of power eventually reconstitute themselves. Curi-

ously the Academic Left stands with one foot planted firmly on the Declaration and the other caught in the quicksand of deconstruction, one giving its political right to exist and the other its ability to undermine the foundations that the philosophy of natural rights asserts. One half of the Left relies upon "self-evident" truths from which freedom derives; the other half denies the existence of an autonomous self and posits instead history as the story of precisely the opposite vision of the Enlightenment—the self's relentless subjection to domination by structures of power. The old adage that truth will make humankind free can hardly be sustained in a postmodern culture that allows truth to disappear into the labyrinth of language where words have no objects.

But is it the case that the foundations of freedom require direct knowledge of truth? The question that remains to be addressed is whether the discoveries of poststructuralist thinkers, supposedly "original," really undermine the premises of the Enlightenment. There was, after all, a skeptical Enlightenment as well as a rational Enlightenment, and if the rationalist René Descartes assumed that the presence of truth could be proven by a self that knows itself in the act of thinking, the skeptic David Hume proved that the absence of truth could be appreciated by a self that knows itself in the act of forming its own "bundle" of impressions. Even with such profound doubts about the faculty of understanding, eighteenth-century skeptical philosophers never considered declaring, as would contemporary poststructuralists, the "end of man" as a conscious, freely determining subject. Exponents of the Scottish Enlightenment, some of whose theories influenced the American Enlightenment, had no trouble dealing with problems that appear to have stymied the Academic Left. Consider the phenomena of hegemony and power, the preoccupations of Gramsci and Foucault.

For all Marx's emphasis upon praxis—the idea that knowledge is realized only in action—Marxism itself paid little attention to the motives for action. People living under the conditions of "prehistory" prior to socialism act from necessity rather than freedom, from wants rather than wishes. Hume and the Scottish philosophers, however, explained the "springs" of human action not in necessity or even reason but in sentiment and convention. The Scots hit upon the idea of hegemony in their search to discover the ethical psychology that governed social relations in an environment of endless change. In *The Theory of Moral Sentiments*, Adam Smith proposed that sympathy and imagination enable men to understand each other's emotions, the deepest of which is the desire to win the approbation of others, and that one does so by behaving according to standards of the presumably worthier classes. In *Discourses on Davila*, John Adams drew upon Smith to insist that "emulation," "the passion for distinction," and the "love of praise" are the most fundamental desires, and that they can be satisfied only by commanding the attention and approval of superiors. The assistant professor who craves the confirmation of a senior scholar should have no trouble understanding this emotion. But it was the playful and sardonic Thorstein Veblen who did the most to establish the anthropological foundations of hegemony and false consciousness.

If emulation is the ultimate aim of avarice, as Adam Smith first insisted in justifying the advent of commercial society, then "invidious comparison," according to Veblen, compels modern man to admire wealth without work just as primitive man envied the predatory hunter and warrior who left the more mundane productive tasks of life to slaves, servants, and women. What distressed Veblen was a phenomenon that neither Tocqueville nor Gramsci perceived: the persistence of the status of wealth and the stigma of work, the very rank and class distinctions of primitive, feudal, and aristocratic society that capitalism was supposed to destroy. Throughout history a contempt for manual labor coincided with the conspicuous show of trinkets, furs, and other useless trappings of wealth. To the extent that most workers would, given the first opportunity, forsake the life of labor as dishonorable as well as boring, unrewarding, and "irksome," the hegemony of the leisure class is not so much imposed as displayed.

Although Gramsci would have been troubled to discover that workers regard their status with a shame more felt than understood, he would have, I believe, singled out Veblen as a model intellectual, one dedicated to making workers aware of the psycho-cultural reasons for their hegemonic confinement, and one who also looked to the technician and engineer as the organizing vanguard for the transformation of consciousness and the reconstruction of society. Veblen's hopes in the engineer may have been misplaced. But the American radical who admired the conservative Hume, the "placid unbeliever" whose skepticism "dissolved everything that was well received," never repudiated the Enlightenment and the promise of science and rational intelligence.[32]

Should the American Left reject the values of the Enlightenment simply because the French poststructuralists have done so? If the Academic Left were to disabuse itself of the Nietzschean-Heideggerian critique of radicalism propounded by Foucault and Derrida, and return instead to America's liberal traditions, it might learn better how to deal with the problem of power. The poststructuralist assumes that the problem remains unresolvable because there exists no rational subject capable of being aware of power and its productions emerging in "structures" hidden to consciousness. But in the *Federalist* there is also no subject—that is, a Cartesian subject, a freely conscious agent capable of arriving at "clear and distinct" ideas and using reason to rise above the "interests" and "passions" that mediate and distort all human action. Not only is humankind irrational, the *Federalist* authors insisted, but political philosophy must pass through the "cloudy medium" of language that renders all discourse "obscure." Yet the authors of this pre-poststructuralist document knew what it took to control power.

The poststructuralist thesis rests upon a curious set of premises: that power and knowledge were at one time seen as distinct; that in Enlightenment thought the act of thinking can prove the existence of the object of thought; that human action is rational and produces what it intends; and that, therefore, man's inherent rational qualities enable him to control his destiny. John Adams did not have to read Nietzsche and Heidegger to know that the mind invents its interpretations and then treats them as discoveries; that historical events are the results of human action but not necessarily human design; that a political text is written to undermine ("deconstruct") the philosophical assumptions of another text ("words lose their signification," Adams complained of Machiavelli's manipulation of metaphors); and that because philosophy cannot lead us to the truth of things, the problem of power must be resolved by something other than reason. Indeed, rather than assuming that knowledge would generate its own opposition to power, Adams advised juxtaposing "power . . . to power, force to force, strength to strength, interest to interest," in a mosaic of checks and balances.[33]

The critique of the Enlightenment put forth by Frankfurt and Parisian thinkers seems like an innocent caricature compared with the deeper skepticism found in American intellectual history. The poststructuralists want to undermine the Enlightenment with their own post-Enlightenment critique. Yet not only did the Scottish and American Enlightenment contain sufficient self-critiques of their assumptions about knowledge, but religious thinkers who approached the Enlightenment from a pre-Enlightenment perspective offered critiques as devastating as anything found in a contemporary Derridian. French poststructuralists have been celebrated as "masters of suspicion" because of their determination to see the illusions and self-deceptions behind all expressions of rational thought. But no minds were more suspicious of reason than those of the New England Calvinists. Who could believe in a rational, self-determining subject after reading Jonathan Edwards's treatise on freedom of the will? No wonder Perry Miller felt it important that Americans understand the "Augustinian strain" of Puritan thought that reaches its finest expression in Abraham Lincoln. Augustine showed that even the best-intentioned exercise of authority may be an act of power and domination, whether in the name of solidarity or in the name of salvation. Seventeenth-century New England was haunted by the "hermeneutics of suspicion," the mind's anguish at never knowing directly the objects it interprets. That skepticism was shared, even though to a lesser extent, by the eighteenth-century authors of the *Federalist*, where the control of power requires knowledge of human nature rather than access to absolute truth.

With many contemporary poststructuralist thinkers, however, the absence of truth can only mean the presence of power, and the prevalence of power over freedom derives from the critique of the Enlightenment solely as an episode in French history, with almost no reference to the skeptical versions in Scotland and America. Thus in much of modern thought power moves mysteriously without a subject, not so much as a force coercively imposed from above as Foucault's "capillary" activity spreading silently into the veins of society like an undetected disease. Alexander Hamilton might remind us, as he did the antifederalists, that only power can produce effect and thus is not the enemy of freedom but its agency. However, modern theorists see all action as power driven, and power is what happens to people, who are less acting than acted upon. With language, communication, and all modes of information regarded as repressing rather than liberating, no wonder the poststructuralist was caught by surprise by the events in Eastern Europe and China in 1989. Obsessed with the omnipresence of power, the Left had no theory of freedom.

The liberal skeptic, in contrast to the Left, had long been familiar with power as a phenomenon that creeps unseen until its effects are felt. But the problem of power became paramount mainly to the ex-Marxist who had the need to supply a non-Marxist explanation. Thus the ex-Marxist James Burnham tried to inform the Old Left, in *The Managerial Revolution* (1940), that ownership and control of property no longer explains who rules whom; and in *The Machiavellians* (1943) he offered thirteen reasons why reason is impotent to end inexorable power struggles, whether open or concealed.[34] But the Left has discovered the permanence of power only because it once assumed its disappearance with the abolition of capitalism. There may be better ways to grasp the phenomenon of power than to see it as oppression and exploitation, or even as submission to authority, or as securing compliance, or as "asymmetrical" superior-inferior relations, or as hegemonic domination, or simply as brute coercion. The liberal skeptic questions both the classical liberal conviction that property must be protected from the power of the state and the orthodox Marxist conviction that society must be liberated from the power of property. Both harbor the illusions of "the children of light," to borrow Niebuhr's description.[35] Bourgeois liberals and social revolutionaries both assume that an answer to the problem lies either in limiting the state or in eliminating capital; and, by contrast, the poststructuralist assumes there is no answer to power, since human activity reproduces structures of domination even in the name of liberation. This preoccupation with the power of structures and systems to the exclusion of the conscious human subject supposedly signifies "the end of man." On the contrary, a clearer understanding of the phenomenon of power may suggest that its activities signify the very definition of man and woman as doer and maker.

A half century before the poststructuralists informed us that the Enlightenment's premises collapse because of its authors' shaky metaphors and indeterminate signifiers, the American historian Carl Becker "deconstructed" the Enlightenment in *The Heavenly City of the Eighteenth-Century Philosophers* (1932). Becker sought to demonstrate that the *philosophes* were engaging in wordplay when trying to make the secular language of "nature," "reason," and "science" carry the same redemptive promise as the Christian language of "Bible," "faith," and "salvation." Earlier, in *The Declaration of Independence* (1922), he also sought to demonstrate that the natural rights philosophy on which the document rested had no valid philosophical foundations. Like later poststructuralists, Becker realized that in a world devoid of philosophical truth there remained only the reality of power. Yet he went on to explain why power cannot be separated from knowledge and why the very meaning of progress presupposes both:

All that has happened to man in 506,000 years may be symbolized by this fact—at the end of the Time-Scale he can, with ease and expedition, put his ancestors in cages: he has somehow learned the trick of having conveniently at hand and at his disposal powers not provided by his biological inheritance. *From the beginning of the Time-Scale man has increasingly implemented himself with power.* Had he not done so, he would have had no history, nor even the consciousness of not having any: at the end of the Time-Scale he would still be (if not extinct) what he was at the beginning— *Pithecanthropus erectus,* the Erect-Ape-Man. Without power no progress.

Power! I now recall that force and compulsion were listed among the words that symbolize my private aversions. It does not disturb me. . . . The significant fact is that the human race, so far from having any aversion from power, has at all times welcomed it as a value to be cherished. Look where we will along the Time-Scale, we see men eagerly seeking power, patiently fashioning and tenaciously grasping the instruments for exerting it, conferring honor upon those who employ it most effectively. Implements of power once used may become obsolete, the secret of their use may be lost for a time; but in general it is true that once possessed of a new implement of power men do not voluntarily abandon it. Regarding it as in itself good, they use it in whatever ingenious ways it can be used, for whatever ends may at the moment seem desirable, never doubting that the desired ends will sufficiently justify the means employed to attain them.

Tools and the Man! Long ago Francis Bacon noted with precision and brevity that human intelligence and implements of power are correlated conditions of progress.

> Neither the naked hand nor the understanding left to itself can effect much. It is by instruments and helps that the work is done. . . . Human knowledge and human power meet in one.[56]

It may have been true, as the poststructuralists insist, that in the French Enlightenment knowledge and power were regarded as distinct. Political power, in particular, was seen as abitrary, coercive, and threatening, and hence the knowledge promised by the Age of Reason would be systematic, uninhibited, and liberating. The notion that knowledge was logically independent from power rested on the assumption that whatever comes to be known must be accepted under conditions free of coercion and distortion. With the Baconian turn in modern thought, however, knowledge becomes instrumental and requires the power to introduce change and experiment on the materials of nature. Knowledge must result in a practical difference. In the American Enlightenment, as opposed to the French, no distinction was made between knowledge and power, and thus the Constitution aimed to control power by dispersing it on the assumption that a "new science of politics" must replace older systems of political philosophy. John Adams even sought to isolate the highly educated members of Congress by having them serve in the Senate, where their talents could be exploited while their power was kept under surveillance. In America's anti-aristocratic political culture, suspicion glared at knowledge as insolence, a barely concealed form of hegemonic domination.

Power is not some alien presence contrary to nature. It is intrinsic to the very constitution of men and women contending with the conditions of history. Poststructuralist philosophers have only described a world supposedly lost to the concealed structures of domination. The challenge the Left faces is not to despair about power but to uncover its hidden operations in order to control it better with countervailing mechanisms. To that challenge the American Enlightenment remains directly relevant. As Hannah Arendt observed, the framers of the Constitution successfully dealt with power because they "abolished" the idea of sovereignty by refusing to believe that any class or faction could be entrusted with undivided authority.[37] One could even suggest that it was in Philadelphia in 1787, and not Paris in 1987, that one finds the first political philosophers of "suspicion." Neither the one, the few, nor the many were sufficiently conscious and capable of seeing that their rhetoric of "virtue" only masked their will to power—or, as James Madison put it, their uncontrollable, passionate tendency to "vex and oppress" others.[38] A combination of Calvinism and Scottish skepticism succeeded in both lowering their hopes and raising their consciousness to the point that the framers were suspicious even of themselves!

As to freedom, it is difficult to see how the American Left can halt its decline and fall unless it returns to the values of the

Enlightenment, wherein both liberal pragmatism and Marxian socialism, the major intellectual ingredients in all four Lefts, derived their heritage. Both philosophies conceive knowledge as a transitive activity requiring the presence of objects to be acted upon by human agents. Knowledge as a transforming practice cannot be carried out without the power to act, and all effective action is an exercise of force, which Dewey saw as indispensable to scientific "method" and Marx aptly called the "midwife" of history in its struggle toward freedom. Knowledge joined to power represents nothing less than the history of life itself, and as long as life continues it seems a bit premature to pronounce "dead" the human subject. To do so is to leave the Left disbelieving in itself, without the power to effect change, without perhaps even the will to live. The American Left was born from the idea of freedom, an idea that implies the power of ideals to be actualized. A noble birth.

> I have felt to soar in freedom
> and in the fullness of power, joy, volition.
>
> —Whitman

Notes

Preface

1. For a valuable resource of intelligently compiled information, see *Encyclopedia of the American Left*, ed. Mari Jo Buhle, Paul Buhle, and Dan Georgakas (New York: Garland, 1990).

Chapter 1: The Left as a Theoretical Problem

1. Isaiah Berlin, *Two Concepts of Liberty* (Oxford: Clarendon, 1958).
2. Herbert Marcuse, "Repressive Tolerance," in Herbert Marcuse et al., *A Critique of Pure Tolerance* (Boston: Beacon, 1965), 81–117.
3. Randolph Bourne, "This Older Generation," *Atlantic*, Sept. 1915, 385–91.
4. David Caute, *The Left in Europe since 1789* (London: Weidenfeld and Nicolson, 1966).

5. Staughton Lynd, *Intellectual Origins of American Radicalism* (New York: Pantheon, 1968).

6. For a critique of Lynd's argument, see John P. Diggins, "Thoreau, Marx, and the 'Riddle' of Alienation," *Social Research* 39 (Winter 1972): 571–98.

7. Daniel Bell, *The End of Ideology: On the Exhaustion of Political Ideas in the Fifties* (New York: Free Press, 1960); on the conceptual ambiguities surrounding this issue, see John P. Diggins, "Ideology and Pragmatism: Philosophy or Passion?" *American Political Science Review* 64 (Sept. 1970): 899–906.

8. In his classic work, *Ideology and Utopia*, Karl Mannheim first pointed out a crucial epistemological distinction that separates the Right from the Left: the former uses ideology to defend the existing order as real and valid, and the Left projects utopian ideas to challenge that order as false and to direct activity toward undermining it. Since "utopian" is so often used as a term of abuse to deride any new radical idea as a pipe dream, it seems more appropriate to use the term "negation." Much of my discussion of this idea is drawn from Leszek Kolakowski's illuminating essay "The Concept of the Left," in *Toward a Marxist Humanism: Essays on the Left Today* (New York: Grove Press, 1969), 67–83.

9. Karl Mannheim, "The Problem of Generations," in *Essays on the Sociology of Knowledge* (London: Routledge, 1959).

10. Robert MacIver, quoted in Seymour Martin Lipset, *Political Man: The Social Bases of Politics* (Garden City, N.Y.: Anchor, 1963), 232.

11. Christopher Lasch, *The New Radicalism in America, 1889–1963: The Intellectual As a Social Type* (New York: Vintage, 1967), ix–xviii.

12. John Reed, "Almost Thirty" (MS, Houghton Library, Harvard Univ.), 8.

13. Max Eastman, *Enjoyment of Living* (New York: Harper, 1948), 15–26; see also Floyd Dell, *Homecoming: An Autobiography* (New York: Farrar and Rinehart, 1933).

Chapter 2: The New Intellectuals

1. Henry James, ed., *The Letters of William James* (Boston: Atlantic Monthly, 1920), 2:100–101.

2. The rise of student radicalism in the 1960s rekindled the debate over young intellectuals that had first been broached by Marxists

in the late nineteenth century. See Lewis S. Feuer, *Marx and the Intellectuals: A Set of Post-Ideological Essays* (Garden City, N.Y.: Doubleday, 1969), 53–69; and Shlomo Avineri, "Feuer on Marx and the Intellectuals," *Survey: A Journal of Soviet and East European Studies*, no. 62 (Jan. 1767): 152–55. The problem is treated at length in Giuseppe Vacca, *Il Marxismo e gli intellettuali* (Rome: Riuniti, 1985).

3. Paul Lafargue, "Socialism and the Intellectuals," *International Socialist Review* 1 (Aug. 1, 1900): 84–101; Paul Buhle, "Intellectuals in the Debsian Socialist Party," *Radical America* 4 (April 1970): 35–58; Lewis S. Feuer, "The Political Linguistics of 'Intellectual,' 1898–1918," *Survey*, no. 78 (Winter 1971): 156–83.

4. Jean Jaurès and Paul Lafargue, *Idéalisme et matérialisme dans la conception de l'histoire* (Toulouse, 1895); Charles B. Mitchell, "Bergsonism and Practical Idealism" *New Review* 2 (April 1914): 224–27.

5. Robert Rives LaMonte, "The New Intellectuals," *New Review* 2 (Jan. 1914): 35–53.

6. William James, *Varieties of Religious Experience* (New York: Longmans, 1902), 157; idem, *Pragmatism and Other Essays* (New York: Washington Square Press, 1963), 187–213.

7. William English Walling, "The Pragmatism of Marx and Engels," *New Review* 1 (April 5, 1913): 434–39; ibid. (April 12, 1913): 464–69; Walter Lippmann, "LaMonte, Walling and Pragmatism," *New Review* 1 (Nov. 1913): 907–9; idem, *A Preface to Politics* (New York: Kennerly, 1913), 282, 303.

8. Max Eastman, "Knowledge and Revolution," *Masses* 4 (Dec. 1912): 1.

9. Max Eastman, *Reflections on the Failure of Socialism* (New York: Universal Library, 1955), 57.

Chapter 3: Strangers in the Land

1. Maurice Merleau-Ponty, quoted in Raymond Aron, "The Myth of the Proletariat," in *The Opium of the Intellectuals* (New York: Norton, 1962), 66–93.

2. Norman Pollack, *The Populist Response to Industrial America* (New York: Norton, 1962), 68–84; see also Lawrence Goodwyn, *Democratic Promise: The Populist Movement in America* (New York: Oxford Univ. Press, 1976).

3. James B. Webster, "A Farmer's Criticism of the Socialist Party," *International Socialist Review* 2 (May 1902): 769–73; Howard H.

Quint, *The Forging of American Socialism* (Indianapolis: Bobbs-Merrill, 1953), 211.

4. Thorstein Veblen, "The Independent Farmer" and "The Country Town," in *The Portable Veblen*, ed. Max Lerner (New York: Viking, 1948), 395–430; Randolph Bourne, "A Mirror of the Middle West," in *The History of a Literary Radical and Other Papers* (New York: S. A. Russell, 1956), 292.

5. George G. S. Murphy and Arnold Zellner, "Sequential Growth, the Labor-Safety-Valve Doctrine, and the Development of American Unionism," in *Turner and the Sociology of the Frontier*, ed. Richard Hofstadter and Seymour Martin Lipset (New York: Basic, 1968), 201–24; Selig Perlman, *A Theory of the Labor Movement* (New York: Macmillan, 1949); Stephen Thernstrom, *Poverty and Progress: Social Mobility in a Nineteenth Century City* (New York: Atheneum, 1970); for an example of the diverse conclusions reached by contemporary scholars studying the mobility question, see Stephen Thernstrom and Richard Sennett, eds., *Nineteenth-Century Cities: Essays in the New Urban History* (New Haven: Yale Univ. Press, 1969); a valuable anthology of interpretations of the fate of socialism is *The Failure of a Dream: Essays on the History of American Socialism*, ed. John H. M. Laslett and Seymour Martin Lipset (Garden City, N.Y.: Anchor, 1974).

6. "Hillquit versus Gompers," in *Socialism in America: From the Shakers to the Third International: A Documentary History*, ed. Albert Fried (Garden City, N.Y.: Doubleday, 1970), 471–95.

7. Theodore Draper, *The Roots of American Communism* (New York: Viking, 1963), 29.

8. Samuel Gompers, quoted in Daniel Bell, *Marxian Socialism in the United States* (Princeton: Princeton Univ. Press, 1967), 43; V. I. Lenin, *What Is to Be Done?* (New York: International Publishers, 1929).

9. Friedrich Engels, quoted in Lewis S. Feuer, "The Alienated Americans and Their Influence on Marx and Engels," in *Marx and the Intellectuals* (Garden City, N.Y.: Doubleday, 1969), 171.

10. Ralph Waldo Emerson, "The American Scholar," in *The Portable Emerson*, ed. Mark Van Doren (New York: Viking, 1946), 24; Charles Crowe, *George Ripley: Transcendentalist and Utopian Socialist* (Athens: Univ. of Georgia Press, 1967), 173.

11. *Harbinger* editorial, in Fried, ed., *Socialism in America*, 161–65; see also John L. Thomas, "Romantic Reform in America, 1815–1865," *American Quarterly* 17 (Winter 1965): 656–81.

12. Edward Bellamy, quoted in Daniel Aaron, *Men of Good Hope* (New York: Oxford Univ. Press, 1951), 112; Horace Greeley, "Association Discussed" (1847), in Fried, ad., *Socialism in America*, 149–60; Max Eastman, "Concerning an Idealism," *Masses* 4 (July 1913): 1.

13. Bill Haywood, quoted in Melvyn Dubofsky, *We Shall Be All: A History of the Industrial Workers of the World* (Chicago: Quadrangle, 1969), 161.

14. James Weinstein, *The Decline of Socialism in America, 1912–1925* (New York: Monthly Review, 1967); John H. M. Laslett, *Labor and the Left: A Study of Socialist and Radical Influences on the American Labor Movement, 1881–1924* (New York: Basic, 1970).

15. Eugene Debs, "Why I Became a Socialist," in *Debs: His Life Writings and Speeches* (Chicago, 1908), 82; John Dos Passos, *The 42nd Parallel* (New York: Random House, 1937), 26; Max Eastman, *Love and Revolution: My Journey through an Epoch* (New York: Random House, 1964), 114; see also the excellent biography by Nick Salvatore, *Eugene V. Debs: Citizen and Socialist* (Urbana: Univ. of Illinois Press, 1982).

16. John Reed, quoted in Charles A. Madison, *Critics and Crusaders: A Century of American Protest* (New York: Holt, 1947), 470.

17. Max Eastman, "The S.L.P.," *Class Struggle* 3 (Aug. 1919): 304–6; Robert Miner to Eastman, April 20, 1919, Eastman MSS, Lilly Library, Indiana Univ., Bloomington.

18. Daniel DeLeon, quoted in Fried, ed., *Socialism in America*, 194; see also Louis Fraina, "Daniel DeLeon," *New Review* 2 (July 1914): 390–99.

19. Dos Passos, *42nd Parallel*, 94; William D. Haywood, "The Fighting IWW," *International Socialist Review*, 13 (Sept. 1912): 247.

20. J. Ramsay MacDonald, quoted in Melvyn Dubofsky, "The Radicalism of the Dispossessed: William Haywood and the IWW," in *Dissent: Explorations in the History of American Radicalism*, ed. Alfred Young (DeKalb: Northern Illinois Univ. Press, 1968), 177.

21. Bill Haywood, and references to him, quoted in Daniel Aaron, *Writers on the Left: Episodes in American Literary Communism* (New York: Harcourt, Brace & World, 1961), 14, 16–17.

Chapter 4: The Lyrical Left

1. Malcolm Cowley, quoted in William E. Leuchtenburg, *The Perils of Prosperity, 1914–1932* (Chicago: Univ. of Chicago Press, 1958), 140; Floyd Dell, *Homecoming* (New York: Farrar and Rinehart,

1933), 356–59; Mabel Dodge Luhan, *Intimate Memoirs,* vol. 3, *Movers and Shakers* (New York: Kraus, 1936), 39, 83.

2. Max Eastman, *Enjoyment of Poetry* (New York: Scribner, 1913), 10–11; Van Wyck Brooks, *America's Coming-of-Age* (New York: Dutton, 1915); Eastman's description of the "Lyrical Socialist" is in his "The Wisdom of Lenin," *Liberator* 7, no. 7 (July 1924): 24.

3. Joseph Freeman, *An American Testament* (New York: Farrar and Rinehart, 1936), 50.

4. Walter Lippmann, *A Preface to Politics* (New York: Kennerly, 1913), 200 and passim.

5. Luhan, *Movers and Shakers,* 264; Mabel Dodge to Eastman, May 10, 1938, Eastman MSS; Randolph Bourne, quoted in Henry F. May, *The End of American Innocence: A Study of the First Years of Our Own Time, 1912–1917* (New York: Knopf, 1959), 244.

6. Max Eastman, *Enjoyment of Living* (New York: Harper, 1948), 355.

7. John Reed, "Almost Thirty" (MSS, Houghton Library, Harvard Univ.), 18–19.

8. Walter Lippmann, "Walling's 'Progressivism and After,' " *New Review* 2 (June 1914): 340–49; idem, "The IWW—Insurrection or Reaction," ibid., 1 (Aug. 1913): 701–6; idem, *A Preface to Politics,* 29; Max Eastman, *Love and Revolution* (New York: Random House, 1964), 126.

9. Dell, *Homecoming,* 251.

10. W. J. Ghent, quoted in Albert Fried, ed., *Socialism in America* (Garden City, N.Y.: Doubleday, 1970), 384.

11. The "wit," quoted in Alfred Kazin, *On Native Grounds: An Interpretation of Modern American Prose Literature* (New York: Harcourt, Brace & World, 1942), 169; a recent study of the period may be found in Leslie Fishbein, *The Radicals and "the Masses," 1911–1917* (Chapel Hill: Univ. of North Carolina Press, 1982).

12. Charles E. Russell and J. G. Phelps Stokes, quoted in Fried, ed., *Socialism in America,* 508–9.

13. Randolph Bourne, quoted in Freeman, *American Testament,* 105–6.

14. On the *Masses* trial I am indebted to Ross Wetzsteon's excellent account, "Revolution American Style: The Masses's Appeal," *Village Voice,* Nov. 15, 1988, 54–58.

15. Randolph Bourne, "A War Diary," in *War and the Intellectuals: Collected Essays, 1915–1919,* ed. Carl Resek (New York: Harper & Row, 1964), 36–47; Eastman, *Enjoyment of Living,* 533–34; John Reed, "One Solid Month of Liberty," *Masses* 9 (Sept. 1917): 5–6.

16. Louis Fraina, *Revolutionary Socialism: A Study of Socialist Reconstruction* (New York: Communist Press, 1918), 62–63.

17. Max Eastman, "The Religion of Patriotism," *Masses* 9 (July 1917): 8–12; Randolph Bourne, "The State," in *War and the Intellectuals,* 65–104.

18. Theodore Draper, *The Roots of American Communism* (New York: Viking, 1963), 109–13.

19. John Reed, *Ten Days That Shook the World* (New York: Random House, 1960), 170–71; Eastman's poem on Lenin appeared in *Liberator* 1 (Nov. 1918): 17.

20. "The Communist Labor Party" (editorial), *Class Struggle* 3 (Nov. 1919): 438–43.

21. Max Shachtman, "American Communism: A Re-examination of the American Past," *New International* 23 (Fall 1957): 225.

22. Reed, "Almost Thirty," 8–18; Bertram D. Wolfe, *Strange Communists I Have Known* (New York: Bantam, 1967), 11–35.

23. Luhan, *Movers and Shakers,* 189.

24. Richard O'Connor and Dale L. Walker, *The Lost Revolutionary: A Biography of John Reed* (New York: Harcourt, Brace & World, 1967); Robert A. Rosenstone, *Romantic Revolutionary: A Biography of John Reed* (New York: Knopf, 1975).

25. Draper, *Roots of American Communism,* 284–93.

26. Eastman, *Enjoyment of Living,* xiv–xv, 15–18, 23–26.

27. Freeman, *American Testament,* 103.

28. Eastman, *Love and Revolution,* 14–16, 125–32; idem, *Marx and Lenin: The Science of Revolution* (New York: Albert Boni, 1927).

29. Max Eastman, *Liberator* 1 (Sept. 1918): 10–13; (Oct. 1918): 28–33.

30. Eastman, *Love and Revolution,* 350–56; idem, *Since Lenin Died* (New York: Liveright, 1925); idem, *Leon Trotsky: The Portrait of a Youth* (New York: Greenberg, 1925), v.

31. Eastman later brought together all his arguments in *Marxism, Is It Science?* (New York: Norton, 1940).

32. Eastman helped Trotsky publish his works in the United States, and he tried to help the exile obtain a visa to enter the country. But the two had a falling out over the issue of dialectical materialism. Eastman to Trotsky, July 9, 1929, Aug. 14, 1933, Eastman MSS; Trotsky to C. V. Calverton, Nov. 4, 1932, Trotsky Archives, Houghton Library, Harvard Univ., Cambridge, Mass.

33. Mario Savio, quoted in Lewis S. Feuer, *The Conflict of Generations: The Character and Significance of Student Movements* (New York: Basic, 1969), 503.

34. Mary Jo Buhle, *Women and American Socialism, 1870–1920* (Urbana: Univ. of Illinois Press, 1981).

35. For a comparison of Gilman and Veblen, see John P. Diggins, *The Bard of Savagery: Thorstein Veblen and Modern Social Theory* (New York: Continuum, 1978), 158–61; see also Ann J. Lane, *To "Herland" and Beyond: The Life and Work of Charlotte Perkins Gilman* (New York: Pantheon, 1990).

36. Richard Drinnon, *Rebel in Paradise* (Chicago: Univ. of Chicago Press, 1961); Goldman is quoted in *The Feminist Papers*, ed. Alice Rossi (New York: Bantam, 1973), 507.

37. Emma Goldman, *Red Emma Speaks: Selected Writings and Speeches*, ed. Alix Kates Shulman (New York: Vintage, 1972), 140–42.

38. Eastman, *Love and Revolution;* idem, "My First Great Companion," in *Einstein, Trotsky, Hemingway, Freud and Other Great Companions* (New York: Collier, 1962), 210–19.

39. Gilman's poem is quoted in Buhle, *Women and American Socialism*, 214.

40. *Crystal Eastman on Women and Revolution*, ed. Blanche Wiesen Cook (New York: Oxford Univ. Press, 1978), 80.

41. Edna St. Vincent Millay, *Collected Poems* (New York: Harper & Row, 1956), 571; Janice R. MacKinnon and Stephen R. MacKinnon, *Agnes Smedley: The Life and Times of an American Radical* (Berkeley: Univ. of California Press, 1988); *Rebel Pen: The Writings of Mary Heaton Vorse*, ed. Dee Garrison (New York: Monthly Review, 1985).

42. Floyd Dell, *Love in the Machine Age* (New York: Farrar and Rinehart, 1930); Walter Lippmann, *A Preface to Morals;* Joseph Wood Krutch, *The Modern Temper* (New York: Harcourt, Brace, 1929), quoted on p. 68; see also Ellen Kay Trimberger, "Feminism, Men, and Modern Love: Greenwich Village, 1920–1925," in *Desire: The Politics of Sexuality*, ed. Ann Snitow, Christine Stansell, and Sharon Thompson (London: Virago, 1984), 169–89; June Sochen, *The New Woman: Feminism in Greenwich Village, 1910–1921* (New York: Quadrangle, 1972).

43. McKay, quoted in *Crystal Eastman*, 34–35.

44. Wayne F. Cooper, *Claude McKay: Rebel Sojourner of the Harlem Renaissance* (Baton Rouge: Louisiana State Univ. Press, 1987).

45. S. P. Fullinwider, "Jean Toomer: Lost Generation or Negro Renaissance?" *Phylon* 27 (1966): 396–401; see also Nathan Irwin Huggins, *Harlem Renaissance* (New York: Oxford Univ. Press, 1971); David L. Lewis, *When Harlem Was in Vogue* (New York:

Knopf, 1979). *My Soul's High Song: The Collected Writings of Countee Cullen, Voice of the Harlem Renaissance,* ed. Gerald L. Early (New York: Doubleday, 1991).

46. Antonio Gramsci, *Selections from the Prison Notebooks,* ed. Quintin Hoare and Geoffrey Nowell Smith (New York: International Publishers, 1971); see also John Diggins, "Gramsci and the Intellectuals," *Raritan* 9 (Fall 1989): 129–52.

47. *Writings by W. E. B. DuBois,* ed. Nathan I. Huggins (New York: Library of America, 1986).

48. The information on and quotes by Robeson come from Martin Duberman's excellent biography, *Paul Robeson* (New York: Knopf, 1989).

49. Van Wyck Brooks's cultural criticism during the Greenwich Village era is conveyed in *America's Coming-of-Age;* the criticism continues as representative of the lost generation in his "The Literary Life," in *Civilization in the United States,* ed. Harold Stearns (New York: Harcourt, Brace, 1922), 179–97.

50. Randolph Bourne, "Trans-National America," in *The Radical Will: Randolph Bourne: Selected Writings, 1911–1918,* ed. Olaf Hansen (New York: Urizen, 1977), 248–64.

51. Malcolm Cowley, *Exile's Return: A Literary Saga of the Nineteen-Twenties* (New York: Viking, 1934), 60–61. Curiously, there has been no historical (as opposed to literary) treatment of the lost generation; for a valuable study of its background, see May, *End of American Innocence.*

52. Walter Lippmann, *Public Opinion* (New York: Macmillan, 1922); idem, *The Phantom Public* (New York: Macmillan, 1925); on intellectuals and fascist Italy, see John P. Diggins, *Mussolini and Fascism: The View from America* (Princeton: Princeton Univ. Press, 1972).

53. The critique of science, technology, and pragmatism is in Lewis Mumford, *The Golden Day: A Study in American Experience and Culture* (New York: Boni and Liveright, 1926), and Krutch, *Modern Temper.*

54. Suzanne LaFollette, *Concerning Women* (New York: Albert and Charles Boni, 1926); on the fate of feminism in the twenties, see Nancy F. Cott, *The Grounding of Modern Feminism* (New Haven: Yale Univ. Press, 1987).

55. John Dos Passos, *The Big Money* (1936; reprint, New York: Washington Square Press, 1961), 520–21.

Chapter 5: The Old Left

1. A "twenty-seven-year-old journalist," in Studs Terkel, *Hard Times: An Oral History of the Great Depression* (New York: Pantheon, 1970), 24.

2. From "East Coker," in "Four Quartets," in *Collected Poems, 1909–1962* (New York: Harcourt, Brace & World, 1963).

3. Leon Trotsky, *The History of the Russian Revolution*, vol. 3, *The Triumph of the Soviets*, trans. Max Eastman (Ann Arbor: Univ. of Michigan Press, 1967), 174.

4. Caroline Bird's phrase, quoted in Terkel, *Hard Times*, 3.

5. Edmund Wilson, "The Literary Consequences of the Crash," in *Shores of Light: A Literary Chronicle of the Twenties and Thirties* (New York: Farrar, Straus and Young, 1952), 498–99.

6. F. Scott Fitzgerald, *The Crack-up*, ed. Edmund Wilson (New York: New Directions, 1956), 79–84.

7. Lawson to Dos Passos, n.d., Dos Passos MSS, Alderman Library, Univ. of Virginia, Charlottesville; Granville Hicks, "Communism and the American Intellectuals," in *Whose Revolution?* ed. Irving D. Talmadge (New York: Howell, Soskin, 1941), 84.

8. Sidney Hook, *Towards the Understanding of Karl Marx: A Revolutionary Interpretation* (New York: John Day, 1933); Louis Hacker, "The American Revolution," *Marxist Quarterly* 1 (Jan.–March 1937): 46–47; idem, "The American Civil War," ibid. (April–June 1937): 191–213; Lewis Corey, "Veblen and Marxism," ibid. (Jan.–March 1937): 162–68.

9. Daniel Aaron, *Writers on the Left* (New York: Harcourt, Brace & World, 1961), 158.

10. Irving Howe, "A Memoir of the Thirties," in *Steady Work: Essays in the Politics of Democratic Radicalism, 1953–1966* (New York: Harcourt, Brace & World, 1966), 357–59.

11. Floyd Dell, quoted in Joseph Freeman, *An American Testament* (New York: Farrar and Rinehart, 1936), 404, and in Aaron, *Writers on the Left*, 217–18; Gold to Calverton, May 4, 1925, Calverton Papers, New York Public Library.

12. C. V. Calverton, "Love and Revolution," *New Masses* 1 (Oct. 1926): 28; idem, "Radical Psychology," ibid., 2 (July 1927): 29; idem, *The Bankruptcy of Marriage* (New York: Arno Press, 1928); H. M. Wicks, "An Apology for Sex Anarchism Disguised as Marxism," *Daily Worker*, June 9, 1927, 4.

13. Sidney Hook, "Marx and Freud: Oil and Water," *Open Court* 42 (1928): 20.

14. Hook, *Towards the Understanding,* 73–114; idem, *Out of Step: An Unquiet Life in the 20th Century* (New York: Harper & Row, 1987).

15. Sidney Hook to John Dewey, Jan. 29, 1929, Hook Papers, Dewey Center, Southern Illinois Univ.; idem, *Towards the Understanding.*

16. Hook, *Towards the Understanding*; idem, *From Hegel to Marx: Studies in the Intellectual Development of Karl Marx* (1936; reprint, Ann Arbor: Univ. of Michigan Press, 1968).

17. Sidney Hook, "Marxism, Metaphysics, and Modern Science," *Modern Quarterly* 4 (May–Aug. 1928): 388–94; Max Eastman, *The Last Stand of Dialectical Materialism: A Study of Sidney Hook's Marxism* (New York: Polemic Publishers, 1934); for a fuller discussion of the debate, see John P. Diggins, *Up from Communism: Conservative Odysseys in American Intellectual History* (New York: Harper & Row, 1975), 39–59.

18. Hook's seminal essay "Dialectic and Nature" is reprinted in his *Reason, Social Myths, and Democracy* (New York: Humanities Press, 1940), 188–226.

19. Max Eastman to C. V. Calverton, June 12, 1935, Calverton Papers.

20. Max Eastman, *Enjoyment of Living* (New York: Harper, 1948), Hook, *Out of Step,* 9–11.

21. Sidney Hook, "What's Left of Karl Marx?" *Saturday Review of Literature,* June 6, 1959, 12–14.

22. Granville Hicks is quoted in *Art for the Masses (1911–1917): A Radical Magazine and Its Graphics,* ed. Rebecca Zurier (New Haven: Yale Univ. Art Gallery, 1985), 135.

23. George Lukács, *History and Class Consciousness: Studies in Marxist Dialectics,* trans. Rodney Livingstone (Cambridge: MIT Press, 1971), 1–24; Arthur Koestler, *Arrow in the Blue* (New York: Macmillan, 1952), 272.

24. Freeman, *American Testament,* 663.

25. Dos Passos's remark is in the important symposium "Whither the American Writer," *Modern Quarterly* 6 (Summer 1932): 11–12.

26. Staughton Lynd, ed., "Personal Histories of the Early CIO," *Radical America* 5 (May–June 1971): 49–85; Theodore Draper, "Gastonia Revisited," *Social Research* 38 (Spring 1971): 3–29; idem,

"Communists and Miners, 1928–1933," *Dissent* 19 (Spring 1972): 371–92; see also John L. Shover, "The Communist Party and the Midwest Farm Crisis of 1933," *Journal of American History* 51 (Sept. 1964): 248–66.

27. "Resolution of the Negro Question in the United States," *Communist* 10 (Feb. 1931): 153–67.

28. Dan T. Carter, *Scottsboro: A Tragedy of the American South* (Baton Rouge: Louisiana State Univ. Press, 1969), 51–103; Diggins, *Mussolini and Fascism*, 306–12; Mark Naison, *Communists in Harlem during the Depression* (Urbana: Univ. of Illinois Press, 1983); Harold Cruse, *The Crisis of the Negro Intellectual* (New York: Morrow, 1967), 365–80.

29. Quoted in Hal Draper, "The Student Movement of the Thirties," in *As We Saw the Thirties*, ed. Rita Simon (Urbana: Univ. of Illinois Press, 1969), 156.

30. The coed quoted ibid., 176; Barbara Foley, "Women and the Left in the 1930s," *American Literary History* 2 (Spring 1990): 82–94.

31. Nathan Glazer, *The Social Bases of American Communism* (New York: Harcourt, Brace & World, 1961); Harvey Klehr, *Communist Cadre: The Social Background of the American Communist Party Elite* (Stanford: Hoover Institution Press, 1978).

32. Theodore Draper, "The Ghost of Social Fascism," *Commentary* 47 (Feb. 1969): 29–42; Diggins, *Mussolini and Fascism*, 213–20.

33. Quoted in Irving Howe and Lewis Coser, *The American Communist Party: A Critical History* (New York: Praeger, 1957), 338.

34. Upton Sinclair, quoted in Frank A. Warren, *Liberals and Communism: The "Red Decade" Revisited* (Bloomington: Indiana Univ. Press, 1966), 116.

35. Robert A. Rosenstone, *Crusade of the Left: The Lincoln Battalion in the Spanish Civil War* (Lanham, Md.: Univ. Press of America, 1980), 114.

36. Hemingway to Dos Passos, 1938, Dos Passos MSS; Dos Passos to Editors of *New Republic*, July 1939, in *The Fourteenth Chronicle: Letters and Diaries of John Dos Passos*, ed. Townsend Luddington (Boston: Gambit, 1973), 527–29.

37. Hemingway quoted in Charles Molesworth, "Hemingway's Code: The Spanish Civil War and World Power," *Salmagundi* 76–77 (Fall 1987–Winter 1988): 99; Albert Camus, quoted in Allen Guttmann, *The Wound in the Heart: America and the Spanish Civil War* (New York: Free Press, 1962), x.

38. Leon Trotsky, "Their Morals and Ours," *New International* 4 (June 1938): 163–73; John Dewey, "Means and Ends," ibid., 4

(Aug. 1938): 232–33; *The Case of Leon Trotsky: Report of Hearings on Charges Made against Him in the Moscow Trials* (New York: Merit, 1968), 356–57, 584–85.

39. Max Eastman, *Einstein, Trotsky, Hemingway, Freud and Other Great Companions* (New York: Collier, 1962), 111.

40. Leon Trotsky to Max Eastman, March 13, 1932; March 22, 1932, Eastman MSS.

41. Howe, *Steady Work*, 117; F. W. Dupee, "Editors Note," in Trotsky, *History of the Russian Revolution*, vii; Dwight Macdonald, *The Memoirs of a Revolutionist: Essays in Political Criticism* (New York: Farrar, Straus and Cudahy 1957), 15; Edmund Wilson, *To the Finland Station* (Garden City, N.Y.: Anchor, 1953), 431–32.

42. Jay Lovestone, "The Moscow Trials in Historical Perspective," *Workers Age* 6 (Feb. 6, 1937): 3.

43. Edmund Wilson, "American Critics, Left and Right," in *Shores of Light*, 643; Waldo Frank, *Chart for Rough Water* (New York: Doubleday, Doran, 1940), 43; Malcolm Cowley, "The Sense of Guilt," *Kenyon Review* 15 (Spring 1965): 265; Malcolm Cowley to John Dewey, June 4, 1937, Hook Papers.

44. Max Shachtman, "Is Russia a Workers' State?" *New International* 6 (Dec. 1940): 195–205.

45. W. H. Auden, quoted in Goerge Novack, "Radical Intellectuals in the 1930's," *International Socialist Review* 29 (March–April 1968): 33; Hicks, "Communism and the American Intellectuals," 107–8.

46. Karl Marx, *Das Kapital*, vol. 1 (Chicago: Charles Kerr, 1906), 837.

47. Lewis Corey, *The Crisis of the Middle Class* (New York: Covici, Friede, 1935); idem, "American Class Relations," *Marxist Quarterly* 1 (April–June 1937): 134–43; idem, "The Middle Class," *Antioch Review* 5 (Spring 1945): 68–87; Max Lerner, *America as a Civilization* (New York: Simon & Schuster, 1957), 465–540; Seymour Martin Lipset, *Political Man* (Garden City, N.Y.: Anchor, 1963), 1–63.

48. John Kenneth Galbraith, *American Capitalism: The Concept of Countervailing Power* (Boston: Houghton Mifflin, 1952), 193; Lipset, *Political Man*, 442; Werner Sombart, quoted in Daniel Bell, *The End of Ideology* (New York: Free Press, 1960), 276–77.

49. James Burnham, *The Managerial Revolution: What Is Happening in the World* (New York: John Day, 1941).

50. Lipset, *Political Man*, 87–126; Max Weber, quoted in Bell, *End of Ideology*, 275.

51. Will Herberg, "From Marxism to Judaism," *Commentary* 3 (Jan. 1947): 25–32; idem, *Judaism and Modern Man* (New York: Farrar, Straus and Young, 1951), 28; Reinhold Niebuhr, *The Children of Light and the Children of Darkness* (New York: Scribners, 1944), 86–118.

52. Herberg, *Judaism and Modern Man,* 8–43; Niebuhr, *Children of Light,* xiii; for the influence of Niebuhr on American liberalism, see the essays by Kenneth Thompson, Arthur M. Schlesinger, Jr., and David Williams in Charles W. Kegley and Robert W. Bretall, eds., *Reinhold Niebuhr: His Religious, Social, and Political Thought* (New York: Macmillan, 1956), 126–75, 194–213.

53. "The Situation in American Writing: Seven Questions," *Partisan Review* 6 (Summer 1939): 25–51.

54. Louis Kronenberger's remark is from the symposium "Our Country, Our Culture," an important intellectual document of the 1950s that ran in three issues of the *Partisan Review* 19 (May–June, July–Aug., Sept.–Oct.): 282–326, 420–50, 562–97; Alfred Kazin, *On Native Grounds* (New York: Harcourt, Brace & World, 1942), 485.

55. Richard Hofstadter, *The American Political Tradition* (New York: Knopf, 1948), viii, 16–17, passim.

56. Daniel J. Boorstin, *The Genius of American Politics* (Chicago: Univ. of Chicago Press, 1953); Louis Hartz, *The Liberal Tradition in America: An Interpretation of American Political Thought since the Revolution* (New York: Harcourt, Brace & World, 1955); see also John P. Diggins, "Consciousness and Ideology in American History: The Burden of Daniel J. Boorstin," *American Historical Review* 76 (Feb. 1971): 99–118.

57. Hartz, *Liberal Tradition,* 32, 309.

58. Lewis S. Feuer, "From Ideology to Philosophy: Sidney Hook's Writings on Marxism," in *Sidney Hook and the Contemporary World: Essays on the Pragmatic Intelligence,* ed. Paul Kurtz (New York: John Day, 1968), 37.

59. Maurice Isserman, *If I Had a Hammer: The Death of the Old Left and the Birth of the New Left* (New York: Basic, 1987).

60. Michael Harrington, *Fragments of the Century: A Social Autobiography* (New York: Dutton, 1972).

61. Irving Howe, *A Margin of Hope: An Intellectual Autobiography* (New York: Harcourt Brace Jovanovich, 1982).

62. James Burnham and Max Shachtman, "Intellectuals in Retreat," *New International* 5 (Jan. 1939): 4–22; Shachtman, "Introduc-

tion," Leon Trotsky, *The New Course*, rev. ed. (New York: New International Publishing, 1943); Burnham, *Managerial Revolution.*

63. Shachtman quoted in Howe, *Margin of Hope*, 107.

64. Interview with Shachtman, June 21, 1971.

65. Michael Massing, "Trotsky's Orphans," *New Republic*, June 22, 1987, 18–22.

66. Dwight Macdonald, "The Root Is Man," *Politics* 3 (April and July, 1946): 98–115, 192–214; see also idem, *Memoirs of a Revolutionist*; and Stephen Whitfield, *A Critical American: The Politics of Dwight Macdonald* (Hamden, Conn.: Archon, 1984).

67. Dwight Macdonald, "Our Invisible Poor," *New Yorker*, Jan. 19, 1963, 82–132, reprinted in Macdonald, *Discriminations: Essays and Afterthoughts, 1938–1974* (New York: Grossman, 1974), 75–98.

68. Isserman, *If I Had a Hammer*, 167–69.

69. Bruce Cook, *The Beat Generation* (New York: Scribner, 1971).

70. Kerouac, quoted ibid., 89; see also Barry Gifford and Lawrence Lee, *Jack's Book: An Oral Biography of Jack Kerouac* (New York: St. Martin's, 1977).

71. The clash between the beats and the academic intellectuals is sensitively described in Morris Dickstein, *Gates of Eden: American Culture in the Sixties* (New York: Basic, 1977).

72. Irving Howe, "The New York Intellectuals," in *Decline of the New* (New York: Harcourt, Brace & World, 1970), 211–65; William Barrett, *The Truants: Adventures among the Intellectuals* (Garden City, N.Y.: Anchor, 1983), 12–13; Hook, *Out of Step*, 509–26; William Phillips, *A Partisan View: Five Decades of Literary Life* (New York: Stein & Day, 1983), 113. The body of memoirs and the scholarship on the New York intellectuals is vast. See Lionel Abel, *The Intellectual Follies: A Memoir of the Literary Venture in New York and Paris* (New York: Norton, 1984); Alexander Bloom, *Prodigal Sons: The New York Intellectuals and Their World* (New York: Oxford Univ. Press, 1986); Terry A. Cooney, *The Rise of the New York Intellectuals: Partisan Review and Its Circle, 1934–1945* (Madison: Univ. of Wisconsin Press, 1986); Richard H. Pells, *The Liberal Mind in a Conservative Age: American Intellectuals in the 1940s and 1950s* (New York: Harper & Row, 1985); Alan D. Wald, *The New York Intellectuals: The Rise and Decline of the Anti-Stalinist Left from the 1930s to the 1980s* (Chapel Hill: Univ. of North Carolina Press,

1987); too late to use for this study is Neil Jumonville, *Critical Crossings: New York Intellectuals in Postwar America* (Berkeley: Univ. of California Press, 1990).

73. Norman Podhoretz, *Making It* (New York: Random House, 1967).

74. Max Eastman, *The Literary Mind* (New York: Scribner, 1931); idem, "My Friendship with Edna St. Vincent Millay," in *Great Companions*, 61–79.

75. Philip Rahv, *Essays on Literature and Politics, 1932–1972*, ed. Arabel Porter and Andrew Dvosin (Boston: Houghton Mifflin, 1978), 128; Lionel Trilling, *The Liberal Imagination: Essays on Literature and Society* (New York: Viking, 1950); *Granville Hicks in the New Masses*, ed. Jack Alan Robbins (Port Washington, N.Y.: Kennikat, 1974).

76. "Our Country, Our Culture."

77. Peter Coleman, *The Liberal Conspiracy: The Congress of Cultural Freedom and the Struggle for the Mind of Postwar Europe.* (New York: Free Press, 1989); for the breakup of the Old Left over the issue of McCarthyism, see Diggins, *Up from Communism.*

78. Bell, *End of Ideology,* 300; Richard Hofstadter, *The Progressive Historians* (New York: Knopf, 1968), 357.

Chapter 6: The New Left

1. Jack Newfield, *A Prophetic Minority* (New York: Signet, 1966), 43; Tom Hayden, *Rebellion and Repression* (New York: World, 1969); the student is quoted in J. Glenn Gray, "Salvation on the Campus: Why Existentialism Is Capturing the Students," *Harper's,* May 1965, 57.

2. Dennis Wrong, "The American Left and Cuba," *Commentary* 33 (Feb. 1962): 93–103.

3. See the interview with William Appleman Williams, by Mike Wallace, in *Visions of History,* ed. Henry Abelove et al. (New York: Pantheon, 1983), 123–46.

4. C. Wright Mills's "Letter to the New Left" has been anthologized in, among other places, *The New Left: A Collection of Essays,* ed. Priscilla Long (Boston: Porter Sargent, 1969), 14–25.

5. For the influence of Dewey and Veblen on Mills, see Rick Tilman, *C. Wright Mills: A Native Radical and His Intellectual Roots* (University Park: Pennsylvania State Univ. Press, 1984).

6. Mills's reference to his "intellectual grandfathers" is ibid., 107; see

also Mills's dissertation, published posthumously, *Sociology and Pragmatism: The Higher Learning in America*, ed. Irving Louis Horowitz (New York: Oxford Univ. Press, 1966).

7. Theodore Draper, *Castro's Revolution: Myth and Realities* (New York: Praeger, 1962); idem, "The Strange Case of Professor Williams," *New Leader*, April 29, 1963, 13–20.

8. Daniel Bell, *The End of Ideology* (New York: Free Press, 1960), 47–74. On Bell's intellectual development, see the recent works by Howard Brick, *Daniel Bell and the Decline of Intellectual Radicalism* (Madison: Univ. of Wisconsin Press, 1986), and Nathan Liebowitz, *Daniel Bell and the Agony of Modern Liberalism* (Westport, Conn.: Greenwood, 1985).

9. Tom Hayden's autobiography, *Reunion: A Memoir* (New York: Random House, 1988), can be supplemented by the account of Hayden and SDS in James Miller's excellent study, *"Democracy Is in the Streets": From Port Huron to the Siege of Chicago* (New York: Simon & Schuster, 1987), 41–125.

10. The text of the Port Huron Statement is reproduced as an appendix in Miller, *"Democracy,"* 329–74.

11. For an examination of the internal disputes of the Madison group, I am indebted to Kyle Cuordileone and her paper "From the Old Left to the New: *Studies on the Left* and the Intellectual Origins of a New American Radicalism" (Department of History, Univ. of California, Irvine).

12. "Symposium: Confrontation: The New Left and the Old" (Tom Hayden, Ivanoe Donaldson, Dwight Macdonald, and Richard Rovere), *American Scholar* 36 (Aug. 1967): 567–88.

13. Jeremy Larner, quoted in "The Young Radicals: A Symposium," *Dissent* 9 (Spring 1962): 129–63; Clark Kissinger, quoted in Steven Kelman, "The Feud among the Radicals," *Harper's*, June 1966, 67–79; Leslie Fiedler, "Reflections on Writers and Writing in the Thirties," in *The Thirties*, ed. Morton J. Frisch and Martin Diamond (De Kalb: Northern Illinois Univ. Press, 1968), 44–67.

14. Randolph Bourne, "Youth" and "Medievalism in the Colleges," in *The World of Randolph Bourne*, ed. Lillian Schlissel (New York: Dutton, 1965), 3–15, 64–68; Walter Weyl, *Tired Radicals* (New York: Huebsch, 1921).

15. Abbie Hoffman, *Revolution for the Hell of It* (New York: Simon & Schuster, 1970); Jerry Rubin, *Do It! A Revolutionary Manifesto* (New York: Simon & Schuster, 1970); Irving Howe, "New Styles of 'Leftism,' " *Dissent* 12 (Spring 1965): 295–323.

16. C. Wright Mills, *Listen Yankee: The Revolution in Cuba* (New

York: Ballantine, 1960), 178; Susan Sontag, "Some Thoughts on the Right Way (for Us) to Love the Cuban Revolution," *Ramparts,* April 1969, 6–19; Todd Gitlin, "Cuba and the American Movement," *Liberation* 13 (March 1968): 13–18; the passage quoted is from James Higgins, "Episodes in Revolutionary Cuba," ibid., 19–25, quotation on 22.

17. Newfield, *Prophetic Minority,* 48–82.

18. Sara Evans, *Personal Politics: The Roots of Women's Liberation in the Civil Rights Movement and the New Left* (New York: Knopf, 1979).

19. On Potter and Hayden, see Miller, *"Democracy,"* 232–33, 265–69; Max Weber, "Politics as a Vocation," in *From Max Weber,* ed. H. H. Gerth and C. W. Mills (New York: Oxford Univ. Press, 1946), 116.

20. Michael Ferber and Staughton Lynd, *The Resistance* (Boston: Beacon, 1971); Michael Unseem, *Conscription, Protest, Social Conflict: The Life and Death of a Draft Resistance Movement* (New York: Wiley, 1973).

21. The following account of the counterculture is drawn from "Youth," *Time,* July 7, 1967, 18–22; "Dropouts with a Mission," *Newsweek,* Feb. 6, 1967, 92–95; Jack Newfield, "One Cheer for the Hippies," *Nation* 204 (June 26, 1967): 809–10; John Luce, "Haight-Ashbury: A Case of Terminal Euphoria," *Esquire,* July 1969, 65–68; Leslie Fiedler, "The New Mutants," *Partisan Review* 32 (Fall 1965): 509–25; Joe Ferrandino, "Rock Culture and the Development of Social Consciousness," *Radical America* 3 (Nov. 1969): 23–48. For an overly enthusiastic, hence uncritical, treatment, see Theodore Roszak, *The Making of a Counterculture* (Garden City, N.Y.: Doubleday, 1969).

22. Friedrich Nietzsche, *The Birth of Tragedy and the Genealogy of Morals,* trans. Francis Golffing (Garden City, N.Y.: Anchor, 1956), 42–43.

23. A perceptive discussion of this problem may be found in Karl Löwith, "Weber's Interpretation of the Bourgeois-Capitalist World in Terms of the Guiding Principle of 'Rationalization,'" in *Max Weber,* ed. Dennis Wrong (Englewood Cliffs, N.J.: Prentice-Hall, 1970), 101–22.

24. Fiedler, "New Mutants," 509–25.

25. For the events at Berkeley, see Hal Draper, *Berkeley: The New Student Revolt* (New York: Grove Press, 1965), and Irwin Unger, *The Movement: A History of the New Left, 1959–1972* (New York: Harper & Row, 1974), 62–81.

26. Having witnessed for three years the escalating demands at San Francisco State, I agree with the historian W. J. Rorabaugh's observations of similar confrontations in Berkeley. Demands were made not necessarily to be met but to force a showdown. "That was why radicals emphasized 'The issue is not the issue.' The purpose of an issue was to create a confrontation in which moderates were radicalized; in 1969 activists exploited the issue of People's Park in precisely this same fashion. Because of this strategy, leftists usually rejected compromise. 'We cannot be coopted because we want everything,' said Jerry Rubin. This wry remark was at the heart of Berkeley radicalism." W. J. Rorabaugh, *Berkeley at War: The 1960s* (New York: Oxford Univ. Press, 1989), 91. On events at San Francisco State, the phase before Thermidor (that is, before Hayakawa), is described in Ralph Goldman, "Confrontation at S.F. State," *Dissent* 16 (March–April 1969): 167–69; for later recollections see the symposium interview "Paradise Lost at San Francisco State," *Academic Questions* 2 (Spring 1989): 48–63.

27. Steve Halliwell, "Columbia: An Explanation," in Long, ed., *New Left*, 200–215; Daniel Bell, "Columbia and the New Left," *Public Interest* 13 (Fall 1968): 61–101; Diana Trilling, "On the Steps of Low Library," in *We Must March My Darlings: A Critical Decade* (New York: Harcourt Brace Jovanovich, 1977), 75–153; Morris Dickstein, *Gates of Eden* (New York: Basic, 1977).

28. Louis Kampf and Eugene Genovese are quoted in David Caute, *The Year of the Barricades: A Journey through 1968* (New York: Harper & Row, 1988), 65, 382.

29. A vivid account of the New Left as a worldwide phenomenon may be found in Caute, *Year of the Barricades*.

30. Irvine Howe, Lewis Coser, and Richard Lowenthal, "The Worldwide Revolt of the Young," *Dissent* 16 (May–June 1969): 214–24; Lewis S. Feuer, *The Conflict of Generations* (New York: Basic, 1969), a thorough study extending back to the nineteenth century; see also Leo Labedez, "The Student Revolt of the 1960s," *Survey*, nos. 1–2 (March 1988): 265–80. On the Weimar analogy see Theodore Draper, "The Ghost of Social Fascism," *Commentary* 47 (Feb. 1969): 29–42; idem, "The Specter of Weimar," ibid., 52 (Dec. 1971): 43–49; Carl E. Schorske, "Weimar and the Intellectuals I," *New York Review of Books*, May 7, 1970, 22–27; idem, "Weimar and the Intellectuals II," ibid., May 21, 1970, 20–24. The Sorbonne graffiti is quoted in Dominique Jamet, "1968–1988: Vingt ans après," *Historia*, no. 497 (May 1988): 54.

31. Dellinger is quoted in Miller, *"Democracy,"* 296.

32. Todd Gitlin's vivid reconstruction of the street warfare outside the Chicago convention has the compelling drama of John Reed and Trotsky writing about St. Petersburg in 1917. See Gitlin, *The Sixties: Years of Hope, Days of Rage* (New York: Bantam, 1987), 319–40; Hayden is quoted in Miller's equally important account, *"Democracy,"* 307.

33. Andrew Kopland, "The New Left: Chicago and After," *New York Review of Books*, Sept. 28, 1967, 3–5.

34. Jervis Anderson, "Panthers: Black Man in Extremis," *Dissent* 17 (March–April 1970): 120–23.

35. Bobby Seale, quoted in Theodore Draper, *The Rediscovery of Black Nationalism* (New York: Viking, 1970), 108.

36. Jerry Rubin, quoted in Robert Nisbet, "Who Killed the Student Revolution?" *Encounter*, Feb. 1970, 10–18; see also James P. O'-Brien, "The Development of the New Left," *Annals of the American Academy of Political and Social Science* 395 (May 1971): 15–25.

37. Cleaver's and other threats are quoted in Anderson, "Panthers," 120–23.

38. Jack Weinberg and Jack Gerson, *The Split in SDS* (New York: International Socialists, 1969) *Young Socialist* 13 (May 1969); *Spartacist*, no. 13 (Aug.–Sept. 1969); *Militant* 23 (July 4, 1969).

39. David Horowitz, "Revolutionary Karma vs. Revolutionary Politics," *Ramparts*, March 1971, 27–33.

40. Randolph Bourne, "Below the Battle," in *War and the Intellectuals*, ed. Carl Resek (New York: Harper & Row, 1964), 15–21.

41. Ralph Waldo Emerson, "Historic Notes of Life and Letters in New England," in *The American Transcendentalists*, ed. Perry Miller (Garden City, N.Y.: Doubleday, 1957), 5–7.

42. Marcuse, quoted in Robert W. Marks, *The Meaning of Marcuse* (New York: Ballantine, 1970), 92, 97; for Marcuse's influence on the New Left, see Mitchell Franklin, "The Irony of the Beautiful Soul of Marcuse," *Telos*, no. 6 (Fall 1970): 3–35; Paul Piccone and Alex Delfini, "Marcuse's Heideggerian Marxism," *ibid.*, 36–46; Ronald Aronson, "Dear Herbert," and Paul Breines, "Notes on Marcuse and the Movement," *Radical America* 4 (April 1970): 3–18, 29–32; Paul Breines et al., eds., *Critical Interruptions: New Left Perspectives on Herbert Marcuse* (New York: Herder & Herder, 1970); Douglas Kellner, *Herbert Marcuse and the Crisis of Marxism* (Berkeley: Univ. of California Press, 1984).

Chapter 7: The Academic Left

1. More than the Vietnam War was involved in the issue of patriotism. The abuse of American symbols explains in part why the New Left failed in its attempt to reach the working class. I once mentioned this point in a talk in Bologna, and it went over well with Italian radical students and young scholars, especially those who took seriously Gramsci's advice that Italy's Left must identify with the country's nationalist traditions. On several occasions I mentioned the same point at conferences of Americans historians, only to be met with stone silence or jeers. For a thoughtful attempt to rescue the concept from the bashing of the sixties generation, see John H. Schaar, "The Case for Patriotism," in *Legitimacy in the Modern State* (New Brunswick, N.J.: Transaction Books, 1981), 285–312.

2. Michael Walzer, "Notes for Whoever's Left," *Dissent* 19 (Spring 1972): 309–14; Jesse R. Pitts, "The Manson Murders: My-Lai of the Counter Culture," ibid., 337–47.

3. Joel Whitebook, "The Politics of Redemption," *Telos* 63 (Spring 1985): 156–65; Paul Breines, "Redeeming Redemption," ibid., 65 (Fall 1985): 152–58; Murray Bookchin, "Were We Wrong?" ibid., 59–74.

4. André Glucksmann, *The Master Thinkers*, trans. Brian Pearce (New York: Harper & Row, 1980).

5. Susan Sontag, "Trip to Hanoi," *Esquire*, Dec. 1968, 131–41; for the attack on Sontag's Town Hall speech, see "Setting the Record Straight" (editional), *Nation* 234 (March 13, 1982): 292; see also Peter Collier, "Another 'Low Dishonest Decade' on the Left," *Commentary* 83 (Jan. 1987): 17–24; on the Washington conference, see Michael Kazin and Todd Gitlin, "Second Thoughts," *Tikkun* 3 (Jan.–Feb. 1988): 44–48; an anthology of memoirs, some of which reflect Left to Right shifts, is *Political Passages: Journeys of Change through Two Decades, 1968–1988*, ed. John Bunzel (New York: Free Press, 1988).

6. James O'Connor, *The Fiscal Crisis of the State* (New York: St. Martin's, 1973).

7. Karen Tumulty, "Corruption Charges Shake New York City Schools," *Los Angeles Times*, Nov. 30, 1988.

8. William Grider, "The Rolling Stone Survey," *Rolling Stone*, April 7, 1988, 34; "Portrait of a Generation," ibid., May 5, 1988, 46.

9. Russell Jacoby, *The Last Intellectuals: American Culture in the Age*

of Academe (New York: Basic, 1987); see also the "Symposium" on Jacoby's book in *Telos* 73 (Fall 1987): 167–90.

10. The controversy over whether the Left or the Right predominates on the campus was thrashed out in Norman Cantor, "The Real Crisis in the Humanities Today," *New Criterion*, June 1988, 28–38; Jon Wiener, "Why the Right Is Losing in Academe," *Nation* 242 (May 24, 1986): 726–28; David Bell, "Ghost of the Leftist Past," *New Republic*, Aug. 11–18, 1986, 17; Stanley Rothmann, "Academics on the Left," *Society*, March 3–13, 1986, 4–8; Roger Kimball, *Tenured Radicals: How Politics Has Corrupted Our Higher Education* (New York: Harper & Row, 1990).

11. James Atlas, "The Battle of the Books," *New York Times Magazine*, June 5, 1988, 24–27, 72–75, 94–95; Gertrude Himmelfarb, "Stanford and Duke Undercut Classical Values," *New York Times*, May 5, 1988, A31; Christopher Hitchins, "Whose Culture, What Civilization?" *Times Literary Supplement*, March 4–10, 1988, 246.

12. Randolph Bourne, "The Cult of the Best," in *The Radical Will*, ed. Olaf Hansen (New York: Urizen, 1977), 193–96.

13. Bruce M. Rappaport, "Towards a Marxist Theory and Practice of Teaching," in *Studies in Socialist Pedagogy*, ed. Theodore Mills Norton and Bertell Ollman (New York: Monthly Review, 1978), 278.

14. "What's Black, White and Red All Over? A Marxist Magazine," *Wall Street Journal*, April 10, 1978; "Success Story, Marxist Division," *New York Times*, April 23, 1978.

15. Bertell Ollman and Edward Vernoff, *The Left Academy: Marxist Scholarship on American Campuses* (New York: McGraw-Hill, 1982), 1:1.

16. Bertell Ollman, *Alienation: Marx's Conception of Man in Capitalist Society* (Cambridge, England: Univ. Press, 1971); for a critique, see John P. Diggins, "Animism and the Origins of Alienation: The Anthropological Perspectives of Thorstein Veblen," *History & Theory* 16 (1977): 117–36.

17. Myrna Wood, "Bread and Roses," SDS Papers, reel no. 38; I am indebted to Eric Olin for bringing this document to my attention.

18. Sara Evans, *Personal Politics: The Roots of Women's Liberation in the Civil Rights Movement and the New Left* (New York: Knopf, 1979); for an overview, see also William Chafe, *The American Woman: Her Changing Social, Economic, and Political Roles, 1920–1970* (New York: Oxford Univ. Press, 1972); Carmichael is quoted in June deHart Matthews's valuable essay "The New

Feminism and the Dynamics of Social Change," in *Women's America*, ed. Linda Kerber and June deHart Matthews (New York: Oxford Univ. Press, 1982), 397–425.

19. Betty Friedan, *The Feminine Mystique* (New York: Norton, 1963).

20. Maren Lockwood Carden, *The New Feminist Movement* (New York: Russell Sage, 1974); Gayle Graham Yates, *What Women Want: The Ideas of the Movement* (Cambridge: Harvard Univ. Press, 1975).

21. Prostitution, pornography, and other carnal issues are fully treated in *Desire: The Politics of Sexuality,* ed. Ann Snitow, Christine Stansell, and Sharon Thompson (London: Virago, 1984).

22. See, for example, "The New Scholarship: Recent Essays in the Humanities," in *Signs: Journal of Women in Culture and Society* 1 (Winter 1975): 435–526; Atlas, "Battle of the Books"; Adrienne Rich, "Toward a Women-Centered University," in *On Lies, Secrets, and Silence: Selected Prose, 1966–1978* (New York: Norton, 1979), 125–55.

23. Thomas Haskell and Sanford Levinson, "Academic Freedom and Expert Witnessing: Historians and the Sears Case," *Texas Law Review* 66 (June 1988): 1629–59.

24. The expression "the power grab" is Mary Ann Dolan's, in "When Feminism Failed," *New York Times Magazine,* June 26, 1988, 21–26, 66.

Chapter 8: Poetry of the Past

1. Ellen Schrecker, "The Missing Generation: Academics and the Communist Party from the Depression to the Cold War," *Humanities in Society* 6 (Spring–Summer 1983): 139–59; see also Kent Blaser's essay "What Happened to New Left History?" *South Atlantic Quarterly* 85 (Summer 1986): 283–96, and ibid., 86 (Summer 1987): 210–28; on Marxism's being the "mainstream," see Michael Denning, "The Special American Conditions—Marxism and American Studies," *American Quarterly* 38, no. 3 (bibliography issue) (1986): 356–80; see also Gertrude Himmelfarb, *The New History and the Old* (Cambridge: Harvard Univ. Press, 1988).

2. Theodore Draper, "Long Ago and Far Away: A Memoir," *Dissent* 33 (Summer 1986): 312–19.

3. Theodore Draper, "American Communism Revisited," *New York Review of Books,* May 9, 1985, 32–37; idem, "The Popular Front

Revisited," ibid., May 30, 1985, 44–50; see also the letters and Draper's reply, "Revisiting American Communism: An Exchange," ibid., Aug. 15, 1985, 40–44.

4. See John P. Diggins, "The Misuses of Gramsci," *Journal of American History* 75 (June 1988): 141–45; idem, "Gramsci and the Intellectuals," *Raritan* 9 (Fall 1989): 129–52. Gramsci's description of America's lacking a "parasitic" aristocracy is in *Selections from the Prison Notebooks,* ed. Quintin Hoare and Geoffrey Nowell Smith (New York: International Publishers, 1971), 285–86, 293. On Hegel's views of America, see George Armstrong Kelly, *Hegel's Retreat from Eleusis* (Princeton: Princeton Univ. Press, 1978).

5. Santayana, "The Irony of Liberalism," *New Republic,* Sept. 24, 1956, 12–15.

6. George A. Peek, Jr., ed., *The Political Writings of John Adams* (Indianapolis: Boobs-Merrill, 1954), 105–63; Tocqueville, *Democracy in America,* ed. J. P. Mayer (Garden City, N.Y.: Anchor, 1969), 506–8; Thoreau, *Walden and Other Writings,* ed. Joseph Wood Krutch (New York: Bantam, 1962), 107–78; Veblen, *The Theory of the Leisure Class* (1899; reprint, New York: Mentor, 1953); C. B. Macpherson, *The Political Theory of Possessive Individualism* (Oxford: Clarendon, 1962); Christopher Lasch, *The Culture of Narcissism: American Life in an Age of Diminishing Expectations* (New York: Norton, 1978).

7. Richard Hofstadter, *The American Political Tradition* (New York: Knopf, 1948), v–xi, 16–17; Louis Hartz, *The Liberal Tradition in America* (New York: Harcourt, Brace & World, 1955), 3–22.

8. Emerson, "Historical Notes of Life and Letters in New England," in *The Transcendentalists,* ed. Perry Miller (Cambridge: Harvard Univ. Press, 1950), 494–502; for Burke's views of Machiavelli, see Conor Cruise O'Brien, *The Suspecting Glance* (London: Faber and Faber, 1972), 33–49.

9. In stressing protest as a moral act (and rightly so), Marxists and to a certain extent republicans seemed to be suggesting that the social and political language in which protest is conducted is evidence of the absence of economic and egoistic motives. Marx believed, in contrast, that in the state of "prehistory" humankind remains alienated and that the "furies" of interests and power dominate social relations. Karl Marx, *Capital: A Critical Analysis of Capitalist Production,* trans. Samuel Moore and Edward Aveling, vol. 1 (Moscow, n.d.), 21.

10. Eugene D. Genovese, *The Political Economy of Slavery: Studies in the Economy and Society of the Slave South* (New York: Vintage, 1965); idem, *The World the Slaveholders Made: Two Essays in Interpretation* (New York: Pantheon, 1969).

11. James Oakes, *The Ruling Race: A History of American Slaveholders* (New York: Knopf, 1982), ix–xiii.

12. Stanley M. Elkins, *Slavery: A Problem in American Institutional and Intellectual Life* (Chicago: Univ. of Chicago Press, 1959).

13. Thomas Jefferson, *Notes on the State of Virginia* (1787; reprint, New York: Vintage, 1964), 155.

14. Eugene D. Genovese, *Roll, Jordan, Roll: The World the Slaves Made* (New York: Pantheon, 1974), 3–7, 67.

15. David Brion Davis, *The Problem of Slavery in the Age of Revolution, 1770–1823* (Ithaca: Cornell Univ. Press, 1975), 558; G. W. F. Hegel, *Phenomenology of Mind*, trans. J. B. Baillie (New York: Harper & Row, 1967), 228–40.

16. Davis, *Problem of Slavery*, 561–62.

17. Tocqueville, *Democracy in America*, 556.

18. Herman Melville, "Benito Cereno," in *Billy Budd, Sailor, and Other Stories*, ed. Harold Beaver (New York: Penguin, 1967), 306; for an excellent analysis of this story in the context of perception and domination, see John H. Schaar, *Legitimacy in the Modern State* (New Brunswick, N.J.: Transaction Books, 1981), 53–87; for a penetrating critique of the moral claims of ruling classes, see Reinhold Niebuhr, *Moral Man and Immoral Society: A Study in Ethics and Politics* (New York: Scribner, 1932), 113–41; and for a historical description, see Frederick Law Olmsted, *The Cotton Kingdom*, ed. Arthur M. Schlesinger, Sr. (1861; reprint New York: Modern Library, 1984), 510–63.

19. Gramsci, *Prison Notebooks*, 277–318.

20. Tocqueville, *Democracy in America*, 346, 375.

21. Genovese, *Roll, Jordan, Roll*, 115.

22. Ralph Waldo Emerson, "Wealth," in *The Complete Works of Ralph Waldo Emerson*, vol. 11 (centenary ed.; reprint, New York: AMS Press, 1979): 91–95.

23. In a chapter whose title is taken from a passage from Revelation, "And Every Man According As His Work Shall Be," Genovese did discuss such matters as "time and work rhythms," the question of "a lazy people," and "the black work ethic"; see *Roll, Jordan, Roll*, 284–324. Almost the entire discussion, however, deals with twentieth-century social theorists like Max Weber and contemporary historians like Eric Hobsbawm. Except for a

reference to Harriet Martineau's observation, Genovese's chapter contains little more than hopeful speculation, and it also seems to contradict his thesis that master and slave were tied together by deep psychological bonds of mutual respect based on a need for reciprocal recognition. The only way slaves could have developed a viable work ethic under an aristocratic culture would have been, I should think, to renounce the master's ideal life-style. Jefferson recognized that "in a warm climate, no man will labor for himself who can make another labor for him," and he feared that even the children of plantation masters could be corrupted by watching their fathers rule as idle proprietors. "Our children see this, and learn to imitate it; for man is an imitative animal"; see *Notes on Virginia*, 155–56. What Tocqueville had to say about master-servant relations in aristocratic societies is even more telling. Although Tocqueville was not discussing plantation owners and black slaves, he saw little evidence of paternalism on the part of aristocratic masters and little evidence of independence and self-esteem on the part of servants: "In aristocracies the master comes to think of his servants as an inferior and secondary part of himself . . . The servants, for their part, see themselves in almost the same way, and they sometimes identify themselves so much with the master personally that they become an appendage to him in their own eyes as well as his"; see *Democracy in America*, 375.

24. Francis J. Grund, *Aristocracy in America* (1839; reprint, New York: Harper Torchbooks 1959), 145–46.

25. Ibid., 149.

26. Olmsted, *Cotton Kingdom*, 466–68.

27. Genovese, as quoted in "Revisionism: A New, Angry Look at the American Past," *Time*, Feb. 2, 1970, 14.

28. Paine, "The Rights of Man," in *Thomas Paine: Representative Selections*, ed. Harry Hayden Clark (New York: Hill and Wang, 1944), 72.

29. Adams to Jefferson, Nov. 15, 1813, in *The Adams-Jefferson Letters*, ed. Lester J. Cappon (New York: Clarion, 1971), 397–402.

30. Herbert J. Storing, *What the Anti-Federalists Were For: The Political Thought of the Opponents of the Constitution* (Chicago: Univ. of Chicago Press, 1981), 15–23, 48–52.

31. "The thought of human misery," Weil wrote of Marx, "distressed him terribly." Yet Marx "took refuge" in his theory of "dialectical materialism" and the supposedly liberating "forces of production," notions that led him and other Marxists to assume

that the weak would inherit the power of the strong without fully considering what oppression had done to the oppressed. See Weil, *Oppression and Liberty*, trans. Arthur Wills and John Petrie (Amherst: Univ. of Massachusetts Press, 1973), x, 144–45.

32. Hartz, *Liberal Tradition*, 145–77.

33. John Locke, *The Second Treatise of Government*, ed. Thomas P. Reardon (Indianapolis: Bobbs-Merrill, 1952), 16–29.

34. Eric Foner, *Free Soil, Free Labor, Free Men: The Ideology of the Republican Party before the Civil War* (New York: Oxford Univ. Press, 1970), 16.

35. "How, we ask now, does it happen that man internalizes his labor, alienates it? How is this alienation rooted in the nature of human development?" With the question dramatically posed, Marx continued, "Let us consider more clearly these relationships." At this point the manuscript breaks off—unfinished. Lloyd D. Easton and Kurt Guddat, eds., *Writings of the Young Marx on Philosophy and Society* (Garden City, N.Y.: Doubleday, 1967), 299–301. Also see John P. Diggins, "Thoreau, Marx, and the 'Riddle' of Alienation," *Social Research* 39 (1972): 571–98.

36. Roy P. Basler, ed., *The Collected Works of Abraham Lincoln*, 8 vols. (New Brunswick: Rutgers Univ. Press, 1959), 2:440; 3:462; 4:24–25.

37. When one considers Tocqueville's observation that servitude can easily lead subjects to "imitate" their masters, one recalls Burke's observation that ambition is the answer to the mimetic bondage of social relations and to the inertia of life itself. "Although imitation is one of the great instruments used by providence in bringing nations toward perfection, yet if men gave themselves up to imitation entirely, and each followed the other, and so on in an eternal circle, it is easy to see that there could be no real improvement amongst them. Men must remain as brutes do, the same at the end of the day that they are at this day, and that they were in the beginning of the world. To prevent this, God has planted in man a sense of ambition. . . . It is this passion that drives men to all the ways we see in use of signalizing themselves, and that tends to make whatever excites in a man the idea of this distinction so very pleasant." Burke, *A Philosophical Inquiry into the Nature of Our Ideas of the Sublime and Beautiful*, ed. James T. Boulton (1787; reprint, South Bend, Ind.: Univ. of Notre Dame Press, 1968), 50. Ambition could lead to freedom and even economic success on the part of slaves who were fortunate to have enlightened and humane masters. It could also lead

to a drive for social respectability that had some ironic turns. See the excellent study by Michael P. Johnson and James L. Roark, *Black Masters: A Free Family of Color in the Old South* (New York: Norton, 1984).

38. For an intelligent criticism of this trendy line of thought, see Gareth Stedman-Jones, "Class Expression versus Social Control? A Critique of Recent Trends in the Social History of Leisure," *History Workshop* 4 (1977): 163–70; the "relations of production" is in Paul E. Johnson, *A Shopkeeper's Millennium: Society and Revivals in Rochester, New York, 1815–1837* (New York: Hill and Wang, 1978), 140–41.

39. For a discussion of the Commons-Perlman school, see Daniel Bell, *The End of Ideology* (New York: Free Press, 1960), 211–26; on the Gompers-Hillquit debates, see Carl Degler, *Out of Our Past: The Forces That Shaped Modern Culture* (New York: Harper & Row, 1959), 263–68, and Draper, *Roots of American Communism*, 24–28; for a full text, see "Hillquit versus Gompers," in *Socialism in America*, ed. Albert Fried (Garden City, N.Y.: Doubleday, 1970), 471–95.

40. David Montgomery, "To Study the People: The American Working Class," *Labor History* 21 (1980): 501; see also idem, "Review Essay: Gutman's Nineteenth-Century America," ibid., 19 (1978): 416–29.

41. Herbert G. Gutman, *Work, Culture, and Society in Industrializing America* (New York: Vintage, 1977), 3–117.

42. Gutman also dramatized the worry of John Adams and other founders that masses of Americans would have little motive to work. From these observations he developed the argument that late-nineteenth-century immigrant workers had to be disabused of their "preindustrial" attitudes and instilled with new attitudes toward the disciplined life of labor; see ibid., 4–5. The deeper issue, as Adams, Veblen, and Sombart recognized, is man's desire for gain and possession apart from work, a desire fed by the emotion of "emulation." Even the European peasant was not immune to the desire to acquire the resources to establish a family house and own land. See Emmanuel Le Roy Ladurie, *Montaillou: The Promised Land of Error*, trans. Barbara Bray (New York: Vintage, 1979), 24–119. Gutman shied away from examining American workers' attitudes toward acquisition and consumption.

43. E. P. Thompson, *The Making of the English Working Class* (New York: Vintage, 1963), 11.

44. R. G. Collingwood, *The New Leviathan* (New York: Oxford Univ. Press, 1971), 282.

45. Michael H. Frisch and Daniel J. Walkowitz, eds., *Working-Class America: Essays on Labor, Community, and American Society* (Urbana: Univ. of Illinois Press, 1983), ix–xvi, 53, 62, 201, 226, 228.

46. C. Wright Mills, "The New Left," in *Power Politics and People: The Collected Essays of C. Wright Mills*, ed. Irving L. Horowitz (New York: Oxford Univ. Press, 1967), 256.

47. Anthony Giddens, *A Contemporary Critique of Historical Materialism* (Berkeley: Univ. of California Press, 1981), 230–52, 281–82.

48. Friedrich Engels, *The Condition of the Working-Class in England in 1844*, trans. Florence Kelley Wischnewetzsky (London: Allen & Unwin, 1936), 124.

49. According to Sean Wilentz, "the moral code of possessive individualism crept into the masters' ceremonial speeches"; see Wilentz, "Artisan Republican Festivals and the Rise of Class Conflict in New York City, 1788–1837," in Frisch and Walkowitz, eds., *Working-Class America*, 52. According to Tocqueville, "materialism"—the "love of money"—could be seen everywhere in America, a country that lacked an aristocracy to disdain it and a "proletariat" to resist it; see *Democracy in America*, 621.

50. Frisch and Walkowitz, eds., *Working-Class America*, 104–283, esp. 264, 266.

51. Wilentz, "Artisan Republican Festivals," 63–64.

52. Tocqueville, *Democracy in America*, 433.

53. Wilentz, "Artisan Republican Festivals," 49.

54. Ibid., 60.

55. E. P. Thompson, "The Moral Economy of the English Crowd in the Eighteenth Century," *Past and Present*, no. 50 (1971): 76–136. Thompson demonstrated that English workers protested high food prices in the new market economy in the name of older rights and customs pertaining to communal welfare. The defense of "the old moral economy of provision" against the harsh impersonality of market fluctuations indicates that English workers had available to them a familiar means of legitimating the justice of their cause, not that they were radical in the sense of placing new political and moral demands on their own behavior. See ibid., 132.

56. Kenneth Burke, *The Philosophy of Literary Form* (Berkeley: Univ. of California Press, 1973), 111–12. On "mystifications" and

"eulogistic coverings," see idem, *A Rhetoric of Motives* (Berkeley: Univ. of California Press, 1969), 104–10.

57. Arthur M. Schlesinger, Jr., *The Age of Jackson* (Boston: Houghton Mifflin, 1945), 18–29, 267–82; Daniel Walker Howe, *The Political Culture of the American Whigs* (Chicago: Univ. of Chicago Press, 1979), 69–95.

58. Bourne, "The Doctrine of the Rights of Man as Formulated by Thomas Paine," in *Radical Will,* 233–47.

59. Eric Foner, *Tom Paine and Revolutionary America* (New York: Oxford Univ. Press, 1976); Sean Wilentz, *Chants Democratic: New York City and the Rise of the American Working Class, 1788–1850* (New York: Oxford Univ. Press, 1986); for a more recent and discerning interpretation of Paine, see Isaac Kramnick *Republicanism and Bourgeois Radicalism: Political Ideology in Late Eighteenth-Century England and America* (Ithaca: Cornell Univ. Press, 1990), 133–62.

60. Tocqueville, *Democracy in America,* 367; Michael Kazin, "The New Historians Recapture the Flag," *New York Times Book Review,* July 2, 1989, 1, 19–21.

61. On the extent of racism in one important union, see Herbert Hill, "Myth-Making as Labor History: Herbert Gutman and the United Mine Workers of America," *International Journal of Politics, Culture and Society* 2 (Winter 1988): 132–200.

62. Tocqueville, quoted in Raymond Aron, *Main Currents in Sociological Thought,* trans. Richard Howard and Helen Weaver (Garden City, N.Y.: Anchor, 1968), 265; Tocqueville, *Democracy in America,* 550–54; Hartz, *Liberal Tradition,* 89–142.

63. Tocqueville, *Democracy in America,* 251; for Tocqueville's remarks on Montesquieu, see Aron, *Main Currents in Sociological Thought,* 258.

64. Tocqueville, *Democracy in America,* 395; for Tocqueville's redefinition of "interests" as "virtuous" and his analysis of egoism and individualism, see James T. Schleifer, *The Making of Tocqueville's Democracy in America* (Chapel Hill: Univ. of North Carolina Press, 1980), 233–59.

65. Just as Hume rejected the classical notion that virtue and commerce are incompatible, Tocqueville departed from both classical and socialist traditions in rejecting the notion that the pursuit of self-interest leads to a society's disintegration. For individualism could not flower unless society already enjoyed "invisible" *moeurs* that would compel men in their economic pursuits to conform to accepted principles of conduct—principles like

honesty, trust, and reliability. But, in light of Henry Adams's more troubled perceptions of post–Civil War industrial America, many of Tocqueville's hopeful assumptions about America's "virtuous materialism" may seem dubious at best. See Diggins, *Lost Soul of American Politics*, 255–59.

66. Tocqueville, *Democracy in America*, 704.

67. Whatever their differences, orthodox Marxists and liberals once believed that the oppressed were oppressed precisely because they had been denied the freedom to determine for themselves their own human development. Some present-day historians, however, come close to arguing that the conditions of slavery and working-class life produced black and white Americans with a mentality sufficiently free and determined to be resistant to capitalism and "possessive individualism." Should the historian, then, rejoice that both slavery and wage labor produced superior moral persons and therefore regret the abolishment of the conditions that presumably created good human beings? On the "delusion" that a specific class or race is morally better than others, see Bertrand Russell, "The Superior Virtue of the Oppressed," in *Unpopular Essays* (New York: Simon & Schuster, 1950), 58–64.

Chapter 9: Power, Freedom, and the Failure of Theory

1. *Power and Knowledge: Selected Interviews and Other Writings by Michel Foucault, 1972–1977*, ed. Colin Gordon (New York: Pantheon, 1980), 39.

2. The scholarship on Gramsci is an endless growth industry; the best place to begin is Joseph Femia, *Gramsci's Political Thought* (Oxford: Clarendon, 1981); Walter Adamson, *Hegemony and Revolution: A Study of Antonio Gramsci's Political and Cultural Theory* (Berkeley: Univ. of California Press, 1980); see also the valuable "Introduction" to Antonio Gramsci, *Selections from the Prison Notebooks*, ed. and trans. Quintin Hoare and Geoffrey Nowell Smith (New York: International Publishers, 1971), xvii–xlvi; and the attempt to update his ideas in Ernesto Laclau and Chantal Mouffe, *Hegemony and Socialist Strategy: Towards a Radical Democratic Politics* (New York: Verso, 1985); on the appeal to intellectuals, see John P. Diggins, "Gramsci and the Intellectuals," *Raritan* 9 (Fall 1989): 129–52.

3. David Held, *Introduction to Critical Theory: From Horkheimer to Habermas* (Berkeley: Univ. of California Press, 1980).

4. Max Horkheimer and Theodor W. Adorno, *Dialectic of Enlighten-*

ment, trans. John Cumming (New York: Seabury, 1972), 3–42 (the original edition, *Dialektik der Aufklärung,* appeared in 1944).

5. Theodor W. Adorno, *Negative Dialectics* (New York: Seabury, 1973), 211–89, quotation on 255.

6. Mark Poster, *Foucault, Marxism and History: Mode of Production versus Mode of Information* (New York: Basil Blackwell, 1984).

7. Michel Foucault, *The Order of Things: An Archaeology of the Human Sciences* (New York: Vintage, 1973), 387; see also idem, *Power and Knowledge.* The literature on Foucault is vast; I have benefited from the following: Charles Taylor, "Foucault on Freedom and Truth," *Political Theory* 12 (1984): 153–83; Mark Philp, "Michel Foucault," in *The Return to Grand Theory,* ed. Quentin Skinner (Cambridge England: Univ. Press, 1985), 65–82; David Gress, "Michel Foucault," *New Criterion,* April 1986, 19–33; and the special issue "Foucault and Critical Theory: The Uses of Discourse Analysis," ed. Mark Poster, *Humanities in Society* 5 (Summer–Fall 1982).

8. While Foucault saw all institutions as power structures, Lasch criticized the rise of professional associations for taking responsibility away from the family and individual and thereby undermining traditional values. See his two essays "The Family and History" and "What the Doctor Ordered," *New York Review of Books,* Nov. 13, 1975, 33–38, and Dec. 11, 1975, 50–54.

9. "Final Interview: Michel Foucault," interviewers Gilles Barbadette and Andra Scala, originally published in *Les Nouvelles,* reprinted in *Raritan* 5 (Summer 1985): 1–13; Bourne, "The Puritan Will to Power," in *Radical Will,* 301–6; idem, "Immanence of Dostoevsky," *Dial* 18 (June 28, 1917): 24–25.

10. Long before poststructuralists sought to demonstrate that freedom could never break loose from systems of power that reside in discourse, the Old Left veteran James Burnham drew on Vilfredo Pareto, Gaetano Mosca, and others to demonstrate that democracy will always be frustrated by systems of power that inhere in society's structural imperatives; see James Burnham, *The New Machiavellians* (New York: John Day, 1943).

11. Jacques Derrida, *Margins of Philosophy,* trans. Alan Bass (Chicago: Univ. of Chicago Press, 1982), 1–27; a full, if difficult, explication of Derrida from the perspective of Husserlian phenomenology is Rodolphe Gasché, *The Tain of the Mirror: Derrida and the Philosophy of Reflection* (Cambridge: Harvard

Univ. Press, 1986); two valuable surveys are Jonathan Culler, *On Deconstruction: Theory and Criticism after Structuralism* (Ithaca: Cornell Univ. Press, 1982), and Peter Dews, *Logics of Disintegration: Post Structuralist Thought and the Claims of Critical Theory* (New York: Verso, 1987).

12. Frank Lentricchia, "Derrida, History, and Intellectuals," in *The Salmagundi Reader*, ed. Robert Boyers and Peggy Boyers (Bloomington: Indiana Univ. Press, 1983), 247–64; William James, *The Principles of Psychology* (New York: Dover, 1950), 1:609–42; George Herbert Mead, *The Philosophy of the Present* (1932; reprint, Chicago: Univ. of Chicago Press, 1980), 24; John P. Diggins, "Thoreau, Marx, and the 'Riddle' of Alienation," *Social Research* 39 (1972): 571–98; Ewa M. Thompson, "Body, Mind, Deconstruction," *Intercollegiate Review* 23 (Fall 1987): 25–34.

13. See, for example, Gayatri C. Spivak, "Displacement and the Discourse of Women," in *Displacement: Derrida and After*, ed. Mark Krupnick (Bloomington: Univ. of Indiana Press, 1983), 169–96; for the debate among women labor historians, see Joan W. Scott, "On Language, Gender, and Working-Class History," *International Labor and Working Class History* 31 (Spring 1987): 1–13; Christine Stansell, "A Response to Joan Scott," ibid., 24–29; an astute critique is Seyla Benhabib, "On Contemporary Feminist Theory," *Dissent* 36 (Summer 1989): 366–70.

14. For a Marxist reservation, see Terry Eagleton, *Literary Theory: An Introduction* (London: Basil Blackwell, 1983).

15. Originally the embracing of language, "the linguistic turn," was the temptation of thinkers on the Right rather than the Left. See Martin Heidegger, *Nietzsche: The Will to Power as Art*, trans. David Farrell Krell (1961; reprint, New York: Harper & Row, 1979).

16. Tom Hayden, "Compared with 1989 in Beijing, Chicago '68 Was a Pacifist Teaparty," *Los Angeles Times*, June 18, 1989, sec. 5, p. 2; Joshua Muravchik, "Bully a Mouse, Kiss a Dragon," *Los Angeles Times*, Dec. 22, 1989, B7.

17. Henry Kissinger, "Push for Reform, Not Rupture," *Los Angeles Times*, July 30, 1989, sec. 5, p. 1.

18. The student is quoted in Esther B. Fein, "Czech Students Rejoice at News of Concessions," *New York Times*, Nov. 29, 1989, A9.

19. "China Passage," *Nation* 248 (June 12, 1989): 800–808; Morton M. Kondracke, "The World Turned Upside Down," *New Republic*, Sept. 18 and 24, 1989, 26–29.

20. The account of the conference on rethinking Marxism and Antin's remark is in Larry Gordon, "Cold War of Words Heats Up," *Los Angeles Times*, March 3, 1990, A1, A36.

21. Václav Havel, "Words on Words," *New York Review of Books*, Jan. 18, 1990, 5–8.

22. Jürgen Habermas, *Legitimation Crisis* (Boston: Beacon, 1975); see also the concise evaluation by Anthony Giddens, "Jürgen Habermas," in *Return of Grand Theory*, 123–39.

23. Jürgen Habermas, *Theory of Communicative Action* (Cambridge: MIT Press, 1984); Habermas quoting Mead is in his "Summation and Response," *Continuum* 8 (Spring–Summer 1970): 126; see also *Habermas and Modernity*, ed. Richard Bernstein (Cambridge: MIT Press, 1985).

24. Richard Rorty, *Philosophy in the Mirror of Nature* (Princeton: Princeton Univ. Press, 1979).

25. Ibid., 357–65, 376–94; Richard Rorty, "Habermas and Lyotard on Postmodernity," in *Habermas and Modernity*, 161–76.

26. Richard Rorty, *Contingency, Irony, Solidarity* (New York: Cambridge Univ. Press, 1989), xvi; George Santayana, *Skepticism and Animal Faith* (1923; reprint, New York: Dover, 1955), 179.

27. Richard Rorty, *Objectivity, Relativism, and Truth* (New York: Cambridge Univ. Press, 1991), 15–17.

28. Randolph Bourne, "John Dewey's Philosophy," in *The Radical Will*, ed. Olaf Hansen (New York: Urizen, 1977), 331–35.

29. Frank Lentricchia, "Rorty's Cultural Conservatism," *Raritan* 3 (Summer 1983): 136–41.

30. Dewey quoted in *Dialogue on John Dewey*, ed. Corliss Lamont (New York: Horizon, 1959), 88.

31. On the dilemmas Dewey faced in grappling with historical experience, see John P. Diggins, "John Dewey in Peace and War," *American Scholar* 50 (1981): 213–30.

32. John P. Diggins, *The Bard of Savagery* (New York: Continuum, 1978).

33. As I try to point out elsewhere, John Adams's critique of Machiavelli "deconstructed" *The History of Florence* by showing how the author's own words betray the intent of his argument; see my forthcoming *The Promise of Pragmatism: Modernity and the Crisis of Knowledge and Authority in America*; Adams on power is quoted in my *The Lost Soul of American Politics: Virtue, Self Interest, and the Foundations of Liberalism* (New York: Basic, 1985).

34. James Burnham, *The Managerial Revolution* (New York: John Day, 1941); idem, *The New Machiavellians*, 251–55.

35. My discussion of the illusions of removing power from the human condition owes much to Reinhold Niebuhr; see his *The Children of Light and the Children of Darkness* (New York: Scribners, 1944).

36. Carl Becker, *Progress and Power* (1936; reprint, New York: Vintage, 1965), 24–25.

37. Hannah Arendt, *On Revolution* (New York: Viking, 1963).

38. *Federalist*, no. 10.

Index

Index

Index

Index

Index